John W. Allen

Legends
&
Lore

OF SOUTHERN ILLINOIS

SOUTHERN ILLINOIS UNIVERSITY PRESS
Carbondale

24 23 22 21   5 4 3 2

Library of Congress Cataloging-in-Publication Data
    Allen, John W.
    Legends and lore of southern Illinois / John W. Allen.—Southern Illinois
    University Press pbk. ed.
    "First edition published 1963"—T.p. verso.
    Includes index.

    ISBN-13: 978-0-8093-2967-0 (pbk. : alk. paper)
    ISBN-10: 0-8093-2967-0 (pbk. : alk. paper)
    ISBN-13: 978-0-8093-8565-2 (electronic)
    ISBN-10: 0-8093-8565-1 (electronic)

    1. Illinois—Social life and customs—Anecdotes. 2. Illinois—History, Lo-
    cal—Anecdotes. 3. Illinois—Biography—Anecdotes. 4. Folklore—Illinois.
    5. Legends—Illinois. I. Title.

    F541.6.A44 2010
    398.209773—dc22   2009047766

Printed on recycled paper ♺

Contents

Foreword

THERE IS NO NEED to introduce *Legends and Lore of Southern Illinois.*
That was done years ago when John W. Allen's early writing on regional
history and folk customs first began to appear in those newspapers of
Little Egypt whose editors knew a good thing as soon as they saw it.

But there still is mighty good use to which this space can be put. That
is to tell things about John Allen which he would balk at telling about
himself. For our author is a modest man. In all his book, the reader will
find almost no reference to John Allen's origin, to his background, his
parentage, his family, his personal experiences—where he has been, what
he has seen, why he has lived the kind of life he has.

A lot of people know John Allen's rugged, kindly presence at historical and civic gatherings in Illinois and elsewhere. But they do not
know where he came from, how he grew up, or what he has done to
earn a living. They do not know what stirred his interest in recording
the everyday habits and notions and doings of our grandparents and great-
grandparents while there was yet time to write them down.

You might walk with John Allen throughout an afternoon on a Historical Society tour around, say, Fort Kaskaskia. You might ask conver-
sational questions about the shape of the grass-covered earthworks and
be surprised at the informed answers. You might speak of the great
banding sweep of the Father of Waters far below the bluff top and evoke
from him fascinating data on the Mississippi's vast flow, its cargo of
commerce and topsoil, and its storied past peopled with De Soto, Marquette, Jolliet, and Pontiac, with Lee, Clemens, Shreve, and Eads. You
might profit from his observations and comments while the sun arches
across the sky—and not hear him use the first person singular "I" even
one time.

And so, although there is no need to introduce John Allen's book,
there is ample reason to talk about its author for a few minutes. While
he is busy on his next column which the Southern Illinois University
Information Service is waiting to send out to grateful editors, we will
take advantage of his preoccupation with legends of the past.

John Willis Allen comes naturally by his concern for other days and
ways. He was born in a log cabin in southeastern Illinois, near the village

of Broughton, Hamilton County. For those who do not know the geography of Little Egypt as well as they should, Hamilton County corners with Gallatin County whose seat of government is the historic old Ohio River port of Shawneetown. The Hamilton County seat is McLeansboro.

The event of John Allen's log-cabin birth was not officially recorded, since the compiling of vital statistics was far from universal in those days. But family tradition has it that the date was October 14, 1887. His father was Benjamin Gwin Allen and his mother the former Rhoda Tyler. The families were from Virginia by way of Tennessee and Kentucky. His Allen line went back to Green Mountain patriot Ethan Allen and his families connect with those of "two Presidents of the United States and one convicted horse thief."

Grandfathers Allen and Tyler both served in the Civil War on the side of the North. His Grandfather Tyler was in the southern Illinois regiment that "disintegrated." He promptly joined another Union regiment and ended the war with a good military record. Grandfather Allen was in the small brigade under General Benjamin H. Grierson on his celebrated 600-mile raid through Mississippi from La Grange, Tennessee, to Baton Rouge, Louisiana, in the spring of 1863.

John Allen's mother was a melodious folk singer. She knew a seemingly limitless repertoire of ballads and sang them as she went about her log-cabin chores. She sang them, too, as she knitted or sewed by the fireplace at night. Sprinkled through the family relationship were other ballad singers, fiddlers, several capacious drinkers of spirits, and two or three preachers of the hardshell (forty gallon) variety.

The Allens moved from that first log cabin home very early in the life of our author, for he cannot remember either the cabin or its setting. His first memories are of the faimly's second log cabin, in Rector Bottoms, Saline County. The move was not a long distance since Saline County is the county south of Hamilton and west of Gallatin. Its county seat is Harrisburg. From the front door of the Rector Bottoms cabin little John Allen looked out toward Ash Pond when flood waters were rising. As he stood in the clearing, he saw wild turkeys come to feed with the chickens.

The next move the Allen family took was into the pioneer home of a prominent settler, John Douglas, close to the Saline-Hamilton County line. John Douglas was a slaveholder who buried one of his slaves in the local cemetery. The settlement of Douglas took its name from him. John Allen remembers his first Christmas in the Douglas house. At its great fireplace he received his first orange and a little red wagon. He recalls, too, the pond in which he drowned an oversupply of kittens, the shed

"tabernacle" in which camp meetings were held, the neighborhood cemetery where flowers were placed on the graves of Civil War veterans in
observance of General John A. Logan's Decoration Day.

Ben Allen kept his family on the move. From the Douglas house they
went into another log cabin near North Fork Creek, in the vicinity of
Texas City, also in Saline County. John Allen dates it with its first red-
top boots, the pet woodpecker that his father brought to him, and the
two-wheeled log cart that passed their place. The log cart's wheels were
so high that the head of a man was about level with the hubs.

Before John was six years old, the Allens moved to the Reeder place,
their first frame house, built beside its predecessor, a log house. There
he learned that he was a social rebel. He went with his parents to a
brush arbor meeting and heard the itinerant preacher describe Heaven
as having streets paved with gold, walls of jasper, and jeweled ornamen-
tation. It may have sounded like an attractive place to most of those
within sound of the exhorter's voice but not so to John Allen. The boy
put Heaven down as substantially inferior to his favorite haunt back
of the Allen garden, where a walnut tree shaded the brook in which he
often went wading. This was the family home when school age caught
up with John, and one morning he set off down a dusty road to answer
his first country school bell. He did not know it then, but it was the
start of a lifetime that has been invested for the most part in school
rooms.

From the Reeder place, with its haunt beside the brook, the Allen
family moved still another time—to the Smith place, near Hardscrabble,
in the northwest corner of Rector Township, Saline County. John had
gone to school only twenty-one days in the first school. In the school of
the Hardscrabble district he received the balance of his basic education.
The shortest distance from the Allen home to the Hardscrabble district
school was a mile through the woods. Since there was no road, not even
a trail, Ben Allen took John and daughter Flora, two years older, to the
schoolhouse on the first morning of their attendance. On the way he
blazed the trees with his axe so the children could find their way home
that afternoon. Their daily trips to and from the school soon wore a
path from one marked tree to the next. Before sister Grace, six years
younger, began school a road that forded the slough had been opened.

The small schoolhouse was crowded with an enrollment of some
eighty pupils of varying ages, sizes, and grades of study, all under one
teacher. The old structure is still standing, but it ceased to be a school
years ago when enrollment declined to four students. Now and then
John Allen hooks a trailer to his automobile and drives to the Hard-

scrabble District school yard and camps there for the night. When evening drops around the old schoolhouse he remembers the teachers he sat under. One was a college graduate who stood out as an unusually able instructor of the young. Another was an excellent violinist. Still others were skilled at the piano. Ciphering matches, spelling contests, debates, and literary society programs all were part of Hardscrabble school days and nights. The boys played bull pen, move up, hat ball, old sow, sling dutch, whip cracker, wolf-on-the-ridge, stink base, and anti-over. It was a memorable day when the wood stove, which heated the school in fall and winter, was supplanted by a coal burner.

The Ben Allen family was one of the last in its area to live according to pioneer ways. The boy John separated lint cotton from the seeds before the fireplace. He helped his mother make hominy and lye-soap. He helped her thread the loom, and he can still hear its thudding sound and the whine of the spinning wheel and the ripping noise of the hand cards. When he tried to give his mother a boy's hand in weaving, she said that he pulled the fabric in too much at the sides. That loom was bought for six bits from Aunt Mary Wilson.

Outside the cabin, John worked with his father in clearing farm land, piling up and burning brush, grubbing stumps, hewing barn timber, chopping firewood, splitting fence rails, riving clapboards, pickets, and tobacco sticks for the family's cash crop. He helped build rail fences and weave "a few miles" of split picket fences. From the forests he joined in wresting a second cash crop of railroad ties. After John and his father hacked ties from logs and delivered them to a railroad station, they collected twenty-five cents for each tie.

John Allen tried his hand at cradling wheat and binding the stalks of grain by hand. He became an expert hay pitcher and learned how to splice hay ropes for other settlers as well as his father. He worked at holing up food for the winter—apples, turnips, potatoes, and heads of cabbage. He helped pull and dry beans and flail them on the floor of an old log house. He was water boy for barn raisings, log rollings, and threshing and ditch digging outfits. He was one of the best marble shooters in the neighborhood, and he grew skilled at pitching washers, only they called it "pitching dollars." Venturesome in a cautious and calculated way, he liked to stand around the older, more talkative men and hear them spin out their tall tales, some inherited, some relating true experiences, and some made up in fertile imaginations.

Here are some of the things John Allen remembers: the first noisy telephone in the Texas City vicinity, the first puttering electric lights at Eldorado, the first buggy in which he went for a ride, the large wooden rake that his father fastened behind the running gears of the wagon to gather up corn stalks. In those days people were "bad off" if the doctor was called. When the Australian ballot brought secrecy to Illinois elections, John Allen's father drew the form of the new ballot and the way to mark it on a board at the end of the log house. As the father drew his diagram, John's mother washed the family's clothes in a wooden tub, by an open kettle, with homemade soap.

After working on the farm and in a logging camp and sawmill, the curious youth began to do unusual things. He helped a pioneer aviator build an airplane. He went to California and served as "a chambermaid to a string of race horses." But he kept going back to schoolrooms as a teacher. His first teaching post came on the heels of graduating from the eighth grade of the Hardscrabble school. To get the new school, he had to pass a teacher's examination. He taught the one-room school for three years and then served as principal of two-room country schools for four years. With this rural educational apprenticeship behind him, he moved into Harrisburg as principal of a ward school. He was there four years and then served as superintendent of city schools for fifteen years—thirteen years in Eldorado and two years at Fairfield. As a teacher and school man, he emphasized the value of legible handwriting. He taught the Palmer penmanship method and was commended for his success in leading boys and girls to become skilful at it.

When World War I came along he volunteered for the Marines. He received training of sorts, was sent to France and attached as a replacement to a badly shot up unit, all within two months. He saw action with the Sixth Regiment and moved to the Rhine in the Army of Occupation. While there he was placed on detached service and sent to the University of London as a sociology student in New College, Hampstead. He gave minimum attention to class attendance and maximum to seeing the British Isles. As he moved about he managed to happen into memorable situations. He attended the funeral of Nurse Edith Cavel. He saw the King of England meet David Lloyd George when the wartime Prime Minister returned from the Paris Peace Conference. He climbed a column at the Royal Art Gallery to watch a parade in Trafalgar Square as the Germans signed the peace treaty at Versailles. He sat by the fireplace in Lady Astor's home and heard Rudyard Kipling tell stories through an evening. He had tea at Windsor Castle and doing so he remembered having eaten the elemental fare of American hobos in their jungles. He kissed the Blarney Stone and tramped along the Scottish-English border. He attended Easter service in St. Paul's Cathedral and went to sleep. He also took a nap in the churchyard at Stoke Poges, scene of Thomas Gray's famous elegy. He saw Clemenceau, Churchill, Admiral Beatty, General Pershing, the Duke of Windsor, and Lord Reading.

When all this rubbing elbows with royalty and the wartime great was over, John Allen returned to Hardscrabble and its talkative people who made up with experiences what they lacked in advanced education. He listened anew to folklore and home remedies, to songs and ballads, to superstitions and odd notions, to the stories of the pioneers and veterans of the Black Hawk, Mexican, and Civil wars. Then about twenty years ago he happened into a meeting of the Illinois State Historical Society. He found that others were interested in the historical things that interested him. So he began to collect the implements and tools of his boyhood and to write down the words of the legends and the lore. He assembled accounts of the crafts, the food, the clothing, the dwellings, beliefs of the people who shaped his own life.

In 1922 John married Johanna Ruppel of Boskydell, Illinois. They have one son and one daughter. Their son, Robert V., did his undergraduate work at Southern Illinois University and graduate work at Yale University, where he received a doctoral degree in Russian history. He now is an Area Specialist (U.S.S.R.) in the library of Congress, Washington, D.C. Their daughter, Betty, is the wife of D. Blaney Miller, mayor of Carbondale, Illinois.

John Allen became a tireless searcher through the past. One organization after another called him to its rostrum. He has served as president of the Illinois State Historical Society, the Illinois Folklore Society, the Southern Illinois Handicraft Society. To these should be added still other organizations, among them the Schoolmasters Club, a Rotary Group, and an American Legion Post of which he was twice commander. In W.P.A. days he supervised the Historical Division of the Museum Project. His second career started in 1942 when he joined the faculty of Southern Illinois University at Carbondale, to collect a museum of handicrafts, implements, and home arts of early times. He reached retirement age and took up the title of "emeritus," September 1, 1956. His retired status has not affected his weekly column, "It Happened in Southern Illinois." He writes it regularly and Southern Illinois University sends it out. Some five hundred articles have been released to newspapers, and it is a selection of these pieces that make up his book.

Such is John W. Allen—rail splitter, building estimator, foreman, superintendent of construction, breaker and trainer of horses, referee of prize fights and sparring partner of Gene Tunney, substitute preacher and maker of more than a thousand talks, tramper of back roads, teacher, friend of youngsters as well as old timers. He admits to being a coward by nature (he means he is shy), but he has an official citation for bravery. He says he is a provincial person and he offers no apologies for his outlook. He does not go for all superstitions, yet since boyhood he has held to the buckeye theory of good luck. A lover of ghost stories, he does not believe in ghosts but he is afraid of them. With the Allen place on Rural Route 1, Carbondale, the center of his universe, he is having "a plum good time" in life. As he pokes into the past, he is always wondering what is going to happen next. And he would like to stick around and see. May it be for a lot of southern Illinois winters and springs and just as many more summers and autumns, with an abundance of bright hiking days in every season to come!

IRVING DILLIARD

Collinsville, Illinois
Decoration Day, 1962

Preface

THIS VOLUME is mostly about southern Illinois, its lore, legends, sometimes strange beliefs and bits of its history. The reader will easily determine the grouping in which each belongs.

In the presentation of this assorted collection of materials, two definite objectives have been in mind. The first is to have those living in the region made more conscious of the heritage it offers and to see it as an essential part of the mosaic that is America. The second purpose is to have those living outside the region come to know it better.

The reader is asked to keep in mind the fact that the first white settlements made in mid-America were those of the French in southern Illinois more than 250 years ago. They were here long before the mass migration that finally settled America began its march from the eastern seaboard to the Pacific. The French and each succeeding wave of settlers brought distinctive cultural contributions. Vestiges of these contributions are obvious to the competent observer.

When settlers began to come in great numbers they came by way of the ever-available rivers and found southern Illinois a convenient region for settlement. The advent of the steamboat and the development of trails and roadways soon lead immigrants to bypass the southern part of the state. It thus was left a somewhat isolated region, a kind of historical eddy. In this region a culture, reasonably advanced at the time of its coming, tended to become static. The customs, practices, and beliefs of the pioneer survived here long after they had passed in less isolated regions.

It is against the background of this distinctive area that the writer would have these offerings viewed.

GRATEFUL acknowledgment is made to Southern Illinois University for financial grants given and for facilities made available in the preparation of this volume. Thanks also are due to the staff members of Information Service of the University for their continued courtesies and helps.

The number of persons, both those associated with the University and those not associated with it, who have given valuable information and suggestions is too great to list in anything resembling entirety. It is the wish, however, to acknowledge the personal encouragements of William H. Lyons, Director of Information Service, and those of Edmund C. Hasse, Assistant Director. Special thanks are due Mr. Hasse for his painstaking reading of the manuscript and for his many helpful criticisms and suggestions.

No acknowledgment would be complete without extending sincere thanks to those students who have so earnestly and competently helped to assort, file, and arrange materials used, and who have so patiently typed and retyped as revisions and alterations were made.

J. W. A.

Carbondale, Illinois
March, 1963

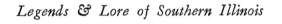

Legends & Lore of Southern Illinois

Chapter 1

Individuals

🏵 *WASHINGTON NEVER SLEPT HERE*

EVERY REGION, DOUBTLESS, has its list of interesting individuals around whom stories cluster. Those who travel over the Virginia-Maryland countryside frequently encounter signs like "Washington Slept Here." One man, statistically inclined or wishing to appear humorous, insisted that all such claims could not be true. He contended that their combined total would be greater than that of all the nights Washington spent away from Mt. Vernon. True or untrue, such signs do indicate a desire to connect a locality with some name great in our history. These local associations intensify the feeling that the men connected with past events were real.

Washington did not come so far west as Illinois, so we cannot erect a "Washington Slept Here" sign. Nevertheless, this region can claim some rather close associations with the great Virginian. One early contact between Washington and men from southern Illinois occurred when unwelcome visitors from here paid a call upon him in 1754. Among these callers were "100 choice troops" with some Indian allies from present-day Randolph County.

It came about in this way. British and French interests had for many years been in violent conflict in various places over the world. The American part of this conflict is known as the French and Indian Wars. In our country it was a struggle for control of the heart of the North American continent. A common objective of both parties was control of the Ohio Valley. The French were in the region early in force and established Fort Duquesne at the site of present-day Pittsburgh. The British, represented by a force of Virginia militia under the command of George Wash-

3

ington, arrived in the same area soon afterwards, intending to establish a fort and thus control the region. When he found the French already there, Washington built a second fort at Great Meadows, not so far away, and named it Fort Necessity.

The French immediately began to gather forces to drive the Virginians away. It was to this gathering of French forces that Major Makarty, commandant at Fort de Chartres in Randolph County, sent a hundred troops accompanied by Indian allies. Other French troops and Indians went from Vincennes to join those coming from posts in Canada. When sufficient French forces had gathered, they attacked Washington and forced him to surrender Fort Necessity at Great Meadows, now Confluence, Pennsylvania, on July 3, 1754. The callers from Illinois contributed to Washington's defeat. By a strange coincidence this surrender occurred exactly twenty-one years before the day on which Washington assumed command of the Colonial Army at Cambridge, Massachusetts.

This sending of troops to attack Fort Necessity does not constitute the only association of Washington with men in our story. A year after the surrender of Fort Necessity, Washington returned to that same vicinity as an aide to General Braddock, commander of British forces sent to occupy that area. The defeat and death of General Braddock and the able services of Washington in rescuing the troops from utter destruction, as well as the part played by the Indian allies of the French, is well known. These Indians, the element that apparently determined the defeat of the British, were directed by Chief Pontiac who later was killed at Cahokia, just south of East St. Louis.

Another man close to Washington came to live at New Haven, in Gallatin County. He had served as Washington's personal baggagemaster during the Revolution and perhaps knew Washington as intimately as it was the privilege of any man to know him. This baggagemaster is buried in a marked grave in the little cemetery about three miles west and two miles north from the Wabash River village.

Another and a better known man associated with Washington ended his days at Shawneetown. This was General Thomas Posey, distinguished alike for his military achievements and as a state and governmental official.

After all, southern Illinois can claim definite, but tenuous, connections with Washington.

🎖 *THOMAS POSEY*

A GRAVE IN Westwood Cemetery at Shawneetown suggests the story of Thomas Posey, who was born in Fairfax County, Virginia, not far from the home of the Washingtons, in 1750. Not much is known of Posey's family beyond the fact that his mother was Elizabeth Lloyd, sometimes suggested as the lowland beauty alluded to in legends about Washington. Her family was one with a social standing above the average. Posey grew up in the way of country boys of that time, with meager educational advantages. No records of his life previous to 1769 have been found. In that year, when Posey was nineteen years old, the family moved to Botetourt County, Virginia, about 175 miles south and west from his birthplace. This migration brought him much nearer the frontier with its constant Indian threats and conflicts.

Posey enlisted in the militia at an early age and thus began a long and active military career. He served as a captain in the forces led by Lord Dunmore and General Lewis in the Indian campaign often designated as Lord Dunmore's War. In this campaign he held the post of Commissary General under General Lewis. In the Lord Dunmore War he was engaged in the battle with the Indians at Point Pleasant near the place where the Kanawha River joins the Ohio in West Virginia. He was at German Flats, Schoharie, Cherry Valley, and Wyoming. At all these places he acquitted himself well and acquired an excellent military reputation. When conflict with the mother country came, Posey became a champion of the causes of the colonists. He was a member of the Committees of Correspondence that sought to keep the colonists informed concerning developments and relations with the mother country.

Throughout his military activities during the Revolutionary War he repeatedly appears as a favorite of General Washington, who recommended or appointed him to increasingly important tasks. At Washington's special request, Posey was assigned to the celebrated regiment known as Morgan's Riflemen, where he rendered distinguished service. He was present as a member of Washington's staff at Yorktown. After the war, he served under Mad Anthony Wayne in some of his campaigns against the Indians.

Posey was present and helped to arrange the surrender of General Burgoyne, the English play-writing general, at Saratoga on October 17, 1777. After Saratoga he had an important part in other campaigns. He was at Stony Point and led the battalion that successfully stormed the

British position. An incident in the Stony Point battle is indicative of his devotion and loyalty to Washington. When asked to lead the storming troops he is said to have replied, "I'll storm hell if General Washington will plan it." It was he who announced the capture of the fort.

After the Revolution Posey moved to Kentucky, where he was elected a state senator and served two years as speaker of that body. He was thus, ex-officio, lieutenant governor of the state. Later moving to Louisiana, he served as United States senator from that state. Upon the retirement of William Henry Harrison, Posey was appointed governor of Indiana Territory and served in that capacity until Indiana became a state. He was then appointed agent for Indian Affairs for Illinois Territory and moved to Shawneetown in 1816.

As a souvenir of the battle of Stony Point, Posey brought with him to Illinois the flag carried by the storming troops. This flag with its seven broad stripes of red and white and its field of thirteen stars arranged in a circle was one of the objects of interest in Shawneetown for a century or more. Much tattered and frayed, it was, a few years ago, still on display in the bank there.

Posey died in Shawneetown at the home of his son-in-law, Joseph M. Street, on March 9, 1818, within a few weeks of the time when Illinois became a state. He is buried about two miles north of the old town.

🌸 PIERRE MENARD

THE HOUSE THAT Pierre Menard built in Randolph County merits a high place on any list of historic homes in the United States. This sturdy old frame house of French colonial design is attractive to look at; its lines and proportions are pleasing. Moreover, it has remained basically unaltered through the years since it was completed in 1802.

It then stood on the east bank of the Kaskaskia River, looking across the stream toward the ancient town of that name. The Mississippi was seven miles away. Today the house, though it stands unmoved at its original location, faces directly upon the Mississippi, continuing to look toward the spot where the town of Kaskaskia once stood, but its view is now obscured by a high levee. This paradox clears when it becomes known that many years ago the Mississippi, while in flood stage, cut a new channel across a narrow strip of land that separated it from the Kaskaskia a few miles above the town and shifted its current to the latter stream. In making this shift the town of Kaskaskia, once the metropolis of the Mississippi Valley, was washed away.

Among the houses that were part of the Kaskaskia scene, only the home that Menard built against the foot of the Garrison Hill bluff remains. It has seen much history and as the years have passed, it has become more and more an object of interest. The house considered alone has its appeal just as does the man who built it. Each alike adds to the legend of the other. Perhaps it would not be improper to say that Pierre Menard and the Menard home occupy a position for Illinois much like that of Washington and Mount Vernon for the nation.

Pierre Menard was born at St. Antoine, near Montreal, Canada, in 1766. He left Canada and went to Vincennes in 1787. This was during the period when many of the French settlers of Indiana and Illinois were moving into Spanish territory west of the Mississippi. At Vincennes young Pierre entered the employ of Col. Francois Vigo, an Indian trader with whom he made at least one trip to Philadelphia to confer with President Washington concerning the defense of the western country. In 1791 Menard came to Kaskaskia and entered a business partnership with Toussaint DuBois. He soon became a prosperous merchant, fur buyer, and Indian trader. Here he twice married into prominent and influential French families.

Soon after coming to Illinois, Menard began to attract favorable attention. He was appointed to command the militia. He was named a judge of the Court of Common Pleas and served ten years in that capacity. He also was appointed to other offices, serving some time as judge in a special orphan's court. His name frequently appears as "next of friend" for someone who otherwise could not gain access to the courts.

Menard served as a member of the territorial legislature of Indiana from 1801 until 1809. In the spring of 1810 he was with Andrew Henry at Three Forks on the Missouri, where they established the first organized trapping venture in that region. He was elected to the first Illinois territorial legislature and became its president in 1812. Though he had come to Illinois as a youth and had been active in civic and political affairs for about thirty years, it was not until 1816 that he was formally naturalized as a citizen of the United States.

When men were selected to frame a constitution for the new state of Illinois, Menard was one of those chosen for the task. The proposed constitution required that the lieutenant governor be a native-born United States citizen, but since Menard seemed to be the best candidate, the constitution was promptly revised to permit anyone two years a citizen of the country to serve in that office. Menard accordingly was chosen as the first lieutenant governor of the state. After completing his term in that office, he retired to his home beside the Kaskaskia to live a quiet life, to entertain his many visitors, and to attend to wide business interests.

At different times, he was called upon to help in dealing with the Indians, whom it is said he "instinctively" understood. The Indians respected and trusted him. There is no indication that Menard ever used deceit in negotiating with them. Neither did they betray him. The same apparently was true in his relations with the whites.

Today a county and a town in Illinois are named for him. A bronze statue, the gift from a son of one of his business partners, stands on the capitol grounds at Springfield with the simple inscription ''MENARD,'' carved on the granite base. His name occurs frequently in the territorial records of both Indiana and Illinois and upon the early state records of the latter.

As has already been said, the home he built on the banks of the Kaskaskia still stands. Visitors may wander through the rooms of the old house, go to the kitchen with its shaped-stone sink, built-in oven, and fireplace with crane and pendant, where the meals were prepared to be carried to the dining room across an open porch.

Visitors also go through the stone-brick building designated as the "Slave House" where domestic servants evidently were quartered. Some years ago, very old people told of the ruins of a row of log cabins that once stood against the foot of the cliff south of the present house. Tradition indicated that these vanished cabins were the quarters where Menard's field slaves lived. Provision has been made recently for needed repairs to guarantee the preservation of the building. Such belongings of Menard's as are available are being brought back to the home. Other articles needed to furnish it will be supplied by authentic pieces of that period. Thousands of visitors now come to see the home each year. With proper restoration it could become an even greater mecca for those interested in the early history of the state and for those who wish to learn more about the culture of that period.

🏵 CONRAD WILL

CONRAD WILL was a Pennsylvania Dutchman. His first name, in compliance with the speech practices of his countrymen in the Quaker State, was pronounced Coon-rod. He may have been in Illinois at an earlier date, but it is known that he was here in 1813 and bought a pair of good boots at the store of William Morrison in Kaskaskia, paying $8.00 for them. A year or so later he moved his family to Illinois. He quickly assumed a position of prominence, and he easily ranks among the able and well-known founders of the state.

Will was born near Philadelphia on June 3, 1779. He grew up in an industrious and frugal home where the language was the German dialect common to Pennsylvania. Through attendance at subscription schools and by personal application he acquired a sound English education, attended medical colleges at Philadelphia, and practiced medicine in Somerset County, about sixty miles southeast of Pittsburgh.

He was successful in his practice and acquired considerable property, but not being altogether satisfied with his location in Pennsylvania, he decided to seek a better one. Reports from the Illinois country impressed him, and he came to investigate.

The quick perception of Dr. Will became evident when he was preparing to return to Pennsylvania after looking at the Illinois country. Having found cattle in Illinois plentiful and cheap, and money scarce, he took some of the gold coin that he had brought with him, bought a small herd of cattle, and drove them back to Pennsylvania, where he made a handsome profit. This is one of the very early recorded instances where cattle were driven from the western areas to the eastern market, a practice that was to become increasingly important.

After returning to Pennsylvania, Will sold his property, closed his business there and moved to Illinois, locating for a short time at Kaskaskia. As his first business venture, he chose the making of salt at a salt spring on the north side of Big Muddy River about three miles west of Murphysboro. Will entered land in the vicinity of the spring and built a double log house with two stone chimneys.

Shortly after moving to his new home near the salt spring, Will journeyed to Pittsburgh and bought thirty large cast-iron kettles to be used in boiling the brine. After the making of salt was abandoned, many of the kettles passed into the hands of near-by farmers. An occasional one may even yet be seen, generally used as a watering trough for livestock or for scalding hogs at butchering time.

The salt content in the springs he found in Jackson County was low, and Will was unsuccessful in his business enterprise. He was highly regarded by those who knew him, however, and when the population of the area became sufficient to warrant it, he was named as one of the committee to locate the county seat. Will was also chosen as one of the county commissioners of the new county and served until the formation of the new state of Illinois in 1818.

Jackson County was allowed to choose two delegates to frame a constitution for the proposed state. There appears to have been only one question for the people of the county to decide: "Who shall go with Conrad Will?"

His vote on the slavery clause of the constitution is not recorded. He advocated the hiring of slaves at the Gallatin Salines, apparently hoping to have the privilege made applicable at the Muddy Salines that he operated. He favored a liberal salary schedule for public officials. He approved a system of indentures and finally voted for the removal of the state capital to Vandalia.

Will was on a special committee to consider a petition from a group at Kaskaskia who wanted the new constitution specifically to state that the Bible was the basis on which the constitution was founded. This committee did not act upon the petition, and it was "tabled until the fourth of next March."

The constitutional convention finished its work on August 26, 1818, and adjourned. It had been in session twenty-three days. Will returned from the convention and was elected as the first state senator from Jackson County. In each subsequent election, as long as he lived, Will was chosen as state senator or representative from Jackson County. He died on June 11, 1835.

Besides being a physician, Will operated a tanyard and built a gristmill and a sawmill on Big Kincaid Creek about three miles northwest from Brownsville. He also kept a general store, taught medicine to Benningsen Boone and carpentry to Alexander M. Jenkins. A large man, always kindly and genial, he was widely known for his enjoyment of practical jokes even though he might be the victim.

Though he had always been successful in seeking public office and was almost universally liked and respected, Will was not successful in business. He signed as surety on too many notes, died a very poor man, and is buried in an unmarked grave in the cemetery near vanished Brownsville.

Perhaps no man in public life in Illinois at that time knew more state officials and men of note in the state than the Pennsylvania Dutchman, Conrad Will.

A BROKEN FRIENDSHIP

NO ONE APPEARS TO know just how the friendship between Morris Birkbeck and George Flower began. It is well known that the friendship ended at Albion, Illinois, but no one except Birkbeck, who neither talked nor wrote of it, could have provided an explanation. All agree, however, that this event was a severe blow to the English settlement in Edwards County.

Morris Birkbeck, son of a Society of Friends minister, operated a farm of 1,500 acres called Wanborough in County Surrey, not far from London. George Flower, son of Richard Flower, lived with his father on an estate known as Marden, a short way north and west of London. Each received better than an average education.

In 1814 Birkbeck, then fifty years old, and Flower, twenty-six, traveled together through France. Much of their journey was over roadways and through regions not regularly visited. Apparently it was on this trip that they formed plans to establish a settlement in America.

After their return to England, Birkbeck published "Notes on a Trip through France," which was widely read. Flower came to America, evidently as part of the plans for the founding of a settlement in the new country. He journeyed as far west as Illinois and went south to Tennessee. He also spent some time at Monticello, home of Thomas Jefferson, to whom he had been given a letter of introduction from General Lafayette.

In the spring of 1817 Birkbeck, who had arranged for the sale of his property and holdings in England, arrived in America with his sons, daughters, and a few others. The group reached Norfolk, Virginia, on May 13, 1817, and was met in Richmond by Flower, who conducted them to Illinois.

It was on this journey, made on horseback from Pittsburgh, that an incident occurred which probably led to the severance of the friendship between the two men. Eliza Julia Andrews, a member of Birkbeck's party, rejected his proposal of marriage and was wed to Flower instead when the party reached Vincennes. The rift, however, did not immediately become apparent.

The entire group went from Vincennes to Princeton, Indiana, where the women and younger members of the party remained while Birkbeck and Flower, with others, went to find a suitable location in Illinois. They chose land, mostly prairie, lying about the present city of Albion.

After they had gone to the United States Land Office at Shawneetown, where Birkbeck entered 1,440 acres of land, Flower returned to England, taking Birkbeck's manuscript, "A Journey in America to the Territory of Illinois." After arranging for its publication and attending to certain business, Flower returned to Illinois. His experience upon reaching the settlement in Edwards County was not pleasant. The house that workmen were to have had ready for him was incomplete; it had neither doors nor a chimney. His party was compelled to camp in the unfinished house and to cook over an open fire built in the space where the chimney and hearth were to be.

In the account of his return to the settlement, Flower expresses sharp disappointment that neither Birkbeck nor any others came to welcome or talk with him, though they certainly knew of his return. He accordingly decided to call upon Birkbeck, little anticipating the strange reception that awaited him. Perhaps the reception received can best be described by a quotation from Flower's account of it.

On the third day after my arrival, I took my horse and rode over to Mr. Birkbeck's cabin. When almost in the act of dismounting, I saw him rise from his seat from under the shade of an oak tree that stood opposite to his cabin door. He passed before my horse's head into the cabin, pale, haggard, and agitated. With eyes cast down and shaking his head he said, "No we cannot meet, I can not see you." Sitting on my horse, and looking at him in wonder, I said: "We must meet, our property is undivided, business is urgent, heavy payments are to be provided for freight and charges." But what! "Stop! Stop!" said he, "let a third person arrange all." "So be it," said I, and rode on. These were the last words that ever passed between us.

Knowledge of the break spread and caused much gossip and comment. Strange to relate, though, neither ever was heard to speak unkindly of the other and no record of the incident is found in their writings beyond that of Flower's quoted above. Both men continued to live in the settlement and to work unselfishly for its advancement. Both alike were reduced to straitened circumstances in their later years, having expended their once rather ample means to promote the interests of the settlement.

Birkbeck was drowned while attempting to swim his horse across the Fox River on June 4, 1825. He was returning from a trip to New Harmony, Indiana, where reports state that he had gone to ask Robert Owen to help in effecting a reconciliation with Flower. Flower, alike reduced in circumstances, left Albion in 1849 and went to manage a hotel in Mt. Vernon, Indiana. He lived until 1862, when he and his wife died on the same day while visiting in Grayville, and are buried there in a common grave.

🏵 DR. GEORGE FISHER

TRAVELERS ON THE highways of our eastern states often are impressed by the number of roadside markers that call attention to points of historical interest. As Illinois grows older, similar markers are appearing in in-

removed. The brothers simply stood out of line and removed the board by remote control. The pistols fired but injured no one.

The notes of Grandmother Tennery tell how the long-handled brass bedwarmer was used to remove the chill from cold beds in the winter. One can almost see live coals being placed in the covered pan of the warmer before it was passed beneath the covers of the bed.

She tells of the English practice of changing from winter to summer-weight clothing at Easter, even though an Easter squall might be in the wind at the time. The parallel practice in America took place on May first, which also was the day when children began to go barefoot. Some oldsters may recall the feeling of fresh air that greeted both body and feet on that day.

Her notes also tell of the way in which leeches were used to reduce bruises in both England and here. She describes how they were used in treating her younger brother, who had come away second best from a frenzied round of fisticuffs. Perhaps the story can best be told by quotes from her notes.

"His face was black and blue from bruises and his eyes were almost swollen shut. We went down to the drugstore and got some leeches, a long flat worm like a fishworm. Grandmother had the maid place them on the bruised parts and leave them there until they were gorged with blood. They were then taken off and laid on a large plate and sprinkled with salt that caused them to throw up the blood. They were then washed with lukewarm water and replaced on the wound." After use, they were returned to the druggist, and his fee of two pence for their use was paid.

She writes about an epidemic of smallpox in their community in Effingham County and of the manner in which the children's hands were balled in cotton so that they could not scratch and scar their faces.

Her notes also tell of a time, shortly after her mother's death, when the father was away and they lived for a spell on corn bread and pumpkin, often with no meat and no salt. Even now the reader sympathizes with them and reacts pleasantly upon learning that her brothers succeeded in trapping some prairie hens and that a kindly neighbor sent his boys with some salt. Her brothers also worked for a neighbor and were paid with a hog that another man helped them butcher.

The hardships she describes evidently were not crushing. She tells of the cherished china ornaments, sea shells, and mementos kept on a shelf above her mother's gay, life-sized portrait against the log wall, as she remembered it lighted by the glow from the fireplace. She tells of the Dutch oven, the trundle beds, the yard with its "many bright pink

though his formal training could have been but little, if any, Fisher is regarded as one of the most capable and distinguished of the state's early physicians. At one time he served as regimental surgeon in the Illinois Militia.

When Randolph County was formed as a part of Indiana Territory, Governor William Henry Harrison appointed Fisher as the first sheriff of the newly created county. His services in that office are recorded as highly satisfactory.

In 1805 Dr. Fisher and Pierre Menard were elected as representatives from Randolph County to the Indiana territorial legislature. As members of that body both of them were definitely in favor of slavery. Fisher was one of the first who urged the separation of Illinois Territory from that of Indiana, advocating such action and signing a petition to that effect. It is evident that he was highly regarded in the Indiana territorial legislature because he was appointed in 1807 to the Legislative Council, a policy-shaping body that worked closely with Governor Harrison.

In 1808 Dr. Fisher distinguished himself during a smallpox epidemic in St. Louis and in the near-by Illinois country. In an effort to control the disease, Dr. Fisher erected a hospital near his home, where he successfully treated many patients. He also made great use of vaccination, discovered and developed by Jenner a few years earlier in England. Despite his success and the high repute he held as a doctor, Fisher discontinued the practice of medicine shortly afterwards and gave his attention to other matters.

In 1812 he was elected to the Illinois territorial legislature and served as Speaker of the House from 1812 to 1814, and again from 1816 to 1818. When time came to frame a constitution to be submitted in connection with the territory's application for statehood, Fisher and Elias Kent Kane were the delegates from Randolph County. They soon became two of the most influential members of that body, Fisher being named to the Rules Committee. Always frank in expressing his attitudes and beliefs, he again sought to advance the cause of slavery during the convention. On August 16, 1818, he was named on the committee to complete the drafting of the Constitution.

Only a few men exercised influence equal to that of Dr. Fisher in the affairs of the state in the twenty years preceding its admission to the Union. He held numerous local and appointive offices and was one of the men who helped to form the Masonic Lodge at Kaskaskia. After the admission of Illinois to statehood, Fisher was a candidate for the state Senate, but was defeated by John McFerron. He died at his farm in 1820.

A more prominent marker to Dr. Fisher's memory was recently placed at the point where Illinois Highway 155 leaves Illinois Highway 3 at the south side of the village of Ruma.

🌿 *JAMES HALL*

WHEN TWENTY-SEVEN-YEAR-OLD James Hall landed from a free-floating boat at Shawneetown in the early spring of 1820, Illinois acquired a valuable citizen, one who was to wield considerable influence through coming years. His influence was to be felt in several fields, including law, state politics, the field of general education, and literature. In the last he was to pioneer in the region.

Hall was born at Philadelphia in 1793. As a youth he received a liberal education. When the War of 1812 came, Hall volunteered for military service and became a lieutenant of artillery. He remained in the military for several years, serving with distinction under Stephen Decatur during that officer's daring campaign in Algiers.

In 1818 Hall left the military and opened a law office in Pittsburgh, where he was only moderately prosperous. Hearing much about opportunities in Illinois, he decided to come to this state. Hall found Shawneetown a prosperous river town, and tells us that there were about one hundred homes there, twelve stores, two excellent taverns, two banks, the United States land office, a post office, and a newspaper. Along with these there were the shops of tailors, shoemakers, bakers, coopers, hatters, blacksmiths, gunsmiths, cabinet makers, and other craftsmen essential to a pioneer community.

Hall states that there were five or six brick buildings, several of frame, and that the others were of logs. The streets were muddy and were filled with pools of water left by receding floods or by heavy rains. There was no sewage disposal, and much debris littered the place, including even a dead animal here and there.

Shawneetown was a typical booming river town—crude, disorderly, and dangerous, as such places often were. There were many fights of the biting, gouging, no-holds-barred variety. Despite these apparent handicaps, it was a center of trade and easily was one of the state's important towns.

There was much about Shawneetown that appealed to Hall. He accordingly opened an office and began to practice law. He also became interested in newspaper work. On May 22, 1820, he bought a half interest in the *Illinois Gazette,* the second newspaper established in the state. His partner in this enterprise was Henry Eddy, a prominent lawyer, businessman, and politician. This partnership remained effective until November 22, 1822, when political differences apparently induced them to dissolve it.

Hall began to attract attention because of his boldness and honesty. In the winter of 1821 he was appointed as prosecuting attorney for the ten southern counties of the state. This was a challenging assignment. Hall's comments concerning his observations and experiences furnish much insight into conditions then existing in Illinois. He tells that there were communities where horse thieves seemed to rule, others where counterfeiting was much in vogue, and still others where the law-abiding element had formed into "regulator" groups to promote the enforcement of the laws.

Hall's reputation as an able and willing prosecuting attorney continued to grow. He apparently worked at his job, even functioning as a sheriff's deputy to apprehend and bring offenders into court, where he assumed the role of prosecutor. His reputation as a successful attorney was much increased by his prosecution of John Darr, who "not having the fear of God before his eyes, but being moved and seduced by the instigation of the Devil" had "stabbed William Thomason to the depth of eight inches, thereby causing instant death." This crime was committed on September 7, 1823. Justice must have been speedy then, for Darr was brought to trial nine days later and convicted of murder.

Hall was appointed as a circuit judge and in March, 1825, began to serve at Shawneetown. On May 14 of that year, Shawneetown was honored by a visit from General Lafayette. Judge Hall had a prominent part in the ceremonies connected with the visit; he delivered the very able welcome address that was repeated by C. K. Roedel on May 14, 1925, when the reception of 1825 was re-enacted.

On February 12, 1827, Hall became state treasurer, defeating Colonel Abner Field, the other aspirant.. Field became very angry at the politicians whom he charged with betraying him, burst into the room where they were still assembled, and before they could escape had soundly thrashed four of them. His ire, however, did not appear to have been directed toward Hall. Politics was quite rugged in those days.

While serving as state treasurer, Hall and others on December 8, 1828, formed the Antiquarian and Historical Society of Illinois, and Hall was elected its first president. Because of the difficulties of attending meetings and because of the lack of funds, this first organization did not survive long.

Near the close of 1828, Hall published the first annual or gift book—one with padded, richly colored covers—issued west of the Ohio River. This publication of 324 pages, 3 by 5½ inches, bound in glossy red silk, contained fifty-eight selected articles. His next literary publication was the

Illinois Monthly Magazine, which appeared in October, 1829, to become the first periodical issued in Illinois.

Hall wrote many articles and books. Among these were *Sketches of the West, Tales of the Border, Notes on the Western States, Romance of Western History, History of the Indian Tribes,* and *Letters from the West.* His writings, perhaps more than those of any other person of that time, served to call attention to the stories and legends of the West. They are still source material on the West of 150 years ago.

In 1833 Hall moved to Cincinnati, where he served as cashier of a bank and continued to write. He died in 1868.

🌑 *NED BUNTLINE*

VISITORS TO THE office of the *Union Banner* in Carlyle, Clinton County, Illinois, see a photograph on one of the walls with the name Edward Zane Carrell Judson beneath it. When they are told the man also was known as Ned Buntline, their interest is aroused and they wonder why his picture should adorn this particular wall. For an explanation one must go back more than a century.

In 1853, for a short time, Judson, or Buntline, was a local citizen and edited a paper in Carlyle. This paper, *The Prairie Flower,* ceased to bloom before long and was discontinued. Judson moved to other fields. Even though his stay was a relatively brief one, it does serve to introduce a strange figure into the southern Illinois story.

Judson easily qualifies as one of America's most colorful figures. He was, by turns, sailor, author, publisher, promoter, playwright, politician, agitator, mob leader, duelist, jailbird, soldier, showman, chiseler, philanthropist, temperance lecturer, drunkard, reformer, philanderer, homewrecker, spiritualist, impostor, and general man about town. He is designated as the father of the dime novel, of which he wrote an almost incredible number.

Though his novels and stories are many and varied, and at times are definitely tall tales, no character in any one of them is so fantastic as the author of the tales.

Born in 1823, Judson enlisted in the Navy at an early age. At fifteen he became a midshipman, commissioned by President Monroe on February 10, 1838. At that time he was serving in the Gulf of Mexico with the American naval forces on patrol to observe the French, who were blockading the Mexican coast.

The next year, 1839, Judson was participating in the Seminole wars in

Florida. At about this time his first story appeared under the pen name of Ned Buntline—the surname being borrowed from nautical parlance, where it is used to designate the bottom rope on a square sail.

Feeling somewhat restricted by naval regulations, Judson alias Buntline resigned his naval commission in 1842 and disappeared for two years. According to his story, this interval was spent with a fur company in the valley of the Yellowstone. Perhaps that is true, but we have only Buntline's word for it, and he was given to tall stories.

In 1844, at twenty-one years of age, Buntline co-operated with others in the publication in Pittsburgh of a magazine known as *The Ned Buntline Magazine,* but it was actually printed in Cincinnati. It shortly became known as *The Western Literary Journal.* In December, 1844, it was moved to Nashville, Tennessee, where it was known as *The Southwestern Literary Journal and Monthly Review.* The last issue of the magazine appeared in April, 1845.

Buntline's stay in Nashville was marked by one of the many dramatic events in his highly eventful lifetime. He was hanged. It came about in this manner. He attended a masked social affair or pageant and met a young married woman, Mrs. Porterfield. This lady's husband became very angry at the somewhat amorous actions of the pair and decided to settle with Buntline. In the shooting affray that resulted Buntline killed his adversary.

For this shooting he was seized by a mob and hanged. Friends succeeded in cutting him down and reviving him. When brought before a jury, his plea of self-defense secured his release, and Buntline immediately left town.

In 1849, at a time when there was intense and bitter rivalry among New York's theaters and stage folk, he was in New York and was a leader in the mob that stormed the Astor Place Opera House, where the English actor, Macready, was to play Hamlet. Before militia quelled the riot, some thirty-four persons had been killed and 131 injured. Once again, Buntline left town.

From New York he went to St. Louis, where he organized a troupe of actors and musicians that toured many Illinois towns. Back in St. Louis he was a leader in riots that occurred on election day in April, 1852, and resulted in much property damage, numerous injuries, and at least one death before the militia put down the disturbance. For his participation in the St. Louis rioting, Buntline was arrested and jailed. Released on bond to await trial, he became impatient at delays, jumped bond, and came to Illinois. For this action St. Louis was out of bounds for many years.

This convenient absence from St. Louis brought Buntline to Carlyle to edit *The Prairie Flower,* a paper sponsored by Illinois politicians. In a short time the Carlyle paper was discontinued as were so many of the political organs of that time, and Buntline again moved on. There are reasons for believing that upon leaving Carlyle, he returned for a short visit to Nashville, Tennessee, to see Mrs. Porterfield, the widow of the man he had killed. If he visited there, his stay was a brief one.

A few years later Buntline was in the Indian country of the West. Here he met a gallant appearing gentleman named William F. Cody, whom he induced to appear in a western play that Buntline produced in Chicago. To the new character that Ned had discovered he gave the name of Buffalo Bill, not an uncommon one on the frontier. Buntline thus launched Cody upon his career as a showman and surrounded him with a wealth of stories, often fanciful.

After sixty-three years, which no one could term other than hectic, Ned Buntline, participant in many a varied venture and much marked with scars from old wounds, died in New York State on July 16, 1886. He left behind a number of broken hearts, a few killings, the dime novel, Buffalo Bill, a stack of legends, and *The Prairie Flower.* All of these have been woven into an interesting book *The Great Rascal* by Jay Monaghan.

Perhaps some copies of the paper Judson issued in Carlyle still exist, and in old attics one occasionally finds a copy of a Ned Buntline story.

🌸 LAFAYETTE

MANY MEN HAVE come to America to live and work and to become staunch defenders of this country and its ideals. Others have come, rendered great services, and departed. Marquis de Lafayette was among the latter. His part in America's war for independence is well known. Less well known are the details and circumstances of his return visit to America.

In 1825, about fifty years after his first visit to this country, Lafayette returned as the guest of the nation he had done so much to free. He was received with great acclaim throughout the eastern states as he revisited many of the scenes connected with his earlier services. When it became known that Lafayette planned to visit the southern and western states, Governor Coles and the legislature of the State of Illinois extended him a cordial invitation.

The invitation was accepted, and on April 18 Lafayette wrote to Governor Coles that he would arrive about the end of the month. He suggested that Kaskaskia, center of the old French settlement, be one of the places visited. Traveling faster than his letter, the distinguished visitor reached the state before it had reached Coles. Only when they learned of his visit to St. Louis did they know he could be expected, so there was at least an element of surprise involved. This late knowledge did not allow much time for making any organized plans.

About one o'clock on the afternoon of April 30 the steamer "Natchez" arrived at "the ferry" or steamboat landing at Kaskaskia with the noted visitor and his party. When they came ashore, they were met by a reception committee composed of many of the most distinguished citizens of Illinois. They were taken to the home of General Edgar, "where refreshments were served" and appropriate welcoming ceremonies were held. Governor Coles made an eloquent welcoming address to which Lafayette responded with due grace. Many persons came to the Edgar home to meet the noted visitor. From the residence of General Edgar, the French guest and many other prominent persons from several states went to the tavern of Colonel Sweet, where, in a flowered and gaily decorated hall, a banquet was served and many toasts were proposed. After the banquet, a great ball was held "at the stone mansion of William Morrison." Many young ladies came to dance briefly with the general. Even now some of the slippers and gowns worn on that eventful evening are treasured as family heirlooms.

About midnight the party ended. Lafayette and the delegation with him boarded the "Natchez" and proceeded on their way toward Nashville, Tennessee.

Leaving Nashville, where a day was spent with General Jackson at the Hermitage, the party returned to visit Shawneetown on May 14. Here a most elaborate program was enacted. A pathway from the steamboat landing to the Rawlings House, where the reception was held, was spread with calico and strewn with flowers. The women of the town were resplendent in gala dress. Judge James Hall delivered the welcoming address, to which Lafayette made a kind response. It was indeed a great day in the history of the town.

At each of the places visited, groups of Revolutionary War veterans came to greet their one-time commander and to extend their welcome. Some of them were remembered by the visitor.

As the centenary of his visit to Illinois came near, it was decided that some observance should be made. Since the town of Kaskaskia and all its landmarks had long since vanished into the Mississippi, it was determined that the re-enactment of the event should be in Shawneetown. Accordingly, this observance was held on May 14, 1925, exactly a century from the day of his visit there. Some of the buildings of 1825, perhaps enough of them to give a measure of familiarity to the scene, were still standing.

Many of the leading roles in the 1825 reception were performed by the descendants of those who participated in the early observance. For example, the part of W. A. Docker, president of the village board in 1825, was performed by his grandson, J. L. Rowan, mayor of the city in 1925. The address of welcome made by Judge James Hall in 1825 was repeated by C. K. Roedel in 1925.

Those of us who were present at the re-enactment in 1925 will not soon forget the occasion. The Lafayette legend received added interest.

❧ *TWO CONFEDERATES*

FEW PERSONS LIVING in the state are aware that two great Confederates did military service in Illinois. One of these was Robert E. Lee.

In 1835 Lee helped to survey the state line between Ohio and Michigan. In 1836 he became a first lieutenant and came to St. Louis, assigned to do engineering work on the Missouri and upper Mississippi. He served on this assignment until 1841. For a part of this time he was stationed at Fort Armstrong, a military post on Rocky Island, now the city of Rock Island, Illinois, where he surveyed the rapids of the river. His name is thus connected with those of other men who later were to attain fame, such as Zebulon Pike, Zachary Taylor, Winfield Scott, and Abraham Lincoln, who saw service in the same area. Illinois can take pride in its association with Robert E. Lee.

The second of these great men was Jefferson Davis, president of the Confederacy. Davis served as a lieutenant at Fort Armstrong during the Black Hawk War. At the same time Abraham Lincoln commanded a company of volunteers in the area. Some traditional accounts would have them meet there, but no convincing evidence of such a meeting has been found.

Davis first came to this region in 1829 to help in the building of Fort Winnebago at the portage between the Fox and Wisconsin rivers. From there he made a journey to the Chicago area in the fall of 1829. The incidents of his arrival at Chicago were almost prophetic. Arriving at a point opposite the station, he found no way to cross the river and accordingly hailed the post. Lieutenant David Hunter responded and took Davis across in a small canoe.

More than thirty years later, Jefferson Davis, then president of the Southern Confederacy, threatened death to this same David Hunter, then Major General Hunter, if captured, for enlisting Negroes for military service. About two years later Major General Hunter sat as president of the council to pass judgment on those charged with conspiracy, including Davis.

Incidentally, Davis was captured in his flight from Richmond in the spring of 1865 by troops from the area of Madison, Wisconsin, that he had first traversed on his trip from Fort Winnebago to Chicago thirty-six years earlier. Davis visited Chicago a second time in 1833, when he surveyed the Chicago and Calumet rivers and Calumet Lake and recommended that the Calumet River and the lake be converted into a harbor.

It was while serving at Fort Armstrong that Davis met Colonel Zachary Taylor's daughter, Sarah. They promptly fell in love, only to find Taylor bitterly opposed to their marriage. Davis soon resigned from the service and Sarah went to visit her aunt in Louisville, Kentucky. They were married there, not with General Taylor's blessing but with a cash gift from him, and went to live on a Mississippi plantation. Two months later Sarah died of malaria, singing in her delirium snatches of a song that was a favorite of hers and of her husband. Today a ruined mausoleum near Baton Rouge marks the final resting place of Sarah Davis. Her noted father, Zachary Taylor, lies in a neglected cemetery near Louisville, Kentucky, and Davis' grave is in Hollywood cemetery at Richmond, Virginia. Perhaps another incident connecting Davis and an Illinoisan should be included. Davis and William H. Bissell, from Monroe County, Illinois, were both elected to Congress after serving in the Mexican War. Davis took offense at a speech made by Bissell on the floor of Congress and challenged him to a duel. Bissell, promptly accepting, chose heavily loaded army muskets as the weapons and set an almost powder-burning distance of six paces. Friends of Davis succeeded in persuading him to forego the duel.

🌼 *LINCOLN AT JONESBORO*

Illinois claims Abraham Lincoln and Stephen A. Douglas among her illustrious sons. Over many years they were political rivals and clashed as such on numerous occasions. One of these significant events occurred at a meeting, September 15, 1858 in southern Illinois.

The place was the fairgrounds, one-fourth mile north of the public square at Jonesboro, county seat of Union County, where a stone marker now indicates the site. It was the third in the series of seven joint debates they were holding in their contest for a seat in the United States Senate— perhaps the most noted series of political debates in the nation's history.

The setting for this meeting was a simple one. There was a crude platform made of rough planks laid across logs in the shade of some large trees. There was no rail about the platform. The seats on it were common, household chairs brought from near-by homes or from wagons where they had been used by those coming to hear the talks or to attend the county fair then in progress.

A large table on the platform was used by the press secretaries making record of the talks. There apparently was no rostrum for the speakers. No bunting or flags draped the platform, and there were few banners in evidence. Except for a small area in front of the platform where planks had been laid across logs, no arrangements had been made to seat the small audience of a thousand or less who listened.

The majority of those present were plain folk of the later pioneer type, generally dressed in their Sunday best—if they owned such—and freshly shaven. Some had trudged in from the near-by countryside, some had come on horseback or in carriages, and still others had taken Illinois Central trains to the adjoining town of Anna.

A great proportion of those present had come in ox wagons. One group consisting of E. E. Trovillion and friends came in this manner from Golconda, in Pope County, more than forty-five miles away, camping by the roadside at night. Altogether, it was a group of rugged but serious listeners.

Lincoln, with a newspaper reporter, his only known companion, had arrived at the Anna railway station on the evening of September 14 and stayed that night at the home of his friend, D. L. Phillips. Much of the evening was passed with friends and admirers at the Union Hotel in Jonesboro, where the time was devoted to telling stories, discussing political issues, forming plans, cultivating friendships, and observing Donati's comet, then a prominent object in the night sky.

Douglas, who had recently spoken in Chester, had arrived in Cairo by steamboat on the fourteenth and spent the night there. On the morning of the fifteenth his special coach and a flatcar were attached to the northbound train. The flatcar carried a small brass cannon attended by two men in semimilitary uniform. It also carried Professor Terpinitz, jeweler and able musician from Jonesboro, and his band.

On the trip north from Cairo, the cannon was fired as the train approached each town, heralding the approach of Douglas and his party. The band would then begin to play. The Douglas group thus proceeded to Anna with a reasonable amount of fanfare. A small crowd was awaiting the Douglas train at Anna with carriages for at least a part of the group. A parade was formed, with the band leading, and the trip to the public square in Jonesboro was completed.

Shortly after the noonday meal, the candidates and their supporters went to the fairgrounds. There was no parade. Douglas, appearing to be fatigued by the campaign, rode in a carriage. Lincoln and some friends walked along the pathway on the east side of the street. An old man, drawing upon his memories, left some interesting glimpses of the tall figure of the Lincoln he remembered, walking among friends, but with no one in particular, toward the place of meeting.

When Lincoln and Douglas met, the contrast in their physical appearance was striking. Douglas, short in stature and rather rotund, wore a broad-brimmed whitish hat, kid gloves, shining shoes, and an elegant suit of clothes. His general appearance is recorded as imperious and haughty. Lincoln's clothes, though tasteful, were not nearly so nice in appearance as those of Douglas. He wore a high topped hat that served to emphasize the difference in height of the two men. Lincoln's carriage, though not so graceful as that of Douglas, was leisurely and relaxed and added to the impression that he was a calm, capable, and confident person. He was easily the more striking figure.

The story of the Lincoln and Douglas debates is well known. The crowd at Jonesboro, much the smallest in the series, was overwhelmingly favorable toward Douglas, but the tenseness that was evident throughout the debates was not relaxed here. Each candidate clearly indicated his high regard for the capabilities of the other. If any incident distinguished the Jonesboro debate, it was the fact that Lincoln succeeded in goading Douglas into an obvious display of temper.

After the debate, Douglas returned to Cairo. Lincoln again spent the night with his friend, D. L. Phillips. The northbound train on the morning of the sixteenth carried the special coach of Douglas and the flatcar with its cannon. Lincoln boarded the train at Anna as a regular passenger.

🌼 LINCOLN FOR PRESIDENT

SOME GROUP, SOMEWHERE, naturally had to be first to formally endorse Abraham Lincoln as a candidate for the presidency. That distinction goes to the Wayne County Illinois Republican Convention that met at Fairfield in early March of 1860.

Lincoln had then been in Illinois twenty-nine years. His experiences here had been varied. He had been a farm hand and rail splitter, helping his father open and fence a farm. He also had been a flatboatman, a soldier, an inventor, a merchant, a postmaster, an attorney, a state legislator, a congressman, and long an active politician. He had contended with Stephen A. Douglas for a seat in the U.S. Senate and lost. He had appeared as an attorney in many courts over the state, several of these being in southern Illinois. He had come to be regarded highly in legal circles.

Almost imperceptibly he had become a national figure—one whose opinions and utterances were awaited and carefully noted. Though no organized political group had formally recorded its approval, there were many indications that Lincoln was being considered, seriously and widely, as the Republican candidate. The movement that brought him to wide attention almost might have been termed a "political ground swell."

It was in this general atmosphere that the Republicans of Wayne County met in the spring of 1860, and on March 3 took the action here indicated:

RESOLVED—
that the Hon. Abe Lincoln is the unanimous choice of the Republicans of Wayne County for the presidential nomination of the National Convention at Chicago.

> Wayne County Republican Convention
> C. Sibley—Chairman
> Wm. H. Robinson—Secretary

No effort to evaluate the effects of the action taken is being made. It is only noted.

On Friday, October 6, 1939, a program was held in Fairfield and a marker was dedicated to commemorate the first recorded action of the early county group. This program began with a parade of floats, bands, and horsemen at 10 o'clock in the forenoon.

After luncheon the public ceremony of dedication was enacted. Dr. Cameron Harmon, then president of McKendree College, offered the invocation, and Mayor Fred Bruce gave the address of welcome.

After the Fairfield High School chorus had sung "Illinois," distinguished guests were presented and the formal dedication was enacted. The address of the day was given by George D. Aiken, then governor of Vermont.

Those who pass through Fairfield often stop to observe the marker on the courthouse lawn and to consider the early tribute paid by the Wayne County Republican Convention to one of the world's most noted men.

❦ *ANN RUTLEDGE*

THE STORY OF Abraham Lincoln is inseparably connected with that of Illinois. From the time of his young manhood when he crossed the Wabash at Vincennes with his father's family until his death, he was personally associated with incidents and persons in the southern section of the state. The story of his life has been fully and interestingly told—so much so that no attempt will be made to do that here. However, one incident of his life closely related to southern Illinois will be set down.

All are familiar with stories and legends about Lincoln while he was at New Salem. Some of those concerning Lincoln and Ann Rutledge raise questions that never have been answered definitely. Perhaps they never can be.

Did Abraham Lincoln love Ann Rutledge? Did Ann love Lincoln? Were they engaged to be married? Were they planning to attend colleges in the same town? Did Mentor Graham teach English grammar to Ann Rutledge at about the same time he taught Lincoln or did Lincoln teach Ann grammar? Did they sing together from the same song book at the local singing school? Did Ann send for Lincoln and did he go to visit her a few days before her death on August 25, 1835?

The story of Ann generally begins with her arrival in New Salem when she was fifteen years old. It is seldom mentioned that Ann, also born in Kentucky, had lived twelve years near the village of Enfield, in White County.

When James Rutledge decided to move from White County to a new location in present-day Menard County, the idea of leaving Ann with her grandmother at Enfield was seriously considered. It finally was decided, however, that Ann should go with the family. Her grandmother remained at Enfield and is buried in the cemetery a short way south of town. Considering the fact that Ann spent more than half her life near the village of Enfield, southern Illinois may justifiably claim more than a casual interest in her. Here she attended the local school at old Sharon Church. Her later years may have brought certain disappointments, but James Rutledge was a prosperous farmer in White County, and we may safely assume that Ann's girlhood years there were happy ones.

Little information that would ordinarily be considered as reliable concerning Ann and young Lincoln has been set down. The information recorded is often in conflict, but at any rate a great deal has been written concerning a great romance between the charming young lady and the tall, popular, and respected young man.

The Rutledges came to New Salem in 1828, where Ann's father built the first house on the site where the village was to be, and when John Cameron later constructed a milldam across the Sangamon River. It was on this dam that the flatboat Lincoln was taking down the river became lodged on April 19, 1831. The delay necessary to free the boat resulted in Lincoln's becoming acquainted with some of the people living there. The ingenuity he exhibited in transferring the boat across the dam brought him to the attention of a number of people and secured for him an invitation to come back and work there.

Lincoln continued his journey with the flatboat. Upon completion of the trip, he returned to New Salem and went to live at the boarding house of John Cameron. In the spring of 1832, he moved to the tavern built and kept by Ann's father and stayed there until he departed in December, 1834, to serve as a legislator at Vandalia.

During Lincoln's stay at the tavern, Ann lived with her parents and helped her mother with the household tasks. Ann and Lincoln thus had opportunity to know each other well. Ann's plan to attend college and Lincoln's known intellectual inclinations would indicate that they had common interests.

Ann Rutledge had grown up in a somewhat intellectual and devoutly Christian home. Those who knew her and recorded their impressions of her are agreed that she was a charming and popular lady of excellent character. She is described by one of those who knew her as auburn-haired, slim, blue-eyed, fair complexioned, about five feet two inches tall and weighing about 120 pounds.

At the time of Ann's death at twenty-two, Lincoln was twenty-six years old. He was tall and impressive looking and had already begun to display the mannerisms and traits that later were to endear him to the world. He was even then known as humorous, kindly, studious, trust-worthy, sober, highly respected and of great integrity, the outstanding young man in the vicinity.

The character of each was such as could well secure the admiration and respect of the other. The extent and depth of any romance that may have developed between the two may never be known definitely, but the names of Abraham Lincoln and Ann Rutledge are inseparably connected in the minds of millions. Whether based on facts or fancy, the legend of their romance is a good one.

🌿 *JOHN A. LOGAN*

"John was a pert little fellow of three years, black-eyed, black-haired and dark-skinned, straight-built and Indian-like, as his father was before him." This is a brief but rather vivid description of a Jackson County tot who grew up to become a national figure and one of the state's most colorful characters. It is taken from the memoirs of Daniel Harmon Brush, a prominent citizen of the long vanished village of Brownsville.

The boy was John Alexander Logan whose father, Dr. John Logan, had come from Ireland to Maryland, then to Missouri, and later settled on a farm where the city of Murphysboro was to appear. Parts of Brush's description of Logan as he appeared in 1829 applied equally well to the famous general of forty years later, when he was pictured as dark complexioned, with very dark eyes, raven black hair worn long, and with a magnificent black mustache. As for his personality, it was said that Logan was a versatile, energetic, affable, impetuous, daring, and dignified man.

In the years that had passed since Brush first observed the three-year-old boy, Logan had lived a somewhat varied and eventful life. His education was rather fitful. He attended the local school, was taught by his father, and had gone for a short time to Shiloh College, in Randolph County, and to Louisville University at Louisville, Kentucky. He also had studied law in the office of his uncle, Lieutenant Governor Alexander M. Jenkins.

Other associations helped to shape the character of young Logan. His father was a great lover of race horses and kept a number of them. He also maintained a track on his farm, where races were regularly held. The boldest and most successful jockey who rode at Dr. Logan's track was his son. Perhaps his associations with horse racing and the usual betting that accompanied it caused John A. to indulge in a bit of gaming and to acquire the nickname of Black Jack.

One indication of Logan's tendency to gaming is shown by an indictment returned by the grand jury of September, 1846. This indictment charges that "on the 4th day of August 1846 John Logan Jr. and Samuel Hays did then and there play together at a game called seven up for money contrary to form of the statutes and against the peace and dignity of the state." The warrant for Logan's arrest was "served by taking John Logan into custody." A bond for $100 was signed by Logan with Jonathan Heiple as surety. The case against Logan was continued many times— in fact so many times that he was able to serve as a lieutenant in the war with Mexico and return with an excellent military record before being brought to trial at the April term of court in 1849.

A second indictment against Logan was returned by the grand jury at the April term in 1847. In this indictment it was charged that "John Logan, Junior, James Jurray and Isaac M. Willis did on the 10th day of October, 1846 unlawfully play together with dollars at a game called pitching dollars for one pint of whiskey of the value of ten cents." In the trial that followed, Logan was found "not guilty as charged."

His clashes with the law, however, did not prevent his being elected as county clerk for Jackson County in 1849. He was serving in that office when the seven-up case was finally settled by his payment of a fine of ten dollars and costs of $17 on September 21, 1850.

His youthful escapades apparently did not handicap Logan, and he continued to rise in public favor. After completing his study of law, he was admitted to the bar and named prosecuting attorney for the Third Judicial Circuit in 1852. In this office he became known as a vigorous and able prosecutor. He was next elected to the state legislature, where he actively supported the legislation enacted in 1853 known as the Black Code, a body of law to restrict slaves and bond servants more severely.

In his earlier political career Logan was a rabid Democrat, supporting Stephen A. Douglas and bitterly attacking Abraham Lincoln. After the election, Logan apparently vacillated in his course for some months. An avowed Southern sympathizer, he nevertheless was a staunch defender of the national union and the ordered course of government.

To back up his stand when there was talk of preventing Lincoln from the office of President, Logan declared that he would "shoulder a musket to have him inaugurated."

In Washington for the special session of Congress in July, 1861, Logan hastened to Bull Run when fighting started there and attached himself to an Iowa regiment. He valiantly but unsuccessfully sought to rally the retreating Union troops and was among the last to leave the field of battle.

Shortly after Bull Run, Logan returned to southern Illinois and in a memorable speech on the public square at Marion, pledged his full support to the national cause. This decided stand by Logan did much to rally the people of southern Illinois to the support of the national government.

At the Marion meeting Logan also began recruiting a regiment and became their colonel in September, 1861. His valiant and capable actions in combat at Fort Donelson won him a commission as Brigadier General in March, 1862. For his brave decisions at Vicksburg, he was made a major general in July, 1863. Upon the death of General McPherson, Logan was made Commander of the Army of the Tennessee.

In combat Logan was an inspiring leader. Daring to the point of recklessness he often, even after becoming a major general, personally led his troops into battle. His admonition to his soldiers—"aim low, it takes two men to carry a man shot in the leg off the field"—was repeated for many years by the men who fought under him. Few military leaders have won and held the great personal loyalty that was given Logan.

After the end of the Civil War, he returned to civilian life and politics. He was elected as congressman at large for the State of Illinois in 1866, then United States senator; he was a candidate for vice-president and was being groomed for nomination as the 1888 Republican candidate for the presidency when he died in 1886. Logan was active in the formation of the Grand Army of the Republic and was twice chosen at its national commander. In this post, he was instrumental in establishing Memorial Day. He was always a vigorous advocate of the interests of the men who had served in the Union forces during the recent war.

Striking in personal appearance, an able and eloquent speaker, energetic, restless, impulsive and daring, Logan retains a prominent place in southern Illinois history.

✿ THE GREAT AGNOSTIC

IN THE 1880's Robert G. Ingersoll was a national figure. He was recognized as one of America's outstanding orators, a very capable attorney, and "the Great Agnostic." To many orthodox churchmen he was a person to be abhorred. Among those who termed themselves liberals he was admired. Few who knew him regarded him in any lukewarm manner. Feelings toward him were better expressed by love or hate than by like or dislike. Whether pro-Ingersoll or anti-Ingersoll, all admired his great eloquence and respected his unquestioned ability as an attorney.

This somewhat unusual character was a product of southern Illinois. Some of the landmarks around which Ingersoll stories are clustered remain. Among these are the log school where he taught in Metropolis, the log house that once served as a school in the now vanished town of Bowlesville, where he is said to have made his first political speech, and the building (now a family garage) that was his law office in Raleigh when it was the county seat of Saline County. There are also numerous stories and legends still extant about him.

Antipathy against Ingersoll came from his criticisms of the church whose orthodox beliefs he often attacked from the lecture platform. Some of his lectures—"The Gods," "Some Mistakes of Moses," "Why I am an Agnostic," and "Superstitions"—drew large audiences and were widely discussed. His eulogy at his brother's grave and that at the grave of a child are still recognized as gems of oratory. All his speeches were widely circulated and commented upon.

Ingersoll, born in New York State, came to Illinois as a youth with his father, a minister. Robert first attracted attention when he taught part of a school term in Metropolis. His somewhat unconventional remarks prevented his finishing the term. According to the local account, Ingersoll was present at the hot-stove session in the local grocery store on a winter evening. The usual group of men had gathered and were discussing religious matters. The point under consideration was the proper method of baptism. Ingersoll's opinion was asked. He replied, somewhat humorously, that it was his opinion the very best method was immersion if the candidate had properly "soaped up" before the plunge. This remark angered some of the churchmen present. They considered it flippant and impious. Ingersoll was dismissed as a teacher.

From Metropolis Ingersoll went to Shawneetown, where he was appointed deputy county clerk. While serving in this capacity, he began to study law and was admitted to the bar when twenty-one years old. It was while he was serving as deputy county clerk that he became a principal figure in a tragedy.

Ingersoll was in the office most of the time when it was open. He thus met and talked with many visitors. Ingersoll remarked to one caller that the daughters of a prominent farmer living near Shawneetown had attracted much attention and perhaps caused some comment by driving down the street in a buggy on the day before, gaily chatting and swapping banter with some young men loitering along the street. This visitor to the county clerk's office passed the remark along. Though the comments made by Ingersoll appear to have been casual and only mildly, if at all, critical, the version that reached the father highly incensed him. Upon inquiry, he learned where the story originated, but he presumed that the county clerk himself was spreading the report. The father immediately set out to investigate and evidently to punish the one who had made the remarks he considered offensive. Deputy Ingersoll was not present when the irate father arrived and the regular county clerk met the visitor. Asking if he was talking to the county clerk and receiving an affirmative reply, the father drew a pistol from his pocket and shot him to death.

For this killing the father was charged with murder. The trial that followed was long and bitterly fought. John A. Logan was the prosecuting attorney. The father was defended by a capable and determined group of attorneys. The case attracted statewide attention and established a precedent in Illinois courts. The defense was based on a plea of temporary insanity, induced by the remarks concerning the daughters. On the basis of this plea, the father was acquitted. After a short period spent in a mental institution, he was released. This is said to be the first case in Illinois courts where a temporary insanity plea was successfully offered as a defense for a killing.

Robert G. Ingersoll, the deputy county clerk who is credited with the original remarks, soon left Shawneetown.

🌿 WILLIAM JENNINGS BRYAN

WHEN SILAS AND Mariah Bryan went to the Centennial Exposition at Philadelphia in 1876, their sixteen-year-old son took advantage of their absence and attended a national political convention. Although he did not have a pass for admission to the convention hall, he did have an affective smile that won the co-operation of a friendly policeman who helped him through a window into the hall.

The national convention was that of the Democratic party at St. Louis in the summer of 1876, and the young man crawling through the window was William Jennings Bryan. This was his first, but by no means his last, attendance at a national political conclave.

The youth was greatly impressed by the men of national prominence he saw. He was also moved by their able and persuasive speeches and by the glimpses of the broad workings of democracy that the occasion afforded.

However, young Bryan could not have dreamed that twenty years later he would appear as the dominant figure at a similar convention, make one of the most noted political speeches in the nation's history, and be nominated as candidate for the presidency—the youngest such candidate of a major political party in American history.

Bryan was born at Salem in Marion County, Illinois, on March 19, 1860. His birthplace is still standing, well-stocked with mementos that recall events of his life. The home, located on a main street about three blocks south of the square, is visited by many people.

When William was five or six years old his father bought a large farm adjoining the town on the northwest. Here the elder Bryan fulfilled a boyhood dream by building a large dwelling of bricks that were made a short way north of the building site. He also built a fine set of outbuildings and enclosed fourteen acres southeast of the dwelling as a deer park. It was the practice of the father, while the building operations were under way, to drive out often and observe the progress being made. On some of these trips young William was allowed to place bricks on a small piece of board and carry them to the masons, thus helping to build the house.

It was on this farm and about this spacious home that William grew to young manhood. It also was here that he received his elementary education, his mother being the teacher. Bryan records that she was a rather stern and exacting teacher, evidently a believer in the philosophy expressed by the old adage, "Spare the rod and spoil the child." William also helped with the farm work and daily chores. The Bryan home was a devoutly Christian one. Family worship services were held regularly three times daily. In later life William spoke of this family custom and indicated the pleasure that the memories of those occasions afforded him. Considering this practice in the Bryan home, it is not difficult to understand the deeply religious cast of William's thinking.

When he was fifteen, William was sent to Whipple Academy in Jacksonville. He continued in attendance at the academy and at the college there until 1881, when he was graduated as valedictorian of his class.

The next two years were spent at Union College of Law or in reading law in the office of Lyman Trumbull, both located in Chicago. He was admitted to the bar in time to open an office in Jacksonville on July 4, 1883. After four reasonably profitable years, Bryan made a business trip to Lincoln, Nebraska. He liked the western town and decided to move there.

He was successful in his law practice at Lincoln, but he was more successful in politics and on the lecture platform. His ability in these latter fields led him practically to abandon law when he was elected to the United States House of Representatives in 1890. In 1894 Bryan was defeated in a contest for a seat in the United States Senate and shortly thereafter became the editor of a paper. But about this same time, his reputation as a platform speaker was becoming nationally known.

In 1896 he was a delegate to the national convention of the Democrats in Chicago. The question of using silver along with gold as a basis for our national currency was before the country. Bryan was one of the staunchest advocates of the plan. When he appeared before the convention to advance the cause of silver, he captivated the audience with his famous "Cross of Gold" speech, which he climaxed with the memorable sentence, "You shall not press down upon the brow of labor this crown of thorns; you shall not crucify mankind upon a cross of gold."

The setting for this speech could not have been better arranged. The crowd was electrified. Five ballots later, Bryan was nominated as the Democratic candidate for president. His station was considerably elevated over that of twenty years before, when a friendly policeman had helped him through the window and into the convention hall in St. Louis. Over many years and at numerous succeeding conventions, Bryan was a dominant figure.

A portion of the Silas Bryan farm where William grew to young manhood has recently been purchased by a citizen of Salem who plans to dismantle the ruins of the old brick home northwest of town. A landmark connected with another of the famous sons that southern Illinois has exported will disappear.

🏵 SENATOR BORAH

SOUTHERN ILLINOIS HAS exported a number of young men who became famous. One of these was William Edgar Borah, a native of Wayne County, later to become dean of the United States Senate and one of the most capable and influential members in its history. Few men have served so long, and surely no one of equally long service has been more independent.

William, one of ten children in the Borah family, was born on a farm six miles northeast of Fairfield in 1865. He grew up there and attended Tom's Prairie School, the oldest one in the county. He also went regularly to the local Cumberland Presbyterian Church, where the father was an active leader.

The Borah home, like most of those at the time, had little reading material. Their library consisted of the Bible, *Pilgrim's Progress, Life of Washington,* Franklin's *Autobiography, Night Scenes from the Bible,* two or three of Scott's novels, an occasional newspaper, and by some strange circumstance a volume of orations by Robert G. Ingersoll. Of course, there was the McGuffey series of readers.

Young Borah had a comfortable and congenial home, a kindly mother, and an intelligent and able father. It was the custom of his father to discuss and attempt to analyze the problems of the day with his son. In later years William expressed great appreciation for the way in which these discussions had influenced his thinking. Though apparently tolerant and broad-minded, the father was uncompromising between right and wrong. To him each issue was to be decided strictly upon its merits, an element obvious in the son's thinking throughout his career.

When William had completed the course of study at Tom's Prairie School, he was sent to Illinois Academy at Enfield for one year. Here he came under the influence of Professor Mark A. Montgomery, a college graduate and a most inspiring teacher. Literature, history, and participation in the activities of the academy's literary society strongly appealed to young Borah. It was while a student here that he made his first political speech, substituting for a scheduled speaker who had failed to appear.

Borah did not return to the academy after the first year but stayed at home to help with the farm work. According to one account, he was away from home three weeks during the year, however, playing the part of Mark Antony with a troupe of Shakespearian actors. This may help to explain Borah's great interest in the theater and his unusual dramatic ability.

In 1883 he attended the University of Kansas, then taught school, and studied law. Among his classmates at Kansas were Herbert Hadley, William Allen White, Fred M. Funston, and Vernon Kellogg, all of whom later attained national prominence.

After admission to the bar in 1889, Borah established an office at Lyons, Kansas. In 1890, having had practically no clients during the previous year, Borah decided to locate in Seattle. But when he reached Boise, Idaho, he found himself practically penniless. A short stop convinced him that Boise offered reasonable opportunities for an attorney, and he decided to begin practice there. In a few years he had the best law practice in Idaho.

Borah's abilities were recognized and he was made prosecuting attorney. In that capacity he conducted the prosecution of Will D. (Big Bill) Haywood and others for the killing of Governor Frank S. Steunenberg during a strike at the copper mines. Clarence Darrow, perhaps the outstanding defense attorney of the nation, was counsel for Haywood. Borah lost the case but was designated by Darrow as "the ablest man with whom I have ever contended."

Borah became interested in politics and entered the race for the United States Senate but was defeated in his first try. In the next campaign, however, he was successful and was re-elected five times.

From his first appearance in the Senate, Borah showed his independence. Nelson Aldrich, powerful senator from Rhode Island, tried to coerce him without success. A portion of a letter that Aldrich received from an influential citizen of Idaho to whom he had written in an effort to have Borah "behave" indicates the new senator's spirit of freedom. A portion of the Idahoan's reply follows: "I want you to understand clearly in any case, I have no influence with Borah, and if you discover anyone in Idaho who does, I would be grateful to you if you would send me his name."

Borah's stature continued to grow. Though many disagreed with him at various times, few questioned his sincerity or integrity, and all alike respected his great ability.

After the close of World War I, Borah opposed ratification of the Treaty of Versailles and led a bitter attack on the League of Nations. It was on the League of Nations issue that Borah appears to have attained his greatest fame as an orator. His opposition speech made in the Senate on November 19, 1919, is considered the greatest of his career. Some consider it fully the equal of any speech ever made before the Senate.

In none of his attacks on the Treaty of Versailles, the League of Nations, or any other measure advocated by President Wilson, did Borah make personal attack on the President as so many others did. Though he strongly opposed many of the policies that Wilson advocated, Borah respected the President and treated him with the utmost dignity. The high plane upon which he conducted his debates won wide praise. Wilson and a companion, driving on the streets of Washington shortly before the death of the former president, passed Borah. Wilson turned to his companion and remarked, "There is one irreconcilable whom I can respect."

Determined, unswerving, incorruptible, hating intrigue, independent, but still cherishing established institutions, the Great Isolationist continued to influence national and world affairs profoundly until his death in 1940.

Serving in the United States Senate during the administrations of seven presidents, a Wayne County boy left an indelible imprint upon national affairs.

🌾 *WILLIAM NEWBY*

ONE OF THE MOST noted cases of confused identity that grew out of the Civil War concerns William Newby, who was living on a farm near the village of Mill Shoals, in White County, at the outbreak of the Civil War. Newby, then thirty-five years old, and two of his brothers enlisted in Company D, Fortieth Illinois Infantry, on August 8, 1861, and soon went away to war.

Their company was encamped on the north bank of Owl Creek, about two miles southwest of Pittsburg Landing and not far from the Tennessee River on the morning of Sunday, April 6, 1862. They were up early, and the men were preparing breakfast when bullets began to whistle about them. The Battle of Shiloh had begun. Taken by surprise, they gathered arms, abandoned camp, and retreated northward a quarter of a mile to form in line of battle. The Confederates followed closely and fighting immediately began.

Several men of Company D were killed or wounded, and the company was forced to withdraw once more. Their dead and some of the more seriously wounded were left on the field. Among the wounded left was William Newby, who had suffered a head wound.

Some of Newby's comrades reported that they last saw him lying on the ground and quivering; others said that they saw him grasping his head and writhing. Still others reported they had seen him crawl to a tree against which he propped himself and complained aloud that he was badly hurt. To this point there is no particular controversy concerning Newby; all agreed that he was alive when they last saw him on the battlefield.

On April 8, the battle had ended and burial details were sent out. More than two days of warm and rainy weather had made it difficult to identify the swollen and discolored bodies. Several members of the detail, former neighbors of Newby, made special efforts to find him, but were unable to do so. Two members of the detail later said the body was identified and buried. Though the reports were indefinite, the records were marked to indicate that Newby had been killed.

In 1891, twenty-nine years later, rumors that Newby was still alive began to circulate. Hezekiah Newby, one of William's sons, heard these and went to McLeansboro to see the four men who had identified a wanderer there as his father. He learned that the man he sought was at the poor farm near Carmi. When Hezekiah arrived there, he called out for William Newby and a man stepped forward in response.

Impressed by the presence of certain scars and features similar to those identified with his father, Hezekiah returned to Mill Shoals and a conference of the Newby family was held. Certain marks were agreed upon which would definitely determine if the wanderer was William.

A few days later Hezekiah, and another son named Tully, and William Newby's brother Whalen, went to Carmi. The man they sought had left the poor farm. He was traced and found on the banks of the flooded Wabash several miles away. Careful investigation convinced them that he was the real William Newby and they accordingly took him back with them to Mill Shoals.

The aged mother, the wife, some of the family, and scores of older persons agreed that it was William Newby and were happy at his return. This condition might have continued indefinitely had it not been decided that he should apply for a discharge from the army, and seek a pension as well as back pay.

When the applicant went to Springfield to advance his claim, he was taken into custody against promises, charged with attempting to secure a pension fraudulently, and lodged in jail. Government attorneys insisted that he was not William Newby but was Daniel Benton, sometimes called "Rickety Dan." An indictment was returned against Daniel Benton, alias William Newby, and date for the trial was set.

The trial began on July 11, 1893, and immediately attracted nationwide attention. Judge Joshua W. Allen presided. Prosecution witnesses were brought from various states at government expense. The court allowed the defense to bring ten witnesses, all to be from southern Illinois, under similar arrangement. In addition to these witnesses, 150 friends, relatives, and neighbors from the vicinity of Mill Shoals went to Springfield at their own expense to testify for the defendant.

Evidence was in sharp conflict. Some identified the defendant as William Newby, while others were uncertain. Still others were positive that it was not Newby. One witness who had written to Newby's wife that he was positive the man he helped bury at Shiloh was her husband, reversed his testimony. A near relative testified that it was not Newby and is alleged to have later confessed that a bribe had been given for false testimony.

Some Union veterans who had been in Andersonville Prison, where the defendant said he was taken after the battle of Shiloh, identified him as a prisoner they had known there and called "Crazy Jack." Other witnesses identified the defendant as Daniel Benton, often spoken of as "Rickety Dan."

When testimony had been completed, Judge Allen gave his instructions to the jury. These instructions were then, and still are, severely criticized as indicating bias on the part of the court. The jury identified the defendent as Daniel Benton whereupon the court sentenced him to serve two years at hard labor in the prison at Chester. A plea for a new trial was denied. Shortly after his release from prison, Newby left Mill Shoals and wandered to the region of Andersonville Prison, where he died and was buried in a potter's field.

The case of William Newby, so far as court action is concerned, was decided in 1893. The great majority of the people living about Mill Shoals thought that a grave injustice had been done. When one comes to discuss the case with older persons now living there, it becomes evident that, despite the passage of sixty-six years since the court decision, sentiment yet runs strongly in favor of William Newby.

It might be of interest to know that the real Daniel Benton was born in White County, Illinois, and went, when five years old, to live with his mother near Nashville, Tennessee, in the same locality where William Newby was born and had lived before he came with his parents to live in the same White County locality where Benton had been born. Their paths crossed; their identities became confused.

A few older persons, among them the writer, recall the stooped figure and shuffling gait of this pathetic old man. Was he Crazy Jack, "Rickety Dan" Benton, or was he really William Newby. I am inclined to believe the last true. Anyway, the case still holds much mystery.

Chapter 2

Names

❧ *EGYPT & SUCKERS*

MOST OF THE STORIES and accounts offered here are associated with the
southern section of Illinois popularly termed "Egypt." Therefore, it may
be meaningful to explain why this region is frequently referred to by
that name and why its earlier inhabitants ofttimes were called "Suckers."
Since Egypt really is far away and the word sucker suggests a fish, perhaps both should be explained.

The boundaries of "Egypt" in Illinois are agreed upon to be the Wabash,
Ohio, and Mississippi rivers on the east, south, and west. The northern
limits, however, are indefinite. There are some, with reasonable territorial
ambitions, who would have it include all the state lying south of an east-
west line in the approximate latitude of Vandalia. Others, perhaps less
imperialistic or perhaps selfish, would include only that part of the state
lying south of the Baltimore and Ohio Railroad, roughly a line from East
St. Louis to Vincennes.

A second term, Little Egypt, often is applied to a smaller area at the
southern tip of the state. It includes eleven southern counties, ending on
the north at about the latitude of the city of Benton, in Franklin County.

Neither of the above terms is recognized as an established geographical
place name, and until comparatively recent years they were little used
outside the area. For a long time, they were convenient colloquial terms.
But, of late, the names have gained wider recognition because they are
handy headline designations for southern Illinois in the metropolitan
press.

The use of these terms, Egypt or Little Egypt to indicate a region so
far removed from the valley of the Nile naturally arouses the curiosity of

outsiders. Several explanations for the use of the names have been advanced. The two cited most frequently deserve comment.

The first explanation states that the region was so named because places bearing the Egyptian names of Cairo, Goshen, Karnak, and Thebes were located in it. The name of Goshen, or Land of Goshen, first was applied to a settlement in the south part of present Edwardsville about 1800. The name of Cairo now applied to the town located at the confluence of the Ohio and the Mississippi, first indicated a bank, the Bank of Cairo, chartered in 1818. This bank, which did not survive long, was located and had its offices in vanished Kaskaskia about one hundred miles northward. The present town of Cairo was planned and a charter was secured by the Cairo City and Canal Company in 1837, at least five years after the name Egypt was in common use. Unless the name Egypt came from "Goshen," "Land of Goshen" or "Goshen Road," all in use in the first decade of the 1800's, it is difficult to support this place-name theory.

The following is a second explanation of the way in which the term came to be applied to the region. This one is supported by documentary sources and by numerous traditional accounts. Perhaps the best explanation of the origin of the term is the one given by Judge A. D. Duff, a prominent attorney, circuit judge, and the person designated as Professor of Law on Southern Illinois Normal University's first faculty. Judge Duff's account appeared in the *Golconda Herald* in the 1860's, having been copied from an earlier issue of the *Shawneetown Gazette*. According to his story, the conditions leading to the use of the term Egypt in relation to southern Illinois began with the winter of 1830–31. This was the "winter of the deep snow," the longest and most severe winter that the residents of Illinois had known. Snows came early, reached a depth of three feet or more, and remained until late in the spring of 1831 and severe frosts continued until May. According to Judge Duff, it was a "very backward spring." The summer was extremely cool and killing frosts came on September 10, making the growing season a short one.

The late spring naturally delayed the planting of crops. The September frost killed much of the unripened corn in the northern counties. Only in those areas lying south of an east-west line approximately through the locality of Benton in Franklin County did corn properly mature. Farmers north of that line were forced to seek corn for their livestock, for the universally used corn meal, and for planting in counties farther south.

When this was happening, Judge Duff was a well-grown lad living beside a much traveled north-south roadway in Bond County. He saw many wagons going south to find corn and returning with the treasured grain. Some of these stopped overnight at the Duff home. Many of the farmers driving these wagons were Bible readers who remarked that they, like the sons of Jacob, were "going down to Egypt for corn." The designation of the southern counties of Illinois as Egypt thus came into use.

No record of the term has been found previous to 1832. Once applied, however, it rapidly came into general use. The journal of Daniel H. Brush, prominent citizen of Jackson County, covering the 1830's, refers to Egypt and indicates the same origin for the nickname.

At times the name of Egypt or Little Egypt has been used in a somewhat derogatory way, though originally the name carried no stigma. In fact, it was worn with reasonable pride.

After southern Illinois had been designated as Egypt, one would naturally expect the inhabitants to have been called Egyptians. This was not the case, however. Instead, they were nicknamed "Suckers," a name that they have very generously shared with all Illinoisans. Though no one seems to point with pride to the name, it still is of interest to know its origin. "Sucker" may have any of several meanings. It can mean a nursing mammal, a lollipop, a sprout on a plant or tree, a greenhorn, a circus or carnival patron, any person, plant, or animal living off another, or a kind of fish. From among these meanings, three have been advanced as a source that first attached the name to southern Illinoisans.

The first one comes from the use of the term "sucker" in the tobacco field. After a tobacco plant has been pinched back or topped, it puts forth suckers in the axils of the leaves. These useless sprouts live off the parent plant, sap it, and thus, stunt normal leaf growth. Since many of the settlers of Egypt were poor folk from the South where planters grew large fields of tobacco, they were compared to the suckers on the tobacco plant. Some planters held that these poorer people lived off the prosperous Southern economy without contributing to it. This appears as a highly improbable explanation since tobacco-growing was followed only to the extent necessary to supply local requirements, or "table use," in southern Illinois at the time the sobriquet was imposed on the population.

Another explanation is that the people of southern Illinois, during a period of great drought in the region were forced to carry long sections of pipe cane that they would insert in crayfish holes in order to get water. This explanation does not sound plausible either. The crayfish holes with which the author had acquaintance were not straight enough to allow the insertion of a long cane. Besides, the crayfish holes usually were located on low ground where it would not be difficult to find a stream with water in it.

What appears to be the true explanation is that the term originated in the lead mining region about Galena in the northwest corner of the state. Many men from southern Illinois would go to work in the lead mines during the summer and return to their homes in the autumn. This influx of seasonal workers began in the 1820's and continued for many years.

During the earlier years of this activity, Galena was in the midst of Indian country, and the miners who went to work there generally traveled upstream on the Mississippi instead of overland. They arrived with the milder weather of spring and returned to their homes as winter came. At about the same time that the men from downstate arrived at the lead mines, the fish commonly known as the sucker would also be making its annual migration upstream to its spawning grounds. The migrant worker and the fish would reach the region at about the same time. It was not unusual then to hear someone remark, "Here come men from southern Illinois; it's time to fish for suckers." If the fish appeared first someone was sure to remark "Here come the suckers; now look for the southern Illinoisans."

For those not fully familiar with the geographical-historical factors in the southern Illinois background, a very brief review may be helpful. Egypt was the first part of the state to be settled, but the French, who came first, and the English, who followed them, contributed little beyond romance to the region. It was not until the coming of Americans from the eastern settlements that a stabilized culture began. Among the earlier Americans in southern Illinois were the soldiers who came with George Rogers Clark to conquer the region for the colony of Virginia in 1778. When they returned to the East, they carried favorable reports concerning the localities in which they had campaigned. These men, with other immigrants seeking new homes, soon began to move into the area.

The first settlers migrated into the area principally by way of the Tennessee, Cumberland, and Ohio rivers. They found it easy to float down these rivers on flatboats but extremely difficult to ascend the Mississippi. For this reason most of them landed at selected points along the Ohio to settle near by, or they crossed the state over trails toward the Mississippi. So many of them located in the rich farmland belt lying along the Mississippi in Madison, St. Clair, Monroe, and Randolph counties that this region became known, and still is referred to, as the "American Bottom." In territorial times and during early statehood it was the most populous part of the state; thus it exercised great influence in early state affairs.

The two factors that did most to change the situation and to halt development of Egypt were the increased use of steamboats and the completion of the roadway known as the National or Cumberland Road, with its western terminus at Vandalia. As the steamboat and the National Road made travel easier, settlers struck out for desirable locations in the unsettled part of the state farther north, along the Mississippi, or in the vast stretches of the West.

The older settled portion of the state, except that near the rivers, was thus bypassed and left in what one might term an historical eddy. With decreased outside contacts to offer stimuli, the settlers in southern Illinois were left with a static or slowly changing culture. This condition remained relatively little changed until modern highways were built.

Because the interior portions of Egypt were thus isolated, its once superior culture was stalemated. Methods, practices, and devices of the pioneer tended to continue in use for a long time. It would be better to call this a period of arrested development rather than one of retrogression.

With the coming of improved roadways and added contacts with other sections of the country, the region began to show a marked change. Now, after a relatively short time, the daily way of life here does not differ materially from that of other sections of the state, though many vestiges of the early culture remain. The songs, stories, games, beliefs, remedies, customs, signs, legends, lore, and superstitions of the early days of Illinois are still found in quantity among older persons, but these, with the people who have knowledge of them, are slowly passing and soon will have gone into the realm of the forgotten. Here and there rail fences, log buildings, and some of the tools, implements, and devices employed by the pioneer remain to indicate a way of life that has all but vanished.

Many places associated with the significant events in the history of the state are located in Egypt and are constantly being brought to attention. Men who wielded great influence in the development of the early state lived here. Their stories, like those relating to the sites with historic significance, are slowly being assembled.

Information and descriptive materials concerning the scenic appeal of the region are likewise being gathered, and its recreational resources are given more attention. Its industrial potentials are being explored. Southern Illinois University at Carbondale is devoting much effort to programs for improving the region. Egypt, bypassed for more than a century, appears to be experiencing an awakening.

It is against this background that we would have these glimpses viewed.

❦ *PLACES MUST HAVE NAMES*

PLACES NATURALLY require names, and one of the tasks in newly settled southern Illinois was to select them. They came from many sources. Some were borrowed from the localities where the earlier settlers had lived; others were from literature, history, the Bible, and from mythology. Still other places were named for individuals or objects, while some come by their names accidentally.

Several places in southern Illinois have names borrowed from the Indians, though such borrowing did not occur here so frequently as in many other states. The Indians' "beautiful river" still is the Ohio, their "big water" is the Mississippi, and "shining water" remains the Wabash. The Kaskaskia River and village with the same name recall the once powerful Indian tribe that lived in Illinois. Even the state received its name from the Indian word "Illini" meaning "real men."

The village of Tamaroa in Perry county derives its name from another vanished tribe, and the city of DuQuoin does honor to John DuQuoin, a literate chief of the Kaskaskia. Makanda, at the entrance to Giant City Park in Jackson County, is said to have been named for the last Indian chief living in that vicinity. Oskaloosa, in Clay County, commemorates the wife of Chief Mohasda. Patoka was an Indian chief that lived in Marion County. The Cahokia gave their name to a mission there more than 250 years ago. Mascoutah in St. Clair County also arouses memories of an Indian, while Shawneetown is named for the Shawnee Indian tribe which once lived in the region. Shobonier, in Fayette County was another Indian chief. Nameoka, in Madison County, is the "place of fish"; War Bluff, Indian Kitchen, Mound City, Indian Gap, the Pounds, and another half dozen Indian forts suggest the prevalence of Indians in early Illinois. Several smaller streams still are called Indian Creek.

People who came here to settle brought the names of their former homes. An English colony settled in Edwards County and called their villages Wanborough and Albion. Alhambra, in Madison County, and vanished Cadiz, in Pope County, suggest Spain. A great battle was fought at Alma in the Crimea in 1854, and that name, then in the news, was given to Alma, in Marion County. The Swiss came to settle in Madison County, and Highland, once referred to as Helvetia, was named. Some sailors home from the seas settled in the community that is now Marine, in Madison County.

A number of community names were drawn from the Bible. The

mountains of Palestine suggested names for Lebanon, in Madison County, and Mt. Carmel, in Wabash County. From Palestine also came Palestine, in Crawford County. A fair and fertile spot in Randolph County became Eden, while Sparta was named for the ancient Greek city. Egypt gave names to Cairo, Karnak, Thebes, and Goshen. Odin was named for a god in Norse mythology. Countless churches answer to the names of Gilead, Zion, Mt. Olive, Bethany, Joppa, Ebenezer, and other biblical names.

Jasper County offers a somewhat unusual association of names of two individuals. The county itself was named for the Revolutionary soldier, Sgt. William Jasper, hero at Fort Moultrie, who was killed later at Savannah. Its county seat of Newton was named for Sgt. John Newton, another Revolutionary War hero. Gallatin County was named for Albert Gallatin, Secretary of the Treasury, as was Galatia once spelled Gallatia. DeSoto, in Jackson County, is for the Spanish explorer of that name.

General John B. Turchin, "the Mad Cossack," a former officer in the Russian army, served with distinction in the Union army during the Civil War. After the war, he formed a settlement in Washington County and called it Radom for his native district in Poland. Randolph County was named for the Governor of Virginia. Vanished Santa Fe village in Alexander County was for the Spanish town of Santa Fe in New Mexico.

French names linger in a number of places. Prairie du Rocher was "field of the rock"; Bellefontaine still is a "beautiful spring" near Waterloo, in Monroe County. LaClede, in Fayette County, is for the French founder of the city of St. Louis. Vanished Belle Rive, in Hamilton County, was for Louis St. Ange de Bellerive, who surrendered Illinois to the British in 1765. Pawnee became "pani" or slave in the French patois and later was used for the name of the new town of Pana.

Fort Massac and Massac County are for M. Massiac, Minister of Marine for France, during the French and Indian War. The Embarrass River, passing near Lawrenceville, and Bonpas Creek (Bumpus), in Edwards County, answer to the names the French gave them as also does Beaucoup (Buckoo) Creek, in Jackson County. Grand Pierre (Grampeer) and Big Grand Pierre, in Pope County, bespeak a French derivation. The town of Equality, in Gallatin County, echoes a part of the rallying cry of the French Revolution. Tonti, in Madison County, was named for LaSalle's faithful lieutenant of that name.

❧ *COUNTIES & COUNTY SEATS*

MEN RATHER THAN women evidently controlled affairs when the counties of southern Illinois were being laid out and the county seats named. This is apparent in the names they have. Almost forty such names do honor to men, and only one county seat pays tribute to a woman.

At different times, however, a total of three county towns have answered to feminine names. One of these, Elvira, in Johnson County, very quietly vanished from the scene. Sarahville, at Lusk's Ferry, seems to have soon wearied of her name and decided to change it—a privilege of women. She first decided to become Corinth. A few days later—apparently upon sober second thought—she decided to become Golconda, and Golconda she still is. Elizabethtown, county seat for Hardin County, thus remains the only county town in the region answering to a lady's name. Even then some of this distinction is removed by a local practice that shortens the title to E'town.

At least twenty-five of the counties and a dozen of their county seats are named in memory of men. Five do honor to presidents of the United States. They are Jackson, Jefferson, Madison, Monroe, and Washington. Jackson County was named for the seventh president while that one was resting—if he ever did such a thing—upon his military laurels and before his elevation to the White House.

Vanished Brownsville, Jackson County's first county seat and an important town in early Illinois, was named for a town in Pennsylvania. When it was voted to move the county seat from Brownsville, one of the members of the committee to select a new site is said to have drawn the lucky number from a hat and thereupon named the projected town for himself and called it Murphy's Borough (Murphysboro).

Jefferson County, named for the third president, apparently wished also to pay tribute to Washington and called its county seat Mount Vernon after the first president's home. Our fourth president provided the name for Madison County, which then chose the name of Edwardsville for its county town, thus honoring Ninian Edwards, territorial governor and later governor of the state.

The county of Monroe was named for the fifth president. Its first county seat, Carthage, was named after the ancient city of Carthage in northern Africa. This seat of government soon was moved, however, to a more centrally located site often referred to as Peter's Town, which shortly became Waterloo while the famous battle of Belgium was fresh in memory.

The remaining county named for a president, Washington, chose the name of Nashville for its seat of justice, borrowing it from the capital town of Tennessee.

One vice-president, Richard M. Johnson (1837–1841), had a county named for him. This naming, however, was a number of years before his election to the vice-presidency and while he was only a colonel of Kentucky militia. This new county borrowed the name of its capital town of Vienna from the town of that name in Austria. The pronunciation of the Johnson County town was somewhat changed, however, and it is pronounced Vie-enna.

Numerous other men who served in the military had counties named for them. General Lafayette, able French soldier and close friend of Washington, had the "La" taken from his name and the remainder of it given to the county of Fayette. When it came to choosing a name for the county seat, it is said that some wag convinced the committee entrusted with the privilege that a once great tribe of Indians, the Vandals, had lived in Illinois. In honor of this mythical tribe, the committee decided that the new town should answer to Vandalia. The town, obviously, has not lived up to its name, though there is a penal farm there.

Lawrence County and its county town of Lawrenceville are both named for Captain James Lawrence, gallant commander of the "Chesapeake" who was killed as he fought the British ship "Shannon" on June 4, 1813. This is the only instance in southern Illinois where one man was honored by having both the county and its county town named for him.

Marion County is for General Francis Marion, often referred to as the "Swamp Fox," able leader of guerilla warfare in the Carolinas during the Revolution. Some say that Salem, the county seat, was named for Salem in Massachusetts. Other accounts would have it named for the city in North Carolina. Since so many of the settlers of this area came from the Carolinas, it is likely that the latter explanation is the correct one.

Count Casimir Pulaski, Polish exile who was killed while serving with the colonial forces at Savannah on October 7, 1779, gave his name to the county of Pulaski, whose county seat, first known as Emporium City, later became Mound City for the Indian mounds that stood there.

General Arthur St. Clair, Revolutionary War general and governor of the Northwest Territory, gave his own name to the first county he created by proclamation in the Illinois country in 1790. The name of Belleville, its present seat of government, is said to have been given it by John Hay, a French Canadian. There is also another account that would have its title given by George Blair, who owned the land where the town began. The first county seat was at Cahokia.

Perry County does honor to the naval hero, Commodore Oliver Hazard

Perry, who built most of the vessels for his small fleet at a rude shipyard on the shore of Lake Erie and on September 10, 1813, with these home-made vessels won a significant naval engagement. His report of the battle, "We have met the enemy and they are ours," has resounded since that time. The county seat of the new county was named Pinckneyville after, "millions for defense but not one cent for tribute," C. C. Pinckney.

Nathaniel Pope, last territorial delegate from Illinois Territory to Congress, conferred his name upon Pope County. Pope was the man responsible for moving the northern boundary of the new state of Illinois from a parallel passing the southern tip of Lake Michigan to its present location, thereby including the site of the city of Chicago in the state of Illinois. Had he not obtained this change, there might not have been any "downstate Illinois." It already has been told how Golconda, the county seat, first was Sarahville, then Corinth and now is Golconda.

White County took its name from Captain Isaac White of Gallatin County, commander of territorial militia, who was killed in the battle of Tippecanoe. The name of the county seat of White County, Carmi, is biblical in origin; Carmi was the second son of Reuben. Clay County was named for the great statesman, Henry Clay. Its county seat was called Lewisville, for a man named Lewis, but a mistake in spelling changed it to Louisville.

Benjamin Franklin, statesman and philosopher, provided the name for Franklin County, and Thomas Hart Benton, noted, long-time senator from Missouri, was honored in the naming of its county seat. DeWitt Clinton had his name given to Clinton County. Some say that its county town was named for the English author, Thomas Carlyle. This does not seem very probable since its name was used in the county long before Carlyle had become at all noted. It is probable that the name came from the town with the same name in England or even more likely, from the one in Pennsylvania.

Gallatin County honors Albert Gallatin, noted official in the early government of the United States. Its county seat of Shawneetown remains as one of two county seats in the region that bear names of Indian origin.

Successful union revival meetings held by ministers of different faiths near Jonesboro suggested a name for the newly created county of Union as well as the clasped hands of the county seal. Jonesboro, the county seat, was named for a family that settled there before the formation of the county. Alexander Hamilton, first secretary of the treasury, had his name given to Hamilton County. Its county seat was named for Dr. William McLean, early-day physician who is reported to have been the first settler on the site of the present city of McLeansboro.

Edwards County, named for Governor Ninian Edwards, once included the eastern half of Illinois above an east-west line through the point where Bonpas (Bon Pas) creek joins the Wabash. The county extended northward to "upper Canada." People then (1815) living in the region of Chicago or Milwaukee and wishing to transact business at their county seat would have journeyed to vanished Palmyra, two miles north of present Mt. Carmel. The second and present county seat of Edwards County was later placed at Albion, called that after the term used to designate ancient England.

The name for Richland County has two explanations. One would have it named for a place where some early settlers of the new county formerly had lived. The second one states that it was named Richland because of the fact that it marked the definite beginning of the rich Illinois prairie. Its "permanent seat of justice," Olney, received that name from Nathan Olney, prominent citizen of Lawrence County before a portion of that county was detached to form the new one of Richland.

This enumeration of place names and comments concerning their origin could go on endlessly. There are hundreds of them. Even Hardscrabble, Hickory Hill, The Shed, Rural Hill, Wildcat, Barefoot, Possum Flat, Horn Owl, Horse Prairie, Pee Dee, and other very local and intimate names yield interesting stories.

❧ A MIGRANT COUNTY SEAT

Counties had county seats that often would not stay put. The story of one abandoned courthouse offers a classic example. The old Alexander County Courthouse in Thebes is a southern Illinois landmark. Begun more than 113 years ago, it still sits serenely on the bluff overlooking the Mississippi River, though it ceased to serve its first purpose more than ninety years ago.

Since serving as a courthouse, it has at times been empty, been used as a church, as a school, by fraternal orders, as a point for political gatherings, and for various other community purposes. Strolling boys found it a favorite rendezvous. Now it is a city hall and houses the village library.

When Alexander County was established on March 4, 1819, five county commissioners were appointed to locate the "permanent seat of justice" and to establish the new county government. They chose the now long vanished village of America that had been platted on the Ohio at the lower end of Hodges Bayou in 1817, and contracted for the erection of a brick courthouse and jail, the latter to be built first.

Their choice of America appeared to be a wise one. The town grew rapidly. One group of promoters built "24 double log cabins and many framed dwellings." Soon there were several hundred people and America gave promise, but these promises were not to be fulfilled. Business failures, a shifting of the river's channel, some destructive fires, a great pestilence, and the removal or decreased interest of influential men combined to dim all hopes. In a decade the village was practically deserted.

A vote to relocate the county seat was taken and carried. The county commissioners accordingly met on March 6, 1833, and took action. They chose a new site for another "permanent seat of justice." The fact is, they seem to have chosen two or three sites. In one report, still extant and bearing their signatures, a site was vaguely designated about three miles east and two miles north of present-day Unity. The name of Vernon was chosen for this projected village. Vernon was to be somewhere in the "southeast quarter and north end of Section 27."

Another report on another loose sheet of paper, also bearing the signatures of the same commissioners, adds to the confusion. This second report would place the "permanent seat of justice" on a tract of land "located in the southwest half of the southeast quarter and north end of Section 36."

This state of confusion was partially clarified on June 13, 1833, when David Hailman and his wife gave the county a deed to twenty acres of land to be used for a county seat. This tract of land was described by metes and bounds "beginning at three white oaks at the northwest corner of section 6." This was definitely not either of the tracts described in the reports mentioned.

A county building that combined both jail and courthouse was built on the tract that the Hailmans had given. It was constructed of logs, roofed with clapboards, and weatherboarded. In 1843 two prisoners contrived to have this building burned as part of a scheme of escape. Plans immediately were made to remove the county seat from Unity.

Chapter 3

Folklore

🏵 *BY WORD OF MOUTH*

IT IS NOT EASY TO give a concise definition of folklore. Perhaps it would be better to explain and offer illustrations. First of all, folklore is old—as old as speech. Primitive men gathered in caves or in the rude shelters they contrived and about open campfires performed their dances and ceremonies, told their stories, related their experiences, chanted their songs, and recited their legends. Primitive woman crooned the equivalent of lullabies to her infants and passed to those younger her meager knowledge of homemaking. Instruction in crafts and skills was passed along. Beliefs and superstitions were repeated along with moral sayings that became laws. Remedies and charms were prescribed and riddles recited.

In early cultures, before language was written, it was only by word of mouth and by demonstration that man could pass on to others his accumulated wisdom. When writing came, uses of the old process slowly declined; but they did not and will not disappear.

Until recent years it was a common custom to go calling on neighbors in the evening and "set until bedtime." There were no telephones, television sets, or radios for entertainment. There were no automobiles nor were there any roads for them to travel. There was practically no place to go. Stories, songs, narration of personal experiences, yarns, pleasantries, mere chatter and gossip filled the evening. Much of what is termed culture grew from such practices. With the waning of this old custom, folklore became background. Nevertheless, it remains essential to a reasonable understanding of our way of life. No thinking person would discard the comforts, conveniences and opportunities that things modern have brought. Likewise, those who would understand the present cannot lightly dismiss the past and its practices. The great mass of materials gathered and passed along by word of mouth cannot be ignored.

In the process of transmitting our lore, those relating it naturally sought to improve upon it by making it more interesting and dramatic. There also was the tendency to give the story a local setting and to relate it to known persons. Many basic stories endured for centuries, being adapted to the local situation and to different individuals. Some well-known stories will illustrate this point. One from German lore was borrowed by Washington Irving, relocated in the valley of the Hudson in New York State, and is known to us as "The Legend of Sleepy Hollow." In it a mythical headless horseman like the one that rode along lonely paths in the Rhine Valley was brought to America to ride beside the wildly fleeing Ichabod Crane. Before this horseman entirely disappeared from the roster of fanciful figures, he came to ride the woodland trail that passed Lakey's cabin on the creek at the eastern side of McLeansboro. Perhaps somewhere in America he still rides.

Hundreds of years ago a young maiden with her clothing ablaze ran shrieking about an old castle in Scotland until she burned to death. Thereafter, the spirit of this girl would return to that castle and to other homes to warn of an approaching death. This was the "wailing of the banshee." Just a few years ago an aged gentleman, with solemn face, reported to the writer that the wailing of the banshee had been heard near his home on the Ohio in Hardin County. To him it presaged the death of a neighbor, then seriously ill. The neighbor died. The old gentleman's faith in the wailing of the banshee, real to him, remained unbroken.

In Scotland, Lord Randall, a young Scottish nobleman, rides "out of the West." In America this Lord Randall became Johnnie Randall, a cowboy. The nightingale of Europe became the mockingbird or the meadowlark. In much this same manner, many stories, songs, and legends from other lands have been accepted and adapted to the local scene.

America has added stock to folklore. One of our distinctive contributions has been that of tall tales, those in which the supposedly impossible is done. Paul Bunyan, fabled hero of the northern lumber camps, strode across the land and left countless footprints that filled with water to form a great chain of lakes across the northern United States. The exploits of Paul Bunyan and his blue ox—forty-two ax handles and a plug of Star Tobacco between horn tips—came to fill many volumes.

Tony Beaver, according to legend a cousin of Paul Bunyan, did the impossible in the woodlands of West Virginia. Mike Fink, an actual man, became the legendary hero of flatboat days. He jumped almost across the Mississippi, but sensing that he would fall a few yards short of his goal, turned back in midair to his starting point. No greater jump has been recorded.

John Chapman planted bushels of appleseeds along the roadways of Ohio and Indiana. Today he lives as the legendary character, Johnny Appleseed. Davy Crockett could ride the sun around the world, and did ride his pet alligator up Niagara Falls. Pecos Bill, cowboy hero, used a mountain lion for a steed and a rattlesnake as a riding whip. Captain Kidd, Daniel Boone, Jesse James, Billy the Kid, Buffalo Bill, Kit Carson, Bat Masterson, Annie Oakley, Calamity Jane, Wild Bill Hickok, Babe Ruth, Jim Thorpe, John L. Sullivan and many other real persons, half-clothed in legend, came to enrich our lore.

Much of our folklore—in the form of tall stories, games, dances, ballads, strange beliefs, signs, and sayings—has passed into the forgotten, and more is passing. Nevertheless, much of the old stock lingers in southern Illinois and the adjacent sections of Indiana, Kentucky, and Missouri. It can be a great source of wholesome amusement and entertainment for those interested in this aspect of our earlier culture.

🌼 *A PHANTOM FUNERAL*

THOSE WHO APPRECIATE the lore of ghosts know that they are only dis-embodied spirits that have returned to the realm of the living. A ghost comes back for one of two purposes—to free itself from a spell or curse cast upon it while it was yet a living being, or it may return to correct some injustice. In the breaking of a curse or the righting of a wrong, the ghost may incidentally bring misfortune upon the living, but ghosts are not cruel.

Most of the stories about ghosts have vanished. Those that linger survive only among older people. Some incredulous persons have never believed in ghosts, but to those who did believe, they were very real—as real as thought could make them. The story given here is only a sample of lore once common.

This ghost story survives among the older persons at Prairie du Rocher, in Randolph County. Perhaps it can be told best by setting it down exactly as it was related by a very old lady and tape recorded by the writer. Here it is in the teller's words.

"This happened between eleven o'clock and midnight on the evening of July 4, 1889. Mrs. Chris and I were sitting in front of her building keeping a vigil over her little dead baby. But 'twas too warm for us to be in the building, so we were sitting on the outside. All at once, I look and I said to Mrs. Chris, 'Isn't that a funeral a-coming down?' She says, 'It looks like it.' I says, 'We'll see when it passes here.' So, when it passed right in front of where we were sitting, it was a funeral.

"There was a number of wagons, all alike, like the little wagons they haul trash in today. I said to Mrs. Chris, 'Do you know any of these people?' She said, 'No, I don't know a one. I don't know who they are.' Well, I counted forty wagons. Then it come to my attention that there wasn't any noise. You'd see the horses raise their hoofs and put them down on the ground, but there was not a sound. You could see the wagon wheels as they were turning, and the people in the wagons seemed to be talking. There wasn't a sound made by anything.

"All this was most strange, and Mrs. Chris said to me, 'Oh God! Oh God! If I wasn't sitting here with you seeing this, I'd swear I was dreaming.' I said, 'Mrs. Chris, I would think the same thing. I wonder if anyone else is seeing this besides us. We'll have to wait,' I says, 'until tomorrow and see. Somebody'll tell us if they have.' But we never found out anything at all from anybody. Only my father, aroused by the howling of our dog, looked out to see what was the matter. He saw the strange procession pass just as we did.

"After I had counted forty wagons, there were thirteen pairs of horsemen. It seemed that it took an hour for the funeral to pass the place, but I know now it didn't. Then we determined that we were going to watch and see if anyone come back after they had had time to go down to the cemetery and bury that party, but there wasn't anyone come back, not one of the forty wagons nor the twenty-six horsemen that followed them.

"A short time after that a lady from DuQuoin came to visit me; and I told her what I had seen. She said her daughter had read a story about the fort here, Fort Chartres, and she said it seemed as though a man that was the most important of all was killed in ambush one night because they didn't want him to continue with that work, and after he was killed, they went to Kaskaskia to learn what to do with the body.

"They sent word that he must be buried at midnight in an obscure cemetery and without any lights. The only light was to be that of the moon. It must have been full moon that very day, for it was a bright moonlight night. We never saw anyone come back from that funeral, and they never did find the man who murdered him.

"Now this funeral can be seen by only three people, and the only time that it will be seen again is when the time will coincide, just like the night it happened on July 4, 1889. It must be a Friday night, with a bright moon shining and between eleven and midnight. Then only three people can see it."

Perhaps this combination of circumstances has never been exactly right since the July night in 1889, for no one has told of seeing the ghostly procession again.

🌸 *WITCHES*

MODERN TALES OF ghosts and witches, those weird images that are associated about like cousins, have slowly faded away, or nearly so. No reliable report of the recent observance of a full-fledged specimen of either has come to attention. Amusing or terrifying, depending upon the beliefs of different persons, the passing of these strange creatures of fancy is almost to be regretted.

Ghosts, as every well-informed person knows, are disembodied spirits that remain among the living. They are not cruel by nature and do no one harm unless it is necessary in righting a past wrong. Witches are different.

A witch is a human being, a woman who has been given supernatural powers through a compact with the devil. She abjures Christ and God and lives only for the evil one. Some witches become such for only a limited time, others for life. In either case, their names are inscribed in the "black book" and all must "sign in blood." Each witch has imps assigned to do her bidding.

After the woman has entered into a compact with the devil, it is very difficult for anyone upon whom she casts a spell to break it. In fact, the magic of a witch can only be broken by countermagic. For example, pins stuck into the image of a witch cause the real witch intense pain. Some hold that "burning in effigy" will destroy the witch. As a desperate last resort, an image of the animal into which she has transformed herself may be shot with a silver bullet.

A witch has the power to change her form and often does so. She may —the better to accomplish her evil purposes—become a rabbit, cat, dog, or any other animal. When thus changed, the witch becomes immune to most dangers. Ordinary rifle bullets pass harmlessly by the witch in animal form.

The author has never had the good fortune to know a witch. As a youngster, he knew those who knew those who insisted they had known a witch. One such very old lady often told of the witch her father and mother had known. According to this lady's story, the witch operated in

Hamilton County, Illinois. That is, she operated there until a silver bullet checked her career. It all came about in the following manner.

This witch, in order to do evil to the storyteller's grandparents, would take the form of a rabbit and raid their garden, eating the lettuce, sprouts of green beans, and other plants. Repeated efforts of the father, a highly skilled marksman, to shoot the rabbit were futile. Coming to suspect that the animal really was the changed form of the neighboring woman whom he believed to be a witch, the father prepared to use countermagic.

When dusk came, the man took his trusted rifle, loaded it with a silver bullet, and mounted guard over the garden plot. A rabbit, really the witch, appeared and began to nibble the lettuce. Not wishing to be responsible for the death of the neighboring woman, even though she might be a witch, the marksman chose to shoot the rabbit in the right front foot instead of a vital spot. The shot he fired was effective, as evidenced by the hobbling gait of the retreating rabbit and by the bloody spots left by the wounded foot. If further proof is necessary, it was furnished by the real witch, who appeared next day with a bandaged right hand carried in a sling. The lettuce and green beans were no longer molested.

There were other witches in southern Illinois. Perhaps the most noted one of all was a woman named Eva Locker. This woman lived on David Prairie in Williamson County. The spells that Eva could cast were many and varied. Among the maladies she could cause to befall her chosen victims were the "twitches and jerks, fits, and rickets," along with other peculiar and terrifying diseases.

Eva could destroy cattle by shooting them with hair balls. Proof of this was the balls of hair found in the stomachs of slaughtered animals. Spells and curses she could also cast upon tools and shooting pieces. In fact, anyone could render a gun practically useless by listening, at a respectful distance, until the discharge of the piece was heard. Then it was only necessary to walk backward into the woods until a small hickory sprout was found. A knot tied in this sprout rendered the gun inaccurate. This spell cast upon the gun, however, could be broken by sticking nine pins in the stock or by pouring the barrel full of lye, corking it and allowing it to stand nine days.

This Eva Locker could milk other people's cows by the simple process of hanging a towel on her rack. It was allowed to hang there several minutes, after which she could take the towel and wring the accumulated milk from its fringe.

Only one person could regularly break the spells that Eva cast. This man, whose name was Charlie Lee, was a widely known witchmaster who lived in neighboring Hamilton County. Lee broke the spells by countermagic, using pins, silver bullets, pictures, effigies, and solemn incantations.

We now laugh at the strange belief that earlier people held in witchcraft. Nevertheless, it was once a serious issue. Records definitely indicate that more than 300,000 women and children were accused of practicing it and were executed in Europe. Fifty or more such executions occurred in the United States, one being a Negro slave in Illinois.

❦ *LAKEY'S GHOST*

LAKEY'S GHOST HAD a definite location, and its story is associated with an actual event. This ghost that once made appearances in the southeastern part of the present city of McLeansboro has a story that even yet is heard in the vicinity.

It centers about a man named Lakey, one of the early settlers in the McLeansboro vicinity. His first name is forgotten. Perhaps it does not matter. For this story it is enough to know his last name and that it was given to the small creek that crosses the highway near the eastern limits of the city.

Lakey was building a cabin on the west side of the stream a short distance south of the ford where the present street—then an old trail leading from the Carmi vicinity toward Mt. Vernon—crossed the creek. He had practically completed the log structure and on his last day alive had felled a large oak tree to make clapboards for the roof. At the close of day, he was bolting this timber.

The next morning an early traveler saw a gruesome sight. Beside a large stump was a human body and near by a severed head—they were Lakey's. A broadax sticking in the stump indicated the manner in which the head and body had been separated.

News of the tragedy spread, and settlers·came to look and wonder. Lakey was a quiet and inoffensive man. So far as anyone knew, he had no wealth that would tempt anyone to commit such a crime, nor did he have any known enemies. There was no evidence of a struggle. There seemed then to be no explanation for the murder that had evidently been committed about nightfall the day before. Indeed, no solution to the murder has ever come to light. Lakey was buried near the site of his uncompleted cabin, and his story was added to the local lore, but this was not the end of the incident.

On the day following Lakey's burial and just at nightfall, two men living west of McLeansboro were passing the Lakey cabin site as they returned from a trip to the Wabash. A few rods east of Lakey's Creek they were joined by a strange and fearful companion. A headless horseman on a large black steed, on the left hand or downstream side, moved along toward the creek with them.

Neither of the awed men spoke. The new rider also was silent. All rode along together down the gently sloping bank and into the water. As they neared the center of the stream, the phantom horseman turned to the left, passed downstream and appeared to melt into the waters of a deep pool just below the crossing. It must be remembered that no ghost can cross running water.

The two men, happy to be rid of the ghostly horseman, rode onward to their homes. They hesitated to tell the story of the unbelievable incident, but they soon had corroborating testimony. The same apparition appeared a few evenings later to other men approaching the stream from the east at nightfall. The story rapidly gained circulation.

Always the rider, on a large black horse, joined travelers approaching the stream from the east, and always on the downstream side. Each time and just before reaching the center of the creek, the mistlike figure would turn downstream and disappear. For a generation or more an occasional traveler would report the strange horseman; but no living witness of the strange rider has been found.

Very old persons still tell of those who declared they saw him. Perhaps he has completely disappeared. Perhaps it is because there is no longer a ford over Lakey's Creek but instead a concrete bridge. It may even be that automobiles move too rapidly for the slow pace of the large black steed. Again, their noise and strange appearance may have frightened him away. Who knows?

BIRDS, BEASTS, INSECTS, & WEATHER

As JANUARY NEARS its end, the groundhog begins to listen for same mysterious alarm clock to sound. According to popular belief, this inaudible alarm sounds regularly each year in the forenoon of the second day of February. Some may claim another date, but those who are really weather-wise insist upon the second. This date must be correct, since the Missouri legislature by appropriate action once set it aside as the proper one. Many in Arkansas hold for the fourteenth, while Illinois shows a divided opinion. (Perhaps this should be called to the attention of our legislature.)

Inquiry among experts shows that on the morning of February 2 Mr. Groundhog abandons the curl in which he has slept for several weeks, turns over, gingerly stretches, and crawls out of his comfortable burrow, never knowing just what is in store for him until he peeks outside. If the sun is shining, he is permitted to return immediately to his burrow for another nap of six weeks. If the sky is overcast and no shadows are to be seen, he must go about the usual business of being a groundhog and struggle along with only cat naps of fourteen hours or so daily. He knows, as well as people know, that bright sunshine at high noon on the second means six weeks more of winter, and that cloudiness at noon indicates that winter is practically ended and a good crop year and a bountiful food supply are assured.

February 2 also is Candlemas Day, a date observed as that on which Christ was presented in the temple. This day is observed at some places in Europe by processions bearing candles—a practice apparently borrowed from the ancient customs of carrying lighted torches about a field to assure a forthcoming bountiful crop. February 2 also was the date on which the Aztec Indians of Mexico welcomed the New Year. No one seems to know just how and when the groundhog first came to assume such a prominent part in the day's observance. Somehow he has managed right well to take it over.

The long-range forecastings based upon observance of woolly worms and groundhogs may be supplemented by observing behavior characteristics of other animals. These are helpful in day-by-day forecastings wherein the groundhog legend offers little help.

When robins repeat their call "three days," it is a sign that rain is coming. When they build their nests near the trunk of a tree, it means a rainy season. If they build low, expect a windy summer. Some, however, do not regard robins as desirable to have about at all and say they had rather see the devil than a March robin. If earthworms make mounds of earth at the entrance to their burrows, it indicates rain. Ant hills, on the other hand, indicate fair weather.

The height of a beaver dam above the waterline of the pond indicates the amount of rainfall to expect. When cows lie down in the field, rain is coming. If they run back and forth across the pasture with tails straight out, expect severe winds. Dew-covered cobwebs on the grass in the early morning also foretell rain. If spiders are observed going up the wall of a room, expect the temperature to fall; if they go down, it will grow warmer.

Many peeping frogs in the early spring indicate a dry year. When a great chorus of them peeps at night, expect rain the next day. Geese flying north indicate spring is near.

If a rooster stands on one foot, expect rain or snow in season. When it begins to rain or snow and hens head for shelter, expect similar weather the next day. When a hen oils her feathers, it is a sure sign of rain; but if she chooses to stay out in the rain or snow, it will be of short duration.

With these and myriad other weather signs available to the observant person, he should not be surprised at any turn of winter weather.

🌸 *FROGS & TOADS*

IN THE GREAT MASS of folklore, there are many thousands of superstitions that cluster about different objects. A realization of this came when a night was spent in a camp-trailer beside a small lake infested with frogs. In a way it was a noisy evening. Shortly after nightfall, however, the increased coldness silenced the songsters, but not until their serenade had suggested some superstitions concerning frogs and toads.

Remembered bits of that lore along with other items collected by the Federal Writers Project in Illinois in the later 1930's may be of interest. According to these superstitions, frogs and toads could work much good fortune or bad. They were a means of foretelling events, of causing both good and bad fortune, and even of correcting some of the very misfortunes they had brought.

All know that the handling of frogs or toads or getting the water from them on the hands will cause warts. Not many, however, know that this same water on hands already wart-infested will cure them. Nor do they know that a leg severed from the frog "while it still quivers" and rubbed over warts will cause them to vanish soon. It is well to know all this, for anyone killing a frog, even by accident, is liable to have warts appear. If no frog is available to furnish the quivering leg or if that remedy does not appeal to the squeamish, a neighbor's dishrag can be stolen, the warts washed with it and the dishrag buried under the same neighbor's door step. This is equally effective as the dismembered leg and less disturbing to the frog.

Felons, that is bone felons, are cured by proper use of frogs. To do this, a small frog from a spring is tied on the felon for several hours. The frog will die, but the felon will be cured. Goiters also can be cured by the frog treatment. There are three ways to do this. In one, a live frog is dipped into hot lard and fried until dead and done. The grease in which

it has been cooked is then rubbed on the goiter. A second method re-
quires that the belly of the frog be rubbed three times across the goiter and
then thrown over the left shoulder. In this case the frog also dies, but
its death appears less cruel. If neither method appeals, the frog can be
worn suspended about the neck. Any of the three methods is thought to be
equally effective.

Toads are a specific for headaches. A woman with this common ailment secures relief by binding a toad on the head. The malady will disappear; moreover, the cure is permanent. This surpasses the wildest claims
of the television-vaunted remedies. Although folklore prescribes this toad
remedy for women, it should, logically, be just as effective with men.

To dream of croaking frogs is a certain sign of approaching good luck,
particularly if the dreamer will begin to work earnestly as soon as he is
awake. Carrying a frog's jawbone in the pocket also will woo the smiles of
fortune. Likewise, the dried breastbone of a toad frog, wrapped in paper
and carried in the pocket, will assure good luck.

When a frog croaks during the day it is calling for rain. The musical
notes of a tree frog at dusk mean rain in three days. If a bullfrog is killed,
the next day will be foul. There always are two freezes after the first
spring croakings.

A young lady can get some assurance in affairs of the heart by observing
toads. If one hops across her pathway, she will see her sweetheart within
a day. He will come from the same direction as the toad. Certain misfortunes may result from even seeing a toad. For instance, warts will
develop unless one spits immediately.

Anyone wishing to bring misfortune upon another can do so by proper
use of a frog. To do this, the frog is captured, placed in a jar and allowed
to starve and dry. It is then ground into powder and some of this
powder is placed beneath the hatband of the intended victim. Blindness
will result.

Frogs figure in many voodoo rites, along with snakes, lizards, bats, and
black cats. Those believing in voodoo think that a tadpole swallowed in
drinking at a spring or branch will grow into a frog in the stomach of
the swallower. It may lodge during the swallowing process and become "a
frog in the throat," sometimes deadly. By proper voodoo ritual, a person
can be freed of either affliction. Observation of a toad by an expectant
mother may "mark" the unborn child, particularly if the mother is
frightened or startled by the experience.

It is universally known that if one of the family kills a toad, the cows
will give bloody milk. A cow that steps on and kills a toad, thereby brings
that curse upon herself. It was over this bit of lore that the writer's faith in

frog signs first began to waver. A cow that stepped on and killed a toad definitely failed to give milk with even the slightest pink tinge. Perhaps she did not know the legend.

Yes, we almost forgot to say that it sometimes rains frogs from the sky. Also, one who kills a toad by design or accident will stub and stumble. His house may even catch on fire. When frogs croak on a battlefield, active conflict will come in three days.

Frog lore sometimes is baffling, becoming more so when one confuses frogs with toads. Superstitions or not superstitions, most gardeners like to see the toads hopping about at dusk.

🐞 *ROOSTERS*

CHICKENS, ESPECIALLY THE roosters, once common in the farmyards, have gathered much folklore about them. As it now is, most young roosters end their careers in the broiler stage, just as they are well on their way to becoming fully vocal. They are thus denied the opportunity to grow up and crow their prophecies. It might be well, therefore, to set down some of the lore that applies to their crowing. With fewer roosters about and more other noises to drown their calls, rooster lore is diminishing.

The crowing of a rooster generally is considered an indication of misfortune. This belief apparently had its beginning because Peter was reminded of his betrayal of Christ by the crowing of the cock. Though the cock's crowing generally has been thought to foretell the disagreeable, its occurrence during the Christmas season indicates good fortune.

A rooster's behavior foretells coming events, particularly changes of weather. He indicates "falling weather" when he goes to roost crowing. An old rhyme says: "If a cock goes crowing to bed, it will arise with a watery head." Crowing before eight o'clock in the evening means rain on the morrow; after eight the rain will be delayed. Apparently, the earlier the crowing, the earlier the rain.

If a rooster crows loud and frequently in the forenoon, the afternoon will be fair. Should he crow early in the morning while sitting on the fence, it is to be fair all day. If he flies to the top of a post to do his early crowing, the listener may expect rain or snow. Crowing as he goes to roost is almost a sure sign of bad weather ahead. Those questioning the rooster's clairvoyant power must not conclude that he proceeds blindly. All will observe that he frequently pauses to cock his head and scan the sky.

The rooster does not stop with forecasting only weather. He foretells events too. When he crows at the gateway or near the front of the house in early morning, company is to be expected. If this is repeated three times, the sign is rated as practically infallible. Should he halt to do his crowing on or near the doorstep, it presages death, particularly if he crows toward the house. The same portent is attached to crowing just as the sun is setting. If a rooster comes into the house and crows—and such happened when chickens ran at large and there were no screen doors—company will come immediately. If the crowing for company is done in the back yard, the company is sure to be a man. Also, if two hens fight in the front yard, expect the visitor to be a woman. In addition to the announcement of company, the quality of that company may be indicated. If, after crowing the announcement, the rooster mounts the fence and crows again with his head away from the house, the company will be unwelcome.

The crowing of the rooster can presage the arrival of news. If the crowing occurs at noon, it will be "hasty" news, that is, it will come very soon. Three crows mean a letter from a friend. The news will come to the one at which the rooster looks after crowing.

There are many other superstitions attached to the rooster. A young lady wishing to win a certain young swain has only to secure a feather from the rooster's tail and hide it in her glove. She then contrives to shake hands with the one sought. Failing in this, she can take the heart of the rooster and toss it over the left shoulder while making her wish. The results are said to be the same. Perhaps doing both would make it doubly effective.

To dream of a rooster at any time is a sign of good luck. A visiting rooster crowing in the yard is a sign of bad luck. If a visiting rooster fights with and vanquishes the home rooster, the flock will not prosper. You may gain something from the visit of a neighboring rooster if you have warts and wish to be rid of them. Prick the largest wart until it bleeds, rub the blood on a grain of corn and feed the barnyard visitor this bloody grain. Give him enough other pieces of grain to total the number of warts to be removed. If you wish to do so, kill the intruding rooster, pluck off his head, rub the bloody stub upon your warts, and then bury it. When it decays, your warts will disappear. Perhaps the rooster's owner would protest the last mentioned remedy.

❦ *WINTER WEATHER*

THE WEATHER IS A popular subject of conversation and a safe one. People have always talked about it with no apparent harm. In this way, a great body of weather lore has come into being to help those who would be weather-wise. Though constant attention and thought have been given to it, the problem of foretelling weather remains a challenge. It is to help those who wish to know more about weather-predicting that a few bits have been selected from the great mass of weather wisdom available. Some of the lore appears in conflict; hence, results can not be guaranteed.

Some already have begun to talk about "next winter" (this is written in August), to express curiosity and to make prophecies. Will it arrive early or late and just what does it have in store for a waiting public? There are many signs and sayings thought helpful in making long-range predictions. A few, relating directly to winter, are given.

It should first be determined just when winter is to make its bow. That is easy; the first killing frost is due exactly three months after katydids start their chirping.

If the sun shines during the first snow—or for that matter any other snow of the winter—more flurries are to be expected on the next day. When the fallen snow lies long in the shadows of protecting objects or embankments, they become "snow breeders" and foretell an added fall soon.

Sometimes it is possible to know in advance the exact day when a snow will come by counting the stars within any circle or halo about the moon and allowing a day for each star.

More is to be said about snow later. Next the would-be weather prophet should determine the general severity of the approaching winter. There are many ways in which this can be done. One of the oldest and most highly rated is to observe the breastbone of a goose. A clear white bone means a mild winter is due. If mottled or dark, it indicates a severe one. The length of the winter is shown by the length of the breastbone.

Other means are available if no goose bone is to be had. Late maturing and slowly ripening blackberries, fruit trees blooming twice in the same growing season, a heavy crop of wild grapes, a bountiful harvest of hazel nuts, tight thick hulls of walnuts or heavier than usual foliage on trees and bushes, all alike mean a hard winter. The depth at which squirrels bury the nuts they store in the ground is in proportion to the low temperatures to be expected.

Fat raccoons and groundhogs, muskrats that store ears of corn and line their burrows with cut cornstalks, beavers that build larger than usual houses, and rabbits that take refuge in brush piles also proclaim a hard winter.

The bird family is helpful. Chickens moulting in August foretell cold winters. The same is true if the lining in the gizzard of a dressed chicken is hard to remove. A rooster crowing about nine o'clock at night proclaims an approaching cold snap. Wild geese flying south, early and high, leave no doubts with the observer. The higher the wild turkey roosts in a tree, the colder will be the approaching winter.

There are other signs that herald colder weather. A cat sits with its back to the fire. Pigs scamper about and squeal while the grown-up hogs carry litter to build beds, occasionally pausing to stand and look northward. Sheep stand with their backs to the wind, while cattle and horses frisk about. Moss grows on the south side of trees in autumn, the husks on corn are thick, and hair on animals, both domestic and wild, is heavy. The observant person is never without plenty of signs.

Late-crawling caterpillars, or woolly worms, are reliable prophets. A plentiful supply of lighter colored ones—except those that are yellow—indicates a mild winter. Darker ones mean colder weather. Those having yellow noses give the omen of early winter cold, but a yellow tail indicates that the end of winter will be severe. A yellow band about the center or along the back likewise means a cold midwinter.

With the passing of winter, signs of spring are sought. A white Christmas means a green Easter. The first three days of January foretell the remaining months of winter. The emergence of groundhogs on February 2 is an accepted and reliable indicator. If March comes in like a lion, it will go out like a lamb. The reverse of this is just as true.

Even though people over the world have collected and passed along a great amount of weather lore and the United States Weather Bureau has contributed its scientific prognostications, the problem of the weather remains a puzzling one. Solution or no solution, it is a good subject for conversation.

🌸 *SNOW*

SINCE CHILDREN AND Santa Claus like snow, it might be well to seek some signs that will tell us when snowfalls may be expected, also their number.

To find the expected number of snows, count the foggy mornings in August and allow one for each. Should one be neglectful in his counting, he may await the first snow storm and reckon the days since the moon was new. Others think it should be the number of days between the first snowfall and Christmas. Perhaps any one of the methods is as reliable as the other.

A number of beliefs are available for use in short-term forecasting. For instance, if the full moon has two circles about it or appears to be "wading through snow," there will be snow within twenty-four hours. A dog serenading the moon with howls presages an early snowfall. Blackbirds feeding together on the ground or snowbirds scurrying along rail fences mean snow. Since rail fences are gone, perhaps the snowbirds should be allowed to scurry along any fence.

If smoke, in winter season, remains near the ground, or soot burns in the chimney, or the wood fire in the fireplace pops gently or makes a crackling sound like that of falling pellets of snow, a storm is brewing. Far-off hollow sounds that "carry well" are signals to those with practiced ears. If one-time frostbitten feet or ears itch severely, it is a sign of approaching cold weather. There are even those who think they can detect a tone in the howling wind that foretells a coming snowstorm. An east wind or frost clinging to the trees late in the morning means snow and adds to hopes or fears.

Once "grandma begins to pick her geese" or to "shake her feather bed" and the sun breaks through the falling snow, more can be expected at the same time on the morrow. A snow that begins with large fluffy flakes will be a heavy one. Also, if wind is strong and the driven snow sticks to the windward side of the trees, expect more.

Snow itself is supposed to be a means of prophecy. A white Christmas not only foretells a green Easter and a good fruit year but also means few deaths and a "light grave yard." If snow falls on the coach carrying a couple to their wedding at a church, they will surely separate, but snow at any other time on the wedding day means that the husband will be good to his wife. Rabbits naturally are not good eating until after the first snowfall.

The first snow of the season brings certain blessings and dangers. Anyone who walks barefoot around the house in this first fall will not be sick during the year. If this procedure is repeated each morning so long as the snow remains, the feet will not readily freeze. A sore throat can be cured by bandaging it with a snowball made from this first snow. One belief about this first snowfall should be kept in mind. Children should be warned not to eat it, for it contains all the diseases of the summer. Paradoxically, though, it was gathered and melted to provide a potent eyewash. The conflict here is not understood, but apparently it was not questioned.

Even dreams concerning snow have their significance. At all times they indicated approaching incidents of importance. If they come when snow is out of season, they mean approaching good fortune; if at other times, they foretell misfortune.

Water from melted snow is looked upon as quite effective for certain purposes, particularly so if it comes from snow gathered at the proper time. If water from snow falling in March is used to wash the hair, it will not fall out. Washing the face in this March snow water is also thought to be productive of a good complexion. It will even remove freckles. If a wart is pricked until it bleeds and is then washed in snow water—the March variety—the wart will surely disappear.

March snow furnishes water particularly good for the eyes. The only water considered more effective is that from the last fall of the year, if it comes in April. Headaches can be cured by washing the face in water that comes from any snow falling after March first. There are even some who hold that March snow water is holy and can be used to bless. Many persons thought water from melting snow was "finer" than other water and accordingly penetrated the high-top leather boots more readily.

This lore concerning snow may arouse only a mild interest, but a careful look at snowflakes through a magnifying glass will intrigue almost anyone.

❦ THUNDER & LIGHTNING

ALL CONCEDE THAT lightning comes before thunder and that it is more exact to say lightning and thunder, but it isn't done that way. Some who wish to express strong feelings use "thunder and lightning" or "thunder" as mild expletives. Critics "give him thunder" when they severely upbraid anyone. In a figurative way, something may move "like greased lightning." In fact, there are many, many, bits of lore associated with thunder and lightning, some of which are given here.

About the most important selfish interest concerning lightning is the best way to avoid being struck by it. Numerous ways of preventing this are offered. One way, no older than Benjamin Franklin, is to stay in a house having lightning rods, which is rather sage advice. But another belief is that the house and its occupants will be protected throughout the year by burning part of a palm blessed and used in church on Palm Sunday, or one can lie on a feather bed, or even sit on a feather pillow. Some believe that crawling under the bed will protect them. One may shield himself somewhat by pulling the covers over his head or shutting himself in a dark closet.

If an ax, spade, or other metal tool is kept in the house, it should be removed upon a storm's approach. Carrying metal objects in the pocket, even so much as a pocket knife, is to invite danger. No one is to stand before an open window, for the draft will carry the lightning in. On the other hand, a closed window affords protection, for the lightning will not strike through glass. No person should be near a tree unless he lies flat on the ground. Special care should be taken to avoid locust trees for they draw lightning more than any other, with oaks holding second place.

Animals, especially cats, draw lightning. In fact, the first cat was born during a thunderstorm and was "marked" by the lightning. Most animals are said to fear lightning, but cats ignore it and walk stolidly along. Men who sit on a fence and curse during a thunderstorm are practically defying the elements.

All reasonable means are taken to prevent being struck by lightning, for a collision with a bolt "breaks every bone in the body." It is a consoling thought that lightning seldom strikes twice in the same place. Should that rarity occur, it indicates that there is a mineral deposit near the surface of the ground. Except for one purpose, the use of wood from a tree struck by lightning brings misfortune; a splinter from such a tree can be used to prick the gum until it bleeds and thus cure the toothache.

The beholder of a lightning flash should realize that the flash did not strike him if he can count ten before the peal of the thunder is heard. If he counts rapidly, the number reached would represent the miles away that flash occurred. (It is better and more nearly accurate to count the seconds between the time when its flash appears and the peal is heard and divide by five.) Some say that thunder can not be heard beyond seven miles.

Thunder before noon means showers in the afternoon. "Thunder in morning is a sailor's warning." Thunder before the leaves come in the spring tells of an approaching cold spell. It also means a good crop year unless it comes on February 12. In that case, it dooms the peach crop to failure.

Thunder and lightning can foretell coming events as well as good and bad fortune. A peal of thunder as a person lies dying means perdition for the soul. If the peal comes immediately after the funeral, all is well. The sign when one hears a peal of thunder at an open grave is not recalled, but we do remember the startled look on the face of an elderly lady when such a coincidence occurred. To dream of lightning indicates approaching misfortune, generally a death in the family. The maid dreaming of thunder after she has taken nine pills made of grated walnut, nutmeg, and hazel nuts mixed with butter and sugar will marry a soldier or sailor.

If a bat comes to roost in one's hair, it will cling there until it hears thunder. It takes a peal of thunder to induce a turtle to relax its bite or a crawfish to release its pincer hold. To "hold on 'til it thunders" indicates tenacity. Some believe that fish, especially catfish, bite better during a thunderstorm while others insist that they do not bite. Perhaps it all depends on hungry fish being offered suitable bait at the proper time and place.

Thunder and lightning sour milk and keep eggs from hatching. No remedy is offered to prevent milk souring, but there are ways to reduce the damage to eggs. If the eggs are in a nest on the ground, they are less subject to harm. Goose, turkey, and duck eggs are sometimes protected by having an iron ring, such as a metal barrel hoop, placed about the nest. In the absence of a barrel hoop or ring, bits of metal placed by the nest are helpful. In the event no metal pieces or hoops are convenient, an empty jug set near by will catch the thunder and afford safety.

When corns, bunions, and rheumatism are more painful than usual, thunderstorms are to be expected. Relief from the pains of rheumatism can be had by finding and carrying a thunderbolt, generally found under a tree after a storm. Just what a thunderbolt resembles, the writer has been unable to learn. There are a hundred other lightning-thunder superstitions from which those interested may select the ones they wish to believe.

❦ THE MOON IS BEING IGNORED

JUST AS THE STAR groups that made up the signs of the zodiac were credited with great influence over man, the moon also was regarded as powerful. In popular beliefs, the moon was credited with power to produce strange effects. These influences ranged from the ebb and flow of the tides to parallel reactions in humans. The moon's effect on the tides remains undisputed. The writer, now seventy-five, has done no recent research into the romantic effects the moon is supposed to have and cannot speak authoratively about it. Perhaps its potency in that field is even now being challenged by inquisitive scientists, and it certainly is being tested by youth.

Many persons all over America formerly thought that the moon exerted great influence in their daily life. This power extended over growing crops, buildings, foods, the weather, and even over the health and emotions of the individual. Some people carefully noted changing phases of the moon and regulated their activities accordingly.

Some crops were planted "in the light of the moon," others "in the dark of the moon." The light of the moon begins with the appearance of the new moon and extends through the period of its visible increase until the time when it is full. In turn, the time between the full moon and the succeeding new moon, that is the time when the portion visible is decreasing, is termed the dark of the moon.

Those crops that grew beneath the ground, such as potatoes and peanuts, were thought to be much more productive when planted in that period when the moon is waning, or the dark of the moon. Any crop whose basic product grew above the ground, including tomatoes and corn, were best planted in the light of the moon, or that period when its visibility was increasing.

Everyone knew that the worm of a rail fence should be laid in the light of the moon. Unless this precaution was observed, the bottom rails would sink into the ground. When laid during the moon's increase, the rails remained on the surface of the ground, lasted longer, and besides, the fence remained a bit higher. Homes and other structures often were placed upon wooden blocks or upon stones placed in shallow holes. If these wooden or stone blocks were put in place during the light of the moon, they were not so prone to settle. The building thus remained level. Plank and corduroy roads were best laid during the same period.

Certain other building operations were best when done during the dark of the moon. If roofing were done during this time, the clapboards would lie flat and not curl up.

A proper time for butchering hogs was likewise observed. Bacon from hogs killed during the light of the moon just naturally fried away, leaving only a thin remnant for eating. To partially compensate for this disadvantage, more lard could be obtained from those portions saved for rendering. The resulting cracklings were naturally harder and drier. Bacon from hogs killed in the waning phase of the moon would retain more bulk when fried. The amount of lard obtained would be slightly less, but the cracklings would be softer and juicier. The butchering problem thus had its moon complications too.

It was widely thought that the moon influenced the weather and that observation of the new moon would enable one to forecast rains. In this case though, there were two exactly opposite schools of thought. One group of prophets held that if the new moon were "lying on its back," it was holding water and that rains were naturally to be expected. Another group contended that a new moon with tilted points indicated that water was being poured out and rain was assured. There is no claim that either of these contentions was ever established.

In the matter of health, particularly mental health, the moon wielded great influence. Sleeping in the direct rays of the moon could induce lunacy. Sleeping in the moonlight and with the mouth open in such a way as to allow the moonbeams to shine into it, was even more dangerous.

Its effect must have been like the distiller's product designated as "moonshine."

It would not be proper to leave off discussion of the moon without calling attention to "the man in the moon." According to the best traditions, this man was put into the moon for working on a Sunday, supposedly burning brush. Those with vivid imaginations declare that they can see the form of the man and his burning brush pile, and even the unfortunate doggie, which, knowing nothing of Sunday, unwittingly scampered about his erring master and was thus deemed guilty by association.

People still moon around, are moonstruck, and of course, reach for the moon.

🌿 *TALL TALES*

WHAT HAS BECOME OF the teller of tall tales, the spinner of fanciful yarns? Along with rail fences, clapboard roofs, side-saddles, ash hoppers, road carts, and red underwear this essential character of any self-respecting pioneer community has practically disappeared.

Before the coming of supermarkets with air conditioning, a few specimens of the vanishing tribe of tale tellers still could be found on wintry days about the hot stoves of quiet and dimly lit grocery stores. On milder days these story-tellers and their listeners met in protected nooks on the sunny side of some sheltering building. In summer they gathered on benches in a kindly shade. If there was a livery stable, and few villages failed to have such an institution, they gathered there, in both winter and summer. Now, only a few somewhat lonely older men, apparently the rear guard of the vanishing troupe of tellers and listeners, are seen about the few remaining haunts where they used to gather.

Their tales were tall, but generally harmless, relatively clean, and always amusing. One wonders why they have so nearly disappeared. Perhaps it is because the actual incidents and happenings of today are so much taller and have dwarfed the most fanciful ones of the earlier days. Anyway, all was good while it lasted.

No one was expected to believe the tall yarns. Perhaps those coming nearest to actual belief were the tellers. Some of these by so earnestly telling and retelling their yarns apparently convinced themselves that their stories were really true. Listeners recognized these self-converted believers and were reasonably careful not to question their integrity. An occasional narrator would resent any expressions of doubt. After all, "a story told three times is true."

Tall tales are to be distinguished from those about witches, ghosts, haunted houses, and the supernatural. They generally told of great feats of strength, of highly developed skills, and of cunning and ingenuity. They also told of unusual turns of fortune, both good and bad, and of the freakish actions of natural forces.

Hunting stories were numerous. One such story related by a man named Andy Groanin is typical of the tamer ones. Andy was returning from a meatless day of trudging through the woods. In the gathering dusk, he spied seven large fat turkeys resting on a limb forty or fifty feet above. Naturally, Andy wished to take the entire seven home and thus be assured of a week's supply of meat. He realized, however, that he could fire only one shot from his rifle and that the birds not killed would fly away.

Andy suddenly hit upon a plan that he thought might work. He quietly crept to a point directly beneath the place where the middle turkey was roosting. Taking careful aim, Andy fired at the limb upon which the turkeys were perched. This shot struck the limb in its center, split wide open the section where the turkeys were roosting, and caused the halves to spring apart. When the limb popped open, the feet of the turkeys dropped through the opening. When it as quickly sprang back together, the seven turkeys were securely held. The hunter was forced to go for his ax and chop the tree down to get the seven turkeys, but it was worth the added labor.

Andy also had some interesting fish stories to relate. One of these concerned a deadly combat between a very large bass and a fighting angleworm. On the spring day when this incident occurred, Andy had gone to the lake, but the fish were not biting. He was particularly incensed at a large bass that calmly swam about but refused to take the baited hook dangled before him. Finally, a loose worm was tossed into the water and promptly snapped up.

Then a brilliant idea came to the fisherman, who had a half-pint of potent moonshine in his coat pocket—a buffer against the chilly day. Why not soak a few worms in this powerful liquid and feed them to the bass, get it drunk and pick it up. Andy thereupon selected the largest and most lively worm and dipped it briefly into the contents of the bottle before tossing it to the bass. The bass came quickly for its prey. The highly charged worm promptly turned, lunged at the approaching bass, and a conflict was on. Andy looked on in amazement as the battling bass and the warlike worm lashed the water into foam. The battle was soon over and the bass floated to the surface, belly up. The worm had succeeded in wrapping itself about the gills of the fish and thus had smothered it. Andy simply lifted the bested fish into his boat and went home. This fish, according to Andy's solemn assurance, weighed exactly eleven pounds and thirteen ounces. This story should provide a conclusive answer to the oft-repeated question, "Does fishing make liars or do only liars fish?"

Snakes also came in for treatment in tall stories. One day this same Andy of hunting and fishing fame had hitched his oxen to a log and was taking it home for winter firewood. The oxen saw a giant rattlesnake lying coiled in the roadway and stopped. Andy, not seeing the snake, applied his goad. One of the oxen moved and the snake promptly struck. The fangs missed their mark and sank into the bow around one ox's neck. Andy seized a large club and promptly killed the rattler, but when he looked around, one of his oxen was lying dead. The powerful charge of venom that the snake injected into the bow had caused it to swell and choke the ox to death.

There were thousands of these stories.

🌸 *A COON TREE*

THE TALL STORIES OF the pioneers had a strange way of surviving. They were passed down to the younger generations and often were carried along by the settlers who moved westward. The following story heard in southern Illinois illustrates the migration of a tall one. It is found among the hunting lore of Ohio and Indiana, and also in states west of Illinois.

The locale, name of the hunter, and even the animal victims may change, but the story remains basically the same. The incident related here took place in Rector Bottoms, a few miles south of Walpole, in Hamilton County. Sam Prentiss, able hunter and trapper who related the story, lived in Saline County, just south of the Hamilton-Saline line.

Each fall Sam impatiently awaited the coming of winter and the hunting-trapping season. In the year when this incident occurred, a hundred years or so ago, the weather suddenly turned cold on an afternoon in late November and it began to snow. In a short time an untracked layer about four inches thick carpeted the ground and our hunter went happily to bed.

Sam arose early the next morning and was ready to start out at daybreak. He first went to a cornfield at the edge of the bottom woodlands to look for the tracks of coons. There he found the trail of one that evidently had feasted on the farmer's corn before going to hole up for the winter. Tracks indicated that it was a large specimen. The hunter decided to trail it to the den, cut the tree and secure a prime pelt.

This trail shortly was joined by another. Then other trails came to join the ones he was following until it took on the appearance of a roadway about two feet wide where the snow was packed "as smooth as a floor."

Sam followed this gradually widening trail for three miles or more until it reached an enormous hollow sycamore tree more than eight feet in diameter.

Our hunter stopped and looked in amazement at the tree. It was moving. It would expand until Sam was sure that it was going to burst and then would shrink to about normal size. He soon discovered the reason. The tree, hollow from the ground up, was full of coons. When they took a deep breath the tree naturally expanded. When they exhaled, it shrank.

Here was a modest fortune in coonskins which commanded a fair price at that time. Sam realized that he must proceed with caution. Should he begin to chop the tree, the coons—not yet in their deep winter sleep—would be aroused and run away. He must use a more subtle method.

Here it occurred to Sam that he might be able to blast the gathered coons to death. He accordingly went back home, yoked his oxen to a wagon and drove several miles beyond the den tree to a stone quarry where he knew there were many kegs of stored powder. He loaded his wagon with a few kegs and hauled them back to the site. A dozen kegs or so were emptied into the space the coons had left at the base of the tree.

Not having any fuse to ignite the charge safely, Sam dug a small trench from the sycamore to a large oak two hundred yards away and sprinkled a continuous thin line of powder in it. From the shelter of the oak, Sam touched fire to the trail of powder. In a second or so the fire had raced along the powder in the trench and reached the tree. There was a terrific explosion and thousands of coons filled the air.

Sam immediately raced toward the tree, only no tree was there. It had been blown into kindling wood and dead coons littered several acres about the place where it had stood. Naturally, some of the coons also had been torn to bits by the force of the blast. Nevertheless, Sam vowed that he hauled away eleven wagon loads of good coons. He also insisted that coon fur continued to fall over the countryside for some days, being reported from Dale, six miles away.

After the first glow of accomplishment, Sam realized that he might have made a mistake. He had killed all the coons in his favorite hunting ground and hence had to wait several years before other coons moved in and repopulated the area. On the other hand, it might not have been such a great mistake. Sam used the proceeds of this mass slaughter to purchase eighty acres south of the farm he owned. If anyone doubted his story, there was the farm to prove it.

❧ THE FIRST OF MAY

A SLENDER POLE covered with a soiled winding of colored streamers was seen leaning against the coal shed of a southern Illinois rural school. This pole had been used for the May Day dance of the year before and was being made ready for use again. The sight of it aroused thoughts of an old, old custom—one that had been practiced by many generations of youngsters. It also suggested some of the magic that folklore once would ascribe to May, particularly to the first day of the month.

No one knows when observance of May Day really began. Such a day was observed by the Romans in honor of Maia, their goddess of fertility and mother of the messenger Hermes. Some features of that ancient ritual may still be discovered in the May Day games of today.

Like so many other sayings, signs, and superstitions, those concerning May would help to foretell the future. High on the list of things that could be foretold were those that dealt with the romantic life of young maidens. Most of these related specifically to the first day of the month. Thus, any young lady wishing to know more of the love life that lay in store for her, could learn of it by employing certain practices on the month's first day.

She could go into the orchard and grasp the tip of a twig and then listen. If a bird was heard to whistle sharply, she would marry within a year. If a cow was heard instead, the unfortunate maid could resign herself to single life for another year. If an orchard was not convenient, equally valid results could be secured by the proper use of a mirror.

The lass would take the looking glass and using it somewhat like the rear-vision mirror of today, walk backward to the well or spring. There, gazing into the mirror over her left shoulder, she would look into the water. Had she properly carried out the ritual, she would see the face of her future husband; if there was no face, there would be no husband. A coffin visible in the mirror meant death would soon be her lot.

If the young lady did not wish to employ the well-spring-mirror formula, she could secure equally valid results by turning over a stone and finding a hair beneath it. This hair would be the same color as that of her future mate. Naturally, this did not afford as positive an identification as that of the mirror's reflection.

If interested in the worldly status of her future husband, the wondering lass could go snail hunting on the first day of the month. If the first snail she found had a shell, the future husband would own a house in which they could live. If the snail had no shell, her husband would be poor. Whatever was found, no girl should marry in May for she would always be sorry.

If the damsel was not beautiful, she could remedy that defect by rising early, walking backward from the house into the grass and bathing her face in dew. Some held that this should be repeated for three mornings and others insisted upon nine. If the girl had freckles, these would disappear, especially if the bather placed her hands on another portion of her body. The freckles would, however, appear where the hands had been placed. Since girls went fully dressed, this part of the ritual was not so important. One girl thus accounted for the freckles on her shoulders. This dew washing remedy was also a specific for pimples.

There were certain other practices that might be termed health measures. Winter woolens could be discarded on May 1 without danger of contracting a cold. Youngsters could begin to go barefoot and the cold would not hurt. Boys who went swimming before sunup on the first would not contract contagious diseases during the summer months. Wading through dewy grass before sunup on the first would assure the wader that his feet would not sweat.

The first day of May also was one on which some crop prophecies could be made. If rain came on the first day, the blackberry crop would be a failure. Watermelons planted on the first would yield bountiful crops. Some thought that they might be planted on any one of the first three days with equally good results. There were a few who thought the ninth day fully as good as any of the first three. Strong contenders for the first day held that the melons should be planted before sunup and that assurance of a larger than usual crop was doubled if the planter still wore his night clothes.

While the first three days were great for planting melons, they were just the opposite for corn. Plant it on any one of the first three days and failure was almost certain. Furthermore, "pumpkins in May all run away."

These are offered as only a few suggestions. Perhaps the reader can gather other bits of May lore that will be equally as helpful.

❧ *ADVICE FOR THE LOVELORN*

FOR A LONG TIME it has been customary for young folks to fall in love, become engaged, and get married. Disregarding the high percentage of casualties that have occurred along the matrimonial highway, the practice remains popular.

In 1955, according to a magazine article at hand, there were approximately one and a half million marriages in the United States. But during the same interval some 400,000 couples were unmarried; that is, there were twenty-seven divorces for each hundred marriages.

This high casualty rate came about despite the well intentioned services of marriage counselors, social workers, ministers, friendly judges, writers of "advice to the lovelorn" columns, and a host of others that might be grouped under the general classification of "do-gooders." Perhaps the failure of many to achieve domestic happiness could be remedied if some untapped source of guidance could be found. Why not tap the neglected stockpile of wisdom still available in the mass of half-forgotten folklore, once in common circulation in southern Illinois, that relates to love, courtship, and marriage.

The amount of this lore would fill volumes. As this is written, 832 signs and sayings already have been found, and there are many more. Even though they may not solve the problem, this new stockpile should provide materials to relieve the monotony somewhat of the usual stock answers and at least provide diversion.

It is not possible here to classify and organize the signs and sayings that have come to attention. The best that can be done is to offer spot samplings. First, it should be known that these gems of wisdom are generally offered for the guidance of girls. Obviously, the boy always has been deemed the more fortunate one, no matter what the fates passed out to him. After carefully looking at what girls marry, we still are of the candid opinion that men use much the better judgment.

It might be well to use a few of the many available bits of guidance in a logical way. For instance, if a girl were definitely marked to be an old maid, she could recognize that fact early, reconcile herself to the fate awaiting her, cease worrying, and resign herself to school teaching or some other cloistered job. Such action would also prevent her complicating the situation for other girls.

Here are some signs of approaching spinsterhood which every young woman should know. The aspiring young lass must not scorch the clothes being ironed. If setting the table, she must be careful not to place two forks at the same plate. (This folk dictum evidently originated before the advent of salad, pickle, oyster, olive, and other forks *ad infinitum* now distributed in ordered sequence.) Should the young lady decide to make coffee, she must not look into the boiling pot. When time comes to drink coffee, she must not curl her little finger while holding the cup; nor must she sit on her foot; neither must she "dunk" her bread or cake. If she drops and breaks a cup, her fate is definitely sealed.

Girls hoping to marry must not develop a fondness for cats. If they bake bread, as they once did, it must not burn. At meals they should not take the last piece of bread or cake. Some held that taking the next to last biscuit likewise would blight matrimonial prospects. With these and about fifty other warning signs, it was indeed an obstacle course that any ambitious girl must follow.

On the other hand, there were some good signs. If a bird flew into the house and the eligible girl saw it first, she would marry before the year's end. Feeding a cat from an old shoe helped along toward marriage. If a cat, for which the aspiring maiden must form no liking, washed its face and immediately afterwards looked at her, all would be well. There were other good signs to cheer the maid along—not so many good as bad, however.

In those cases where signs had not definitely assigned spinsterhood as her lot, the question of "Just who?" naturally arose. Could she pick and choose or should she be satisfied with less than her choice? Able to meet certain requirements, the choice was hers. If she could, with thumbs and fingers alone, split an apple into halves, no man could escape her grasp. Lacking the physical strength indicated, a weaker girl could eat a four-leaf clover and acquire the same coveted power. If clover were out of season, she could walk, unassisted, seven lengths of railroad irons without stepping off. If neither railroad irons nor four-leaf clovers were at hand, she could eat the raw heart of a chicken or, better yet, one from a duck.

These are only a few samplings of the bountiful lore that related to love, courtship, and marriage. There were signs and sayings to guide one at every turn. Perhaps the wisdom embodied in these bits of old lore could provide new thought for those who would advise. At least they are different. Some, however, will ignore all suggestions and later listen only to the voice of experience.

There were many other ways for a girl to win a choice package, if any man could be such.

❦ *JUNE WEDDINGS*

In ADDITION TO being the month of roses, June also is the favorite month for marriages and has been so since ancient times. Many of the wedding customs, beliefs, and superstitions found in southern Illinois today may be traced to the Romans. To the stock of beliefs and superstitions they left, others were added during the Middle Ages and, even yet, new ones may be added as older ones are forgotten or are proved unreliable.

In the Middle Ages, a maiden agitated the water of a spring with her hand and looked upon its rippling surface to see the reflection of the one she was to wed. Today, a young woman looks into a well to see the image of her man. Ofttimes she may do this by peering into a mirror and over her left shoulder to see the water. She may even drop a pebble into the well to make the water ripple. The old belief or hope persists.

Long ago, a maiden prepared a meal and sat down alone to eat it, believing that while eating she would glimpse the man she would wed. Tales of the "dumb supper" are heard occasionally even now.

Then it was considered unlucky for the wedding party, as it went to the church to meet a monk, priest, dog, cat, snake, or funeral procession. It still forebodes misfortune to meet some of these. It was then considered lucky if the wedding party saw a wolf, spider, or toad.

Weddings were avoided on penitential and fast days then, and still are. Couples wed in the forenoon were supposed to be more fortunate. There once were laws against night marriages, but gypsies always wed by moonlight.

Earlier peoples made a great deal of noise to express their disapproval of matches they considered unsuited. The present-day shivaree (charivari), now with a different meaning, grew out of that custom. Engagement and wedding rings are used today just as the Anglo-Saxons used them, but it was cheaper then, for the same ring served both purposes. It was worn on the right hand as an engagement ring and on the wedding day was transferred to the left hand, there to remain for life.

In medieval times, the father of the bride gave one of his daughter's worn shoes to the groom, who was privileged to strike the bride on the head with it—lightly we hope. Today an old shoe may be hurled and lucky is the bride it hits. The throwing of rice as an emblem of fertility was practiced by the ancients. Hundreds of years ago, bouquets were carried to ward off mischievous spirits. Some of them contained garlic. Bouquets are in fashion today, but they smell of orange blossoms instead

In Scandinavian countries, the losing suitor sometimes would gather a band of friends, arm them with torches and spears, fall upon the wedding procession and kidnap the bride. To prevent any such occurrence, the groom often would select and arm his friends as a band of "best men." Best men still appear at weddings—unarmed.

The bride five hundred years ago sought to catch a glimpse of the groom before he spied her. This was supposed to give her greater influence over him thereafter. The groom in Scotland used to be creeled— that is, loaded with a creel or bag of rocks and made to carry the load until he treated his tormentors. The bride could rescue him by overtaking and kissing him. Today's groom still must treat the boys.

If a younger sister married before an older one, the older was required to dance, wearing green stockings, in a pig's trough. The unmarried older sister still is, figuratively at least, "left to dance in the pig trough."

One of the privileges of an early Welsh groom has been taken from him. Though he always was pledged to treat his wife kindly, he could still legally administer physical punishment. The extent of this mild castigation was defined by law. He could use a stick no longer than his arm and not thicker than his middle finger. With this he was allowed to strike her three times on any part of the body he chose except over the head.

Lore concerning the color of wedding dresses is old and long has been expressed in rhyme:

> If it be white, all will be right;
> Married in red, wish yourself dead;
> Married in black, wish yourself back;
> Married in blue, love always true;
> Married in brown, live out of town;
> Married in yellow, ashamed of your fellow.

Anyone at all versed in the lore of marriage knows that the bride should wear "something old, something new, something borrowed, something blue." Whatever the color of dress she wears, the groom should not see her in it until the wedding day. Above all, blood must not fall upon the wedding dress before it is worn. Should that occur, the husband would murder his wife.

Once upon a time, it was deemed unlucky for the betrothed to kiss before the wedding day. Also, the engaged couple were not to be photographed together from the time when their engagement was announced until the wedding day.

Hundreds of other wedding "rules" could be given, but they might tend only to confuse and discourage young lovers.

❧ *SHIVAREE*

PRANKSTERS NOW ATTACH long festoons of brilliantly colored crepe paper, cowbells, tin cans, "Just married" signs, old shoes and other assorted impedimenta to the getaway car of newlyweds. The practice of decorating their car and of giving them a noisy send-off comes from an earlier one that has all but disappeared. These take the place of the charivari, of French origin. It was a common practice of the pioneers, and it also provided one of the deadly words of spelling-match days.

No one seems to know just when the custom began, but early references to the *charivari* in France indicate that it first was practiced to express disapproval and derision. Transplanted to America, its intent to disapprove or deride lessened. In many rural communities the newlyweds, and even those moving into a new home, who were not shivareed felt that they had not received full social recognition.

The shivaree itself was a serenade of "rough music" made with horns, wagon thimbles, kettles, pans, tubs, tea trays, ticktacks, dumb bulls, guns, circle saws, conch shells, and in fact anything conducive to noise-making. The quality of the performance was measured by its loudness, confusion, and discord. "Decibels" were then unknown.

Those who were to participate in the observance gathered at some designated place to await the time when the couple to be shivareed had gone to bed. They would then quietly gather about the house and await a prearranged signal to "cut loose." This beginning signal might be a gunshot, tub thump, or a resounding whoop.

The onset was usually terrific and startling. In one case the writer recalls that the husband, a "tongue tied" man, dashed madly out to inform the noisemakers that "Thuthie" (Susie) had fainted.

After the din had been kept up for a reasonable length of time, the door was supposed to be opened and the celebrants admitted. An occasional stubborn couple would not open up. In winter time, such stubbornness was easily overcome. One of the celebrants would climb to the roof, place a plank over the chimney or stovepipe and "smoke 'em out."

The husband being shivareed was supposed to treat the crowd. In a village he might take them to the tavern. In our rural community with no drinking place in ten miles, settlement was made for apples, steaming coffee, or "what have ye." In one case it was raw turnips and popcorn, both thoroughly enjoyed. If the husband "got tough" he might be ridden on a rail or carried to the pond and ducked, even in bitter cold weather. A shivaree was often followed by a rousing dance or play party. When parties or dances were planned to follow the noise-making session, the girls and women would gather at some near-by home and be ready.

We have not heard of a real old-fashioned shivaree in many years. Has this old custom, known in different regions as shivaree, charivari, belling, horning, bull-banding, or callithumping, disappeared along with "the run for the bottle" and the "infair dinner"?

❧ HOME REMEDIES

IT WAS ESSENTIAL TO a pioneer's success that he have reasonably good health, but his control over it was very limited. He little understood the principles governing health, and many of the early doctors knew but little more than the layman. Both alike turned to folk remedies, sometimes even to superstitions and charms that the race had accumulated. An occasional one of the great collection of remedies or practices used then comes to mind even now. Some of these are jotted at random here.

Not many years ago a child came to the first grade of a rural school in southern Illinois wearing a neat white cloth bag, which the grandmother had arranged, tied on a blue string about its neck. Inspection revealed that the bag contained the right front foot of a mole. The child was "croupy" and this was the means employed by the grandmother to ward off attacks. This incident suggests a time when the employment of folk remedies and charms was common, particularly with children.

Other objects often were worn for like purposes—that is, to cure or ward off diseases. A ball of asafoetida (another of the deadly words of spelling-match days) worn in the same way was supposed to ward off almost all diseases. It may have been more effective than appears upon first thought. The rancid odor it gave off kept people at such a distance that the child could not so easily become infected. Gum camphor also was worn about the neck by youngsters as a means of promoting the general good health of the wearer. Though camphor may not have been any more effective than asafoetida, it was not so offensive to smell. This remedy also had an added virtue assigned to it. If the child wore it throughout the winter, the usual sulphur-molasses course "to thin the blood" the following spring was not necessary.

Other ailments called for other objects to be worn. A cold was relieved by wearing a spider or woodlouse tied in a sack and hung about the neck until it died. Others would have the victim wear a bunch of live "ground-bugs," species not known, hung in a sack about his neck. If all these failed, the child could drink a tea made of white ants. These last two were considered extra good for whooping cough, which could also be treated by rubbing fresh garlic on the spine or even by giving the child a very small dose of a mixture made of crushed garlic, bruised lobelia leaves, and red pepper in "good whiskey." Perhaps such a vile mixture was also offered to discourage all craving for whiskey.

If none of these remedies gave relief, the child could be passed three times through a warm horse collar, be given a small lump of alum to lick, some Indian turnip ground in molasses, or a mixture of the juice of garlic and onions. Should all these remedies fail, the child still could crawl toward the east under a double rooted raspberry briar.

If the ailing child suffered from only a cold and ordinary sore throat, fat meat and pepper could be bound on the throat, preferably by a sock or stocking that had been worn.

Whooping cough could be cured by eating a castoff snake skin, or by drinking white-ant tea, or by drinking the water used to boil nine eggs that had been bought from some married woman who had not changed her name in marriage. Mare's milk also was a good remedy, or tea made of blue clover blossoms. The child could even be placed in the hopper of a mill and allowed to sit there until the grain had run out. There was no danger in this procedure since the small opening through which the grain dribbled would not admit the baby's feet or hand. Nine fishworms could be put in a bottle and the bottle hidden or the worms tossed into the water. If the worms were fed to fish, the disease would be transferred to them, as evidenced when the fish came to the surface to gulp air or "whoop." Any child who had kissed a Negro before becoming a year old would never have the whooping cough.

The baby must never be left alone with a house cat, which perhaps was not bad advice. A puny baby, however, could eat from a cat's dish and grow strong, but the cat would die.

A mixture of ground flax seed, licorice, raisins, sugar candy, and white vinegar was good for a child's cold, too. In all cases the throat and chest were to be greased liberally with goose grease. Some considered this more effective if the grease came from the goose cooked for Christmas. If none of the remedies already suggested were available, the youngster might take bitters made with bloodroot, or ground cherry bark peeled upward from the north side of the tree. Should all these prescriptions fail to relieve the distressed one and fever arose, sweating should be induced. This was done by putting the youngster to bed, covering him well and administering hot tea made from snakeroot, dogwood, willow, or sassafras. It helped some if the child ate from a blue dish, wore a bit of blue ribbon —better if stolen—or drank from a blue bottle.

"Summer complaint" was a common and dangerous ailment of children. It was treated with poultices of crushed peppermint or tansy leaves. Either mullen or bloodroot steeped in milk was good, likewise, syrup made from rhubarb. The child should eat ripe blackberries, old cheese, or fresh ham.

A child subject to bed-wetting could be helped by feeding it a fried mouse pie, burned hog bladder powder, or by spanking it with a baker's oven ladle—temperature not stated.

Ordinary contagious diseases were considered an inevitable lot of children. All must have measles, and the children often were willfully exposed, in the spring of the year if possible, after the blood had been thinned properly and ridded of "winter humors." Should the measles not break out promptly, the process could be hastened by giving saffron or sassafras tea or tea made from sheep droppings. Inflammation of the eyes incident to measles could be prevented by poulticing them with slippery elm. Rags soaked in strong sassafras tea also were thought good for the inflamed eyes.

Many children then had the seven year itch, now known as scabies. Adults might even be attacked. Itch was treated by hot water and soap applied with a corn cob until the skin was a rosy red. This was followed by salving with a mixture of sulphur and lard or gunpowder and lard. Water in which pokeweed root had been boiled was considered an effective but severe remedy.

Should a child be born with a birthmark, that could be removed by rubbing the spot with the hand of a corpse, or with the head of a fresh live eel on each of three successive mornings. The heads of the eels then should be tied together and buried under a stone beneath the eaves of the house.

Washing the face of the babe in its baptismal water would make it pretty. Stump water, water secured in a cemetery, or even whey from curdled milk would remove freckles. In each case, the one going for the water must not look back after collecting it.

A baby's hair should not be cut before its first birthday, for this would shorten its life. If its nails were cut before nine weeks, it would become a thief. It was unfortunate for a child under nine months of age to see itself in a mirror. Should its empty cradle be rocked, colic would result, but this could be cured by a dose of scrapings from a table cover or a teaspoonful of baptismal water.

When the baby began to crawl, it must not be allowed to go between table legs or chair posts for that would stop growth unless it retraced its course. Should that not be done, the child could be measured by a length of string that then was tied into a loop through which the child was to be passed three times. Afterwards, to completely break the spell, the string should be tied about a grindstone and left there until worn away.

Yellow jaundice ("yaller janders") was cured by a spoonful of scrapings from a horn comb mixed with honey. Bitters of many and varied kinds were considered effective in about the same ratio as their bitterness. Nosebleed could be stopped by chewing paper or putting a dime or a small roll of paper under the upper lip. Three drops from the bleeding nose could be allowed to fall upon a heated shovel or the pocket knife changed from one pocket to another.

The great proportion of young children's graves in old cemeteries is enough to convince all thinking persons that the practices given above and countless other similar ones really did little to assure the good health of children.

🐍 SNAKE BITES

IT IS AN AGE-OLD custom for snakes to bite people. If snakes could speak in the matter, they would doubtless insist that they bit only in self-defense. However that may be, snakes have long been biting, and people have just that long been seeking cures for the bites.

The hazard of snake bites, particularly in sections infested with rattlers, was a serious one in earlier days. Newspapers opened their columns to subscribers with something to say on the subject. It is in the 1848 file of the *Prairie Farmer,* even then circulating widely in southern Illinois, that much of the following is found.

Perhaps the most popular remedy was the alcohol treatment—naturally to be taken internally. By this method, the victim was given copious, very copious, swigs of strong drink. According to published accounts, the alcohol treatment began in South Carolina during the Revolutionary War in the following manner.

A highly intoxicated soldier from a regiment stationed at Charleston fell upon a rattler and was bitten several times. This soldier was not too far under to take a few more drinks, and thus became "dead drunk." Reports state that when he sobered up no injurious effects whatever were to be noted from the bite. The venom "had lain in massive inactivity until its strength was lost." A short time later another soldier, likewise intoxicated, was bitten by a rattler. The regimental surgeon, according to the account, recalled the wonderful recovery made by the soldier previously bitten. He accordingly gave the second soldier "whiskey by the pint," until unconsciousness resulted. According to the report there was complete recovery without any harmful effects. Accounts of these two cases spread rapidly, and the treatment gained popularity. There are reports that men would take along an ample supply of the prescribed antidote when they hunted poisonous snakes.

Another widely acclaimed treatment was a combination of a plantain and horehound juices. The juice of the plantain was to cure the bite and that of the horehound was to counteract effects of the plantain. This plantain-horehound remedy originated about 1800, when a Virginia slave walking along a pathway came upon a toad and a poisonous spider in deadly combat. He observed that the toad would, immediately after being bitten, retire from the fray and nibble a bit of leaf from some near-by plantain. Being curious, the slave wished to determine whether the plantain was really the effective remedy it appeared to be. Accordingly, while the frog and spider were in active combat, he pulled the plantain and threw it away. Shortly thereafter, the toad was bitten again and turned to the place where the plantain had stood, only to find none there. Without its antidote, the toad promptly turned upon its back and died. As a reward for his discovery, the slave is said to have received his freedom and a pension of $300 a year.

Plantain was considered as highly effective. It was said that a rattlesnake covered by its leaves would show evidence of great agony and shortly die. Also, plantain leaves bound about the ankles would discourage the striking of the most vicious rattler.

A reader wishing to use this plantain-horehound remedy gathers equal amounts of each kind of leaves, crushes them thoroughly, squeezes out a tablespoonful of the juices and swallows it. The juice from the plantain alone, one-half tablespoonful, is considered as effective as the combination. Without the addition of horehound juice, however, the patient may become nauseated.

Other remedies were available. Ira Jewell of Hickory Grove, Illinois, suggested that the parts affected be rubbed with a solution of indigo and chamber lye. He said a poultice of indigo or indigo-lard also should be bound on the wound. Others prescribed an indigo-alcohol salve. Jewell also said that snake bites produce fever and that the one bitten should be given doses of epsom salts, rhubarb tea, or castor oil.

R. Ferguson from Perryton, Illinois, advised the prompt and vigorous use of a very sharp penknife. He stated that he always carried one and had not failed in fifty cases to save the bitten victim. According to this remedy, one should vigorously jab away until blood flowed freely. Watery blood, or blood with a yellowish tinge, indicated that the injected poison had been released. Doctor M. C. Strong of Pulaski, Illinois, strongly urged that the wound made by the snake be cut out completely. He cited cases in which he had done so with success. These men apparently were on the right track.

Other remedies were used. The half of a freshly killed chicken, slit vertically and lengthwise and applied immediately, was deemed excellent. A paste of alcohol and gunpowder was rated highly. A toad cut or pulled in two was about as effective as the half of chicken. The same madstone that was applied to the bites of rabid dogs also was rated as an effective remedy for snakebites.

The aftereffects of a snake bite were unpleasant. At yearly intervals a painful rash, or ulcers would occur. A child bitten by a poisonous snake might go about catching flies between his forefinger and thumb, employing a very quick, striking motion like that of a snake. These aftereffects could be avoided by having the victim drink cold tea from the roots of silene inflata or cucubalus behen—plants of the catchfly family.

❧ *WARTS*

No ONE SEEMS TO know exactly what causes warts; even doctors are puzzled. You just look one day and there it is, acquired perhaps from handling toads. That explanation sometimes does not hold well, for girls who squeal and flee before they are near enough to prod the toad with a stick, and also timid boys, are found to be just as warty as toad-catchers. Perhaps these fearful ones have been splashed with water from which chickens have drunk, or been tricked into untying knots in strings or ribbons they have found. They may also be guilty of counting warts. Anyway, they have violated some basic rule applicable to warts.

The startled host to a plump new wart even now has only to mention or display it and then choose from suggested remedies. A popular German remedy has enough mystery about it to make an appeal and is supposed to be known only to a select few. The "remover" draws a circle about the wart with his finger and mumbles a few words that the listener can never understand. The wart is supposed to disappear in a few days. This power to remove warts and the secret words can be passed on only to a member of the opposite sex if it is to remain effective.

Some who employ this method moisten the fingers with spittle or stump water while others deem it necessary only to dry-finger encircle the spot and slightly moisten the wart before the pow-wowing. Others think it just as effective to moisten the wart for nine successive days with stump water or for three days with spittle and omit the magic words. A few persons think that water which condenses on a window pane is more effective than either spittle or stump water. Plain castor oil or the juice from a broken milkweed stem does well. A wart immersed so deeply in water that it cannot be seen will shortly disappear. Those with great faith have only to pretend to wash in an empty pan.

If someone having warts counts them, he will shortly have twice as many. Should someone else count them, he will acquire the same number. This misfortune can be avoided if the one counting pays the owner a penny which is to be thrown away.

Another way to be rid of warts is to take a piece of string, or blue ribbon, tie a knot in it for each wart and drop it in a roadway. The warts will disappear only to appear on the finder of the knotted ribbon if he unties the knots. Three buttons tied on a string and dropped into a coffin is a sure method. Lacking buttons, one can rub a pebble on the wart and drop it into a newly dug grave. Should he neglect to do this, he can go to a new grave at midnight and ask the devil to take his warts. Touching a wart to a corpse or giving it three light strokes with an undertaker's hammer will remove it.

A piece of salt bacon tied to a string, rubbed on a wart, swung thirty times about the head, and then buried under an oak tree is a favorite with many. A piece of fresh pork can be stolen where hogs are being butchered, rubbed on the wart and buried under a stone in damp ground, taking care that the stone is located where no one is likely to step on it. Rubbing the wart with the tail of a terrapin is effective only in the month of May.

Chickens, blamed for causing warts, can also help toward their removal. The most stubborn wart will disappear after being rubbed three times with the lining from a chicken gizzard. Seven grains of corn can be rubbed on warts and fed to a neighbor's rooster. If the wart is pricked until it bleeds and corn is stained with the blood, one grain is sufficient. If the pricking is done through a wedding ring, using a gooseberry briar, no corn at all is needed.

A few drops of blood from a wart can be placed on a handkerchief to be dropped in the road. The finder acquires the wart. A bean can be split, rubbed on the wart and dropped in the well or buried beneath the eaves of the house.

A wart can be rubbed with three bean leaves and the leaves thrown where no one will find them. A green grasshopper can be captured and induced to bite the wart. You can spit upon a small stone picked up at midnight and put it on a rafter in the attic. A seventh son of a seventh son can blow warts away.

A piece of dishrag should be rubbed on the wart then dipped in a pig's blood and buried. A stolen dishrag rubbed on the wart and buried under the doorstep is just as effective. A wart will disappear when a small incision made in the bark of an apple tree heals, or when a strawberry rots after being placed in the bowl of a clay pipe and buried. A pin should be rubbed on the head of a wart and thrown away. A pin placed, "unbeknownst," in the hem of a garment worn by a lady having warts becomes an effective remedy when it drops out. A chalk mark on an oven door is effective when it vanishes. Rubbing with a matchhead or toothpick helps.

To the writer's personal knowledge, the matchhead remedy, slightly changed, once actually worked. The possessor of a husky wart was going to rub it with the head of a match. Friends convinced him that it would be more effective if the head of the match were carefully crumbled, piled upon the wart and ignited. He was told that it might burn "just a little." Since the wart was on his hand and he could not well perform the task unaided, those present agreed to help, even to "steadying" his hand when the crumbled pile was ignited. Before the victim could wrest his hand away, the wart was practically consumed. That remedy worked, but it is not recommended. It angers the victim.

There were many other remedies, perhaps fully as good as the ones described.

MADSTONE

Hydrophobia, or rabies, has been known since ancient times. The fact that it is transmitted by the bite of some rabid animal, generally a dog, has likewise been known. It has also been common knowledge that once contracted, the disease is fatal. Since ancient times, men have sought frantically for ways to prevent or cure it. Suggested remedies have been as numerous and varied as those for snakebite. They have ranged from the magical to the heroic. Many could have had no helpful effects, but they constitute an interesting section of our medical folklore.

Perhaps the best of the early treatments practiced for rabies was the one advocated by an early Greek physician. He advised that some sharp instrument be used to enlarge the wound and increase bleeding, after which the wound was cauterized by the use of a red hot iron. It was a painful remedy, but it appears to have been the only ancient one with a scientific basis.

Many of the older folk remedies vanished and newer ones took their places. One remedy persisting until very recent times was the use of mad-stones. The source and type of these stones varied. Some were obtained from the stomach of a white deer; doubtless they were hairballs similar to those occasionally found in the stomach of a cow. Others were bones from various animals, one from the head of a fish. Others were found among field stones or in mines. Just how it was determined which were madstones is not told.

One madstone kept and used until recent years was in the possession of a family living in Pope County. This stone is said to have come from a mine in Italy. It was brought to Illinois from Tennessee by Matthew Trovillion before 1870. It is roughly rectangular in shape, about one-half inch in length, and slightly less in width and thickness. It is black, some-what fibrous in appearance, and apparently is a piece of cannel coal.

This stone has been the center of considerable legal litigation. The circuit court records for the March term of 1911 show that a man named John Breedlove brought suit again Susan Boos, Maggie Meyer, Will C. Gullet, Charles Gullet, and John Gullet. Breedlove contended that he had an equity in the stone and that he had been deprived of its possession, profits, and use. Breedlove asked that the court appoint a receiver, that the sale of the stone be ordered, and that the proceeds of the sale be divided among those holding equity. It was Breedlove's contention that the proceeds from the use of the stone amounted to more than three hundred dollars a year. He also stated that the stone had been effective in all except one of hundreds of applications. In this instance, Breedlove stated that it failed in the case of a man named Leatzen who had been badly bitten about the face and died en route to a hospital in Evansville, Indiana. The court records for 1911 also state that this stone had been an issue in a lawsuit in 1892 and that at that time its custody had been as-signed to two families in turn. Breedlove's suit of 1911 did not win him custody of the stone nor did the court appoint a receiver or order its sale.

The Pope County stone, according to the beliefs of those holding it, is effective not only against the bites of rabid animals but also against those of poisonous snakes and of insects. A regular procedure is followed when the stone is used. The wound to which it is to be applied should be an open one. The stone is placed on the wound, where it adheres. It is allowed to remain one hour unless it drops off sooner; next it is placed in clear water until it begins to give off bubbles, then it is reapplied. This process is continued until the stone no longer adheres. When used on snake or spider bites, or on insect stings, it is said to show a slight change in coloring.

In an issue of the *Golconda Herald* for April 18, 1887, there is an account of a trip made to this stone by E. V. Nelson of Hamletsburg, when his wife was bitten by a rabid dog. The stone adhered eight times. A letter from Mrs. Nelson's granddaughter states that Mrs. Nelson did not contract rabies.

There have been other madstones in southern Illinois, but none seems to have acquired the fame of this one. When the development of the Pasteur method of treatment, the use of madstones and other folk remedies for the prevention of rabies has practically disappeared. Today anyone bitten by an animal suspected of being rabid hastens to consult a physician.

❧ SIGNS OF THE ZODIAC

"THE FAULT, DEAR BRUTUS, is not in our stars, but in ourselves, that we are underlings." These are the words that Shakespeare has Cassius saying as he urges action to curb the power of Caesar in Rome two thousand years ago. They indicate a belief, then common, that the fate of a person was profoundly influenced by the stars.

In talking with elderly persons, and with others not so old, vestiges of the ancient beliefs in the influence that stars are supposed to wield sometimes come to attention in southern Illinois and in fact, wherever one may go in America.

This belief in the stars is very old and was quite prevalent even among ancient peoples. It was an accepted belief among the Chaldeans five thousand years ago, likewise among the early Egyptians. It was current among the Aztec Indians in Mexico, even before their contact with white men. In our own country, the signs of the Zodiac are even yet occasionally referred to for counsel and prophecy.

These signs refer to twelve early groupings of the stars that are located on the approximate plane in which the planets move about the sun. Each of the twelve groupings or constellations covers thirty degrees of celestial longitude. The twelve thus complete the circuit. The constellation opposite the sun at any given time is the one supposed to be most potent. The twelve constellations, each in ascendency for a month, are named for star groups that early people fancied resembled some known object, often an animal.

The belief in the power of the stars seems to have come into being slowly. The sun, moon, and planets appear to have first become associated in people's thinking with some known metal. The sun was linked with gold and we still have "golden sunshine." The moon still is the "silvery moon" of romance. Saturn and lead, Venus and copper, and Mercury and quicksilver indicate other associations. The star groupings likewise become linked with animals and with certain minerals to give us birthstones.

In their association with men and with lower animals, each individual star group or constellation was somehow assigned a strong influence over a particular part of the body. The first sign, Aries or the Ram, thus was allocated to the head, and the last, Pisces or Fish, to the feet.

During the period when the constellation of Aries was opposite the sun, the head was most sensitive. Injuries to it were to be avoided. Mental derangements were more frequent. Diseases centering in the head were most likely to make their onset. Young animals fretted more if weaned during this sign. This general plan operated for each of the other signs in turn. The temperament of an individual born under a particular sign was considered as greatly influenced by it.

Extensive lore built up about the signs. Great power over plant life also was ascribed to some of them. Trees were most easily deadened on newly cleared ground if girdled when the sign was "in the heart." Grain planted during the time when the "sign was right" and during the light of the moon carried a practical guarantee of a bountiful crop.

Today, most of these old beliefs have been laughed away, but not all are gone. Astrologers still set up to forecast coming events and to advise people concerning their daily actions. Many newspapers carry "Stargazer," "Horoscope," or some similar features. Inquiry reveals that these features are read by many, some of whom say of the newspaper scribe, "He's nearly always right."

The people who set up the system of signs and allocated a particular interval for their powers to be most effective did not have knowledge of the exact time that it takes the earth to complete a circuit of the sun. Thus, at the time when the sign is supposed to be in power, the star group is not actually opposite the sun. Perhaps this discrepancy should not be cause for worry since the earth, sun and the constellations will again be in the original line-up about twenty-six thousand years from now. Then, without doubt, "the sign will be right."

WATER WITCHING

DESPITE THE HEAT OF a June day, a Union County farmer holding a forked peach twig in the approved manner was seen walking with slow and careful tread across the large yard in front of his home. A second man, apparently much interested, stood watching the first.

The scene aroused the writer's interest and revived memories of a time when the ritual then being observed was common. These men were dowsing or "water witching." A stop was made in order to observe the procedure, to chat with the farmers and perhaps to test any aptitude the writer might have for that ancient art. It was learned that the well located between the farmer's yardway and the adjoining pasture was failing and that he needed more water than it supplied. Before digging a new well, however, he was making use of an age-old test, thought by many to be an effective one, to locate flowing underground water.

The use of divining rods is not new. The fact is that they have been used for many hundreds of years and for various purposes. The Scythians, Medes, and Persians made use of them. Marco Polo found such devices in use in China when he traveled there during 1271 to 1295. They had their place in the lore of the early Germans, the Turks, and the Scandinavians. A figure using a dowsing rod appears in a mural decorating the city hall in Oslo, Norway.

In earlier times they were used in efforts to accomplish varied objectives. They were considered effective in the location of minerals, underground flowing water, missing persons or objects, buried treasure, as a cure for certain diseases, and even to analyze the character of an individual.

In America their principal use has been to locate underground water and occasionally to locate hidden treasure or mineral deposits. "Divining rods" are of various materials and different arrangements. One may now buy manufactured devices that the sellers say are effective in the location of minerals and buried treasure, but no purveyor of such equipment seems willing to sell on an installment plan and take his pay from the treasure located.

The divining rods used in America generally are the forked twigs of the peach, willow, hazel, or witch hazel, here listed in order of their reputed efficiency. Each branch should be from sixteen to twenty-four inches long and reasonably pliable. In fact, younger growth is considered more desirable and responsive.

With the upper arms held gently against the sides, and the forearms extended with palms upward and level, the operator grasps the free end of each branch in either hand in such way that the main body of the twig points upward. With the dowsing rod thus properly positioned, he walks slowly and smoothly forward. When a stream of underground flowing water is approached, the end of the rod where the branches unite begins to sweep forward and despite the utmost efforts of the holder, makes a half rotation and comes point downward when the dowser is directly over the spot. Some operators contend that they can tell the depth at which the water will be found and also gauge the amount available.

Can water witching really be done? Opinion is much divided and few are neutral. Many condemn the idea but offer little to refute it. Others ardently support the belief but offer scant proof. Some prominent churchmen have condemned the practice while others, equally eminent, have practiced it. Numerous books and articles have been written concerning it. Five hundred seventy-three such publications are listed as appearing before 1917. Herbert C. Hoover's translation of an old text on mining includes four pages concerning the use of divining rods in mining practices. The Smithsonian Institution and the U.S. Geological Survey have each investigated and published reports concerning water witching.

Ask your neighbor if he knows of a water witch.

❦ ALAN BANE

AN OCCASIONAL STORY concerning some incident that occurred during the early days in southern Illinois has been preserved in the form of a ballad. These ballads generally are romantic and tinged with sadness, but they are always highly sentimental. This story concerns one such ballad entitled "Alan Bane," popular ninety years ago. It grew out of a murder committed near Benton, in Franklin County, and is based on the events briefly sketched here.

During the Civil War, two men came to Benton. One of these men was David Williams, and the last name of the other was McMahan. They were often seen together about Benton and seemed to have been partners of sorts. One day McMahan, who was known to be carrying a considerable amount of money, disappeared. Shortly afterwards, the body of a murdered man was found in a fallen tree about two miles southeast of Benton. His pocket knife was found in the dead man's pocket, and no one appeared to question that the victim was the missing McMahan. Williams, who was the last person to be seen with McMahan before his disappearance, was suspected of murder. He was arrested, indicted, and brought to trial. The case against him, based on circumstantial evidence, was definitely convincing. As the case drew near its end, it appeared certain that Williams would be convicted.

At this point, though, the trial took a dramatic turn. McMahan walked into the court room. With the "murdered" man alive and present, the case naturally collapsed and Williams was set free. His appearance in court came about because a resident of Benton saw him on an Illinois Central train at Tamaroa some twenty miles away and explained the perilous situation of his friend. McMahan left the train, secured a horse, and hurriedly rode to Benton, arriving just in time to save Williams from what appeared certain conviction.

The identity of the murdered man remained a mystery for many years. A boy who had seen the killing committed remained silent under threat of death until the slayers were dead. He then told the story. The victim was found to be a Union soldier who was on furlough and was going to visit relatives in Hardin County.

Three of the twelve stanzas of the ballad concerning the incident are given here. McMahan is the Alan Bane of the title. It is easy to see that they are somewhat crude in construction, but they do include some of the highlights of the story and indicate the manner in which it was handled. The actual ballad begins about where the court records leave off.

ALAN BANE

1

They're taking me to the gallows, Mother.
   They're goin' to hang me high.
They're goin' to gather around me there,
   And watch me till I die.
All earthly joys are vanished now,
   And gone each earthly hope.
They'll draw a cap across mine eyes,
   Around my neck a rope.

2

The crazied mob will shout and groan,
   The priest will read a prayer,
The drop will fall beneath my feet,
   And leave me in the air.
For they think I murdered Alan Bane,
   And so the Judge has said.
They'll hang me to the gallows, Mother,
   Hang me till I'm dead.

.   .   .   .

II

But hark, I hear a mighty murmur
   Among the jostling crowd,
A shout, a cry, a roar of voices,
   Which echoes long and loud.
There dashes a horseman on foaming steed
   With tightly gathered rein.
He sits erect, he waves his hand.
   Good Heavens, 'tis Alan Bane!

❦ *DOORS*

A YOUTHFUL ACQUAINTANCE stopped to call. When leaving he said, "The next time you are down our way, Grandad wants you to come and see him. He said to tell you his latchstring was always out." Since I was hanging a screen door at the time and thus was door-minded, the mention of the latchstring served to recall some dimly remembered lore about doors.

To include in an invitation the words, "my latchstring hangs out" was another way of saying "you will be very welcome." My youthful caller did not know of the expression's origin. He was interested to learn that early cabin doors were put together with wooden pegs and hung on wooden hinges and that the more common type of these latches was operated from the outside by a string attached to the inside bar of the latch and passed to the outside through a hole higher in the door. When this latchstring was hanging out, anyone was free to pull it, lift the latch, and enter. Should the string be pulled in, it meant "Who are you?" It was necessary for the visitor to knock, halloo, or otherwise announce his presence and await a welcome.

Another expression occasionally heard is, "It's Katie bar the door." This likewise originated from a manner in which doors were fastened. When the householder wished to make his house secure against forcible entry, he pegged a bracket on each side of the opening and placed a sturdy wooden bar across the door.

There were numerous other expressions about doors that indicated attitudes and action. Some such that are still heard are "The door is wide open," "Don't let him get his foot in the door," "Show him the door," the door was "slammed in his face," "He used the back door," and "I'll never darken his doorway again."

Many superstitions also were associated with doors. Bad luck certainly, perhaps even death, might come if a new doorway were cut into a recently built house. To change a door into a window or a window into a door in any house would bring misfortune. Mysterious rappings, generally in threes, along with apparently causeless opening or slamming of doors aroused dread. No haunted house was complete without its creaking door hinges.

A spider climbing up a door foretold a visitor. If he spun a web across the door, the visitor would be a welcome one. Dogs, doors, and visitors also were related. If the family dog lay in the doorway with his head inside, company was to be expected. With his head outside, someone from the house would go on a journey. A cat cleaning its face in the doorway would look in the direction from which company would come. A strange dog howling in front of a door foretold death (perhaps the dog's). To allow any dog to howl about the front door brought misfortune.

A piece of hard dry bread placed in a bag above the kitchen door would bring work into the house. A miner's wife once declared that this practice kept them employed during a trying mine strike. Another stated that tomato peel placed above the door would bring money to the house within four days.

A broom falling across the door opening meant that someone in the house would travel to a foreign land. A broom across the doorway also would keep witches out. A pair of old shoes was just as effective; the witch could pass neither. Old shoes were effective in another way. If a wife would bury a pair of her husband's discarded shoes in the front yard with the toes pointing toward the door, that husband would stay at home and not go wandering about. Salt sprinkled about the front door would keep unwanted persons away.

It was bad luck to walk backwards out of a room, for you would not be welcomed back. There must be something to this, because in 1919 the writer backed out of a room where King George and Queen Mary sat in Windsor Palace and never has been invited back.

Chapter 4

Indians

🏵 *TEN-THOUSAND-YEAR-OLD TOOLSHED*

A DENSE INDIAN population that had passed before the coming of the French once lived in the American Bottom, that area lying near the Mississippi in the vicinity of East St. Louis. The few Indians found by the French in the region knew nothing of the earlier ones that had vanished, leaving behind the world's largest earthen mounds.

Long, long before the Indians who built these great mounds came to occupy the fertile lands of the American Bottom, other and more primitive men lived in shelters along the bluffs that border the Mississippi. There they left tools, implements, ornaments, bones—including their own—and other artifacts mingled in the dust and sand beneath the shelving rocks that gave them shelter between Prairie du Rocher and Modoc.

Contemporary man came to store tools and implements beneath the same shelters, thereby giving us a continued story of man's way of life over a period of ten thousand years. Though these artifacts and relics tell much of interest about the various peoples that lived in this vicinity and their cultures, many questions remain.

Surface explorers who follow close against the base of the cliffs, often through a tangle of brush, briars, tall weeds, and vines, can still find many objects that arouse memories of times not too long ago when farming methods differed much from those of today.

Pulleys, old well pumps of the chain, bucket, and lift type with parts of an old wooden pump indicate the method of solving the water problem in pre-electric days. A large wooden rake, complete with its long trip pole that followed behind a farm wagon to rake cornstalks fifty years or

99

more ago is badly decayed. Near by are horse-drawn hay rakes, wooden and steel remnants of an old hand rake, a hay tedder, a wagon hay frame, pitchforks, the sneed of a scythe, sickle blades, and a rusted bundle of bale ties that tell of long hot days in the hayfield. A farm wagon, a sleigh, some old buggies, a sled or two, a surrey, buggy shafts, poles and neck yokes, the bolster of a log wagon, one of the heavy cross timbers of a mudboat, large apple-wood wagon hubs, some wagon hounds, buggy fifth wheels, and tire irons remain to remind visitors of farm transportation a century ago.

The irons of a new-ground plow, bits of a harrow, a single shovel plow used to lay off corn ground, with a rectangular stone slab having a hole in one corner so that it could be dragged down the furrow to cover the dropped corn, are remnants of earlier field tools. There are one-row corn planters, two-row planters with their checking attachments and quarter-mile-long knotted wires, well rusted, to tell of progress in agriculture. There are some double-shovel plows, both wooden and steel stocked, to remind an occasional oldster of the vicious manner in which they could kick. There are wooden beamed breaking plows, diamond plows used to bar off corn, walking cultivators, riding cultivators of both disc and shovel type, each suggesting part of a story. So much for the unburied archeology that adds reality to the more recent past.

Before men first came to live along these bluffs, the ground level was much lower. Through the ages that he lived here, the surface has been built up many feet by accumulations of earth, ashes, charcoal from old campfires, bones, shells, and stones. It is this accumulation that holds much of the story of the remote past. As this is removed, layer by layer, the record of man's life here is turned backward.

In 1954 a party from the Illinois State Museum worked here, uncovering reliable evidence that men lived here 10,000 years ago. Though they removed more than twenty feet of sand, dust and ashes, they did not reach the bottom of the deposits over and around the long dead campfires. Another year of digging brought added knowledge. Specimens of recovered objects on display in the Illinois State Museum at Springfield amply reward those interested.

One can only guess at what may yet be revealed. It is indeed a site of great promise, just as are other places in the southern section of the state. Competent authorities believe that one of America's great fields for archeological research lies in this region.

❦ *INDIAN PICTURES & INSCRIPTIONS*

SOME PERSONS ARE familiar with the stone, shell, and bone ornaments, weapons, and tools used by the Indians of southern Illinois. Not many, however, are acquainted with the carvings and colored pictures they left on walls beneath some of their rock shelters and on rocky ledges. It generally is not difficult to understand the purpose and use of their tools and weapons, but the petroglyphs and colored pictures are not so easy to comprehend.

There still are many places where their crudely drawn pictures and rough carvings are found, but only a few complete pictures are left. Most of them are only faded fragments and splotches, generally in one color.

One of the more interesting of these is on the wall of a low bluff in Gum Spring Hollow about two miles north of Simpson, in Johnson County. It is a picture of a buffalo about four feet long and two feet high; it is outlined by a shallow groove and is now faded to a pale rust color. Since settlers first came to the vicinity, it has been known and referred to as the "Indian Buffalo Painting."

There are some other pictures beneath rock shelters in Clarida Hollow in Pope County. They represent men, wolves, turtles, and lizards; all are faded and fragmentary. Their better preserved parts indicate that they once were richly colored.

The carvings left by the Indians are naturally better preserved than the pictures, and are found more frequently. One of the finest groups is on the west side of Big Hill near the Mississippi, about four miles north of Grand Tower. One gets to them over a somewhat rugged path. After such a trip, one visitor said that it was a half-mile downhill from the car to the carvings and two miles uphill to get back to the car.

These carvings include encircled crosses and swastikas, concentric circles, queer eyes that seem to look past or through the visitor, geometric designs that may be attempts to make a map, and also arms and hands of mysterious significance. In addition to these shallow carvings, there is a great scooped-out place that some think was made for a throne.

One who stands at the proper place near these carvings, finds that the rocky walls of the bluff serve as a kind of amplifier that gathers sounds from the Missouri shore more than half a mile away and makes them audible. The rippling of water around jetties on the Missouri side and the sound of voices there are easily heard. One wonders if perchance the Indians stopped at the same spot, heard similar sounds, thought it the abode of a great spirit, and therefore set it aside as a shrine.

Another group of carvings is found at the north end of Big Hill about a quarter of a mile east of the place known as Fountain Bluff, where people long have gone for picnics. Here one sees carvings of birds, wolves, deer, staring eyes, crosses, circles, human forms, and geometrical figures, along with the names and initials of young picnickers, chips in the rock wall made by those using some of the bird carvings for rifle targets. This group of carvings, about a mile south and west of Gorham, may be reached easily by a pathway leading from the gravel road and across the railway track to the bluff not more than a hundred yards beyond.

Another small Jackson County group that one may visit easily is at Turkey Track Rock, about a half-mile north of the place where State Route 151 leading toward Ava leaves Route 3. Here one finds carvings of human tracks, hand imprints, circles, the everhaunting eye, and "turkey tracks." Again there are the initials of moderns. Still other carvings in Jackson County are in the bed of Rock Creek about one mile east and three miles north of Ava. Here are footprints with the great toes turned at right angles, arms, hands, face profiles, snakes, lizards, and chiseled trenches.

Another area with interesting carvings is about four miles south and three miles east of Vienna, in Johnson County. There are footprints of adults and children arranged in rows as though standing in formation. A hand holds what may be a votive offering. Other carvings suggest that a turkey walked across the flat stone. On several near-by rocky ledges there are depressions or rounded stone pits where the Indians pounded corn. Some of these depressions are eight or ten inches across and equally deep. They are not so large, however, as those near the place known as the Indian Fort on the southern edge of Saline County, and east of the village of Stonefort.

When one pauses to view these strange remains, he can but wonder what the artists who made them meant to say. After the Atom Age and hydrogen bombs, will other beings come to ponder the meaning of the ruins left by present-day man?

🌼 *FORTS OR POUNDS?*

ARCHAEOLOGISTS RECOGNIZE southern Illinois as a region rich in significant Indian remains. Some express an opinion that no section of the mid-United States affords students a richer field. Only a small part of the known sites where Indians lived have been excavated and the findings studied by competent scholars. Many other known ones await the attention of those who would learn more concerning the manner in which early man lived.

Places where their villages once were located are widely distributed and materials for study are varied. There are many mounds, both burial and ceremonial. There are ashes of burned-out campfires along the bases of bluffs and outlines of palisaded walls that enclosed long-gone villages. Remnants of pots that they used for storing and cooking their food are found in kitchen middens. Mounds of flint chips and camp refuse show where they fashioned implements and weapons. Bone needles suggest the manner in which they made clothes.

Sunken spots in the hills west of the village of Mill Creek were once deep pits where Indians dug for flint balls or nodules which were split and chipped to forms desired. Strange carvings upon rocks cause the curious to look and ponder. From some points of vantage the trails that the Indians followed across the wooded hills are still visible. Ornaments, decorations, crude jewelry and statuettes are found at their burial sites. Strange objects and structures cause even those most versed to pause and give thought.

Among the larger structures left by the Indians are a number of "forts" or "pounds." At least nine of these ruins are known in the hills of southern Illinois. There may be others whose walls have been removed to ground level. The latest discovery was made recently about three miles east of Cobden only when its foundation was accidentally observed.

These walled places, forming a broken line across the state, have one thing in common. Each is located on the top of a high bluff and on a projecting portion or finger of the bluff. Each can be reached on the higher level over gently sloping ground. Each, except at the narrow part where a wall was built, is bordered on the remaining sides by sheer cliffs. In most cases a man could scale those cliffs only by careful and strenuous effort. They thus have many of the characteristics that would make them into desirable forts. In each case, however, unless it be the one in southern Saline County near Stonefort, all lack water supplies.

The walls of these forts or pounds were built of loose stones of one-man size. Part of the stone used was collected from the beds of brooks flowing along the foot of the cliff. These walls are without mortar.

They were not insignificant structures, and the amount of manual labor required was great. From earlier records and from careful inspection of their foundations and sections of the original walls, it may be determined that they were originally six feet or more high and about as wide. Very old persons who knew the walls before farmers hauled much of the stone away give this report. The many thousands of trips necessary to be made from the brook bed to the top of the bluff, often two hundred feet or more above the creek level, represent a stupendous effort for primitive people—the more so when it is considered that some of these walls were six hundrd feet long.

Each wall sets off a plot of ground, perhaps the smallest one being that discovered south of the highway and east of Cobden by the Thomas brothers a few years ago. The largest area walled off is at The Pounds near the southern side of Gallatin County.

In addition to the two walls already mentioned, the locations of seven others have been marked. One of these is about three miles east and a mile south of the village of Stonefort. It has long been referred to as the Old Stone Fort. The wall at this place was about 650 feet long and formed half of an accurate ellipse with axes of 450 and 190 feet. It is not easy to explain how this wall could be laid out and built so accurately in a forested area.

Other walls are on Draper's Bluff, in Johnson County, at Indian Kitchen, on Lusk Creek south and east of Eddyville, on War Bluff, two miles east and one mile north of the village of Raum, on Cornish Bluff, in Johnson County, and at Trigg Stone Fort, also in Johnson County.

One other stone fort, perhaps the easiest one for visitors to reach, is the one marked in Giant City State Park, near Makanda. An inspection of this structure gives a clear idea of the general plan followed for all of them.

Mystery surrounds these old structures. One wonders who built them, how long they have been there, and just how they were used. Were they forts or pounds, or did they serve some other purpose? What is the significance of the stone cairns and pits near their old gateways? Visit them and wonder.

❦ BIRD OF EVIL SPIRIT

PEOPLE PASSING ALONG the river highway north of Alton see a strange painting on the smooth face of the bluff. This picture is about thirty feet long and eight feet high. It represents a strange creature widely known in Indian legends as the Piasa (Pi-a-saw) or Bird of Evil Spirit.

The present picture, placed there a few years ago, is a faithful reproduction of the original one made by the Indians and carefully sketched by an artist on April 30, 1826. The first picture really was a shallow carving or petroglyph that had been painted in red, green, and black. It remained well preserved until the winter of 1846–47, when the rock was quarried away.

The monster pictured must have been hideous indeed. Its body resembled that of an alligator. Each foot had enormous talons, like those of a bird of prey, and, according to legend, strong enough to carry a buffalo. The head of the beast on an upright neck, was much like that of a man. The ears were pointed, eyes red and staring. Its teeth were large and sharply pointed. Its antlers resembled those of a deer, and its beard that of a tiger. It bore a fiendish look.

The body was covered with scales or feathers of assorted colors. The tail was long enough to return over the back and head, then underneath the entire length of the body, ending like that of a fish. The enormous batlike wings were carried erect. The picture is said to have been so horrible that few of the most daring Indians could look long upon it.

According to Indian legend, this bird or beast had its home in a high cave in the bluff. At first its diet was serpents, and the Indians did not fear it so greatly. One day, however, while two tribes of Indians were engaged in a fierce battle alongside the bluff, the Piasa swooped down, seized two warriors, carried them away, and feasted upon them. Having tasted human flesh and found it pleasing, the eating habits of the beast changed. It no longer hunted serpents. Adults and children alike, often several in a day, were seized and eaten. It appeared that all might be devoured. The Indians accordingly were filled with a great dread.

After their medicine men had tried many devices but had failed to control the beast, a young chief of the powerful Illinois, named Wassatoga, began a solitary fast, seeking a way to overcome the Piasa. After many days, a vision came to him. The tribe could be saved only if a brave would stand as a living sacrifice. Massatoga called a council and told of his vision. He agreed to offer himself and, if necessary, to give his life to save the tribe. On the day chosen, the young chief and twenty of the most trusted warriors repaired to a prominent rocky point. Armed and in gorgeous war dress, Wassatoga took position on an exposed rock where he easily could be seen from great distances. His sturdy warriors, with their most powerful bows, hid themselves in the niches of the near-by rocks. All awaited the coming of the Piasa.

In a short time, Wassatoga beheld the monster perched upon a distant point of the bluff. Standing very erect and in full view of the Bird of Evil Spirit, Wassatoga began his death chant. With a great shriek and with each swoop of its wings giving off the sound of thunder, the Piasa dived toward its intended victim. Bolts of lightning flashed from its eyes. The young chief stood defiantly atop the rock. When the beast had come very near, the twenty warriors hidden among the rocks near by loosed their arrows with all the force the powerful bows afforded. According to the legend, these "quivering arrows pierced the monster through to their feathers." The Piasa fell dead against the rock upon which Wassatoga stood. The tribe had been saved. The Indians, to commemorate their fortunate rescue, carved and painted the picture of the beast high upon the face of the cliff.

The first records mentioning the Piasa were those Father Marquette set down in 1673. Fathers Hennepin and Dousy mention it in their accounts. Father Gene Saint Cosme tells of seeing it in 1699. No other mention of it had been found, until more than a hundred years had elapsed.

This picture of the Piasa was accounted as the greatest Indian painting found in North America. It apparently was an outgrowth of the widely-held belief of all North American Indians in the Thunder Bird, or god of storms.

🌑 LEGEND OF TOWER ROCK

A SMALL ROCKY ISLAND near the Missouri shore of the Mississippi opposite Grand Tower, in Jackson County, has borne several names. First it was known as the Rock of the Cross for the large crucifix erected on its crest by Catholic priests, missionaries to the Indians. It later became Tower Rock and appears on the map as such. Locally, it is "The Rock." Whatever the name used, it still is one of the most noted landmarks along the Mississippi.

Many stories, some based on facts and others on fancy, cluster about the rocky islet. Earlier ones come from Indian legends that were old when the white men arrived. The later stories are from the records and lore left by travelers who journeyed along the river or from settlers who came to live in the vicinity. The Rock is a natural setting for stories.

The river is narrowed here and the current is rapid. Only a small channel separates the island rock from the Missouri shore. At certain river stages, the rapids that swirl about Tower Rock are dangerous to river craft. Indians in their canoes took care to avoid them. They said that an evil spirit dwelt there to seize upon unwary passers-by. White men also learned to avoid the perils.

When river stages make access to the Rock reasonably easy, some persons like to go to its top for a long view of the river and its interesting shorelines. It is worth the effort. Legend relates that this also was a frequent diversion of the Indians.

Bits of several Indian legends and at least one of their complete stories survive. It concerns an Indian brave and the maid who loved him. A condensed version of the story taken from the *Cairo Delta* of June 13, 1848, is given here.

According to this account, attributed to J. Milton Sanders, a Wyandotte brave named Woncasta had spent a night in the relative safety and seclusion that the island top afforded. Early the next morning he arose and stood upon the highest rocky point to welcome the coming day with voiced thanks to the Great Spirit and solemn smoking of his ceremonial pipe. Woncasta did not tarry long, for he was on a definite mission. Making his way to the Missouri shore, he traveled westward through the forest. Before noon he had reached a glade near the dwelling place of a tribe of Fox Indians.

Here Woncasta paused and drew forth a reed whistle. With this he sounded one piercing note, and listened. Soon he saw an Indian maiden approaching from the Fox camp. It was Ya-Roh-Nia, daughter of Chieftain Tamandegue. The shrill note Woncasta had sounded was the signal for their rendezvous. The Wyandotte brave at once began to relate to the Fox maiden the story of his prowess as a warrior and to declare his love for her. She, in turn, told of her love for him, but she revealed that her father intended to give her as a bride to a brave of the Fox Tribe. They continued to talk and to make plans to thwart those of her father.

Within an hour, however, an intruder appeared. Ye-Wong-Ate of the Fox Tribe entered the glade. He was the brave to whom the father would give Ya-Roh-Nia. After directing a few barbed remarks toward each other, the two braves fell into furious combat. When it appeared that her lover was to be killed, Ya-Roh-Nia deftly struck the knife from the Fox warrior's grasp. The fight continued furiously until the great medicine man of the Fox Tribe appeared in the glen. He at once commanded the fighters to cease their struggle. After listening to their stories, he decreed a method by which the issue should be settled.

On the next morning at dawn the two warriors were to be on the top of Tower Rock where Woncasta had spent the previous night and where he had stood that very morning to welcome the new day. There each in turn was to smoke from the pipe that the medicine man carried. Each would blow the smoke upward. The one whose smoke ascended to the greatest height in an unbroken mass was to have Ya-Roh-Nia for his bride. These arrangements were made without the maiden's consent.

The next day the two warriors and the medicine man were at the appointed place on the top of Tower Rock. The ceremonial pipe was filled and lighted. The Fox warrior was first to try his skill. The smoke he blew rose in an unbroken mass until it seemed to blend with the sky. It was now Woncasta's turn. The smoke he blew upward had hardly left his mouth when it broke into bits and vanished. By decree of the medicine man, Ya-Roh-Nia would become the bride of the Fox.

Events now took an unexpected turn. A shout was heard from the brink of the rock not far away. When the medicine man and the two warriors turned, they saw Ya-Roh-Nia standing upon a projecting ledge of rock above the river. She had stealthily followed them and had observed the outcome.

Awestruck and powerless, the seated men heard her proclaim that she loved only Woncasta and would not abide by the decision of the medicine man and be the bride of the Fox. She then turned and leaped into the muddy river a hundred feet below. Woncasta rushed to follow her. The place from whence they jumped still is pointed out as one of several such leaps in southern Illinois.

These stories are so common that one can almost believe that some Indian maiden must have leaped from some cliff because of thwarted love. Anyway, they are good stories.

❧ PONTIAC

THE LEGENDS OF A few great Indians are widely known. Perhaps no name among these brings to mind more associations than does the name of Pontiac, chief of the Ottawas, who was killed at the village of Cahokia, a few miles south of East St. Louis, in the spring of 1769. No other Indian of record ever wielded more power than he. There are many who consider his the greatest mind among the natives of North America during the period of its settlement.

Pontiac easily fulfills a boy's complete dream of an Indian. He is described as of medium height, somewhat darker than the average of his race, very muscular, and vigorous. His features were stern, bold, and irregular. His bearing was forceful, haughty, and imperious. He was crafty, cruel, relentless, and was a great orator. In fact, almost any characteristic ascribed to an Indian, good or bad, could be found highly developed in Pontiac.

The date of his birth is not known definitely, but it was about 1713. Historians are not agreed concerning the tribe into which he was born. Most, however, say that it was either the Sacs or the Ottawas, with the evidence somewhat favoring the latter. The first mention of Pontiac has him leading the Ottawa warriors in the campaign that resulted in the defeat and death of General Braddock near Pittsburgh, Pennsylvania, on July 9, 1755.

Pontiac was the mastermind in the Indian uprising extending from about 1760 to 1765 and known as Pontiac's Conspiracy. This action was intended to drive the white settlers, especially the English, from the lands west of the Alleghenies and perhaps from the continent. In his efforts to accomplish this objective, Pontiac traveled over a great expanse of territory and was a frequent visitor at Fort de Chartres, in Randolph County.

After the French had ceded this territory to the English in 1763, the French commandant, Saint Ange, remained in command of the post to await the arrival of an English garrison, which did not come until 1765. During this interval, Pontiac went to the fort and urged Saint Ange to give him guns and ammunition to be used against the English, but Saint Ange did not comply with his request.

The fortunes of war were against him and Pontiac failed in his conflict with the English. Realizing that his cause was hopeless, he went to Sir William Johnson, sued for peace, and pledged loyalty to the English. Pontiac then disappears into the forest and little is known concerning him until the spring of 1769, when he appeared at the Spanish post in St. Louis; the post was commanded by his old friend Saint Ange, who had entered the Spanish service. Pontiac was welcomed at the fort and a reception was given in his honor. He attended dressed in a French military uniform that had been given to him by General Montcalm before the fall of Quebec in 1759. It is recorded that Pontiac never wore this uniform except on those occasions when it was in good taste.

After a visit of a few days with Saint Ange and other Frenchmen he knew in St. Louis, Pontiac learned that a social gathering of some kind was being held in the village of Cahokia across the Mississippi from the fort. Against the advice of Saint Ange and others, he decided to go, stating that he had nothing to fear. Many of the English mistrusted Pontiac, and one of their traders then in the village saw this as an opportunity to do away with him. The trader found an Illinois Indian who agreed to kill Pontiac for a barrel of whiskey.

At nightfall, after several hours of feasting and drinking, Pontiac left the village and started toward the near-by forest. He was heard, as he passed in the darkness along the trail through the woods, singing the Indian's song of magic that was supposed to ward off all danger. The next morning the body of Pontiac was found in the pathway. His skull had been crushed by a blow from a tomahawk. He lay where they found him until his friend, Saint Ange, came to claim the body and to bury it near the Spanish fort in St. Louis. Thus ended, in the village of Cahokia, the career of one of the greatest and most feared American Indians.

🌳 *WILLIAM BIGGS*

SOME OF THE MEN who served in George Rogers Clark's small army, which won possession of Illinois from the British in July, 1778, liked the region. After their military services, they returned to make their homes in the new land. Their first settlement was about a great spring called Bellefontaine, about one mile south and just west of Waterloo, in Monroe County.

For about thirty years after its formation, this settlement was harassed by the Indians. Many persons were killed and scalped. Others were carried into captivity. A few of those who were captured escaped, but others were brutally slain or met unknown fates; a few were ransomed. Among those whose freedom was bought was William Biggs, a Virginian. Biggs had served as a lieutenant in one of Clark's companies and had returned in 1784 to settle near Bellefontaine.

In a letter written in 1789 from "Grandruseu," a name then applied to Piggott's Blockhouse, about a mile west of the present town of Columbia, and addressed to a brother in Virginia, Biggs describes part of his experience. More is told in an account that he dictated in 1826. His letter and the more extensive accounts are interesting both for the facts that they record and for the quaint manner in which he records them.

In his letter, Biggs mentions "Preasant and Past surcomstance" and laments his misfortunes since coming to Illinois. He says, "I have been Very Unfortunate . . . in Regard of losses and Crosses." He tells that he was "taking Prisoner by the Indians on the 27 of March [1788] as I was Riding the Roade from Bellefontain to Cahokia." He tells of the surprise meeting with Kickapoo Indians in early morning a few miles from Bellefontaine, and says they "shot fore balls into my horses boddy which freightened and startled my horse." In addition to the shots striking the horse several bullets pierced Biggs's clothing. He relates that "my saddle not being girted nor cruppered which the horse threw me with the saddle onto the ground."

Biggs held to his horse's "Maine" for about thirty "passes," "meanwhile making several Etempts to back him but all was in Vaine." He then released his hold on the horse, which ran on some six hundred yards and fell dead. In his attempt to escape on foot, Biggs was handicapped by his great coat that continually tripped him. He was also carrying a large bag of beaver fur.

He soon was overtaken by the Indians. The first one to reach him claimed Biggs as his captive. To indicate that he was to be as a captive and not killed, the Indian rubbed the handle of his tomahawk on Biggs's right shoulder and down his right arm. His captors assured him that he was safe in their hands, that they were good Indians and would not kill him. Tying his hands securely behind him, they took Biggs on a hurried march toward their village in Indiana. Biggs's companion, John Vallis, escaped on horseback, but died six weeks later of the wound he had received.

Each night Biggs's legs and arms were bound. He was roped to stakes and an Indian slept across each rope. The Indians continued to treat their captive about as well as he could expect under the circumstances.

Despite the warning of the other Indians, a Potawatami youth who had attached himself to the Kickapoo group made two attempts to kill Biggs. In accordance with the practice of Indians on the war path, this youth was taken from the group and shot.

Nine days and about 250 miles away, the Indians reached the first of their villages. During this long march, Biggs apparently had only three full meals, one of these being an entire large fat duck. Part of the time he went hungry because he could not eat the Indian food. At other times no food was available. Most of his clothing was taken from him. He arrived at the Indian camp with only moccasins, leggings, a breachcloth, and an "old, lousy, dirty blanket" that an Indian squaw gave him.

At the Kickapoo village in Indiana, Biggs was untied and told he might move around freely as long as he did not leave the village. By appropriate ceremony he was adopted as a member of the tribe. Biggs was a tall and handsome man. They gave him better clothing, more comfortable living quarters, a razor for shaving, and ample food.

The Indians were insistent that he take an Indian wife. For three days an eighteen year old squaw followed him about or stood just outside the doorway to the cabin where he was staying alone. Despite the fact that she was very fair and very "shapely" Biggs remained faithful to his wife at Bellefontaine.

Biggs continued the narrative of his stay in the village by saying: "I was but three weeks in thare Coustidy of the savage I then made Interest with a french trader that was at that town from Creadit and got goods and Purchased myself from the savage my Price was 107 bucks (deer-skins) or dollars." (Does this explain our present-day use of the term bucks for dollars?)

Three weeks later Biggs had found passage on a boat going down the Wabash. At Vincennes he met John Rice Jones and through him relayed a message to John Edgar at Kaskaskia. Edgar immediately notified Biggs's wife at Bellefontaine. Ten weeks after his capture, Biggs was once more at his home. His friends had given him up for dead.

Biggs afterwards attained reasonable prominence. He was the first sheriff of St. Clair County, served two terms in the legislature of Indiana Territory, and was a member of the legislative council or Senate of Illinois Territory. He became judge of the Court of Common Pleas, and also served several terms as a justice of peace. He died in 1827.

🌿 *WHO KILLED TECUMSEH?*

INDIAN SUMMER, WITH its hazy and colorful days, comes to southern Illinois each autumn and is a proper time to recall a great Indian who paid the region at least one brief visit. This was Tecumseh, a chief of the Shawnee and one of the most famous of American Indians. Born in Clark County, Ohio, about 1768, he early become known for his prowess in battle. He was convincing in argument, a competent judge of human beings, a great organizer, temperate, and possessed a great self-restraint.

Tecumseh believed that all lands belonged to all Indians and that no tribe had the right to cede any part of it to the white. He advocated a federation of all tribes and the formation of a government by elected representatives. He believed that his race was doomed unless such an organization was created and vigorous action taken to stop the encroachment of white settlers.

Associated with him was his brother, The Prophet, likewise a great chief but not the equal to Tecumseh. It was he who provided the religious fervor that added force to the movement. The Prophet demanded strict monogamy and required all Indians living with the whites to return to their own people. Their food, clothes, and even their dogs were to be only those of the Indians. There must be no buying and selling, only barter. The Prophet also insisted that those violating these practices be considered evil and not allowed to live.

To carry out his plan to unite all Indians, Tecumseh first visited the tribes of the north and obtained assurance that they would co-operate. He then set out to enlist the help of those in the south and southeast. This journey began at Vincennes, where he had conferred with William Henry Harrison, governor of Indiana Territory. From Vincennes, Tecumseh traveled by way of Bone Gap, in Edwards County, toward Frankfort, in Franklin County, and to the vicinity of Marion, in Williamson County.

It was here, near the edge of the prairie south of Marion, that John Phelps found himself surrounded by Indians one day in the summer of 1811. When Phelps learned that the group included Tecumseh and twelve of his warriors, he feared for his life and was much relieved when the chief engaged him in friendly conversation, making inquiry concerning the trail of Fort Massac.

On his journey toward Fort Massac, Tecumseh held conferences with the Wautaugas and Uches, then living in the southern end of the state. It was this latter tribe that helped him and his band across the Ohio as they proceeded on their journey to confer with the Creek, Cherokee, Choctaw, and perhaps with lesser tribes.

The great chief of the Shawnee found a sparse Indian population in southern Illinois and seems to have gained no recruits. Some, however, believe that his visit led to a later attack on settlers near Jordan's Fort and to the killing of a man named Moore and his son on Moore's Prairie, in Jefferson County.

While Tecumseh was in the South seeking to have the Indians there join in his projected confederation, Governor William Henry Harrison raised several companies of militia, including some from southern Illinois, and marched to the place where The Prophet and his forces were encamped on Tippecanoe Creek in Indiana. In the battle that followed, the Indians were defeated and The Prophet killed. This reverse did much to wreck the plans of Tecumseh and perhaps caused him to become more closely allied with the British. In fact, most of Britain's earlier success in the West during the War of 1812 can be attributed to the help given by the Shawnee chief.

Tecumseh was made a brigadier general in the British army and was in charge of the Indian troops at the Battle of the Thames in Canada. This battle, in which numerous southern Illinois men fought, occurred on October 5, 1813. Very early in the fray, the British troops under General Proctor fled and left the Indians to fight alone. Tecumseh must have suspected some such action on the part of the British troops when he discarded his British uniform for Indian dress and gave his sword to a friend before the battle began. Tecumseh was killed.

An old question, "Who killed Tecumseh?" remains without a conclusive answer. At least two men claimed that distinction. One was Eli Short, a Baptist minister living near Steeleville, in Randolph County. Another was Colonel Richard M. Johnson, able leader of the American attack and later vice-president of the United States. Short's claim was the earlier one. Johnson's was made when he was campaigning for the vice-presidency.

🌿 *THE TRAIL OF TEARS*

In March, 1839, the last group of the exiled Cherokee Indians passed through southern Illinois over the route known as "The Trail of Tears." In the interval since that time, books and articles aggregating millions of words have been written concerning the migration. Stories connected with it are yet heard among the older Cherokee of the Great Smokies and those in Oklahoma. Still other bits of their story come from local lore gathered along the trail they followed.

This route, eight hundred miles long, extended from the Great Smokies to present-day Oklahoma. It passed through Tennessee, Kentucky, southern Illinois, Missouri, and Arkansas. It was well named "The Trail of Tears," for the journey over it was a heartbreaking one.

Perhaps no part of the long trail held more of tragedy than the section lying in this state, for it was here that thousands of the unfortunate travelers were forced to halt for several weeks between mid-December, 1838, and early March, 1839, because of floating ice in the Mississippi.

The crude camps marking the trail in southern Illinois were strung along at intervals from Golconda, on the Ohio, through Allen Springs (now Dixon Springs), Wartrace, Vienna, Mt. Pleasant, and Jonesboro to the crossing of Dutch Creek on the road leading westward toward Cape Girardeau. These makeshift camps provided poor shelter against the unusually severe winter weather.

Transportation was available only for the very old, the infirm, small children, and perhaps an occasional Indian who was able to pay for it. About eight thousand of them were left to plod the entire way on foot, sometimes without shoes or moccasins.

The Indians were thinly clad and their bedding was light. Medical care was poor and was at a minimum. Rations were meager and monotonous. This is indicated by the oft repeated entry in journals of "salt pork and meal." There is some evidence that coffee and sugar were occasionally given to favored persons or could be bought by those with sufficient funds.

These ten thousand Indians represented the forlorn tribe that had been gathered from their homes by a force of seven thousand soldiers made up of regular army men, militia, and volunteers. The troops employed were under the command of General Winfield Scott. As they were rounded up, the Indians were placed in stockades near the United States Indian Agency on the Hiawassee River not far from the present town of Charleston, Tennessee.

The method by which they were gathered was a ruthless one. Their homes were surrounded and they were given little or no opportunity to collect personal belongings. The items that a few did succeed in gathering often were ordered left behind when the trek began. Indians seized at their homes frequently saw their buildings burned to the ground and their property destroyed or taken by plunderers before the owners had passed from view. The Indians had already traversed about half of the bitter trail when they entered Illinois at Golconda on December 15, 1838.

The Cherokee were perhaps the most civilized of the larger tribes in America. They had their own written language. The alphabet for this language had been developed by the brilliant Sequoya, for whom the great trees of California were later named. The alphabet that Sequoya devised is still in occasional use and compares very favorably with any alphabet man has developed. The writer has a newspaper using this alphabet printed in the Cherokee language in 1950.

They had well established churches, and their schools were comparable to those of the whites. Many of their leaders had received a college education. They lived in settled abodes. Their houses were as well built as those of the whites. An occasional one of their houses might, for that time, be termed pretentious. There are some who credit the Cherokee with an independent development of the pioneer type of log cabin.

They regularly paid taxes and owned property, even slaves. One of these slaves, a quadroon girl, was sold by one of the chiefs to Basil Silkwood of Mulkeytown, to become chief character in the Priscilla story. The Indians regularly elected representatives to govern them. They had a code of recorded tribal laws, and a court system to administer them. They were not a degenerate or backward people; they were a well-organized nation.

Tragedy began when the Georgia legislature decided to take the portion of Cherokee lands within that state. Laws were accordingly enacted to permit seizure of this property and to set aside the tribal laws and established government of the Indians. Gold mines opened on the lands held by the Indians were promptly declared property of the state. Farms, long occupied and cultivated by the Indians, were allocated by lottery to white settlers. A law was passed saying, "No Indian or descendant of an Indian . . . shall be deemed a competent witness . . . in any case in court . . . to which a white person may be a party." Other states in which parts of the reservation lay enacted similar laws.

A treaty of cession was arranged with a few handpicked Indians, not regularly selected representatives of the Cherokee nation. Many of these were made drunk and bribed by land grants, money, and often only promises. Andrew Jackson, then serving as president, lent full support to their removal. About two thousand of the Indians emigrated to the West under this arrangement. More than fifteen thousand others did not recognize the arrangement as binding upon them. It was from these fifteen thousand that the group passing through southern Illinois came.

Every effort was made to capture all the Indians on their eastern reservation. Many succeeded in evading the soldiers and hid in the hills. Others escaped from the stockades where they were gathered. Some fled from the group as it moved along, and still others returned from Oklahoma. The descendants of these Indians that hid, escaped, or returned, yet live about Cherokee, North Carolina, and each year they re-enact the pageant, "Unto These Hills," which depicts the tragic incidents of their forced removal. Perhaps no other Indians were treated more severely nor unjustly.

Chapter 5

Early Travel

🏵 *THE FIRST ROADWAYS*

THE FIRST WHITE man came to the Illinois country on the lakes and rivers, the area's natural roadways. With rivers on three sides, southern Illinois was easily accessible by floating downstream. Early arrivals came in this manner and settled along the streams at Vincennes, in Indiana, and New Haven, Shawneetown, Cave-in-Rock, Elizabethtown, Golconda, Kaskaskia, Prairie du Rocher, and Cahokia, in Illinois.

Some trails had previously been made in the area by Indians and wild animals. The early animal trails generally were those between their seasonal feeding grounds or to those spots where buffalo, deer, and elk came to lick salty earth. Older persons used to point out these distinctly worn trails that converged at the salt licks—trails that tended to vanish after the woodland was cleared for farming. These earlier pathways seldom were located to serve the best purposes of the settlers, however.

Some of the great animal trails like those of the buffalo around the southern end of Lake Michigan and similar ones that led through the passes in our eastern highlands were much used by the Indians and later by whites. There also were some trails made by the Indians as they passed between their villages and hunting grounds or went trading.

There still are small areas in the wooded hills of southern Illinois where bits of animal and Indian trails remain visible. One is among the hills lying south of the deserted roadway leading eastward from the vicinity of Potts' Tavern, in Hardin County, to the crossing of Saline River near abandoned Saline Mines. A second place where one may see traces of old pathways is in the hills bordering Big Muddy River above Rattlesnake Ferry, in Jackson County. A third place is near Little Muddy

River, southeast of Elkville. This one leads toward a shallow spot where the stream could be crossed more easily. The places mentioned are reasonably accessible, but it may be difficult for the unskilled stranger to find them.

The first overland trails laid out by white men in this section of the state were those beginning at places already named along the Wabash and Ohio rivers and converging upon the Cahokia-Kaskaskia region or leading to Mississippi River crossings. Perhaps earliest of these was the one from Fort Massac to Kaskaskia. It achieved early importance and continued in use for a long time. As other crossing points were established on the Ohio, trails leading from them were merged with the one from Fort Massac to Kaskaskia making that trail increasingly significant.

These trails or traces were hardly roadways. They seldom were marked in any way and often were so little worn that they could be followed only with difficulty. When roads and trails were marked, it generally was by infrequent blazes on trees along the route. Moreover, road locations often were changed with changing seasons and with shifting patterns of settlement. A seasonal change in location still is pointed out on the old Ford's Ferry–Gallatin Salines roadway near Nigger Spring. The one on the lower level was the regular roadway, and the one on an upper level still is referred to as the "High Water Road."

At first there were no bridges nor established ferries, and it was necessary to cross waterways at shallow places or on crude ferries or rafts built at the site. Early accounts tell of the difficulties thus encountered. John Reynolds, later to become governor of the state, tells of the grave situation that arose when an ax was lost in Little Muddy River west of Hurst while a raft was being constructed.

Following these early trails and pathways often was a difficult task. This is indicated by the fact that George Rogers Clark, and his band of expert woodsmen—guided by a man named Duff, whom Clark had engaged—became lost on the Williamson County prairie as they moved to capture Fort Gage, at Kaskaskia, in early July, 1778.

When men first began to lay out roads between settlements, the territory had not been surveyed and there were no land lines to follow. Trails wandered from point to point. Wherever convenient, roadways followed contour lines. Hills and swamps alike were avoided when possible and roadways were laid out to cross streams at the less difficult places. Ash Ford, Rhine Ford, Island Ripple, Fish Trap Shoal, and Pull Right are the names of a few of the early crossings. An occasional old ford, sometimes surfaced with concrete, still is found along the roadways in the

Shawnee Forest. In a few places trails still follow along the beds of the streams.

Sections of these very early roadways, deserted and overgrown, are in view beside the present paved highways. Some excellent bits of such an old roadway are seen on the west side of Highway 1 south of the Saline River.

❧ *LAND OF GOSHEN*

NAMES FROM FAR-AWAY Egypt came to Illinois very early. Three of the older towns in the southern section of the state, Cairo, Karnak, and Thebes, still answer to the names from that ancient country along the Nile. Many years before these Illinois towns were in existence another Egyptian name was prominent in the state. This was the name of Goshen, used in biblical times to designate that land, fertile and free from plagues, where the Israelites dwelt in Egypt from the time of Jacob's going there until the Exodus.

The name of Goshen first was used in Illinois when it was applied to the region lying south of the present town of Edwardsville. The designation was given to that area by the Reverend David Badgly, representing an eastern congregation, who had come in 1789 seeking a suitable place to establish a settlement. Badgly found the land near Edwardsville to be fertile like that of ancient Egypt, and he judged it would be a healthful one in which to live.

When the group for whom he had served as scout received his report, they began moving to the new land in 1800. As early as 1802 their community was somewhat widely known as Goshen settlement. It differed from other settlements in that there was never a distinct village here, so it was always referred to as the settlement, or more often, "the Land of Goshen," and the roadway to it was Goshen Road. Maps prepared by U.S. land surveyors as early as 1808 show this roadway and name.

❧ *HAZARDS OF TRAVEL*

THE FOREST ROADWAYS of southern Illinois were lonely ones and ofttimes hazardous. This is suggested in the early records of Randolph County by recurring entries like, "For holding an inquest over a body found on Ford's Ferry Road — 10 dollars."

That an item of record for the Cave-in-Rock region should appear in the Randolph County record may seem strange, but it should be remembered that Randolph County then included practically all of southern Illinois. The first mention of Ford's Ferry Road thus appears in the Randolph County records at Chester. When references to this road are assembled, they add up on one fact—it was not a safe one to travel.

Ford's Ferry Road received its name from a ferry located just below the present Ohio dam about three miles above Cave-in-Rock. It was operated by James Ford, who regularly lived in Kentucky. At one time, however, he lived in and was a citizen of Illinois. This is shown by the fact that he served as overseer of the poor for Cave-in-Rock Township. His crossing was the best and most used ferry along that section of the river.

To make travel by way of his crossing more attractive, Ford established a good tavern beside the trail on the Kentucky side a few miles south of the Ohio. Another man, William Potts, built a second one at the north end of the improved section of roadway in Illinois. Potts' Tavern was located beside a fine spring at the southern slope of a hill still called Potts' Hill. A farmhouse stands a short distance west from Illinois Highway 1 where the tavern once was located. The first building was a large two-story double log house with a hallway or "dog trot" between. This place became one of the most widely known in all the region. The length of roadway between it and Ford's Tavern in Kentucky was called Ford's Ferry Road.

James Ford and William Potts, operating taverns about twenty miles or a day's travel apart became well acquainted. According to tradition, they even became associated in certain operations like robbing unwary travelers. By their plan, each robbed independently as opportunity afforded, but not wishing to see a prosperous appearing traveler go unrobbed, a kind of mutual help service was established.

According to stories surviving, if a traveler whose appearance indicated that he might be a good prey came to either tavern, the owner made all reasonable efforts to relieve him of his valuables. If, however, opportunity did not arise to do so, a messenger would be dispatched to the other tavern ahead of the visitor with information concerning him. Potts, thus, would notify Ford concerning travelers from the north, and Ford in turn would relay information concerning those coming from the south.

There are indications that others in addition to Ford and Potts profited unduly from these travelers. Anyway, there is a strange coincidence in the fact that a certain respected citizen in the area often advertised a "stray horse" for sale about thirty days after the recorded disappearance of a traveler. The law required that anyone taking up a stray should hold it thirty days, then advertise it for sale to reimburse himself for the feed bill. Possibly stray horses just liked to go to this man's place, which was some miles from the road.

Today's traveler on Illinois Highway 1 south of Saline River sees some bits of an abandoned and overgrown trail that once was Ford's Ferry Road.

❦ THE LEGEND OF WILLIE POTTS

RECORDS AND ORAL traditions tell of numerous tragedies that occurred along Ford's Ferry Road. One of these concerns William Potts's son, generally called "Willie." According to this story, Willie succeeded only too well in the plans he made to play a joke upon his parents. His success cost him his life, caused his parents many years of sorrow, and left to the region one of its most interesting legends.

It was not strange that Willie, growing up in the environment of the tavern his father kept, would be inclined toward a career of violence. Men engaged in robbery along that trail loitered about the tavern. Willie mixed with them, heard their stories, and naturally became interested in their activities.

According to one version, Willie selected for his first victim a prosperous looking traveler coming north from Ford's Tavern in Kentucky toward his father's tavern in Illinois and rode along with him for some distance before attempting to rob him. The stranger, who had become suspicious and alert, was first on the draw and shot young Potts in the shoulder. The wound was not too serious and the would-be robber rode away at great speed.

A second account says that Willie met his prospect as they journeyed in opposite directions along the road and was robbing him at gunpoint when two farmers, not friendly to Willie, came upon the scene. Fearing exposure, Willie decided to leave the country.

He did so and was gone for a number of years, during which time it is said that he plied his trade with success in other regions. Then, very much grown up and changed in appearance, Willie thought it would be safe to visit the scenes of his boyhood. He was now a very large man and would not be readily recognized. He also had grown a heavy dark beard that would add to the difficulty of recognition.

Members of the gang with which young Potts had once operated observed the apparent prosperity of the stranger when he stopped at Ford's Tavern in Kentucky on his way home. One of the men to whom he revealed his identity informed the others that the supposed stranger was their old confederate, Willie Potts; whereupon the plans already formed to rob him were dropped and he was welcomed back by the group. The next day young Potts went on to his father's tavern at the northern end of the road, arriving there later in the afternoon. Neither the mother nor father recognized the stranger as their son. Willie, enjoying the success of his plan, decided to wait until the morrow to tell them who he was. He and the elder Potts sat talking until bedtime.

Young Potts, being thirsty, asked for a drink of water. His father, as was his custom, suggested that they go to the near-by spring for a fresh drink. When they reached it, young Potts knelt, placed his hands upon the stones as he had done so often in earlier years, leaned forward and began to drink. The father, seeing the opportunity offered, drew a dagger that he always carried and plunged it into the unsuspecting drinker's back, below the left shoulder blade. The victim died at once.

The elder Potts took the large roll of bills that he found, removed the body of his son to a near-by hillside and placed it in a shallow grave among other victims. He then returned to the tavern and went to bed. Measured by his standards, it had been a successful day.

The next morning some of the group with whom his son once had associated came to the tavern from Ford's place in Kentucky. They had come to celebrate the return of their former associate. When the new arrivals inquired concerning Willie, the mother and father were puzzled. They thought that a joke was being played and appeared to resent it. Further questioning and a description of the one sought aroused grave anxiety in both Potts and his wife. They began to suspect that the stranger of the night before was their son.

After the departure of the puzzled visitors, Potts took a spade, went to the newly-made grave and began to remove dirt. His consternation and remorse may be imagined when the body was uncovered and careful examination revealed a tell-tale birthmark. This mark was a dark figure shaped like a four-leaf clover, once called "the lucky mark," just above the point where the dagger had pierced.

🌼 *END OF A LONG TRAIL*

THERE WERE MANY early roadways of note in southern Illinois. To tell of them all would require a book, but a few must be included. One of these, among the most historic in America, was the Cumberland or National Road that ended at Vandalia, in Fayette County, where an impressive memorial stands to mark its ending.

For those whose interests are historically inclined, such statutes or memorial markers beside a highway arouse interest. They often suggest interesting stories and may tell parts of them. The stories they bring to mind, though often local, almost invariably are connected with significant events in our national history. One such prominent southern Illinois marker is the Madonna of the Trail that stands beside Highway 51 on the corner of Statehouse Square in Vandalia.

The site for this statue of a pioneer mother was chosen by the National Old Trails Association and the Daughters of the American Revolution. Unveiled with much ceremony on October 26, 1928, it is one of several that the groups mentioned have placed across the country to call attention to famous trails and roadways of earlier America. In the dedication ceremony of thirty years ago, the scheduled speaker for the occasion was Judge Harry S. Truman, who was then president of the National Old Trails Association. Mr. Truman, however, was unable to attend, and the address was given by Frank A. Davis, of Rosedale, Kansas, the association's secretary.

The monument at Vandalia, as the inscription on its base indicates, is to mark that town as the western terminus of one of America's greatest roadways, the National Road. This highway also has answered to several other names. It has been called the Cumberland Road, Ohio's Road, Great Western Road, Uncle Sam's Road, or simply The Road. It is said to have been the first roadway built by the United States government. Beginning at the town of Cumberland, Maryland—the point from which General Braddock set out on his ill-fated expedition—it extended through southwestern Pennsylvania, across the states of Ohio and Indiana, and was planned to continue across Illinois to the site of present-day East St. Louis. It provided a passable route by which settlers could reach the West. It also would serve to bind the western states more firmly to the union. Perhaps no highway in America or the world ever led to a land of greater opportunity or carried a people with more hopeful hearts.

This roadway was authorized in 1806, when President Jefferson appointed a commission to locate and build it. It was lengthened and improved year by year from its eastern beginning toward the west and carried millions toward the growing West until about Civil War days. Extensions were made from its eastern beginning at Cumberland, Maryland, to the cities of Washington and Baltimore. The portions of the roadway east of Terre Haute were cleared of timber, graded, surfaced with rock, and its streams were spanned with stone bridges. It was a good road, though it was never all good at the same time. Much of the section from Terre Haute to Vandalia was cleared and some improvements were made before work was discontinued. Vandalia thus became the western terminus, and the Madonna of the Trail was placed there to mark its ending.

The impressive statue shows a mother striding forward with a babe in her arms as another small tot clings to her skirts. With face slightly uplifted, she looks steadfastly and hopefully westward toward an ever-receding horizon. It is intended to typify the thousands of pioneer mothers who moved along the National Road toward new homes and renewed hopes.

The Road may have ended at Vandalia, but many thousands who passed along it did not stop there. Branch roads led from there to other Illinois towns or continued toward the beckoning frontier. The main mail route from the East ended at Vandalia, but numerous stage lines and other mail routes extended as far as Shawneetown. In fact, Vandalia was a principal travel center of the moving West.

Although it was designated as the terminus of the roadway, in reality it was not so. The trail was extended westward by state and local efforts to East St. Louis, then known as Illinois Town, and eventually to the far Pacific.

There still are, at irregular intervals, sections of this old road that one may see beside the pavement as he journeys westward from Vandalia along U.S. Highway 40 through Greenville, Pocahontas, Highland, and Collinsville, or eastward through Teutopolis, Greenup, Martinsville, and Marshall toward Terre Haute. At times he even will be driving over the old roadway along which a million immigrants have passed.

It is interesting to pause at convenient spots where the original trail touches the present pavement and to conjure up images of the assorted traffic that the road once knew. To a great extent, it was a one-way street. Going westward there were the "footpads"—then used to mean tramps or itinerants—who would be carrying their meager belongings in a "bindle" on a stick or a handled tool flung across a shoulder. There were those trundling wheelbarrows or pushing two-wheeled carts on which their few possessions were carried. There were those driving or leading pack animals such as cows, steers, mules, or horses laden with personal belongings.

It is recorded that even turkeys and geese sometimes were driven westward over the roadways, along with hogs, sheep, and other animals, to stock planned farms. There were canvas-covered two-wheeled carts, farm wagons, and the great Conestogas with their upswept ends and white canvas covers that somehow reminded one of ships and sails, so much so, that farther west they were called "prairie schooners." They were driven by the picturesque, profane, and highly vocal drivers who chain smoked their long slender cigars that still are called stogies. There were drovers—

just as vocal and tough as the Conestoga drivers, moving livestock on foot to eastern markets. The drovers were forerunners of the cowboys of the West. Some came by horseback and others among the later tide that surged along the Road traveled by stage.

There were groups from eastern settlements that traveled together. There were numerous other groups that came from Switzerland, Ireland, Germany, and other European countries, bringing with them the customs of their native lands, sometimes with a few of their treasured personal belongings and a wealth of lore. It was indeed a motley throng that traveled the old trail.

❧ *HALFWAY HOUSE*

TRAVELERS ALONG THE early trails and roadways of southern Illinois required stopping places where food and lodgings could be had. Numerous taverns sprang up to meet this need. Many of these stopping places became noted. Only one of these original taverns is known to be inhabited today, but the abandoned ruins of two or three others remain to add their bit to the story.

One of those abandoned is a dilapidated two-story log house that stands on the north side of Illinois Highway 50 about nine miles east of Salem, in Marion County. A sign above its front doorway says "B U I L T 1818." Signs at either end of the house offer additional bits of information. We learn that it was once Halfway Tavern, a widely known southern Illinois stopping place and stage station.

It came to be called Halfway Tavern because it was about midway between Vincennes and St. Louis. It did not, however, enjoy a monopoly of that name. There were other taverns and other stations on other roads that likewise were halfway between important points. This one apparently was the most noted of those so designated in southern Illinois.

In its more prosperous years, there were other buildings grouped with the original log structure to form the tavern and stage station. Three additional two-story houses were joined to this edifice that still stands, and they extended westward to form a building more than one hundred feet in length. A continuous front porch on both levels combined to present an impressive appearance.

The old well, now wearing a concrete curb, is the one that furnished water to the tavern and stage station. Equipped with a sweep that was standing within memory and a convenient watering trough, it also supplied the needs of travelers and livestock being driven along the roadway.

A large barn that sheltered the stage horses as well as those of travelers riding or driving their own, stood near by with fenced lots to impound driven livestock for drovers moving herds along this road to eastern markets. A gnarled cedar, the remaining one of the conventional pair so often seen across the walkways to front doors, still survives, and one somehow wishes it could talk.

The present decaying house is all that remains of the tavern begun by John Middleton in 1818, the year that Illinois became a state. It is about eighteen feet square, with one room above the other. There once was a side room or kitchen at the rear of this building. The manner in which the oak logs were notched and fitted at the corners indicates careful and competent workmanship. Much of the timber chinking used to fill the spaces between the logs is still in place. The clay-lime daubing, now almost rock hard, shows remarkable resistance to weathering and makes one wonder what else may have gone into the mixture.

The siding that was added to cover the logs also is unusual. It was made by splitting oak into clapboards, or shakes, about four feet long and applying them as weatherboarding. The square-headed nails of earlier times still are in evidence. Much of this weatherboard yet clings to the logs, well over a century after it was applied. There is no evidence that the exterior ever was painted.

The original floor of the lower room rotted away many years ago and was replaced by one of concrete. The bottom logs or sills likewise have disappeared and the building has settled until a tall man must stoop as he walks beneath the lowered ceiling. Evidence indicates that the inside walls of the first-floor room were first the bare logs with their chinking and daubing. The walls are now boxed or ceiled with rough-sawed vertical planks about a foot wide; at one time they were papered. The ceiling that originally exposed its log joists is now lathed and plastered.

A narrow, well-worn stairway leads to the upper room with its floor of wide undressed oak planks and ceiling of narrower boards painted white. Tacks about the edges of the floor indicate that it originally was carpeted. The walls of this second floor were plastered on handmade lath and later were painted a dull red, thus offering a tempting surface on which to scratch names, dates, and legends. This practice evidently began about 1895, perhaps earlier. A later scribbler recorded the fact that "C. B. Hill lived here in 1898." Persons from other states, perhaps returned natives, came to leave their names and addresses.

While the old building remains, it is more than a rotting log house. It is an emblem of a vanished era in the history of the Midwest. The trail leading past this point was old even before the tavern was established. It was the one over which the French journeyed between their settlements at Vincennes and Cahokia. It was in this vicinity that the branch trail leading to Kaskaskia was joined. It was also at or near the tavern site that George Rogers Clark and his intrepid band passed in the midwinter of 1778–79 on their daring march to capture Fort Sackville, at Vincennes.

Many thousands of immigrants and tradesmen passed here. There were those, including the footpads, hopefully trudging along on foot. Some trundled carts, others drove or led such pack animals as horses, mules, oxen, or even cows that pulled sleds. The passing travelers were an assorted lot, varying from those seeking new homes to those fleeing justice.

In early days, a man wishing to operate a tavern was required to secure a license from the county court. He also furnished a bond guaranteeing that he would "as a tavern keeper be at all times of good behavior and observe all the ordinances which are or shall be in force relating to innkeepers within the state." The same court that licensed the tavern keeper also fixed rates that he might charge. In 1823 the rates allowable at Halfway Tavern were as follows:

Breakfast	25 cents
Dinner	25 cents
Supper	25 cents
Keeping horse overnight	50 cents
Single feed	25 cents
Lodging	12½ cents
Whiskey—½ pint	12½ cents
Rum—½ pint	25 cents

From time to time, the county commissioners' court might make slight changes in these rates.

Halfway Tavern still attracts the attention of travelers along the highway and many stop to peer about the old log house; none, however, to lodge for the night. In a few more years, it will be gone, and another bit of early Illinois history will have vanished.

❦ COVERED BRIDGES

EARLY ROADWAYS, JUST as now, encountered streams that had to be crossed. So far as possible, they were crossed by fording at a shallow place. At larger streams it often was necessary to build rafts or rude ferries. With increased traffic, men began to build bridges at some of the more important crossing places, many of which they covered.

Such bridges, once common over the eastern half of the United States, have almost disappeared. One of the few that remains is across Mary's River, on the route of the old plank road that connected Chester and Sparta, in Randolph County. The building of this bridge was promoted by the Randolph County Plank Road Company, chartered by the state on February 11, 1853.

Designed to replace older roads corduroyed with poles, plank roads were strange structures. They were made by cross-laying the roadway with planks about three inches thick, from eight to twelve or more inches wide, and not less than eight feet long. These planks were placed on stringers laid parallel with the roadway and flush with the earth. The floored surface thus provided was an excellent one over which heavy loads could be hauled. Provisions for the passing of vehicles meeting on plank roads were provided by building wider sections at somewhat regular intervals.

Stations for the collection of tolls from those using these roads were located at points along the way. One of the toll stations on the Chester-Sparta road was on the south side of the highway at Bremen about two miles east of Mary's River and was kept by a family named Hartman.

The bridge across Mary's River was opened to traffic in 1854. It remained a part of the toll road until purchased by Randolph County in October, 1872, at a cost of two thousand dollars. It was continued in use as a part of the highway system of the county until the completion of the concrete pavement in 1930; thus it served about eighty years. Through efforts of interested citizens and with funds provided by the Chester Chamber of Commerce, the old bridge and some near-by ground were purchased and given to the State of Illinois.

This bridge, resting on stone piers and flanked with stone approaches, reaches across the river with a single span about ninety feet long. Its overall height is about twenty feet and it is twenty feet wide. A side view of the structure reveals that it is slightly swaybacked, but those acquainted with it for many years state that they have not noted any increase in the dip during their memories.

The large hewn timbers of oak and the ingenious manner in which they are assembled will intrigue those who are even mildly interested in building construction. Skilled workmanship and good engineering practices are illustrated, especially in the large timbers that form the curved tops of the trusses that carry the bridge. Careful inspection of the entire bridge indicates that those who designed and built it were highly competent.

One may wonder why bridges were covered. One purpose, perhaps the principal one, was the preservation of the structure, because the cost of such bridges—made of large, shaped timbers—was considerable. Secondly, nearly all livestock was then driven to market and they could be more easily urged across a covered bridge. Perhaps this may have been taken into consideration. The roof of the bridge also provided a shelter for those journeying along the roadway. Too, a covered bridge would present a more attractive appearance than the bare framework, though it is doubtful if any would be covered for that reason.

It is interesting to walk under the covering of this old bridge and see some of the advertisements painted upon the timbers, along with fragments of bills once posted there and thousands of tacks that held other bills and posters. The names of assorted products, then common but now only memories, will be found. The same may be said about the names of individual and business firms. Some names and initials carry dates. Others occur in pairs often encircled with hearts or geometrical figures, proclaiming the fact that romance bloomed even then.

Picnic facilities make the covered bridge a pleasant place to stop for a while.

❧ *LIVERY STABLES*

STAGE COACHES, LIKE buses, trains, and street cars of a later time, ran over regular routes and more or less on schedules—though these routes and schedules sometimes were not adapted to the particular needs of a traveler. To meet these special requirements, an institution known as the livery stable was born, and these establishments became widespread. About the turn of this century, there were thousands of them over the country. Nearly every little village had one, and there were several in the larger towns. Today it is doubtful if there is a genuine livery stable left in all the United States.

Few persons under seventy years of age remember much about them. Fitting so naturally into their environment and taken for granted, artists and writers gave them scant attention. Their disappearance was so gradual and natural that little notice of it was taken. With increased use of the automobile, those needing local transportation simply took a "jitney" or taxi to save time, and left the buggies and hacks standing by. A few of the keepers of old-time livery stables added automobiles to their stock of vehicles and thus were in the jitney business.

In pre-automobile days, passengers alighting from the behind-time train heard the cry "Hack! Hack!" This cry might come from the one who drove the bus or hack that delivered prospective guests to the hotel. It also might be that of a driver from a livery stable looking for prospective customers, just as the present-day driver calls "Taxi?" The conveyances that regularly met trains were assorted, but the horses drawing them had one thing in common that distinguished them from other animals: they refused to become excited as the trains ground, clanged, and hissed to a stop.

Livery stable operators naturally gave attention to the buying and selling of horses and mules. These stables were centers where men gathered to sit in the shade of the central driveway, in the office by the pot-bellied stove, or on benches in the sun alongside the stable walls, the choice depending upon the reason and the weather.

The typical livery stable conformed to an established architectural pattern. The front, or façade, was a partially false one, rectangular in shape, as high as the ridge of the barn roof, and generally as wide as the entire building. A wide driveway high enough to admit a buggy without lowering its top was in the center, and an enclosed room was at either side. Almost all were of frame construction.

The floor plan of the barn included a wide passageway throughout its length, with stalls for horses and spaces for carts, buggies, surreys, buckboards, and assorted other vehicles—sometimes even a sleigh—on either side. One of the rooms at the front served as the office. The other generally was a storeroom. In this room one found feed, surplus or special harness, saddles, horse blankets, lap robes, fly nets, buggy and blacksnake whips, storm curtains, foot warmers, neat's-foot oil, wool fat ("it contains lanolin"), horse medicines and liniments, currycombs, brushes, twitches (to attach to the unruly horse's upper lip), hand rakes, scoops, pitchforks, shovels, feed baskets, buggy wrenches, wheel jacks, axle grease, castor oil, leather washers for buggy hubs, and perhaps a spare fifth wheel.

The office was regularly supplied with a pot-bellied stove that seemed always to be either glowing hot or clammy cold. A cot where the keeper could nap at night while he awaited the late return of rented rigs was a standard fixture. There were a few unmatched chairs in various stages of disrepair, a venerable table, a worn broom standing in the corner, and naturally spittoons. On the wall one would frequently see lithographs of buggies or of noted horses like Lou Dillon, Dan Patch, or Jay-Eye-See, a calendar that might be two or three years old, advertisements of spavin and gall cures, and a few old clothes hanging on nails. Stud or jack posters also adorned the wall along with farm sale bills.

This livery stable office knew a particular breed of men: men who could horse-trade, chew tobacco, or tell tall tales. Often the stories had been gathered from traveling men, who always had a stock of yarns and purveyed them. The stable also was the gathering place for petty politicians and just plain loafers. Always it was a fountainhead for news, rumors, and town gossip.

No livery stable could be properly described without mention of two characters invariably found there. One was a teen-age boy considered a yokel by some, but acknowledged by all as wise in the ways of horses. The other was the livery stable dog. Like the boy, the dog wore a detached air and seemingly stayed around because he liked horses, often forsaking the comforts of the office to sleep in the stall of his favorite.

Regular customers of the early-day livery stable were the traveling salesmen—then called drummers. They would appear in town with so many sample cases that a buckboard might be necessary to carry them about. Those carrying smaller sample cases used a buggy. These traveling salesmen generally were accompanied by a driver from the livery stable whose duty it was to take care of the rig, to help handle the sample cases, and to guide the salesman to isolated country stores.

The brands of buggies were as well known as the names of cars today. Some early-day ones were the Studebaker, the Moon, the Dexter, the Elkhart, the Allen, the Columbus, the Murray, and the Bradley. The writer's first one was a Studebaker, the nameplate of which he still has.

A young man who did not have a buggy available to take his girl to some affair would rent a livery rig. The rig would include the horse, or a team if the roads were bad, the buggy, and all necessary accessories.

There were certain advantages in renting a rig from the livery stable. The horse was a well-trained animal and would return to the starting point with a minimum of guidance. Secure in this knowledge, the young swain, removed the buggy whip from the socket, tied the lines at proper length, hung the lines over the dashboard, and replaced the whip. Thus, there was no danger that the lines would fall off the dashboard and be out of reach. This freed both hands to point to the stars, make appropriate gestures, or perhaps to insure the young lady against a possible fall from the buggy over rough roads. Some insist that the built-in facilities of the horse-buggy combination made it preferable to present one-arm driving.

Chapter 6

Early Business Activities

🏵 *THE GALLATIN SALINES*

THE FIRST WHITE men coming to southern Illinois found a great salt spring near the south bank of Saline River, about three miles east of Equality. In its vicinity they discovered evidences that the Indians had been making salt there for centuries. Many pieces of their broken pots and pans were found. The markings upon them, along with tools, weapons, and ornaments found in the litter covering near-by camp sites, definitely indicated that the workings went back to antiquity. The first white visitors also noted the location of a large salt lick about four miles west of the spring.

In the summer of 1952, Irvin Peithman, then Curator of Archeology at the Museum of Southern Illinois University, dug some exploratory pits at one of the sites where the Indians worked at the old spring. These small pits yielded much significant material and aroused the active interest of several widely known archeologists. A thorough investigation of the sites where the natives worked would doubtless yield much more information than has yet come to light.

There is a persistent legend that the early French who knew of the spring and lick came here and made salt, but no positive proof that they did so has been produced. Perhaps they may have obtained salt from the Indians. The earliest mention of white men making salt here was in the spring in 1778. A later writer states that in 1796 this was the only place west of Marietta, Ohio, where a supply of salt could be obtained.

Official records concerning Old Spring, at other times called Great Spring, Nigger Spring, or Nigger Furnace, indicate that in 1803 William Henry Harrison, the governor of Indiana Territory, leased it to a Captain

Bell, of Lexington, Kentucky. In 1807 it was leased to John Bates, of Jefferson County, Kentucky, and in 1808 to Isaac White.

In 1801 a man named Butler became connected in some manner with the making of salt at the salines. He and White had some difficulties that resulted in one challenging the other to a duel. Their seconds arranged that the duel should be fought with horse pistols at a distance of six feet. Butler declared than such an arrangement was equivalent to murder and refused to proceed.

In 1810 the principal salt-making operations had become centered in the lick west of Equality where fourteen wells were pumping. These wells were dug square and walled with timbers, much like the one still to be seen at Old Spring. These first wells were from thirty to eighty feet deep. When machinery became available later, it is said that some were drilled to a depth of two thousand feet.

Salt-making operations required more labor than the locality had available. Negroes were brought to meet this increased demand. Some were held as slaves, others were slaves rented from their masters in other states, and still others were indentured servants. There also were some free Negroes. Legends of almost unbelievable cruelties practiced upon the Negroes working at the furnaces indicate that their lot was a bitter one.

The origin and naming of Half Moon Lick, west of Equality, has also been explained. According to legend, this depression, several feet deep, some two hundred feet wide, and about an eighth of a mile long was caused by the animals that came and licked away the earth to obtain the salt it contained. Animal trails leading into the lick once were visible that might partially justify this explanation. It was named Half Moon Lick because of its shape, roughly that of the new moon.

In 1814 salt production at the Gallatin Salines rose to 124,885 bushels. State income from this source was considerable. In the two-year interval from December 31, 1820, to December 31, 1822, the state treasury received $10,673.09 from leases, approximately one-seventh of its income. When rentals declined somewhat, it was decided to sell the reservation and divide the proceeds among the several counties of the state.

The last operator of Old Spring was John Crenshaw, who erected a pretentious residence on a hill north of there. This house, still standing, is widely known as the Slave House. Small attic rooms where Negroes are said to have been confined are pointed out to visitors, and legends of salt-making days are recounted. The last men to operate at Half Moon Lick were Joseph Castle and Broughton Temple, who secured possession of the facilities there in 1854. Operations were continued until 1873, with production amounting to about five hundred bushels a day.

Only a few ruins now mark the location of a great industry, at that time the greatest in Illinois.

❧ *HALF MOON LICK*

HALF MOON LICK, NEAR Equality, once was the main source of supply for salt in the Mississippi Valley. Until Illinois became a state, Old Spring and Half Moon Lick with the lands lying about them remained in the possession of the United States government. From time to time they would be leased to an individual or company to operate for a term of years; generally, the rental was a portion of the salt made. Because of its importance, the government wished to encourage the development of the industry. A rectangular tract of land ten by sixteen miles was set aside along with a strip about three miles wide running to the mouth of the Saline River. To assure a supply of fuel wood for the salt furnaces, this tract was withdrawn from settlement and designated as the Saline Reservation.

At first, all operations were centered in the immediate vicinity of the spring and lick. Fuel requirements soon exhausted the near-by forest, however, and required the hauling of wood from a distance. This problem was partially solved by establishing new furnaces away from the spring and wells and conveying the brine to them through pipelines.

Necessary pipes were made of logs from ten to sixteen inches in diameter and sometimes more than sixteen feet long. The logs were bored lengthwise with holes about four inches in diameter, first by hand, but later by a horse-powered device. The logs were then reamed at one end and tapered at the other. With iron bands placed around the reamed end to prevent splitting, the logs were jammed tightly together to form a wooden pipeline. A map prepared about 1816 shows seven of these lines leading from Half Moon, some for more than two miles.

Pits now mark the sites of old wells in the Half Moon Lick area. Some of these pits have large trees growing within them or on their edges to indicate that they were abandoned long ago. More well pits, filled and stacked with brush, are seen in a newly cleared field north and west of the lick, where additional wells outside the depression were sunk in efforts to obtain stronger brine.

Many of the workmen at the lick, both slave and white, lived in houses near Half Moon Lick, while others came from the village of Equality. On a walk across the newly cleared field already mentioned one may see numerous spots where assorted bric-a-brac and discolored stones show that dwellings once stood here. In another field on the eastern side of the wood-land, a few wells and cisterns show where workmen once lived.

A recently constructed dam across the outlet of Half Moon Lick has made a lake covering the site and some thirty or forty additional acres of land. Half Moon Lick is in the deeper part near the dam.

There can be nothing particularly wrong with the placing of this dam. The deer and buffalo, evidently millions of them, that once came along the now dim trails to lick the salty earth have been gone for a long, long time. Gone also are the Indians who came here to hunt or to make salt for themselves. Even the white men who came here to establish the first saltworks, for many years the most important industry in the region, have been gone since 1873.

None of the buildings that served the early industry is left. The derricks, towers, tanks, furnaces, offices, shops, pipelines, and dwellings have all disappeared. To the casual viewer, little remains to indicate the extent of the once flourishing industry.

Some very old persons can still point out the site where Castle and Temple, last operators of the works, had their office. These same persons will help you find bits of low crumbling walls that were the foundations upon which the kettles and pans were arranged to boil the salty water. About these sites one also finds bits of broken kettles and pans and iron fittings that now puzzle the visitor.

That the salt-making industry near Equality was important beyond the income it brought in is indicated by the fact that it, more than any other one factor, served to shape the policy of the new state concerning slavery and encouraged the movement in 1824 to open Illinois to slavery.

A book could be written about the Gallatin Salines. Materials are easily available.

❧ COAL

THE INDIANS KNEW OF coal and often fashioned charms and ornaments from the kind we call cannel. Some of these objects, among the most symmetrical and finely finished of Indian artifacts, are highly valued by collectors. No evidence has been found to show that the Indians used coal as a fuel. The sites about their ancient campfires, often almost against outcroppings of coal, show no waste coal or cinders to indicate that the Indians used it.

Records concerning the first findings of coal by white men in the United

States are vague and fragmentary. None seems to indicate its having been noted before the coming of the first French explorers to the Illinois country. Louis Jolliet and Father Marquette are said to have found outcroppings of coal, *charbon de terre,* on the hillsides along the Illinois River when they crossed the state in 1673. Father Hennepin, another Jesuit missionary, mentions coal in his journal for 1679 and locates a mine on a map he drew. This mine was on the Illinois River near the present city of Ottawa. Another map drawn by the French explorer Thevenot in 1681 shows a mine in the same region.

On each of these maps they are indicated as "mines" and not as deposits or outcroppings, thus indicating that they were actually worked. There also are references in other records to indicate that coal was secured locally and used in the forges at the French posts in the Starved Rock area. Some reports of groups sent out to search for mineral deposits report with apparent disappointment that neither gold, silver, copper, nor lead was found—"only coal."

The first reported use of coal in America was made by blacksmiths. Charcoal was used to smelt ores, a practice continued at Illinois Furnace, in Hardin County, until the early 1880's.

The first commercial coal mine of record in the United States began production in Virginia in 1750. Richmond coal, then widely and favorably known, came from this mine. Production on a commercial scale in Illinois began in 1810, when the first shipping mine was opened in Jackson County. It was among the first coal mines of the Midwest. The shaft for this mine, really a slope or tunnel directly into the exposed vein, was against the high eastern bank of the Big Muddy River south of the place where old Illinois Highway No. 13 crosses the stream. A metal marker on the north side at the eastern bridge approach marks the site and briefly tells the story.

This outcropping was conveniently located and permitted loading of the coal directly on barges for shipment. Some of the coal from this mine was shipped in that manner to New Orleans, as shown by its port records for 1810. The claim that the Big Muddy mine was the first commercial one in Illinois appears a perfectly valid one.

Mining was continued beside Big Muddy for many years. In 1822 the Jackson County Coal Company was formed and activities were increased. A number of Scotch miners came, and a settlement known as Scotch Town grew up about the mine. According to meager records and tradition, Scotch Town had its full quota of eccentric and unusual individuals. In many ways it resembled the mining towns that were to spring up in the West a generation or more later. With the exhaustion of this coal outcropping, the miners moved away and the village disappeared. Now it is difficult to find traces of it.

A few years ago, when some excavations were being made in the rise of ground known as New Hill, just east across the Big Muddy from Murphysboro, one of the tunnels of the old mine was found. The entries and rooms of the abandoned mine were much as the miners had left them more than a century before. There were still a few decayed chunks of the old timbers, bits of track over which the crude cars carried coal to the barges waiting in the river, remnants of broken and rusted tools lay about, and there were even parts of an oil lamp once used by some departed and forgotten miner.

Passageways often were littered by stone that had fallen from the roof. There was a musty smell, and dust covered everything. It was distinctly an unsafe place even though an experienced miner served as guide. Strange shadows from his light made the long-abandoned mine an eerie place.

In addition to supplying coal needs, this mine and another later one at an outcropping in the hills near Belleville encouraged the building of the first two railroads in Illinois. The one at Belleville, built in 1833, carried coal from the mine there to the Mississippi River. It is recorded as the first railroad in the state. The one at Murphysboro carried coal from the mine to a point just below Fishtrap Shoal, a mile or so downstream and enabled the mine to continue shipment when low river stages would not allow barges to pass upstream over the shoals. The Murphysboro road consisted of wooden rails with straps of iron nailed on them. The motive power was provided by a mule, and the entire train crew consisted of one man, Valentine Taylor. The date when this road began to operate has not been definitely fixed. It may have been the first railroad to operate in the state. We are inclined to believe it was.

This small mine beside the Big Muddy marked the beginning of a great industry in Illinois. The abandoned workings still offer mute evidences of the crude methods of early mining. Three-fourths of Illinois still is underlaid with recoverable coal, and the world will always need coal.

🌣 *A MINING CAMP*

Now it is uranium, and Geiger counters are clicking over the rocky spots of Illinois. Perhaps it would be more nearly correct to say Geiger counters are failing to click. Whichever it may be, click or no click, men are still seeking treasures to mine.

The first white men—mostly Frenchmen—coming to explore Illinois looked for metal deposits. They were disappointed in their quest for gold and silver; they did, however, find lead, coal, and zinc deposits, and salt springs. They needed the lead—for it could be made into bullets—but zinc was considered a waste product. Salt was a necessity, but the sparse population required only a small amount of it. Lead offered the great mining opportunity and accordingly was developed early. Blacksmiths, the prime users of coal, needed only small amounts of it.

Workable deposits of lead were found at two places in Illinois—one in Jo Daviess County and the other in Hardin County—separated by the length of the state. The deposits in Jo Daviess County were the more plentiful and more easily mined. They were, therefore, the first exploited.

The Galena lead deposits were mentioned in reports by the Frenchman LaSeur, about 1700. He located them on the "River of Mines . . . a small river that entered the 'Great River' in its east bank." He indicated that the Indians were working there.

Records give evidence that lead has been mined there almost continuously from that time until the present. Many men came to the region seeking fortunes. By the 1820's mining was a booming industry, and Jo Daviess County had become a typical mining region much like those of the West a generation or so later.

Winters in the Galena region were severe, and mining during that season was difficult. It therefore tended to become a seasonal occupation. Many of the men coming to mine lead came in boatloads or companies each spring, and left in groups as winter approached to better protect themselves against the hostile Indians.

Those from downstate Illinois were called "Suckers," a term they did not particularly appreciate. The Suckers therefore retaliated by calling their fellow miners from west of the Mississippi "Pukes," saying the region from whence they came had taken a vomit. Because some of a third group from Wisconsin lived in pits that had been burrowed into the hillside to mine small pockets of ore, they were called "Badgers" after an animal of the region that lived in hillside burrows. Badgers and Suckers are still mentioned. Pukes, not sounding so nice, is less often applied. In addition to the lead it exported, Galena thus exported three widely used nicknames.

A few large, modern mines still operate in Jo Daviess County and process their ores for smelting. There also are numerous small mines— sometimes operated by farmers as a spare-time job. These dig ore from the pockets found on their farms and take it to the larger plants for processing. The worthless zinc of earlier days has now become more valuable than the lead first sought.

The roistering air of the early mining days is gone. Some records and a rich lore of those earlier times remain, however. Those driving over the countryside about Galena or tramping the stony fields may yet see many sunken pits and waste heaps which the grass is struggling to cover.

All the romance of the western mining camp once was to be seen in Jo Daviess County, and that long before the West knew a single mining camp. Those hectic days of lead mining are now long past, as are the picturesque men who came to work there. Many ruins remain, however, to enable those with a reasonable degree of imagination to glimpse much of the region's past.

Lead mining has had a somewhat parallel development in Hardin County at the extreme southeast of Illinois. With the mining of lead in Hardin County, however, has been coupled the mining of zinc and fluorspar, single mines often yielding large proportions of each.

🌿 *KAOLIN*

A FEW YEARS AGO southern Illinois began to break out in a rash of centennial celebrations, but some occasions for such observances have slipped by unnoted. One neglected opportunity would have been to mark the opening of the state's first kaolin mine about one mile south and two miles west of Cobden, in Union County.

Failure to observe the kaolin centennial was remissible, however, because the industry is gone. Except for one lonely house, several times worked over, the village of Kaolin, to which the product gave a name, has vanished. Only a few of the now aging men who worked there in the declining years of kaolin mining are left to tell about it. A few lingering traditions of better days are heard, and scars left on the hillsides still are unhealed.

This earlier Illinois industry apparently resulted from the activities of the Kirkpatrick brothers, competent and skilled potters, who came to set up shop on a site near the present post office at Anna in the 1850's. Their company made the conventional products of the early potter such as churns, jars, jugs, milk-crocks, bowls, and bed chambers. They also made less conventional pieces, like mugs with frogs seated on the bottoms to meet the startled gaze of the drinker when he had finished his draught.

They made demijohns with symbolic snakes wound about them. Inkwells, castles, ornamental shoes to set upon the marble tops of old-time bureaus, and inscribed decorative vases were among their products. They also mass-produced many thousands of clay pipes, the kind that used stems of pipe cane. Many of their less conventional products had artistic merit and are sought by collectors.

With their pottery in operation, the Kirkpatricks began to seek better materials for use in it. They found an outcropping of excellent kaolin on a hillside about five miles northwest of Anna and opened a pit there. For some time they hauled this clay to their pottery in Anna by ox wagon. Its principal use was in the making of the distinctive glaze that identified their products.

Kaolin from this locality was much sought by other potters over the country, and shipment was begun over the railways. Machinery was installed to dig clay from the large open pit. A new railway about a half mile long was laid from Kaolin station to the mine. A drying, processing, and loading shed three hundred feet long and sixty feet wide was built. Additional open pits and some tunnel mines were opened to the north and east of the original one. Drying, bagging, and shipping sheds were erected at the railway tank town of Mountain Glen about a mile and a half north of Kaolin. Mining continued an active industry for many years.

When World War I started, kaolin was found to be of strategic value, and mining was increased until several hundred men were employed. With the close of the war and the development of glazes using other materials, however, kaolin mining declined. The original pit that had expanded to cover about three acres was abandoned and allowed to fill with water. The decreased demand for the clay was met by sinking vertical shafts in deposits found on the north side of the hill.

Men who had come to work at the mines moved away. The post office and stores of the village closed, the railway station and switch were removed, and the shipping shed was allowed to fall down. At the time of its centennial, the industry has entirely ceased. The large pit, once about a hundred feet deep, has filled with silt from the surrounding hills until it is now about thirty-five feet deep. Only when the visitor looks at this lake and considers that about a half million cubic yards of clay were taken from it alone, does he realize the magnitude of the industry that centered here.

A few years ago, beavers came to live at the lake. Tree stumps they gnawed along the margin of the lake are there with sections of the logs they cut. Now, even the beavers have abandoned the site. Fresh cuttings show that they are busy, as beavers should be, along the near-by creeks.

In addition to the appeal that the story of kaolin offers to those historically inclined, the site offers many other things of interest. Those who would bird-watch will find many species of birds that are not common, such as a kingfishers, chuck-will's-widows, and crow-sized pileated wood-peckers. There is also a great variety of plant life.

If the visitor is interested in Indian remains, one of the ancient Indian campsites is found on either side of the gravel road leading south near the railway curve west of Mountain Glen. Indian Chimney, about a mile west and south from the site of vanished Kaolin, presents an unsolved mystery. Those interested in gathering fossils will find a nice deposit of them beside the roadway about a mile east of Mountain Glen.

The village of Mountain Glen itself should appeal to those who would glimpse something of the vanished calm of a country village of fifty years ago. The friendly people living there will pause to talk about the times when kaolin was important.

One strange fact connected with the kaolin mining industry is most notable. Despite the number of men employed, the years during which work was carried on, and the hazards naturally connected with mining, no one could recall an accident that cost a man's life.

🌿 *IRON*

THE LAST FIRES WERE pulled and the equipment removed from Illinois Furnace in 1883. Now some piles of weathering iron ore, broken chunks of limestone, and a few low mounds containing charcoal are found on a hilltop. The ruins of a blast furnace stand close against the steep side of the hill some sixty feet below, and bits of slag lie scattered about it. Large trees grow near the furnace, one seven or eight inches in diameter even grows on top of it.

All these help to tell the story of an important industry established near Hog Thief Creek, about four miles north of Rosiclare, in Hardin County, in 1837, the same year that the county was formed. During the first thirty-seven years after it was built, Illinois Furnace was in almost continuous use. From 1874 to 1883 it was in operation only at intervals.

Many records relating to the furnace were destroyed when the court-house at Elizabethtown was burned in 1884. Enough remain here and there, however, to tell much of its story. Also, one of the workmen, the late Joe Piland, who helped to dismantle the machinery in 1883, contributed much information concerning its closing.

The old furnace was being operated by Chalon Gard and Company of Indiana in 1839. By 1872 it had passed to the Illinois Furnace Company, a corporation chartered in Indiana on April 6 of that year. A. G. Gloud, later to become a prominent businessman and banker in McLeansboro, was bookkeeper at the furnace.

Iron ore was obtained from deposits found in the near-by hills where the pits from which it was taken are still seen. Known as limonite, it was about 50 per cent metallic iron. Mining was done by various individuals, and the ore, for which the company paid $1.75 a ton, was hauled to the hilltop, just above the furnace, in wagons.

A number of men also were engaged in providing charcoal for fuel. This was burned at places convenient to the wood supply and hauled to the furnace. When the furnace was in full operation, about 1,800 bushels of charcoal were required daily, for which the producer was paid four cents a bushel.

At capacity, Illinois Furnace produced an average of nine tons of pig iron each day. During the Civil War it was a principal source of supply for iron used at the United States Navy Yards in Mound City. The pig iron was hauled by wagon to shipping points on the Ohio River. Some of the iron "pigs" even today are found on farms over the county. Numbers of them once were found near the ford across Hog Thief Creek, where tradition relates that the teamsters slyly dropped them to lighten their loads for an easier crossing.

Ruins of the old furnace are sufficient to show many of the details of its construction. It is approximately fifty-two feet high. The round core or lining of the furnace in which the ore was melted is eight feet in diameter. Markings on the firebrick with which the core was built show that they were made in Pittsburgh.

The core of the furnace was enclosed and strengthened by a sturdy limestone structure about thirty-two feet square at the base and sloping to a smaller size at the top. This protecting structure was badly damaged about 1933, when workmen blasted some of it away for use in building roads. Parts of masonry foundations and the large bolts used to anchor machinery in place are still there. Arched openings in the base of the furnace show the places from which the molten iron and slag flowed and others indicate where the air blast entered. Power for operation of the furnace machinery was supplied by steam engines.

Since few of the natives possessed the skills necessary in the operation of the Illinois Furnace, many of the workmen came from regions where the iron industry already had been developed, some even coming from European countries. A small village grew up across the roadway from the furnace.

A post office named Illinois Furnace was established on October 2, 1846, and Charles T. Gard was appointed postmaster. This village had the usual country stores, a tavern or boarding house, and the ever-present saloon. The sports and pastimes of the village, typical of these times, were rough—like bouts with the Irish shillalah. One story tells of a shillalah contest between Colonel Ferrell, a prominent local character, and an Irish workman. This workman offered to wager a jug of whiskey that no one could strike him with the prescribed club. The Colonel, thinking it would be an easy way to collect a jug of whiskey, accepted the challenge. The Irishman appeared with his weapon, Colonel Ferrell secured a similar one, and the contest was on. The strokes and thrusts that Ferrell made were cleverly blocked by the Irishman. Exasperated at his failures, the Colonel became more vigorous than discreet and began to lay about with considerable force. The Irishman skillfully parried the blows and knocked the stick from Ferrell's hand, severely rapping some knuckles in the process. Colonel Ferrell paid his wager and vowed he would not try it again for two jugs of whiskey.

When the furnace closed, the village melted away. Today only one well remains to mark its site, and some imagination is required to realize that an important industry was once operated here.

❧ OIL

SOUTHERN ILLINOIS WAS not one of the very early oil fields in the United States. Nevertheless, it tried to be.

The existence of petroleum in some places was known long before there was an oil well in America. It had been found oozing from the rocky ground in a few locations. Since this was a somewhat unusual occurrence, the Indians considered the oil as magical. They carefully skimmed it off pools of water where it had collected or mopped it off rocks with their blankets to use as medicine.

White men copied the Indians' ideas and also used the crude petroleum as a remedy for many and varied ailments. It definitely was an excellent antidote for vermin. A few older persons may recall the bottles labeled "Seneca Oil," one of the trade names under which the product was offered. Assorted substances to give it a sting or a more enticing odor were mixed with the crude petroleum.

When a method of distilling petroleum was developed in 1855, new uses were found for it and men began to seek a more bountiful supply. On August 27, 1859, Col. Edwin L. Drake, working in the face of much harsh ridicule, accusations of insanity, and even veiled threats, struck oil at Titusville, Pennsylvania. Drake's well, sixty-nine and a half feet deep, is hailed as the first successful one in America. The strike he made also is recognized as the particular event which launched the petroleum industry in this country.

An earlier well, perhaps not intended primarily for petroleum, was dug at Burkesville, Kentucky, in 1828. Oil flowing from this well, known as the National Well, was also collected, bottled, and sold as medicine.

Drake's success had a highly stimulating effect. An "oil fever" spread over America and men began to search for it. In 1866, seven years after the Titusville well, the search for oil began in southern Illinois. The first record found concerning any systematic search tells of activities near Mt. Carmel, in Wabash County.

The early group of Illinois promoters around Mt. Carmel was made up of twenty-two men. They went about their work systematically and extensively, as is indicated by the fact that they used printed forms to take options. One of these options was executed between the group of promoters and Silas Keneipp on April 6, 1866. It covered land in the southeast corner of Section 19, now included in the west part of Mt. Carmel. This lease was for a period of twelve years. The company was to begin drilling within six years after the lease was signed. They were to drill for "petroleum and coal oil."

Drilling was to go to a depth of 835 feet unless oil was found at shallower depths. No metal casing was required, but the well was to be cased to bed rock by the use of cypress timbers. The landowner was to receive "one in thirty barrels" of oil. This is far less than the one-eighth now considered standard. The landowner also was to receive one-twentieth of the stone coal or other minerals taken.

No oil was found at Mt. Carmel as a direct result of the 1866 venture, and no known log of the hole has been found. There is mention of a still earlier drilling made for oil at almost the same spot in 1862. Oil was discovered, however, at Allendale, a few miles north and east in 1912, forty-six years later, and at Mt. Carmel in 1940, more than eighty years after the first venture. The judgment of the early group was correct in that there were oil pools in the vicinity. They simply drilled in the wrong places. Many wonder just why these men concluded there might be oil there.

This chapter could hardly end without another note of irony in early oil drilling. In 1866, while prospecting was under way at Mt. Carmel, Colonel Drake—who had been by turns a farmhand, a steamboat clerk, a hotel clerk, an express agent, a railway conductor, an oil company representative, and a well driller—was living in near penury in New York City. He had not profited from his successes nor secured patents on any of the devices he made or processes he developed. His neglect and misfortune were somewhat relieved, however, when the Pennsylvania legislature in 1873 granted him a pension of $1,500 yearly.

❧ THE SANTA FE TRAIL

AT ANY TIME A marble slab, grave size, lying prostrate above a burial place will attract the attention of passers-by. If there are two such slabs at the same grave, with the second one supported above the first one on six nicely turned marble columns about two feet high, even the most casual observer pauses. Such an arrangement is to be seen near the memorial shaft erected by the State of Illinois in the cemetery on Garrison Hill, in Kaskaskia State Park. Markers in this cemetery commemorate those first buried in the old one at Kaskaskia and later removed to the present location when it became obvious that the Mississippi was to wash away the old town and its burial ground. The marker already mentioned is at the grave of William Morrison, son of Sir John Morrison and prominent citizen of Kaskaskia when that city was at the peak of its importance.

Morrison, born in Bucks County, Pennsylvania, came to Kaskaskia some time previous to August, 1790, as a representative of the trading firm of Bryan and Morrison. He prospered there and in about 1800 opened another store in Cahokia. About 1801 he erected a large stone residence in Kaskaskia. This home, along with that of Pierre Menard, east of the Kaskaskia River, became a prominent social center. Lafayette was a guest in the Morrison home when he visited the city in 1825.

The activities of Morrison covered a wide area, extending from Wisconsin to New Orleans and from Pittsburgh to the Rocky Mountains. Most of the ventures in which he engaged prospered and Morrison became a wealthy man, one of the most successful traders in the West.

In 1804, the year after the United States had purchased the Louisiana Territory from France, Morrison stocked a trading expedition, under charge of a French Creole named Baptiste La Lande, to go to Sante Fe, New Mexico. Morrison's was the first American trading expedition over the route that later became noted as the Sante Fe Trail.

Little concerning that long journey, much of which was through hostile Indian country, is known. It is recorded, however, that the expedition arrived safely in the vicinity of Sante Fe and that a messenger was sent forward to notify the Spanish officials of its presence. A group of horsemen came out to welcome La Lande and his men and to escort them to a friendly reception in town. The first commercial venture over a route that was for more than fifty years to remain one of America's most storied trails had been completed.

La Lande sold the merchandise that had been entrusted to his care at a good figure. He liked the country, the women were "kind to him," and the Spanish gave him much land. La Lande accordingly decided to remain in Sante Fe. Also, he decided that he would keep the proceeds realized from the venture.

During the next several years, Morrison tried to collect from the wily La Lande. He enlisted the efforts of Dr. John Robinson, a surgeon accompanying Captain Zebulon M. Pike on his exploratory trip to the West. When Captain Pike's expedition neared Sante Fe, Dr. Robinson was ordered to go ahead into Sante Fe and, among other things, to try to collect the debt owing to Morrison. Robinson failed in his efforts, as did Captain Pike a short time later.

La Lande remained a citizen of New Mexico. No punishment of any kind seems to have overtaken the rascal, and he lived out his life at Sante Fe where he left "a great family of great wealth." If Morrison derived any satisfaction from his venture, it must have come from the knowledge that he had sent the first commercial venture over the trail that looms large in the history of the West.

❦ MERCHANT PRINCE

MORRISON CONTINUED to live at Kaskaskia and prospered, becoming the merchant prince of a region as large as several states. In addition to his eminence as a merchant, he was a land speculator, a politician, and a great promoter.

He sent out special trading expeditions from Kaskaskia. In co-operation with Pierre Menard, able Indian trader and often a business rival, Morrison joined in 1807 to send an expedition far up the Missouri to the mouth of the Big Horn. Two years later, he and Menard co-operated in founding a fur company that did much to make St. Louis the world's greatest fur market for more than a century.

Many of the daybooks and records of the Morrison store at Kaskaskia are still in existence and offer glimpses of early merchandising methods and of individuals then prominent in Illinois affairs. The names appearing on his store records could well have been taken from a *Who's Who* for Illinois at that time.

John Edgar, largest landholder in Illinois and one of its wealthiest men, often traded at Morrison's Kaskaskia store. Almost every week one finds the entry of "Mackerel" indicating Edgar's faithfulness to the tenets of his Catholic faith. Various other entries concerning Edgar appear. They show that many of Edgar's purchases were made by Camillia, sometimes spelled Camilla, Cammile, or Camily, a mulatto girl. She buys "cloth, muslin, three papers of pins, sugar, and coffee."

The name of Nathaniel Pope also occurs frequently. He is charged with "1¼ yards of cambrick — 1.87½ bought by Negro girl." Another entry reads: "Nathaniel Pope, Esquire — a bottle of brandy sent for by his Lady per Isaac, a Negro boy." "1½ gallons of ale at .75 — 1.12½. ½ yard cambric — 1.00." "Two skeins of silk," "one sweeping brush — 1.00."

William Rector, later to become United States Surveyor General for several states is charged with 10 pounds of sugar at 25 cents a pound. At the same time, Morrison sold sugar to a French boatman for 50 cents a pound, and to an Indian for 75 cents a pound. Conrad Will, founder of the salt works of Brownsville and long prominent in public affairs as state senator and representative, bought a pair of boots for $10.00.

Judge Thomas, prominent citizen of that time, is charged for "a bottle of wine sent for by Judge Stuart's Negro boy." Benjamin buys a bill of goods for "Governor Edwards." Michel Bienvenue buys "1 lb. of coffee and one pound of sugar — 1.00." Widow Geaudross is charged with "cotton, 2 threads 1.00." Other well-known names and quaint entries appear on Morrison's books.

An interesting series of entries indicates Morrison's practice of renting slaves and servants to those needing their labor. Some of the laborers he rented were held as slaves. Others were bond servants.

Morrison not only hired out slaves to others; he also hired the slaves and servants from others as he needed them. Labor seems to have been considered a commodity. On July 10, 1812, he credits Baptiste Gendreau Guion with $3.75 "on account of his Negro going to the mouth of the Ohio and Cahokia." He also credits Michel Bienvenue with $60.00 for a voyage by his Negro boatman to New Orleans and charges him with $10.00 given to the boatman at New Orleans.

The following are typical entries in the Morrison records. November 26, 1813: "This day hired Negro, Clem, to Frank Dize, at $10 a month." An addition to this entry says "Returned home December 26. Due $10." On May 6, 1814, Morrison charges Pierre Menard with $10.00 "Cash to his Negro at Orleans." He credits Menard with his Negro's service, but does not indicate the amount.

Morrison's landholdings were great and extended into nearly every county of southern Illinois. The building that formerly housed the cafeteria of Southern Illinois University is located in the northeast corner of a section of land he once owned.

From Morrison's grave on Garrison Hill, the visitor may look across the river that now washes over the site of the old town, but Kaskaskia and Morrison's stone mansion are gone. Bits of legend concerning him, however, are still to be heard.

❀ SELLERS' LANDING

G. ESCHOL SELLERS came to southern Illinois shortly after 1850, selected a site beside the Ohio in the eastern part of Hardin County, and built a nice home. For a generation or more this was known as Sellers' Mansion.

Sellers, the son of one of America's great mechanical engineers, is recorded as one of the region's unusual personalities, an important man in two towns. In his varied career he had built locomotives, paper mill machinery, and equipment for the United States mint, at Dahlonega, Georgia, and at New Orleans, Louisiana. Sellers had also manufactured steel wire and cable, pioneered in the manufacture of extruded lead pipe, built an improved forging hammer, developed a direct traction locomotive (whatever that is), and another one to operate on three rails for steep grades. He had also served as mechanical engineer for the Panama Railroad Company.

Shortly after locating on the Ohio, he built and operated a paper mill there. This mill made paper from the pipe cane that grew in the surrounding brakes. Portions of the mill's stone foundation with large anchor bolts embedded may still be seen. The mill flourished until it was found that the cane did not reproduce itself rapidly enough to provide a supply sufficient for continuous operations, and the plant was closed.

In 1854, Sellers became president of the Saline Coal and Manufacturing Company and went to live at Bowlesville, in Gallatin County, where he gave his attention to coal mining. He was a new type of person in the area and represented a culture that was not common. Mark Twain came to know Sellers and considered him a proper person for a character in *The Gilded Age,* a story on which he was working.

When the first copies of Twain's book appeared, Sellers was referred to by his proper name, G. Eschol Sellers. Infuriated at the manner in which Twain had portrayed him, Sellers paid a visit to the author in his office. Realizing that his caller was determined to bring suit for libel, Twain agreed to change the name in all future printings. Sellers, in turn, agreed that if the name were changed, he would not sue. Twain accordingly changed G. Eschol Sellers to Mulberry Sellers. Perhaps Twain won the argument after all.

For several years after his removal from Hardin County, Sellers lived in Bowlesville and operated the Bowlesville Mines. Very old people who knew him there, told of his driving about in a glassed-in carriage, or riding in his personal coach which operated on the narrow gauge railroad from Bowlesville to Shawneetown. They remembered his dog, Joe, a constant companion, his French gardener-coachman, and the oft-repeated phrase credited to him by Twain, "There's millions in it."

In his later years of residence in the region, Sellers became a great collector of Indian artifacts. When he left for Tennessee, in the 1880's, it is said, he took two railroad cars loaded with relics that he had gathered in Gallatin and Hardin counties, many of them being from Old Spring, near Equality.

A post office known as Sellers' Landing was established on April 6, 1864, and his son Frederick H. Sellers, was appointed postmaster. This office was discontinued some time between December 1, 1874, and March 1, 1875, and was re-established on August 1, 1881.

Sellers' Landing, on a sharp bend of the Ohio, afforded excellent anchorage for boats and was used to gather barges of coal for river shipment. Great iron rings attached to the rocks along the river bank are still there. But only one building of the original village, the old boarding house, remains. Sellers' Landing has long been on the list of once hopeful but now vanished villages of southern Illinois.

❧ PACK PEDDLERS

BEFORE BENEDICT ARNOLD became infamous as the betrayer of his country, he was a highly successful pack peddler. Collis P. Huntington, who was one of the richest men in American history and a great railroad builder in the West, began his business career with a peddler's pack. Jim (Jubilee) Fisk, prominent in the development of the Erie Railroad, likewise peddled in his earlier years. He sold Paisley shawls.

These and numerous other men who rose to prominence were one-time peddlers. Bronson Alcott, Yale scholar and noted American thinker, peddled for several years. Mason Locke Weems—Parson Weems, who wrote the biography of Washington that is said to have greatly influenced Lincoln—was a peddler or "chapman." Weems also was a preacher and proficient fiddler for hoedowns. It is recorded that Lincoln, just before he began his journey to Illinois as a driver of an ox team, obtained a stock of needles, thread, and notions to be sold to housewives along the way.

Pack peddlers, followed by wagon peddlers, once were numerous in this region. Several successful businesses in southern Illinois can be traced back to peddlers who decided to quit their role as wandering salesmen and settle down.

The typical pack peddler, once frequently seen trudging along the trails and rude roadways all over America, has disappeared. Some older persons, however, can recall such men carrying their heavy packs and hand trunks slowly along the country roads from house to house.

The packs these peddlers carried were marvels of compactness, and they offered a wide assortment of merchandise. Their packs included such articles as sewing needles, thread, thimbles, crochet hooks, knitting needles, straight and safety pins, combs, cloth, hair brushes, scissors, knives, and perhaps razors and razor straps. Soap, handkerchiefs, pencils, nutmeg and nutmeg graters, spices, flavorings, and medicines guaranteed to be "good for men or beast" were parts of their stock in trade. Some peddlers also had Bibles with space for the family record, bull rings, calf weaners, galluses, garters, and sleeve bands. Some might have shaving soap, shoe-strings, bay rum, flake white, indigo, assorted dyes, and other articles too numerous to mention.

It was a never-ending source of wonder to see a practiced road merchant open his pack and display his wares. His sales talk was likewise interest-ing. It was apparently the studied effort of the peddler to have each woman—for most of the buyers were women—feel that she was receiving special consideration. She was often told, "You are a lady of good judg-ment, and I'm sure you'll like this." Or, "I have only one of these left, and I don't think I can get any more." The article being pushed might even be "a bit heavy to tote." Needless to say, all members of the family, even grandpa, gathered around to view the peddler's stores.

The practice of pack peddling in America began in New England, where families often made some article as a spare-time job on long winter evenings—a kind of home industry. It was naturally necessary that their things be sold, so they were offered for sale, or money being scarce, for barter at other homes.

Pack peddlers are gone. Until about fifty years ago they were frequently seen in isolated communities. Some older persons will remember the last of them, mostly older men apparently absorbed in deep thought as they plodded along the dusty or muddy roads.

The last old-time peddler remembered by the writer was a man named

Charley, who had regularly visited the community for more than thirty years. He had spent the night before with Uncle Bill Stevens, on whom he had called faithfully through the years. After leaving Uncle Bill's, he had stopped to call on the Buxtons, the Millers, the Barnetts, the Browns, and the Pembertons and was on his way to see the Cholsons, the Porters, the Wilsons, and the Allens when he paused under the shade of a tree on the school playground. There the smaller boys gathered about him and tried to lift his two heavy packs.

After the last of his calls for the day, Charley disappeared down the woodland road that led through the bottoms toward the Murray settlement two miles to the south. He must have spent the night in the woodland along the way. Such was not an uncommon practice when the weather permitted. So far as is known, this trip of Charley's marked the passing of the pack peddler in that community. In some places they may have put in appearances for a few more years.

Their prices were whatever they thought the traffic would stand. One old peddler said they were satisfied with any profit from 33 to 300 per cent.

🌑 *ITINERANT CRAFTSMEN*

FOOT PEDDLERS WHO lugged heavy hand trunks along early roads and trails have disappeared. Likewise, the itinerant craftsmen who passed along these same paths are no longer seen. Both of these, the outright peddler and the artisan, were products of the times they served. Both alike filled a real need, at least until pioneer conditions had definitely ended.

Before enough settlers had located in a new region to support a specialized craftsman, these workmen of the road brought needed skills beyond those found in the usual farm family. Their crafts were many and varied. They ranged from those of the artist, basket-maker and chair reseater to those of weavers, whitesmiths, and even whittlers.

The wandering weavers, tailors, hatters, and shoemakers were among the first to go. The last of these workmen of the road to quit their rounds were the chair reseaters, commonly called chair bottomers, and clock repairmen.

As more people were supplied with clocks and the market for new ones decreased, repair work on those already sold became more important. This brought into being the professional clock repairman, or "clock-fixer." By selling many clocks over the countryside, the Sam Slicks of peddling days really created the situation that prolonged the existence of the repairmen.

Some persons in Saline County will recall an old gentlemen named Neal Jones who, until well past eighty years of age, made regular trips over the county in his two-wheeled horse cart and cared for ailing clocks. It must have been a healthful trade to follow for Uncle Neal lived beyond one hundred years despite the fact that he was rejected for military services in the Civil War on the grounds that "You have consumption and won't be around long."

The coming of the clock repairman was a treat to the curious and inquisitive boy, especially if he were allowed to watch the craftsman go about his work of tightening, loosening, or clipping the fan to vary the speed of the chimes, contriving and replacing minor parts, or driving pinions along shafts to bring wear upon new places. He watched each part of the brass works as they were carefully cleaned by being vigorously scrubbed with a mysterious mixture of white powder in some liquid. The works were then reassembled and oiled with whale oil applied with a slender splinter or a straw from the family broom. The movements were replaced in the case, proper adjustments were made, and the clock set to ticking merrily once more. The repairman collected his small fee, assured his patron that he would return "in a year or so" and moved on, seeking other clocks in need of his services.

Another workman who had regular rounds—if yearly calls could be called regular—was the chair-seater, or chair-bottomer. This craftsman, almost without exception, was also a basket-maker and had plied that part of his trade during the winter months at home. Some of these baskets he carried along for sale when he went chair-bottoming.

On his wagon or back he also carried several large bundles of folded splits made from young, clear, straight-grained white oak. When he found a job of reseating, he would place one of these bundles in water, which made the splints more pliable and easier to use.

Some householders reseated their own chairs, using hickory or elm bark as well as white-oak splits. Some used corn husks torn into shreds and twisted into a slender rope. When binder twine and baling wire came into use, they were pressed into service, too. In the same area where Uncle Neal Jones repaired clocks, the Hafford brothers went about bottoming chairs. They were recognized as skilled craftsmen.

At about this same time, or a bit earlier, it was not uncommon to see an itinerant shoemaker trundling his findings and equipment along the roadway on a handcart, or sometimes on his back. The necessities he carried consisted of little more than a few hog bristles, some beeswax and tallow, a few small hanks of linen thread, two or three knives, about the same number of awls, a lapstone, a couple of hammers, and a few lasts of persimmon wood. All these could be wrapped in his apron and slung from his shoulder. The householder generally furnished the leather, which he obtained at the local tanyard.

The last known itinerant shoemaker in southern Illinois was Uncle Richmond Inge, a former slave who lived near present-day Thompsonville, in Franklin County, and went out to make shoes in the homes of that region. Several years ago very old people would tell of the times when they had seen this elderly shoemaker plodding from place to place over the country. He received fifty cents a pair for making shoes. Inge must have prospered, however, since he was able to buy his wife from slavery in Missouri and to own a well-kept eighty-acre farm.

Sometimes one of these wandering craftsmen would find a promising location and settle down. Such a one was Bill Burton, who came to the vicinity of Broughton, in Hamilton County, at about the time of the Civil War and opened his small shop. The picture of this old gentleman sitting on his bench or harness horse, busily stitching or pegging away and glancing up over spectacles worn very low on his nose, still is etched in the memory of a few boys who went there to have the soles of their high-topped leather boots repegged many years ago.

Bill Burton also was called "Uncle." We wonder why so many of these early craftsmen were referred to by this title.

❧ *SHAWNEETOWN BANKS*

VERY LITTLE MONEY WAS available in pioneer southern Illinois. About the only media of exchange were deer skins and the pelts of various fur-bearing animals. After a fashion, these served the purpose, but they were surely a cumbersome currency. Lacking money for trade was a definite hardship.

John Marshall, living at Shawneetown, saw the need for a better means of exchange and petitioned the legislature of Illinois Territory for authority to establish a bank. This privilege was granted by legislative action approved on December 28, 1816. The first bank in Illinois Territory thus came into existence. Its charter was to expire on January 1, 1837.

This newly established bank was housed in the Marshall residence, still standing against the levee, about two hundred yards down-river from the point where State Route 13 joins the main street of the old town. The safe for the new bank was a heavy timber box, iron bound and thickly studded with iron spikes. A somewhat ponderous lock completed it. This box, or safe, is now in the Museum of the Chicago Historical Society. To further guarantee the security of the bank's assets, according to tradition, a watchman slept on the safe at night.

Marshall's bank, legally designated as the Bank of Illinois, came into existence in late 1816 and immediately began operations. In fact, Marshall seems to have been personally discharging many of the functions of a bank previous to receiving a charter. Marshall's bank suspended operations for a time in 1823–24, but that did not cease its legal existence. This is shown by the fact that on February 12, 1834, its charter was extended another twenty years.

In a few years, the Shawneetown State Bank was established along with another at Edwardsville. Both these banks were designated as banks of issue; that is, they could issue their own currency. The Illinois legislature took a very friendly attitude toward these establishments and passed laws that practically forced acceptance of their currency.

The bank at Shawneetown could charge only 6 per cent interest. It would be penalized 12 per cent if it failed to redeem the currency it had issued. Both the Shawneetown and the Edwardsville bank were designated as depositories for funds received from the sale of public lands by the government land offices. The Shawneetown bank was able, after considerable delay, to repay the land office there for funds it had received, but the land office at Edwardsville lost about $54,000 when the bank there defaulted.

The money issued by each of these banks must have been somewhat crude. Many men thought they saw an opportunity to make some easy cash, and a wave of counterfeiting swept the area. The court records of Gallatin and other river counties in particular indicate numerous charges of counterfeiting and circulating spurious money.

Banking was so successful in Shawneetown that the city was referred to as the financial capital of the state. According to a story current in Shawneetown, a group of Chicago men came down in the 1830's seeking to borrow $10,000 for use in the development of their upstart village. After listening to the plea of the Chicago group, the bank officials retired and duly deliberated. They returned, so tradition reports, to say "Gentlemen, we are sorry we can't grant the loan. You are too damned far from Shawneetown to ever amount to anything."

In 1838 a new bank building was begun in Shawneetown and completed in 1840. This building, constructed at a cost of $80,000 still stands as one of southern Illinois' most noted landmarks. The five massive stone columns at its front are considered by competent judges as the finest of their kind in America.

During the Civil War, it was feared that Southern forces might raid the city and seize the bank's assets. It was temporarily closed, therefore, and Thomas S. Ridgway used the building as a residence. Banking was resumed on the first floor in 1865 and continued until the 1920's.

After banking was discontinued there, the building served various purposes and agencies. It is now owned by the State of Illinois and is in process of restoration. A large sign on the side next to the highway tells something of its story. Viewed in its setting, the old building is impressive and bespeaks the glory that once was Shawneetown's.

Chapter 7

Farm Life

🌼 *MARKING LIVESTOCK*

CERTAIN PRACTICES IN farm fencing have reversed themselves since southern Illinois was settled. Early farmers fenced their cultivated fields and turned their livestock loose to range. Now pastures are fenced and cultivated fields often are not.

Livestock kept in pastures is not so difficult to identify. When stock ran at large and was seen only occasionally by the owner, identification was not so easy. Herds sometimes combined or an occasional animal would leave one herd to join another. That is why owners adopted a system of brands and marks.

The term "brand" refers to marks made by burning a design on the skin of the animal with a hot iron. The animal treated thus was "branded." This system of identification was carried to the western prairies and even now is practiced in many places. Branding was in limited use in southern Illinois, mostly for horses and cattle.

Livestock here was marked by cutting the ears of the animal. The basic cuttings were simple and comparatively few in number. By varying their arrangement, however, the identifications that could be made were almost unlimited.

One of the common ear marks used was the "crop," where a considerable portion of the ear, generally the tip, was cut away. Sometimes only the upper or lower portion of the ear tip was removed. This was called an upper or lower half-crop.

Another mark was the "bit," a rounded gap, perhaps three-fourths of an inch across, cut from a designated place on the edge of the ear. If cut from the upper edge, it was an over-bit: when cut from the lower it was an under-bit.

A "swallow fork," named for its resemblance to a swallow's tail, was a larger and longer forked cut, generally in the end of the ear. There were other marks like "holes," "notches," and "slopes." Holes and notches are self-explanatory. Slopes were smooth diagonal cuts, really crops which might be "over-slopes" or "under-slopes." By combinations of these standard marks, and by using the right or left ear or both, an almost infinite number of identifications could be made.

So long as livestock ran at large, brands and marks were used and recognized as the legal means of showing ownership. They were required to be registered with the clerk of the county where the property was owned. Before being recorded, a check of registered marks was made to be sure that the particular one being registered was not already in use.

According to the territorial laws in effect in 1815, any person who altered the marks of another's livestock in a way that would indicate an intent to steal was subject to a fine not less than $50.00 or more than $100.00. The offender also would receive not less than twenty-five nor more than forty lashes "well laid on," on the bared back.

Another section of the law provided that if one altering brands or marks on a horse, mare, or colt, or on neat cattle or hogs was prosecuted within six months—a queer provision—the guilty person was obligated to pay the rightful owner the full value of the stock on which marks had been altered plus $5.00 for each animal. He also might receive forty lashes plus two hours in the pillory and be branded with the letter "T" in the palm of the left hand. The "T" signified thief and was in common use. Anyone knowing of alterations made in livestock markings and concealing the fact was subject to a fine of $10.00.

Livestock was to be branded or marked before reaching stated ages. Horses were branded before they were eighteen months old, cattle twelve months, and hogs six months. Disputed ownership was settled by the records of registered brands and marks. When stock was traded or sold, the new owner was to change marks within eight months to indicate change of ownership. Re-marking was to be done "in the presence of two creditable witnesses."

If anyone slaughtered hogs in the woods, as sometimes was done, it was required that the person killing them take the head with attached ears before a Justice of the Peace for inspection. The hides of cattle with attached ears and any brands undisturbed, must likewise be presented. In all cases, this was to be done within three days. If it were not convenient to take the head and ears of hogs or the hides of cattle to a

Justice of the Peace, they could be submitted to "two substantial free-holders" who must properly certify their inspection. To have a hog without ears was considered convicting evidence of theft.

Times have changed. It is probable that the Society for the Prevention of Cruelty to Animals would intervene if the practice of ear-cropping was revived.

❦ STOCK DRIVES

MENTION OF CATTLE trails generally brings to mind pictures of the great herds that were driven along the routes that led from the open ranges of the West to a shipping point on some newly built railway. Some of these trails were hundreds of miles long, and the herds driven along them included thousands of animals.

Much of the legend, romance, and folklore of the old West is associated with these cattle trails. The drives were large ventures, and the term used on the old-time circus posters could well be applied to them. They were "stupendous, colossal, and magnificent." Dramatic possibilities were present along with danger and suspense.

Some think that the livestock drives began with the roaring West, but the practice was an old one by the time it had come to the western plains. As early as 1800 numerous herds of livestock were driven to market over eastern roadways and along the woodland trails. Those early eastern drives included horses, cattle, hogs, and sheep. After early housewives began to grow numbers of turkeys and geese, with the help of the children, these birds—with wings properly clipped—were "carried" to market in a similar manner. The practice of collecting cattle in southern Illinois and driving them to an eastern market was used by Conrad Will, a physician from Pennsylvania, as early as 1813.

Will's decision to buy and drive meat animals and horses to distant markets doubtless came from his observance of the practice in his home state. Records indicate that many herds of cattle, hogs, and horses were then being driven long distances to eastern terminal markets. Cattle and hogs were driven from Ohio and Indiana to Baltimore. Most of the hogs and cattle killed in the Detroit area in 1826 were those driven there from Indiana and Kentucky. At about this same time, cattle were being taken from Missouri to Baltimore.

The progress of driven stock was slow. Horses could be moved about twenty miles a day. Three-year-old cattle, intended to be fed for another year nearer the eventual market, would cover about nine miles a day, while four-year-old cattle, termed fat, could go about seven miles daily. Hogs—even the razorback, apparently built for speed—would average only about five or six miles a day. Drives thus were time-consuming.

Plans and preparations for these long trips were made carefully. The cattle and hogs were gathered at some central starting point. There they would often be herded about over the fields and pastures and along the woodland roads so that they might become accustomed to each other and to being driven. Unskilled drivers also would learn from the more experienced men.

Each drive would be in the charge of a boss-driver on horseback. This man or another on a mount would flank the herd and return to it any stock that strayed or bolted. Stock accustomed to being herded also was used to lead. Sometimes the lead animal was a cow or steer wearing a bell. Streams might be crossed by ferries, but stock generally was forced to swim.

Each nightfall it was the task of the boss-driver to select and arrange a place to stop. This might be in the open or at some farmstead where there was a fenced lot and where feed could be obtained. Stock-drovers, like wagon trainmen, seldom stopped at taverns.

Driving days were long; herds often started to move at dawn. Wages of the drovers, many of them only boys, averaged about fifty cents a day with food furnished. When the drive was ended, they were given seventy-five cents a day for the time that should be required for their return to the starting point. The days required for this were determined by dividing the miles to be traveled by thirty-three, considered a standard daily rate. Rapid walkers sometimes averaged more and counted the gain as profit.

Pioneer stock drives passed from the American scene long ago. The writer, however, remembers arising at 1:00 in the morning to help drive hogs five miles to the railway loading pens at Broughton. He also remembers the time when men driving a great flock of two thousand geese stopped at his father's farm six miles north of Eldorado and kept their honkers in the barn lot. Other older persons have told him of seeing great flocks of turkeys and geese being driven along roadways toward St. Louis.

All that remain of this are a few bits of the old songs and lore with which those taking part in such drives beguiled themselves about their night fires.

❧ *HOG-KILLING TIME*

THE ONCE COMMON practice of hog-killing has about disappeared along with apple and turnip holes, rail fences, clapboards, and cattle-marking.

Hog-killing was an almost ritualistic procedure for which careful preparations were made. First, the farm sled was pulled into place for use as a platform. And that reminds us: What has become of the farm sled? A wooden scalding barrel leaned at the proper angle was set against the side of the sled. The lower end of this barrel was placed in a shallow pit and the top leaned against the platform, with chocks on either side to prevent its slipping or rolling.

Iron kettles, often holding as much as thirty gallons or more, were placed on rocks or suspended at the proper height from a strong pole supported by forked posts set in the ground. Plenty of dry fuel, often old or broken fence rails, was gathered. If the kettles and scalding barrel were not near a well or pond, other barrels with water stood by. Pieces of old carpeting with scraps of quilts or blankets were gathered for insulating the scalding barrel or to serve as scalding pads.

Hogs to be killed were placed in small near-by pens the night before. Kettles were filled and fires built beneath them about day break. Helpers brought their best butcher knives, carefully sharpened. Whetstones and a rifle were at hand. "Gamble sticks" were prepared; at least one for each hog to be killed. In the event no meat cleaver was available, and it usually was not, a sharp ax served the purpose.

If there was no rifle to shoot the hog, it was knocked in the head with the pole of the ax or with a hand hammer. In either event, the unconscious hog was quickly turned on its back and stuck with a knife.

The one performing this function plunged his long, clean blade into the center of the hog's throat, pointing it somewhat backwards and perhaps giving the tip of the knife a deft flip to insure the cutting of a main blood vessel. Sticking hogs was considered an art. To secure and retain a reputation as a skilled sticker, it was necessary that he remove a clean knife from the wound. Blood on the handle or blade was indicative of an inept performance.

Next the recently killed hog was plunged headfirst into the barrel of scalding hot water, where it was churned up and down and turned from side to side by men holding its back feet and perhaps its tail. After a few plunges and turns, one of the men would grasp a handful of hair on the portion being scalded as it was raised from the hot water. When this hair slipped easily, the ends were reversed and scalding completed. After this had been done, the hog was withdrawn and placed on the platform for scraping, and the barrel was covered to keep the water hot for the next scalding.

Second-string butcher knives, shaped scrapers, mower sections, and even the workman's hands were used to rub, scrape, or pluck the hair away. If some spots, wrinkles, depressions, or places protected from full effects of the scalding failed to yield the hair, pieces of old blankets or pads of hair already removed were placed over the spot and scalding water poured on. When plucking showed that the obstinate hair had been loosened, the spot was scraped.

The proper temperature for scalding water was determined by rapidly sweeping the fingers through it. If more than three such sweeps could be endured, it was too cold and boiling water was added.

Some sprinkled powdered resin over the hogs before scalding, thinking that it helped to loosen the hair, made the skin firmer, and left the carcass whiter. The whole idea was to remove the hair entirely and not to shave it off. A workman who cut the gashed the skin while scraping was poorly rated.

After scraping was completed, it was time to hang the hog. This was done by making vertical slits low in the back of the hind legs and raising the tendons sufficiently to insert ends of the gambrel. The actual hanging of the hog required strenuous efforts, since its nose had to be a foot or so above the ground.

Hogs usually were suspended from a strong pole, one end of which was chained to a tree or placed in a crotch of proper height, and the other end was supported by a fork made of crossed rails or small poles. Once hung in place, the hog was splashed with water and gently brushed to remove any clinging dirt or hair. Then the entrails were removed. After a brief cooling, the carcass was laid upon a sturdy clean table or perhaps on the scrubbed scalding platform to be cut up. The head was removed and the snoot and the lower end of the jaw were chopped off. The head was then ready for processing, much of it going into "souse." The hog was then halved by cutting along each side of the backbone. The ribs were next removed, the ham's side and shoulders cut apart and properly trimmed. After the meat had been allowed to cool thoroughly but not to freeze, it was ready for salting down. By this time, nightfall was near. The neighbors who had volunteered their help went home laden with ribs, backbones, and livers. In a few days, they also would kill hogs, and the man they had aided would volunteer his help and, incidentally, get some fresh meat to take home. Hog killing was a swap-work affair.

Parts of the hog remained to be worked the next day—the sweetbread (pancreas), the kidneys, the heart, and other portions often were thrown away. The "lights" (lungs) were left hanging where the chickens could pick them. The feet were cleaned for cooking or pickling. The brains were kept and fried with eggs, the intestines could be used for sausage casing or become "chitlin's" (chitterlings). Anything remaining that was adaptable became soap grease.

When all this had been done, the task of making sausage and rendering lard remained. "Cracklin's" from lard-making were good in shortnin' bread. Obviously, little was wasted and "a good time was had by all."

🌿 *SOFT SOAP*

As CIVILIZATION advances, so do standards of cleanliness. It might be just as true to say that as standards of cleanliness advance, so does civilization. However it may be expressed, there always have been those who appeared to fear cleanliness.

In the February, 1848, issue of *Prairie Farmer,* a writer says: "There are persons who suppose that soap of any quality is injurious to the skin, and who use it only under compulsion." That writer was not speaking of small boys, either. Many of those living then and acquainted only with the wood-ashes–scrap-fat soft soap of the pioneer era would doubtless choose it only as the lesser of two evils.

No one seems to know definitely when soap first was used. References to it in ancient writings are infrequent. The Bible mentions it twice, the first time as "sope" and the second time as "soap." The first known soap manufactory was in the ancient city of Pompeii that was buried and preserved under ashes from the volcano Vesuvius in the year A.D. 79.

With no radio soap opera to popularize it, the use of soap spread slowly. Its use in Italy and Spain is indicated as early as 750. About five hundred years later, records indicate its use in France, where it received its present name because it made the hair glisten. A short time later, it became popular in England, where the soapmakers' demand for wood ashes hastened the near disappearance of the magnificent forests that once covered much of Britain.

German and Polish craftsmen coming to Virginia in 1608 brought the soapmakers' art to America. Here, the boundless supply of wood for ashes and the ease with which scrap fats, sometimes from wild animals, could be gathered, encouraged soap-making. In early America, it became a home industry, practiced in nearly all households.

The materials and equipment needed were not difficult to obtain. Soap was made of lye from the wood ashes of household fires or from burned log heaps, and scrap fats from animals slaughtered for the home meat supply and from wild animals killed for food or skins. The needed articles of equipment were an ash hopper, a wash kettle, and some stoneware vessels.

When winter came and household fires were kindled, an ash hopper was built and roofed to shield its contents from rains. The inverted triangular hopper, the most common type, had a chopped-out trough at its bottom. By the time spring arrived, hoppers had been filled with stored ashes.

When soap-making time came, a bucket or two of water was poured over the ashes each day until they became saturated and the water, rich in lye, began to drip from the trough at the hopper's bottom. This liquid, dark brown and highly caustic, was collected in guarded containers, preferably of stoneware, and from time to time, as these filled, their contents were poured into the wash kettle. A fire was built beneath it, and it was generally kept well covered. As leaching continued, the solution grew paler in color and weaker.

Despite safeguards, an occasional inquisitive chicken roaming about the yard would thrust a beak into the container at the hopper for a sip, register consternation and then rapidly depart, wiping a burning beak on the grass. Children are known to have swallowed the liquid with sometimes fatal results. Painful burns could result if lye was splashed on the bare skin.

After a few gallons of the lye (sometimes spelled ley) water had been poured into the kettle, it was tested for strength. If a fresh egg floated in it, it was considered strong enough. By another test, a downy feather was quickly dipped into the boiling lye. If the down and tip of the feather's shaft were dissolved, it was considered strong enough to use.

After the meat scraps—enough to supply about two pounds of fat for each gallon of soap—had been added, the mixture was kept boiling and regularly stirred, preferably with a sassafras paddle. Sometimes sassafras twigs or other aromatic substances were added to disguise the soap odor. In regions where they grew, bayberries often were thrown in.

When the practiced eye and nose of the housewife determined that the soap was about done, samples were taken and tested to see if it produced a good lather. When it did so, cooking was discontinued. At this stage it was soft soap, ropy in texture and having a dark brown color. It was indeed a potent product. Often it was used in this condition.

If the housewife chose, this soft soap could be hardened and cut into bars. To do this, salt was added to the boiling soap as the cooking process was ending. This caused a part of the water and various substances in the soap to settle to the bottom of the kettle. The soap cake was next removed and the bottom was scraped to clean it. It was then remelted without the salty water and poured into flat pans to be cut into bars. A little powdered resin sometimes was added to give the soap a nice yellow color.

Many older persons can recall the brown, soft soap and the distinctive odor of clothes laundered with it. They also can recall the tingle it gave the skin and the relative ease with which it removed almost any dirt from their hands.

In addition to serving in the laundering process, soft soap sometimes was used as a lubricant, particularly for loose wooden bearings. Hence the expression "soft-soaping."

HOLING UP FOOD FOR WINTER

MISCHIEVOUS BOYS still make sly and unannounced visits to watermelon patches. News of such a visit would not be unusual, but it would be uncommon to hear that a group of boys had raided a farmer's apple hole. Such excursions have ceased. Boys may be the same, but the apple holes aren't. They have disappeared along with the practice of holing up food for winter.

Once upon a time in late fall, it was the custom of farmer folk to gather and store certain of their winter food supplies. After heavy frost, but before the first hard freezes of the winter had come, the frugal farmer began putting away reserve supplies of potatoes, cabbage, turnips, apples, pears, celery, and sometimes pumpkins and squashes. Most farms did not have cellars, there were no locker plants, the home freezer had not appeared, and refrigerators were unknown. Small-town grocerymen did not regularly stock fresh vegetables. Therefore, if families wished to have a dependable supply of such food, they had to hole up their own.

The holes for the storage of these reserve foodstuffs really were not holes; they were conical mounds or pointed ridges of straw and earth. It was the practice to store each product separately. The size and number of mounds seen in a householder's garden, therefore, would rather reliably indicate the family's prospect for eating well during the winter.

The construction of these storage places was more or less uniform. A spot where water did not stand was selected, and a heavy layer of straw, leaves, or grass was laid down. The product to be stored was carefully arranged in a conical heap or in a sharply pointed ridge, and a thick layer of straw or dry leaves was thrown over it. A layer of dirt, eight inches or more thick, was next added from a ditch dug around the base of the growing mound. Boards or planks often were leaned against these mounds as additional protection against expected rains and snows. The purpose of this method of storage was to keep the product dry and cold, but not to let it freeze. This crude but effective cold-storage method kept foods throughout the winter months.

Foods to be stored were not especially prepared, but care was taken to store only sound and clean products. Some who stored apples would arrange them with the smaller and knottier ones at one side or end of the mound so that they could be used first while the better ones would be saved for Christmas time or even later.

Cabbage was pulled with root stock attached. It was then arranged with the roots upward to retard any tendency of the cabbage to grow. When cabbage was removed for cooking, the stalks were cut off near the head. If one wished to grow early cabbage leaves for greens or to grow seeds, these stalks were set out. Those which were not planted were prized by youngsters who peeled them, dipped their tips in salt, and ate them. Some oldsters may recall eating those tasty stalks in their youth.

In addition to providing food for the family, a well-stocked apple hole had about it a certain social factor. This was especially true if the owner was of a generous nature and treated visitors. He would hand a bucket or pan to his son and say, "Boy, you and John take this bucket and get some apples. Be sure to stuff the straw back in the hole and put the boards back." It made for a pleasant evening.

SASSAFRAS TEA & SALLET

Good health was vital to the pioneer, and he went to extreme lengths to keep himself fit. When measured by present-day standards, he was not a healthy man, and he had a very limited knowledge of better health practices. However, he did have strange beliefs, antidotes, a considerable stock of remedies, and even health superstitions. Since these were all he had to guide him in the matter of health, he followed them.

As spring came each year, the pioneer began to look about for a spring tonic. This might vary from a mixture of sulpur and sorghum molasses to sassafras tea and sallet. He believed that his blood had become thick during the winter and needed to be thinned, and that his system needed cleaning out.

There were accepted ways in which these objectives could be accomplished. He could take sulphur and molasses, though this popular remedy seemed to have been reserved mostly for youngsters. Another common and less objectionable remedy was sassafras tea, which people drank in copious amounts each spring. They thought sassafras tea was an effective blood-thinner particularly so when made from the roots of red sassafras.

Naturally, a sufficient quantity of roots should be used to give the brew strength and color. The amount needed to produce a half-gallon of tea would be represented by ten or twelve pieces about the size and length of a finger. These were allowed to simmer long enough to bring out the best flavor. The tea was then given a minute or so to settle. Sweetened to taste, it was an agreeable drink for most persons, and also was an agreeable way to "thin the blood."

To assure the best tea, the roots were dug in early spring while the trees were dormant; that is, before the sap had begun to rise. Some insisted that roots should be taken only from the north side of the tree. Some even held that those dug during the dark of the moon were more flavorful. All alike agreed that roots from more mature trees, three inches or more in diameter, were more aromatic. Digging sassafras in early spring became almost ritualistic. Only the rough outer bark of the roots was removed. Larger roots were split rail fashion, and diggers generally discarded the central portion of larger sections. When properly gathered and stored, roots retained their flavor for weeks. Properly brewed and allowed to settle, the tea had a most attractive rosy tint. The scent of brewing tea filled the house with a delightful odor.

A similar drink was made from the broken twigs of the spicewood bush. The writer once drank some of this tea in a home that rated it above the sassafras drink. The lingering memories of this one experience, however, are dim among the more vivid ones of sassafras brew.

Each spring now one finds small bundles of sassafras root in rubber bands on sale at grocery stores, even in nationally known chain stores and supermarkets, but something seems to be lacking. It may be that those gathering the roots do not select a sufficiently mature tree. Perhaps they are collecting white sassafras, or possibly they forget to dig only those roots north of the tree. However it may be, today's tea hardly measures up to those memories of yesteryear. Perhaps an explanation may lie in a friend's remark, "That boyish appetite is gone."

Sulphur and molasses and teas from sassafras and spicewood hardly were sufficient to fully thin the blood and clean the system. A supplement of wild greens, or sallet, was necessary. This yearning of the pioneer for green food is not difficult to understand. There were no frozen foods and no fresh vegetables from the South. The first green vegetables that the pioneer could have were those that grew on the farmstead, in the fence rows, and about old fields, where the housewife went to gather sour dock, pokeberry, lamb's quarter (generally pronounced lam-squarter), dandelion, narrowed leaf plantain, wild beets, wild lettuce, young sprouts of elderberry, wild onion, and perhaps other plants not presently popular.

Each family burned an early lettuce bed and often set out stalks of the cabbage that had been holed up in earthen mounds the previous autumn. They gathered the shoots from such sprouting stocks as well as the tops of any turnips that had survived the winter. There also would be an early planting of mustard. If newly planted beets were thinned, their tops were used. Greens thus became plentiful, but no later varieties could replace the first wild ones which were gathered as early as they appeared and cooked with a slab of fat bacon or hog jaw. Memories of these greens, supplemented with crackling bread may cause some oldsters to indulge in a bit of reverie. Some may recall the refrain of a song: "Corn bread, buttermilk, and good old greasy greens."

🌿 FORAGING BOYS

A BOY HAS JOKINGLY been defined as an appetite with skin around it. Nowadays, to demonstrate that the definition is nearly correct, a boy visits the refrigerator, the coke or candy-bar machine, or the corner confectionery. Refreshments were not so easy to come by before the days of bottled drinks and the candy-vending machine. The grocery store often was miles away and even if it were conveniently located, nickels were very scarce. Two things, however, were as common then as now—the ever present sweet tooth of a boy and his efforts to satisfy it. One source that provided a means for catering to this craving was the maple tree, the hard or sugar variety. Such trees were common in the woodland.

To benefit from the sweetened sap of sugar trees, it was necessary to tap them. In this area, that could be done at any time after winter had come and weather conditions were right. One did not have to wait in southern Illinois, as in New England, for the end of a long and continuous winter. It was necessary only to have nights cold enough to freeze, followed by mornings warm enough to thaw. At such time throughout the winter and spring months, sap flowed freely—that is if the wind did not blow too much from the south and east to dry it up. Don't ask why wind from one direction was any worse than that from another; nevertheless it was so. When the time and season were right, it was a common sight to see a boy or group of boys, often undersize, carrying an oversize chopping ax on their way to a place where sugar maples could be found.

These trees were tapped on the level at which boys could operate most effectively. The bottom of the notch being cut was intended to be leveled across the tree. From there the notch was sloped downward and inward to provide a basin that would catch and hold the flowing sap. The chopping of this notch was done in a careful manner; the heel and toe of the ax were used to full advantage. A few misdirected strokes at the bottom could destroy the storage capacity of the notch. The upper portion of the cutting did not matter so much. Another rule was that the notch should not extend into the heartwood. Just what the bad effect was is not remembered, but care was taken to avoid it. Many notches would hold a half pint or more of sap. Occasional surviving specimens of sugar maple trees are found showing the scars made by tapping them a generation ago.

Boys soon learned that maples with darker bark produced the sweeter sap. The writer remembers a large scarred tree with a very dark bark that stood on the bank of Wilson's Branch and was the last tree left from a large grove where a sugar camp once operated. To drink the accumulated sap from these notches, the boys carried the hollow stem of some plant. A section of pipe cane was the best of all and was standard equipment in the pockets of many boys.

Tapping maple trees served several purposes. It furnished a good outlet for the energies of boys and taught them to find and skillfully tap the better trees. Above all, it demonstrated the enormous capacity of a boy to absorb the delightfully flavored maple sap. There was little likelihood of getting too much sweets, since the best sap contained only about 5 per cent of sugar.

Another springtime diversion of boys wandering through the woods was the pulling and roasting of sweet roots. This practice was less common, however, than the tapping of maple, perhaps because it often required more effort. Sweet roots were those of young hickory sprouts up to about two feet tall but often having a taproot three feet or more long. To indulge in this practice, the would-be forager would equip himself with a section of a small pole about his own length. Knots and rough places were smoothed out and one end was sharpened to a smooth wedge. Having selected the sprout he wished to pull, he would thrust the wedge end of the pole forcibly down on different sides of the tap root to sever any side branches and thus make the task easier. If there was much difficulty in pulling, the section of the pole was laid beside the sprout which was then wrapped about it and tied or held in place. The pole was then used as a lever. This process was repeated until the desired number of roots had been collected. Pulling sweet roots was done only in spring when the ground was thoroughly water-logged and soft, and the roots had a good stock of sugar stored to start new growth. The gathered roots were roasted in a fire, perhaps one that the boys had kindled, or they were taken home to be baked in the hot ashes of the wood-burning stove or at the fireplace. After roasting, the bark was peeled and the roots were chewed. They were surprisingly tender, juicy, and sweet.

Different seasons provided the prowling boys with other provenders. They could have persimmons, paw-paws, wild goose plums, inedible crab apples, black haws, red haws, berries of assorted kinds, and many varieties of nuts, each in its season. Oldsters who sample the same delicacies now insist that the flavor is not what it once was. Perhaps age has dulled it.

❦ GRITTED MEAL

THE PIONEER'S PROBLEM of securing breadstuff was a continuous one that sometimes became acute. One of these times of shortage occurred when the corn grown the previous year had been exhausted or perhaps the meal made from last year's corn had lost its flavor and tasted stale. The new crop of corn had not matured and dried sufficiently to be ground into meal, so householders had to rely upon grating, more often called "gritting."

When corn became hard enough to grate, it meant that the strong, slightly rancid flavor noticeable in bread made from old meal would soon be gone for another year. The bit of variety that this new meal offered made a big difference in eating enjoyment, because corn bread was practically the universal bread of the pioneer. Any improvement in its taste and flavor was welcomed. Even in prosperous homes, biscuits made of wheat flour were common only for breakfast. In the humbler households, biscuits were on the menu for Sunday breakfast only, hence bread made from corn meal grated by hand was high on the list of family staples, and its preparation was all-important. It was warmly welcomed.

Making corn bread from grated meal required a device known as a grater or gritter made from a piece of sheet metal, often coming from a tin bucket or a metal box. This metal was flattened, cut into a rectangular shape and punctured with a sharp instrument, often a nail filed to a point, and a hammer. The punctures were set at intervals of about a fourth of an inch and in rows about that far apart. The area punctured depended upon the size of the sheet metal used. Usually it was about six or eight inches wide and about twelve inches long. After the punctured metal had been bent into a curved form with the projecting points on the outside, it was attached to a board of proper width and two or three feet long. The completed device very much resembled the familiar nutmeg grater, though it was much longer. With this equipment, the householder was ready to grit meal. Men sometimes condescended to do this task and youngsters seemed to enjoy it, at least until the novelty wore off or they had skinned their knuckles on the roughened metal.

The corn was ready for use when it had become reasonably hard but had not dried sufficiently to shell easily. The grater was held vertically; the lower end resting in a pan, upon a cloth, a paper, or a clean smooth surface. The ears of corn, also held vertically, were rubbed somewhat vigorously upon the grater in an up-and-down motion. The individual doing this task quickly learned to be careful that his fingers did not come in contact with the sharpened projections of the grater.

Bread was made after the usual manner of making corn bread. Because the grated meal was already somewhat moist, it did not need as much liquid as that ground at the grist mill. Neither was as much soda necessary. There may be a possibility that the bread made of grated meal was not much better than that made from grist meal, but the author's recollections of it are wonderful. Tried as recently as last fall, it still seems to be tastier than any other kind of corn bread.

❦ *SORGHUM*

In September of each year, sorghum-making time comes in southern Illinois. Perhaps it would be better to say it once came, for sorghum-making has diminished almost to the vanishing point.

Once there were many molasses mills in Egypt, and almost every farmstead had its patch of sorghum intended to provide the major source of winter sweets. Now the mills and cane patches alike are scarce. Boys wandering over the countryside can no longer pause to gather a stalk of cane, peel it, and chew the sugary juice from the pulp. Neither can they visit the sorghum mill and scrape the candied molasses from the sides of the pan with small wooden paddles and eat it. Some older persons with lingering memories colored by youthful appetites will recall such occasions with pleasure.

Some who remember sorghum mills and fresh sorghum compare it with maple syrup for use on hot buttered pancakes or flapjacks. If, however, one is forced to eat hot biscuits, the kind that mother made, many insist that sorghum stands supreme.

Sorghum once was a staple crop. Old time one-horse grain drills were equipped with special plates for drilling the seed. At that same time, Sear's catalogue offered large steel rollers to crush the cane and pans in which to boil juice. In fact, one could order a complete mill from Sears.

Harvest-time cane patches were attractive. The leaves took on a tinge of yellow, and the stalks became blotched with a golden bloom like that seen on some ripened fruits. Large seed clusters nodded from the tops of the stalks. Stripping and harvesting cane was not an easy task, but boys did not seem to mind. It gave them opportunity to design and make their own strippers—swordlike wooden implements about three feet long and often notched along the working edge. Occasionally one of these strippers is yet found tucked on a rafter of some old shed or barn. After the leaves were stripped from the stalks, the seed cluster at their top was clipped off with a corn knife and saved to feed chickens. The cane was then cut and gathered into small, carefully ordered piles and hauled to the mill. It was necessary to harvest cane before cold weather arrived, for even a light frost, if followed by a shower or heavy dew, would "run down into the cane and ruin it." If the weather became cold enough to freeze, cane stored in the yard at the mill was likewise ruined.

When time came for making molasses and the stalks were crushed between steel rollers, the juice went to the the large evaporating pan placed on a stone or brick foundation, which served as a furnace. This flat shallow pan some four feet wide and having baffles across it often was twenty or more feet long. Juice fed into it at one end and boiling vigorously was skillfully stirred around the baffles toward the other end. The scum that arose was skimmed off and sometimes fed to pigs. Skimmings gathered near the finish ends of the pan were quite sweet and often were used to make California beer—a mild home brew.

The refined molasses, by now a rich amber color, was drawn off at the chimney end of the long pan and carefully stored for winter use. The container used was often a wooden barrel made by a local cooper. It was a mark of a good cooper to be able to produce barrels that would hold boiling sorghum.

In addition to being mixed with butter as a spread for pancakes or biscuits, sorghum was used in several other ways. A favorite use was to make molasses candy. For this purpose a small amount of water and a cup of brown sugar sometimes were added with a lump of butter, though these additions were not necessary. This mixture was cooked in a skillet until it "haired." At this point, some candy-makers stirred in a pinch of baking soda, but too much soda spoiled it. As soon as the hot mixture quit foaming, it was poured into buttered tins or plates.

When sufficiently cooled, the candy would be cut into blocks like fudge, or removed from the containers and pulled. If the hands were carefully buttered, the warm candy could easily be pulled into golden-colored taffy, and formed into long twisted rolls that were cut into sticks. In addition to the nourishment that molasses candy provided, its chewing afforded considerable jaw exercise. It also helped to gum up all who handled it.

Another popular use of sorghum was for the making of popcorn balls. To do this, a large pan of corn was popped, and boiling sorghum that had been cooked to candy consistency was poured over it. Balls were then molded. When cooled, they were firm and could be carried about, even taken to school in the lunch pail, or occasionally in a boy's coat pocket wrapped in oiled paper. They were a popular confection.

The use of sorghum didn't end here. Combined with ground black pepper, grated ginger and vinegar, it was made into a cough syrup or cold remedy. Whether effective or not, it certainly was pungent. Also, nothing excelled sorghum as sweetening for gingerbread or ginger cookies. The writer still seriously questions whether real gingerbread can be made without sorghum.

The strangest use ever made or sorghum to my knowledge was in the Gallatin County Courthouse at Shawneetown. When time came to paint murals on the walls of the circuit court room, it was necessary that portions of the wall be primed or sized before the artist did his work. Sorghum was the primer.

❦ PERSIMMONS

PERSIMMONS APPARENTLY have suffered a loss of popularity. They once were, after a few good frosts, a favorite delicacy for wandering boys and for hunters, particularly those who hunted possums at night. By combining the fruit of the *Diospyros virginiani,* the scientific name for the lowly persimmon, with turnips gleaned from an isolated patch or with apples found in the heavy grass beneath a rusty-coat tree at some deserted farmstead, the night hunter fared well. Persimmons also were a favorite food of the possum. Thus, both the hunter and the hunted were drawn towards the fruiting tree. Birds came by day to peck at the fruit, and flying insects came to suck the sugery juice. Pigs and sometimes dogs also ate them. In fact, they were popular with both men and beasts.

In addition to eating the fruit out of hand, other uses were made of it and of the wood of the tree. It was a practice of some to gather the fruit for making persimmon beer and for puddings. We thought both processes had entirely vanished, but several recipes for each have appeared recently.

Persimmons for making beer are best when gathered after they have fully ripened and are sugary. About a bushel will make a barrel of brew. The gathered fruit is placed in an open barrel and crushed in just enough water to make a thick mushy mixture. Clear water is added to make a total of about twenty-five gallons. A few brewers add new sorghum, saying that it makes a stronger beer. No addition is necessary, however, if well-ripened and sugary persimmons are available.

A cup or so of kitchen yeast is added, and the contents of the barrel very thoroughly stirred. It is then left in a warm place to ferment. From time to time it is skimmed as conditions may indicate. After a period varying from a few days to three weeks or more, the mixture ceases to "work" and the amber-like liquid is drained off, placed in jugs and jars, and stored in a cool place.

Our single experience with the product left us of the opinion that the drink was mild and delicious and could be taken without getting the bad after effects of stronger drinks. The slight sampling that Ernie Robb and the writer took from his father's stock is remembered pleasantly. No bad effects whatever are recalled.

Persimmons also are used in puddings, once a common dish in season. Perhaps persimmon pudding is making a comeback, since it has been found listed on the menu at two eating places this fall. Two recipes also have been received for making the pudding. One of them, which the lady giving it called a "receipt," is given here.

PERSIMMON PUDDING

2 cups brown sugar	1 tsp. baking soda
1 cup shortening	½ tsp. salt
2 eggs	1 tbs. cocoa (when she has it)
1 qt. persimmons that have been rubbed through a colander	nutmeg, cinnamon, cloves or vanilla as desired to "spice it up"
3 cups flour	

The sugar, shortening, and eggs are thoroughly mixed or, as the lady termed it, "creamed." The milk and persimmons are added. The dry ingredients are next stirred in along with the chosen flavoring materials. Baking is done in a "tolerable hot" oven. The donor of the recipe assured us that if properly done, the product would be scrumptious.

Even though puddings are off the writer's diet list, he tried one of the two persimmon puddings found in restaurants this fall. It was indeed really good.

The wood of the persimmon trees served a few particular uses. Excellent gluts for splitting fence rail were made from it, slowly dried by scorching beside an open fire, and then oiled. The wood also was used for making the queerly-shaped spool shuttles used by hand weavers. Occasionally one of these shuttles, worn glassy smooth by a million passes between the threads in an old loom, is found where it was stored a lifetime ago. Persimmon also was a favorite wood for the making of shoemakers' lasts. Today the heads of many golf clubs are fashioned of it.

All uses for persimmon did not end here, however. If the seeds were opened in the proper manner (undetermined), a knife, fork, and spoon would be discernible and a wish made at this point would come true. A handful of the inner bark of the tree could be placed in a pint of water and boiled down to a half-pint. The addition of some sugar and a small lump of alum to the liquid converted it into a potent remedy for thrush, a sore mouth of children. The bark also could be chewed for a sore throat. Anyone trying either of these remedies should remember that the bark is most effective when peeled from the north side of the tree with an upward motion. However peeled, it doesn't taste good.

🌾 *EGYPTIAN COTTON*

EACH SPRING FINDS many plots of ground in the extreme southern end of Illinois being seeded to cotton. After the ground has been prepared for planting and the seeds drilled, the young plants will come up in rows across the field and cotton-chopping, hand hoe cultivation, begins. Soon the plants will bloom, and cotton bolls will appear. All the while cotton-chopping goes on.

About mid-September these bolls will begin to burst, and ranks of cotton pickers trailing long sacks will move down the rows. It is cotton pickin' time again. Wagons with high sideboards appear along the roadways leading to the gins that operate during the season. At the gin, the ends of flexible pipes are lowered into the wagon and the cotton is sucked into large bins. From these bins it passes through the gin where the seeds are removed and the cotton pressed into bales weighing about 500 pounds each. Long rows of these burlap-wrapped bales gather on the loading platform of the warehouse.

Seeds removed from southern Illinois cotton go to a plant in Portageville, Missouri, for processing. Delightful odors, as intriguing as those from the street corner popcorn stand on a chilly night, make many passers-by think they are hungry.

When winter comes, a few stray bolls missed by the pickers will remain on the stark branches of the dead cotton plant, and cotton growers will turn to the discussion of next year's crop.

In earlier years, cotton was not a major crop in this area but was grown to meet the need of the home weaver. There was only this limited growth until the Civil War. Then, with the regular cotton supply of the South not available, a great expansion of cotton-growing came. Farmers saw an opportunity to profit, and cotton became a major crop. Within three years, the crop produced many millions of pounds. The government encouraged its growth and provided seed.

Cotton-growing flourished as far north as Randolph County, where several gins were located. The center of the industry, however, was farther south. Perhaps the most important cotton town in the state was Carbondale. Throughout the season gins were busy. They turned out about 4,000 bales or two million pounds of ginned fiber in 1865.

With a peak cotton price of eighty-seven and a half cents a pound in 1863, it is easy to see why farmers turned to growing it. The price continued to be good until the end of the war; it then decreased rapidly. In 1866 a plentiful supply of cotton from the South was available once more and prices in southern Illinois went down to twenty-two and a half cents a pound. Cotton-growing rapidly decreased, but it did not entirely disappear.

As late as 1873 there still was much cotton growing in the vicinity of Carbondale. This is indicated by some Jackson County court records of 1874. In that year the estate of George W. Felts, who operated a gin about where Attucks School is now located, and the estate of a Mr. Scurlock, who also operated a gin in Carbondale, were both being settled. These court records show that in the interval between September 25, 1873, when the gin of George W. Felts opened for the season, and May 15, 1874, when the records close, Felts ginned 309,435 pounds of cotton. The same records indicate that Scurlock's gin during the same interval handled more than 480,000 pounds of cotton. These records state that seed cotton was then selling at the gin for only four cents a pound.

Today some scattered fields of cotton, mostly within a radius of twenty-five miles from Cairo, are seen in southern Illinois. Parts of small crude gins made and used by the pioneer are sometimes found in attics or smokehouses. Hand cards and spinning wheels are occasionally displayed. They help to tell the story of cotton's one-time importance.

❧ *TOBACCO*

AMONG THE CROPS brought to southern Illinois by its earlier farmers was tobacco. Many of these settlers came from Virginia, Maryland, the Carolinas, Tennessee, and Kentucky, regions where tobacco was an important crop. Practically all of them were acquainted with its growth, even though it may have been only for "table use." They began to grow small crops for family consumption and finding that a surplus was readily salable, increased their plantings.

By 1840 tobacco-growing had been well established, so much so that the crops marketed in the area during that year amounted to more than a half million pounds. Twenty years later it had increased to approximately seven million pounds and had become the principal cash crop of the section, bringing the farmers some $700,000, no inconsiderable return for that time.

Tobacco-growing provided the farmer with almost year-round employment, much of which was necessary at what would otherwise have been slack-work periods. As soon as danger of frost was past, seed beds were prepared. The best sites for these were well-drained southern exposures in a sunny woodland. The spot selected was cleared of all weeds, leaves, and trash. It then was covered with carefully arranged brush to be burned. In some cases a fire of poles and brush was started at one end of the plot selected, and dragged at intervals toward the other end by the use of long poles with prongs. The purpose of burning was to kill weed seeds and insects, to hasten warming up of the plot, and to sterilize the soil, though it is doubtful if the farmer knew the latter purpose also was served.

The burned plot was hoed and raked with a hand rake until it was in fine tilth before the seed was sown. Since the seeds of tobacco are very small, a tablespoon full would amply seed a bed ten by twenty feet. These seeds generally were mixed with fine ashes or dust before being sown in order to assure a more even distribution. After sowing, the ground was gently pressed down with the flat side of the hoe or the prongs of the hand rake, or they might be tromped in. To avoid having wandering live stock walking across the tobacco bed, a barricade of poles or brush was erected about it. A few brushy limbs might even be laid directly on the bed. In May, the plants should be ready for setting in the field.

Tobacco grew best on a well fertilized, carefully tended ground. After thorough preparation, the field was laid off by cross furrows about three feet six inches apart. If time allowed, tobacco hills were made at the furrow crossings. When this was not done, the plants were set on corresponding corners at each intersection. When the field was ready, planters awaited a rain which would thoroughly wet the soil. In the event this did not occur, water was carried to the tobacco plot and poured into the holes made for the plants.

An early trip, often before breakfast, was made to the beds to pull plants which had been kept in the shade and protected. They next were dropped and set out. This transplanting was not an easy task, and the one who could set two acres, more than seven thousand plants, in a day was a good hand. Anyone who could set eight thousand between sunrise and sunset on a May day was justified in mildly boasting.

A summer of scraping, hoeing, plowing, topping, worming, suckering, and cutting followed. Then came the curing process that began with yellowing on protected racks followed by curing in the old-time tobacco barn. Sometimes the curing process was hastened by firing. Later, during some rainy or foggy spell, the tobacco would come in season. It then was stripped, assorted into trash, lugs, and leaf, tied into hands, and hauled to market over the bad roads of winter.

When the grower arrived at the market, it was not unusual for him to find several wagons already in line, awaiting their turns to unload. This is not difficult to understand. For many years, each of the markets at Galatia and Raleigh, in Saline County, handled about a million pounds of tobacco a year. At these markets, the tobacco was stemmed and prized into great hogsheads weighing as such as one thousand pounds each. Before the coming of railroads, these hogsheads were hauled on wagons to the river at Shawneetown. The drivers of these wagons generally combined them to form picturesque, slow-moving, ox-drawn trains which camped alongside the road at night.

By 1890, production of tobacco had begun a sharp decline in southern Illinois. More than fifty years ago the barns at Raleigh and Galatia ceased to operate. In 1955, Uncle France Hall, 97 years old, was the only remaining tobacco buyer at Raleigh who worked in the markets there during their heyday.

🌿 CASTOR OIL

IT IS APPARENTLY natural that neighboring towns became rivals. Many present rivalries center around high school athletic teams, but some towns were rivals long before high schools had competing sports.

Sparta and Chester may be cited as a pair of pre-athletic contenders. They have been vying with each other on various issues for more than a hundred years. Almost from their beginning they have been contending for the trade of Randolph County farmers. Each has enjoyed a measure of distinction as a place for the production of farm implements and vehicles. Each has had its plow and wagon factories.

When it seemed that the county seat was to be removed from the old village of Kaskaskia, Chester and Sparta challenged each other vigorously for the new location. They later were rivals for the location of railroads and industries. Each has long striven to excel the other in educational and cultural attainments.

The above mentioned bases for rivalry may be considered commonplace ones, but an additional competition that continued for several years between the two towns could easily be classified as unusual. In the 1840's the two towns tried to outdo each other in the production of castor oil, each striving to merit the title of castor oil capital of the United States. Neither is known to have announced any such ambition in explicit terms and neither appears to have been clearly entitled to that distinction. There was a time, though, when they might have combined their claims and easily have held the honor. According to an article appearing in the *Prairie Farmer* at that time, the center for the production of castor oil in America was in Randolph County, with Sparta and Chester operating several presses.

The first commercial production of castor oil in the state did not begin in this county but at Edwardsville, in Madison County, in 1825, when Don Adams set up a press and produced 500 gallons of oil that sold for $2.50 a gallon. This encouraged Adams to continue and expand the industry until he was operating two presses and producing 10,000 gallons of oil in 1830.

It must have been the evidence of Adams' prosperity that induced Richard B. Servant, of Chester, to promote the production of castor oil in his vicinity. Servant did this by furnishing the farmers with seed, instructing them in the best methods of growing and caring for the crop, and promising to buy the beans they produced. Many began to grow the crop, and they sold it to Servant, who heated the beans and extracted the oil in powerful presses operated by horses hitched to long sweeps. Servant prospered in the industry, and in the later 1830's "had more ready money than any other man in the county."

The firm of Holmes, Swanwick and Company, of Chester, also dealt extensively in castor beans, accepting them in exchange for merchandise. Part of the beans they bought were processed in Chester, others were sent by river to St. Louis or to New Orleans, or even were shipped to Philadelphia.

At about the same time that the castor oil industry began to prosper at Chester, James McClurken, of Sparta, became interested in it, set up the first press there, and the rivalry between the two towns was on.

The production of oil seems to have been greatest about 1849, when several presses were operating in the county. Farmers found the castor bean a profitable crop since they were able to produce an average of twenty bushels to the acre, for which they received about $1.50 a bushel. The demand for "tight barrels" in which to ship the oil also encouraged the cooper trade. Castor beans brought prosperity to the region.

Much of the castor oil produced in the Sparta-Chester region was not for the kiddies but was used as lubricating oil.

With the discovery of petroleum and the development of oils from it, the demand for castor oil decreased and the industry became less profitable. Fewer beans were grown, many of the presses ceased to operate, and a one-time lucrative industry died out. Today a castor bean plant is occasionally seen growing in a farmyard or in a flower garden. The last field noted was one of about ten acres near McClure, in Alexander County, in 1942.

RAIL FENCES

RAIL FENCES, ONCE A universal feature of the southern Illinois landscape, have almost disappeared. Of the thousands of miles of such fences that existed in the region, it is doubtful if enough remain to reach a mile. Only in isolated spots beside some old roadway or at a country home where sentiment or a desire for the picturesque has influenced the family are there remnants of the old fences.

The very fact that they were so common and that they gradually vanished along with their builders may have made their disappearance less noticed. Until the introduction of barbed wire and hedges, rail fences were practically the only ones used. They appeared on the earliest farms opened in the area and are common in the memory of older persons.

When the writer came to Southern Illinois University, then Southern Illinois Normal University, in 1908, the site where the University School stands was part of a cow pasture with a rail fence about it. The area now included in the athletic field, McAndrew Stadium, the physical plant building, and the portion of the University farm between the old state highway and the Illinois Central Railroad was crisscrossed with rail fences. Being a member of an early field class in ornithology that clambered over these old fences, the author retains a vivid memory of them. Since there was an equal division of boys and girls in this early class, there were girls to help across the fences, and this, naturally, is not difficult to remember.

It would be conservative to say that one-third of the farmland of southern Illinois was at some time encompassed by rail fences. Each square mile thus enclosed and divided into eighty-acre fields—which was quite a large farm tract at that time—would require eight miles of fencing. With other enclosures for pig pens, calf lots, barns and door yards, gardens, truck patches, cemeteries, and other special plots, it is likely that the area had at least 50,000 miles of rail fencing, enough to encircle the earth twice at the equator. It must also be remembered that rails decayed and were replaced.

If this amount of fence is converted into individual rails, about seven thousand to each mile of good fence, it will be seen that 350,000,000 rails would be needed. If these rails could have been preserved until today and divided among the people living in the area, every man, woman, boy, and girl would find himself the proud possessor of more than three hundred rails.

Without any intent to appear frivolous, it might prove interesting to make some comparisons and conversions. The effort required to produce these rails might be measured in man-days of work. A skilled and capable rail-maker would have to apply himself diligently to average 175 rails a day. Such a master rail-splitter working steadily at the task could produce the needed rails in two million days. If this rail-splitter took Sundays off and spent Saturday afternoon at the country village, thus working only only three hundred days each year, he could have completed the task in 6,667 years.

Some help might be given this lone rail-splitter and the time shortened accordingly. If sixty equally capable men had undertaken the task in 1783, when the region was acknowledged as ours and settlers in numbers began to come, the task indicated could have been completed in time for the group to have knocked off slightly over 110 years later and to have gone to the Chicago World's Fair in 1893.

Another unprescribed but popular use of fence rails was to cross-lay or corduroy miry spots of roadway. If the rail fences of southern Illinois had been converted to this use, they would have been ample to have solidly corduroyed more than 16,000 miles of roadways, surely enough to have lifted southern Illinois out of the mud.

If the timber used for rails were available and converted into lumber, there would be enough to build 125,000 five-room dwellings and to make clapboards for their roofs, which should be sufficient to relieve the region's housing shortage.

Though rail fences are gone, some of the expressions to which they gave rise continue. Politicians spend time and effort in "mending their fences" and strive to "leave no gaps down." They are accused of "straddling the fence" and invited to "get down off the fence." They try to "keep their fence rows clean," and not to get caught in the "crack of the fence." To many persons, "the grass is greener on the other side of the fence," but sometimes "over the fence is out." Some situations one would "not touch with a ten foot rail." These expressions as well as countless additional ones like "spite fence," "rail-splitter," "fenced in," "skinny as a rail," "long as a rail," "put the bars up," and "crooked as a fence worm" remain in use long after the picturesque features of our landscape to which they refer have disappeared.

❧ HEDGE FENCES

ALONG WITH THE disappearing rail fences went hedge fences that once were common on Illinois prairies. These were made of Osage orange which the early French called *bois d'arc* because they found Indians using it to fashion bows. Before barbed wire came to supplant them, the landscape of Illinois was crisscrossed by thousands of miles of hedges; here and there evidences of them remain as overgrown fence rows or as lone specimens grown to tree size.

Gone are the dense trimmed hedges that once were common. Such sections of these old fences as are still in service show thin places that have been patched with rails, planks, wire, or poles. Apparently, there are no more "pig-tight" hedge fences in use.

Fencing was a major task on early farms. Persons settling in the woodland found timber for rails convenient. As settlers advanced miles into the open prairies, the task of fencing became more difficult. If rails were used, it was necessary to haul them perhaps for miles by sled or wagon from the woodlands. When livestock was allowed to run at large, it was necessary to protect croplands by fencing them. Some farmers, not wishing to have their livestock on the open range, also fenced their pasture fields.

With rails increasingly difficult to procure, farmers sought other means of solving their fencing problem. Some built sod-trench fences. By this method, the sod was removed and piled in a narrow levee-like mound about the field. This mound was planted with grass and shrubs. Early use of this method was made in the English settlement about Albion. Others built a low fence of posts, rails, and pickets on the top of a low mound. Either of these fences was effective since the approaching animal would have its front feet in the ditch, a poor jumping position. Both types of fences required much labor. When smooth wire became available, some farmers made fences of it, but they generally were not satisfactory.

The idea of using hedge apparently came from Europe, perhaps from England, where hedges long had been used. Various shrubs and trees ranging from arborvitae to walnut were tried. The two proving most satisfactory were the buckthorn and, even better, Osage orange. Much of the experimental work that established the desirability of the Osage orange was done by Professor J. B. Turner, of Jacksonville, who often wrote and spoke on the subject. The *Prairie Farmer* also encouraged use of the Osage orange plant.

Though hedge fences first came into general use on the prairie, they were often planted on farms in cleared woodland areas. A few speciman trees on lands south of Southern Illinois University indicate where hedges once grew. A row of sturdy Osage orange trees grows near Half Moon Lick at Equality. A quantity of hedge flourished northeast of Eldorado sixty years ago. Even earlier, it pervaded much of Egypt.

Growing a hedge was not an easy task. This is shown by instructions given in various farm papers of a hundred and more years ago. Much of the seed used came from Texas. It was best if planted in the autumn in prepared seed beds, but seeding could be done in the spring. Seed were planted about an inch apart in rows a foot apart. In this way, a half-million plants could be grown on an acre. A half-section of land would thus produce enough plants to make a tight, double-row hedge around the world at the equator, with ample transplants left.

Year-old plants were set in a prepared strip where the fence was to be and cultivated for three years or more. They were spaced eight or ten inches apart. Better results were obtained where the setting was made in two rows a foot apart with plants set alternately a foot apart in each row.

One year after setting, the plants were slipped to a height of eighteen inches and were pruned one foot higher each year until the desired height was reached. The resulting fence was about "rabbit-tight." A few older persons will recall these formidable barriers.

On many farms new hedges are being planted. Now, however, they are multiflora roses. They evidently are not intended to confine livestock but more to serve as snow fences and game shelters, and to soften the landscape. Perhaps the boys still can go down the leeward side of these new fences after a drifting snow just as other boys went along the vanished hedges of Osage orange with the old muzzle loader to shoot the "setting rabbit" which had taken refuge in the hedge's shelter.

All this induces a certain nostalgia. Believe I'll take such a saunter if a drifting snow comes this winter, providing I can find the hedge, a muzzle loader, gunpowder, shot, high topped leather boots—and the energy.

🌿 *FARMER'S UNION*

IN SPEAKING ABOUT things around the farm, it would not be well to leave the subject without mentioning one of the major farm movements that had its beginning in southern Illinois. The Farmer's Union, said to be the first farm anti-trust organization formed in America, came into being at Grange Hall north of Murphysboro in 1900. This organization spread over many states of the Midwest and became an important factor in the farm movement. Yet its beginning was without fanfare.

At the spring election held at Grange Hall in April, 1900, a number of men were listening to J. M. Schroeder as he discussed with his neighbor the methods used by large organized businesses, generally termed trusts, in their dealings with farm folk. Farmers in general were resentful at the injustices, real and imaginary, that were practiced upon them. All agreed that something should be done, but what? W. D. Crews suggested that the way to fight a trust was with another trust and said that there should be a farmer's trust. This proposal appealed to those present.

A few nights later a group of interested farmers from Somerset, De Soto, Carbondale, and Murphysboro townships met at Brush Creek School west of De Soto. A. J. Cross was elected chairman of the group, and they settled down to business. Numerous ideas were advanced, but no definite plan was adopted. The chairman appointed W. D. Crews and Charles Piper to work out some criteria for a suitable organization and to report at the next meeting. These two men gathered information concerning farmers' organizations in other parts of the country, but found little of help.

Crews, using some of the adaptable ideas that he and Piper had gathered, proceeded to write an entirely new plan for the formation of the Farmer's Social and Economic Union. This plan was submitted and adopted at the second meeting of the group, and the first unit of a new farmer's organization came into existence. While it was legally established as "The Farmer's Social and Economic Union," it generally was known as "The Farmer's Union."

Officers of this first unit were A. J. Cross, president; E. B. Hunter, vice-president; Jacob Miller, secretary; James Piper, business agent; and W. D. Crews, organizer. Crews was empowered to appoint additional organizers whenever he thought it necessary. For his first helper, he chose Edward Deason. They established the second unit of the new organization at

Grange Hall where the election-day discussion that led to the launching of the movement had begun. Within a few weeks, six units had been organized in Jackson County and were combined into the first county organization.

Crews and his helpers then went to Williamson County, found the farmers there interested, and established the seventh unit of the new union at Goreville School. Others were formed in Williamson County and a second county organization was established. This process was repeated in other counties of southern Illinois.

These organized counties next formed a state association with headquarters at Brush Creek School. In a short time, the headquarters of the state organization was moved to Murphysboro, where E. B. Hunter, who had been elected state secretary of the union, lived. Unions were soon operating in Missouri and Indiana after the manner that had been followed in Illinois. These all were combined into a national organization with headquarters still in Murphysboro.

In 1902 the Farmer's Social and Economic Union began the publication of a paper known as *The Union Farmer*. This is designated by some authorities as the first farmers' union paper in America. W. D. Crews, editor and publisher, continued its publication in Murphysboro until 1914.

After the new organization had made progress in the three states named, Crews went to Nebraska and established the first unit in that state, about seventy-five miles northwest of Lincoln. He also trained others to do organization work there. Crews later visited other sections of the country where various farmers organizations were in existence to study their methods and to see if the efforts of all could not be better co-ordinated.

This Farmer's Social and Economic Union, began at Grange Hall in Jackson County, later was united with the Farmer's Education and Cooperative Union that had headquarters in Raines, Texas, through the efforts of Newt Gresham, of Marion. This combination greatly strengthened the whole Farmers' Union movement.

By 1930 the organization begun in Jackson County had been merged with other similar ones over America and its identity lost. However, the movement that was started at Brush Creek School in the spring of 1900 may justifiably be considered an important factor in the farmer movement of the United States.

Chapter 8

Early Schools

🌿 *RECTORVILLE SCHOOL*

THE EARLIEST RECORDS found for schools in southern Illinois are those for subscription schools. They were operated under contracts with parents who agreed to pay the teacher a stated amount for each pupil sent. One of these old contracts, found in Broughton, shows that in 1823 J. W. Dewees agreed to teach a subscription school in the vicinity of the now vanished village of Rectorville, in southeastern Hamilton County. So far as available records indicate, this was the first school in that vicinity. Fragmentary records and tradition indicate that this practice of conducting schools on a subscription basis continued for many years.

In 1838 a number of men living in that same section decided to organize a school district. They did so and built a log schoolhouse on the east side of the north-south roadway. The newer portion of the Gholson Cemetery, about a mile south and a half mile east of Broughton, now occupies the site of the school.

The house they erected served several generations of local youth. When it became inadequate, a new one was built about a mile to the northwest, where the village was growing up. The old building was sold to a local farmer who removed it a short distance to the southwest and used it as a residence. After many years of use in its second location, it was again sold and removed, this time to a place one-fourth mile north and one-fourth mile west of the place where State Highway No. 142 crosses the Hamilton-Saline county line. It remained there during the rest of its existence.

In its third location it continued to be used as a residence, being occupied in succession by a number of families. The last person to occupy it was Frank Dillsworth, who was living there in the 1930's. After Dillsworth's departure, it was used for the storage of baled hay, corn, and farm equipment until it was torn down in 1943.

Many older persons knew of the school and something of its history, but it was during a visit in the 1920's of a very old man who had been a pupil there during its earlier years that many details concerning it were learned. This visitor was a Mr. John Harkrider, past ninety years old, whose home was in Arkansas. He had returned to the vicinity of Broughton to visit relatives and friends and was at Gholson Cemetery on Decoration Day. While there, he pointed out the locations of the homes of several early settlers as well as other landmarks. Among objects he recognized was a large oak tree which marked the site of the schoolhouse built in 1838. He continued for some time to reminisce about the log school.

Another old man who knew something of the story of the school asked Mr. Harkrider if he would like to see it again. His delight in the thought of such an opportunity was evident. A group of persons accordingly drove the mile or so necessary to the old house, still in use as a residence. Once there, Mr. Harkrider spent considerable time in describing the interior of the building as it was during the days when he attended classes in it. He pointed to holes in the wall where pegs once were inserted to hold two writing desks, one for larger and one for smaller pupils. Attention also was called to two other holes beside the door for pegs that supported a smaller shelf for the wooden water bucket and its accompanying drinking gourd. Rows of holes in other logs were for pegs upon which the pupils might hang their wraps. Some of these had portions of the broken pegs still in them. The split log benches used as seats for the pupils as well as the larger one used for a recitation bench were no longer there, but he described them in detail.

Mr. Harkrider told of the teacher's desk and directed attention to the two holes in the wall above the place where it had stood. It was upon pegs stuck in these holes that the pointers and switches inseparably connected with pioneer schools once rested within the teacher's easy reach. Mr. Harkrider stated that the windows, even then small, were larger than they originally had been. Careful inspection revealed that each of the two windows had been lengthened about fifteen inches at the bottom.

It was apparent that nearly all the timbers in the building were the original ones. Many, like some of the roof rafters, had been split out and others showed by marks upon them that they had been sawed by an up-and-down saw, like the one used at a near-by water mill that began to operate in the same year that the school was built. The visit of Mr. Harkrider was a rare occasion for those fortunate enough to be present.

Many persons knowing the old house and its history naturally regretted to see its passing after 105 years. Before it was torn down, however, photographs were taken and careful measurements were made. Using this data and the information given by Mr. Harkrider, by Mr. Will Owen who lived near-by, and by the writer's father, who attended school there for a short time, a faithful scale model of the original building and its fittings was constructed.

✤ OTHER KINDS OF TEACHERS

THE TEACHERS OF EARLY subscription schools often were wanderers who came into a community, organized a school, taught the three R's for the term, then passed on. There also were those who went about teaching some special skill, like penmanship or singing.

This particular type of the wandering pedagogue apparently began with Platt Roger Spencer, a country boy who attended a log school at Conneaut, Ohio. Young Spencer, at the age of fourteen, became intensely interested in penmanship and began to teach a fancy style of writing to other pupils in the school he attended. Successful in this, Spencer began to wander over the state of Ohio, gathering interested groups in homes and schools and teaching them to write the flowing style of penmanship that became known as "Spencerian."

Many of those he taught also became itinerant teachers of the "Spencerian method" of penmanship. Spencer became a teacher of penmanship in a college and, in 1848, published copybooks for use in schools. Dog-eared copies of these books are occasionally found among discarded papers in old trunks or attics. Long after his death in 1864 the influence of Spencer continued to affect the handwriting of America. This was before the days when vertical, Palmer, or manuscript writing came into vogue.

This area of Illinois had its apostles of Spencer who went about peddling penmanship. One of these men would come into a community and secure a number of subscribers to a writing school. Classes were generally held at night in the local schoolhouse. Each pupil provided his own equipment, consisting of a light—often a candle or taper set in a turnip— some paper, oak-gall ink, and writing quills. Girls as well as boys attended these schools, which thus served a double purpose, educational and social.

The scrolls, flourishes, and shaded curves executed as exercises were impressive, particularly to an awkward youth. A glowing border done in colored crayon high on the walls of a country school by Mel Clark remains a vivid memory even though it was covered by plaster more than fifty years ago. Clark was a skilled penman, and his fresco, made up of proverbs, sayings, and interesting bits of information, was in the best Spencerian style.

Perhaps the most widely known of these earlier teachers of writing in southern Illinois was a man named Pickett, who went about for many years teaching Spencerian penmanship in writing schools. At that time no one could be more highly complimented than to have it said of him: "He can do the curves as well as Pickett." Occasional specimens of the exercises used in Pickett's schools showing scrolls, birds, intricate patterns of freehand flourishes, and delicately shaded curves are found among school books laid away fifty years or more ago. When judged by its flourishes and sweeps, the penmanship is interesting, but the misspelled words glare just as badly as they do in the penmanship of today.

In addition to the writing master, there were other purveyors of education and culture. Among these were the men who taught singing schools. The singing master's method of starting a school was much like that used by the writing master—a subscription plan. He needed and carried about with him little equipment.

The essentials for a singing school were a man with a reasonably resonant voice, a tuning fork, and a cloth chart with musical staffs on which he placed the musical characters needed as his course progressed. He often carried enough song books to meet the needs of his class. In later years, a reed organ might be available if a competent helper could be had to play it.

The method of teaching in these schools seems to have been rather stereotyped. The charts of staffs with notes spaced upon them were displayed. The tuning fork was struck, the tone sounded by the teacher and echoed by the class. With the instructor leading, the group did a reasonable amount of singing up and down the scale, even skipping about somewhat at the behest of a pointer wielded by the master. This pointer was also used to beat out time.

It was at this skipping about point that, musically speaking, the separation of the singers and nonsingers began. The time element was introduced, explained, and demonstrated, with variously valued notes and rests. Recalling these classes to memory, it now seems apparent that little or no attention was given to diminuendos or crescendos; everyone generally sang at the top of his voice. A person without ample sound was just naturally a poor singer.

At about this stage in the progress of the school, the teacher further complicated matters by taking up sharps and flats. Many of those who had not formed social attachments that transcended the purely musical considerations of the school dropped out of class. Those with some musical aptitude stayed on and did surprisingly well. Many good church choirs resulted from these singing schools.

One of the last of this group of music masters was Uncle Bill Holloway, who lived south of Eddyville, in Pope County. Even when past ninety years old, Uncle Bill still kept the chart, pointer, tuning fork, and song books he had used for a lifetime.

🌳 *ILLINOIS' FIRST ACADEMY*

ONE SUMMER DAY IN 1825 the Reverend John Milcott Ellis, an educational missionary sent out by Old South Church in Boston, was riding along the roadway between Lebanon and O'Fallon, in St. Clair County. A church in Boston had given him the task of establishing "an institute of learning that shall bless the West."

A few miles beyond Lebanon he came upon a workman shaping timbers for a building that evidently was not to be a dwelling or barn. After an exchange of salutations, Ellis asked, "What are you doing here, stranger?" The workman replied, "I am building a theological seminary." And that was exactly what he was doing.

This workman that Ellis had found also was a minister, the Reverend John Mason Peck. Peck likewise had come from the East as a missionary. His principal objective was, like that of Ellis, to advance the cause of education in the newly settled region.

After five years of somewhat successful work in Missouri, Peck moved to Illinois in the early part of 1822. Here he bought a half-section of land and established a farm at a place known as Rock Spring. The proceeds from his farming operations, plus the five dollars a week sent him by a missionary society in the East and occasional donations from churches where he served as pastor, enabled Peck to devote much of his time to the promotion of better schools.

The two men who had thus met by chance soon found that they had much in common. Each was a minister sent to the region by eastern missionary groups. Each had been instructed to make an earnest effort to advance the cause of education. Each was a capable, high-minded, unselfish, and devoted man.

The school that Peck founded beside the roadway where Ellis had found him became Rock Spring Seminary, the first institution of higher learning established in Illinois. A few years later the academy Peck had begun was moved to Alton and named Alton College. Later the name was

changed again and it became Shurtleff College. The educational efforts
of Ellis resulted, a year or so later, in the establishment of Illinois College
at Jacksonville.

The Methodist Church observed the work of these two men and decided
to establish a third institution for advanced learning in Illinois. They felt
the need of such a school to train men for their ministry. This third
school was located at Lebanon, not far from the place where Peck had
established Rock Spring Seminary. The Methodist school founded, now
well into its second century of service, survives as McKendree College.

Information concerning Rock Spring Seminary appears in the *Quarterly
Register* of the Educational Society for November, 1830. It indicates that
there were two departments of the school. One was much like the traditional New England academies or our present high schools. The other
division was a seminary for the training of those preparing for the
ministry.

Except for brief intervals, Peck continued to live at Rock Spring until
his death in 1858. During his thirty-six years in the state, he remained a
powerful influence in many fields and numbered among his close friends
practically all the great men of Illinois.

Peck was an ardent and devoted churchman, an eminent historian, an
author of note, an active and influential opponent of duelling and
polygamy, an inspiring teacher and minister, a temperance leader, a newspaper editor and publisher, a champion of education for Negroes and
Indians, secretary and general agent of the American Baptist Publication
Society, one of the founders of the Illinois State Lyceum, a forceful and
convincing speaker, and an advocate of a process of examinations for immigrants before their admission to the country.

He strongly opposed slavery and was among those most active against
it in the election of 1824, when an effort was made to have Illinois become a slave state. Peck was instrumental in the formation of committees
to campaign against slavery in practically all counties of the state. Few did
as much as he to defeat the proposition. Though bitterly antislavery, Peck
urged observance of the Fugitive Slave Law and urged the formation of
foreign colonies to which Negroes might be sent.

In 1829 Peck assumed editorship of a newspaper published at Rock
Spring, the eighth one in the state. He became its owner and publisher in
the fall of that year. Shortly thereafter, it was converted into a church
paper, perhaps the first one published in Illinois.

Peck also wrote and published extensively outside the realms of his
newspaper operations. In 1831 he published a *Guide for Immigrants* that
was reprinted in 1836 and again in 1837. The wealth and accuracy of

information in these books is amazing, and they still are consulted by those studying conditions at that time.

His *Gazetteer of Illinois,* published in 1834 and republished in 1837, was likewise a valuable book. The two books doubtless did as much as any others published to bring settlers to Illinois before 1860.

In 1835, working with John Messinger, another prominent early Illinoisan, Peck published an accurate sectional map of Illinois that embodied many new and valuable features. In 1847 he turned out a biography of Daniel Boone, who had been a regular attendant at the Missouri church where Peck was pastor. *Annals of the West,* written by James H. Perkins, was edited by him, revised, and published in 1850. In addition to these works, Peck wrote many articles, kept a most extensive journal, carried on wide correspondence, and collected an immense amount of historical materials. His collection, including notes, relating to the Midwest, was recognized as being one of the best ever gathered, but unfortunately it was destroyed by fire.

Peck died at Rock Spring in 1858 and, in accordance with his request, was buried there. Twenty-nine days later, for some strange reason, his body was exhumed and taken to a cemetery in St. Louis where another funeral service was held and the body reinterred.

Rock Spring Seminary, Alton College, Shurtleff College, and John Mason Peck surely left their indelible imprint upon the region.

❦ *SHILOH COLLEGE*

NEW YEAR'S RESOLUTIONS often result in something well worth while. This was the case when a group of men met at the home of John B. Burke, near the present-day village of Shiloh Hill, in Randolph County, on January 1, 1836. They met for the "purpose of drawing up Articles of agreement" for the building of a school and meeting house. Thirty-eight men signed the document and pledged a total of $123. With hardly an omission, these pledges were paid in full and several were overpaid. While some of the men pledged cash, others pledged their labor at the rate of fifty cents a day. The services of those furnishing teams and wagons were figured to be a dollar a day.

Little time was wasted in putting the plan the men had formed into operation. Work on the building was begun on January 19, 1836, and Benjamin Culley began a nine-month term of school in the new building on April 4 of that year. There were twenty-eight pupils for this first session.

The school movement in the community progressed rapidly. On April 30, 1836, the citizens of the vicinity met and signed a petition asking the Randolph County authorities to create a public school district to be known as Shiloh School District.

On May 28, the district trustees met to let a contract for the digging of a well. John Barrow, one of the trustees, cried the sale. There were no bidders, so the board of trustees decided to do the work themselves. Barrow and James Gillespie, another trustee, seem to have done the actual digging and were credited with contributing sixty-two and one half cents a day to the project by their labor. Others helping with the well received fifty cents a day in cash or credited to their pledge.

The trustees met again on June 17, 1836, "to examine the school and scholars as the law directs." After the inspection had been made, it was "proposed that they spell a heart lesson and dismiss." It was also agreed at this meeting that only the teacher should correct a pupil. It was "motioned that we record the progress of the children as to be good and that the teacher has given general satisfaction."

The old record books tell of other inspections by the board of trustees, when prizes were offered pupils for their accomplishments, free textbooks were provided, land was bought for the school, and teachers were employed.

On November 23, 1839, a group of men met and petitioned the legislature to incorporate an institution to be known as Shiloh College. On January 8, 1840, the charter was granted by the state legislature and signed by Governor William L. D. Ewing.

The first building they erected was of logs and stood until 1933. In later years it was used as a store and at last as a barn. The present stone and brick structure was built by Brinkman and Brotter, who used bricks burned at the site. It was completed in 1881 at a cost of about $7,000.

The old building among large trees on a hill at the edge of the village is rather impressive. Viewing it, one feels a high regard for the settlers who so loyally supported the movement for better schools.

🏵 ONE HUNDRED YEARS AS A COLLEGE TOWN

ON MAY 1, 1957, Carbondale had been host to a college for a full century. The town was young when it took on the role, having been platted and its first dwelling erected in late 1852. In 1856 it was incorporated as a village. One year later, only five years after arrival of its first settler, Carbondale welcomed a college.

On May 26, 1856, a committee from the Alton Presbytery, appointed at its recent meeting at Decatur, had come to Carbondale seeking "a site to establish a seminary of learning of a high literary character in southern Illinois." They met with a group of interested citizens at the West Side School, then standing about where the gymnasium of Brush School is now.

This committee apparently was impressed by the new town and by the advantages it offered. They noted the fact that the founders had set aside certain town lots that would be given to groups wishing to erect church buildings and also that a nice frame schoolhouse had been built by popular subscription. They found that a provision in the deed to each town lot forbade the sale of alcoholic beverages on the premises. The visiting committees took note of these and other advantages the location offered.

After careful consideration, they decided that Carbondale was the best site available for their "seminary of learning." A subscription form accordingly was circulated locally and pledges amounting to $1,045 in cash, seven town lots, and 494 acres of land were made.

Three weeks later another meeting was held and fifteen trustees were selected. Eight of these were present at the time and held their first business session that day. They named a committee composed of the Reverend W. J. Post, J. M. Campbell, and D. H. Brush to supervise the erection of a suitable building on a thirty-acre tract donated by Henry Sanders where Lincoln Junior High School now stands. The name they selected was Carbondale College.

It was decided to open the college even before a building was completed. Accordingly, at a meeting of the board of trustees held on October 27, 1856, it was requested that J. M. Campbell finish the third floor of his store building for "academic purposes"; work there was completed on April 6. The first term of Carbondale College began the first day of the following month with the Reverend W. J. Post as principal and William Sheriff as teacher. Except for a short time during the Civil War and another in the late 1860's, Carbondale has remained a college town since that day.

With the school in operation, plans proceeded for the erection of suitable permanent buildings. The architectural services of a Mr. McClure were engaged. Thomas Thornton contracted to burn "400,000 merchantable brick" on the grounds for $4.50 a thousand. Despite coaxing, money advanced, and "possibly threats," Thornton fell sadly behind in performance and was released from his contract.

Shortly afterwards, Ezra and Isaac Burdick contracted to build the foundations of "a chapel and culinary department" at a cost of three dollars a square yard, plus extra for dressed or brushed stone. They were to be paid with college bonds drawing 10 per cent interest and due in one year. They also were to take over the work of making and burning the necessary bricks.

Money was scarce and progress was slow. Nevertheless, a contract was made for the erection of the walls "all lime, sand, labor and necessary equipment being furnished for $4.50 a thousand bricks laid." The Burdicks were later released from their contract. J. M. Campbell and D. H. Brush then took over and completed the building; they had it ready to turn over to the trustees on September 30, 1861.

The coming of the Civil War and the disruptions that resulted brought many difficulties to the college. Money necessary for the operation of the fledgling school was not available. Men interested in the project were entering the military services. Creditors began to press their claims in court until a judgment was secured and the property ordered sold to pay debts. After this was done, there remained an unpaid balance of $2,561. Apparently without any legal obligation to do so, Campbell and Brush paid this amount in full. After little or no use, the building was abandoned to become the gathering place of tramps and prowlers.

On September 8, 1866, the college property was sold to the regional conference of the Christian Church that already had been granted a charter to establish a college at De Soto, six miles north of Carbondale.

The name was changed to Southern Illinois College. The Reverend Clark Braden, of Centralia, was selected as principal, and his wife became preceptress. Reverend Braden announced the opening of the college for October 6, 1866. On that day, five students were present. They were Butler Hall, Ben Johnson, Hayes Mulkey, Mollie Yost, and Robert Yost. The disrepair of the building was so great that Braden and his students decided to delay the opening for one week and to give their time to making very necessary improvements and in giving the building a general cleaning.

After a week of renovation, it was found that eight additional students had come. Not to be deterred by superstition, the first term of the college was opened on October 13 with thirteen enrolled. Additional students continued to arrive, and before the end of the term, their number had reached fifty-four. During the winter term, it reached seventy-five and, in the spring term of 1867, it was more than a hundred. During the first year, 142 individuals had enrolled—eighty-eight men and fifty-four women.

During the second year,1867–68, a total of 315 individuals were in attendance. Detailed enrollments for the next year have not been found.

It is known, however, that 250 were reported during the spring term of 1869. This would indicate an enrollment of about 370 individuals during the year. It was not an insignificant school.

Students engaged in varied activities. There were at least four literary societies. Volume One, Number One of a school paper, *The Young Ladies' Friend,* appeared in November, 1867. Another one, *The Egyptian Marvel* began publication January, 1868.

An old handbill announced that there would be "Splendid entertainment at Southern Illinois College, under the auspices of the Matheson, Egyptian and Adelphian Societies, at the College Building on Thursday and Friday evenings, June 30 and July 1, 1870. Doors open at 7 o'clock— performance begins precisely at 8 o'clock. Admittance 25 cents. Private boxes and opera glasses for rent." Dramatis personae, scenery, etc., are described. It must have been a gala evening.

In the late 1860's, the establishment of Southern Illinois Normal University became assured. Since the "Normal" was to be located in Carbondale, support for Southern Illinois College dwindled, and it did not operate after 1870. It was thirty years or more, however, before the enrollment of the state school equaled that of the older college at its peak.

After the Christian church ceased to operate the school, the buildings and grounds were sold to the city of Carbondale for about $15,000 and were included in the city's bonus given to secure the location of the state school. Later the grounds and building were repurchased by the city and used for high school purposes. It was generally referred to as the "College" until about 1906, when it became Lincoln School.

🍃 CHANGES AT SOUTHERN

A BIT OF BROWSING in an old diary, plus tramps across Southern's campus, remind the writer that many changes have come to this school since that day in late March of 1908 when he first became a student here. Fresh from a term as teacher of a country school, he was admitted and classified as "Normal," whatever that may have meant. It was an impressive day.

Now, fifty-five years later, he is again impressed. This time, however, it is by the many and varied changes evident. Enrollment, for instance, has increased somewhat since April 8, 1908, when President Parkinson made an announcement that found its way into the writer's diary.

The faculty and student body had met in the regular daily assembly and chapel services on the third floor of Old Main. Attendance had been checked to see that each was in his assigned seat. A song had been sung, Scriptures read, prayer had been made, and announcements were in order.

At this point, President Parkinson stated with evident pride that the enrollment as of that day stood at 328. He then added in a somewhat subdued voice, "including those in high school." It was not necessary to announce the number of the faculty. One only had to count the nineteen seated in an orderly row on the stage and add the three necessarily absent to help student teachers ride herd on the grade school pupils in the "practice school."

Now, 1963, the on-campus enrollment at Carbondale, "not including those in high school," soon will be four hundred times that of the record enrollment in April, 1908. At that time, nearly every student knew each faculty member and some members of the faculty knew all the students. The general atmosphere was family-like. With the present enrollment, naturally, acquaintance cannot be so all-inclusive.

Also, the campus has expanded since then. University School stands on ground that was at that time a cow pasture, enclosed with rail fences, to which some faculty members brought their cows to pasture, returning to drive or lead them home at milking time.

Another farm, much criss-crossed with rail fences, lay just south of a few houses that faced north on Harwood Street. This land later became the "state farm." The University power plant and shops now stand on part of it. It was across this farm that the writer, as a member of the first field class in ornithology, was privileged to wander. This class of four boys and four girls was admonished not to trample the patches of rhubarb, strawberries, asparagus, and other truck crops growing there.

A few houses and barns stood along the roadway leading east toward Snyder Cemetery. A high and narrow foot bridge across Piles' Fork enabled pedestrians to cross at flood times. The writer knows about this, for he lived across the branch, where he paid $2.75 a week for a room and board. The Dowdell farm was a good one with one nice harness horse and a wonderful Jersey cow that served as the laboratory specimen in dairy-cow judging. Portions of the present campus lying south and west of the original twenty acres were looked upon as hinterlands. The Normal indeed had a rural setting.

Changes also have come in the curriculum, better to say curricula. There were then no numbered courses. A few were designated "High School." On the "Normal" level, pedagogy began with "E," geography with "C" and algebra with "D." "B," arithmetic, was considered a difficult course. Class periods were forty-five minutes long. Since it was not necessary to rush long distances between buildings, classes were in session forty minutes and the shift was made in five. Teachers asked many questions, students stood to recite, and there was little lecturing.

As the end of the academic year neared, class spirits and rivalries, even then, began to appear. Class numbers were painted and pennants were flown, sometimes in queer places. A class pennant atop the rod at the pinnacle of Old Main was outstanding. Perhaps President Parkinson unknowingly aided and abetted.

At intervals it was the custom to take groups of students to the tower in order that they might see "all the way to Carterville." One bright day about mid-May of 1908, the President conducted such a tour. Some in the group must have come along to "case the joint." Anyway, three or four days later, a class pennant attached to a cane fishing pole appeared wired securely to the portion of the rod extending above the directional letters at its base. The lad who placed it there incidentally was among those who had gone aloft with the president's tour to have a "wonderful view." Perhaps the fact that the pennant-placer lived out his allotted three score years and ten should be credited to an equally daring chap who went to the star's rescue when muscular cramps froze the hero on the pinnacle; the rescuer, using ropes, lowered the amateur steeple jack.

Girls taking physical education dressed primly, if that term properly designates a costume made up of a greatly oversized blouse, voluminous bloomers and long stockings, all in deepest black. Their figures were completely draped. One daring young lady was observed on a hot summer day, trailing well in the rear of the teacher, and out of that person's line of observation—with bloomers pulled just above and stockings rolled just below attractive knees. The teacher must have seen, for the next day, the student was, like others of the class, completely draped.

Research intended to reveal the habits, attitudes, and beliefs of students had begun even then, and questionnaires were circulated. Only one question, somewhat personal and impertinent, is recalled. It was: "Do you bathe regularly each week?" (Yes, the school had showers for P.E. students.) Physical tests and measurements also were coming into vogue. Again, only one score—290 cubic inches of expired air—is recalled.

One meeting for "men only" was held in a classroom. It proved somewhat disappointing, for the president talked only about points of etiquette and good manners. Yet, this meeting might have been helpful for two young chaps who began tipping their hats the very next day. Later their comparison of notes revealed that each had made his initial doff to the same library helper, a redhead.

It would be fun to live another fifty years and see what other changes are in store.

❧ A FEMALE SEMINARY

MARKERS TO INDICATE the location of historic sites and to suggest something of their stories often are to be seen beside Illinois highways. One such marker is at the village of Old Du Quoin, in Perry County.

It marks the site where Du Quoin Female Seminary once stood. This seminary, according to a statement in the catalogue of 1866, was the first institution of higher learning for females which was successfully established by a Protestant group in the section of the state generally known as Egypt.

People living in the vicinity of the old village about 1850 had difficulty in obtaining a trained and competent teacher. They accordingly asked an educational society in the East to help. It was the custom for these groups to send out teachers somewhat as educational missionaries, even paying part of their expenses. In response to the request of the local citizens, a well qualified and competent young lady named Eliza Paine was sent from Massachusetts. She arrived in time to begin a school term at the district school in the summer of 1852.

Miss Paine's achievements must have provided encouragement to those interested in education. Anyway, a group of seventy-two persons met in August, 1853, signed "Articles of Compact," and pledged $1,134, then considered a substantial amount, toward the establishment of a female seminary. Those signing the articles met again soon and elected a board of directors consisting of eighteen members.

On November 18, 1854, this board of directors selected Miss Paine, who had been conducting a private school after her first year in the vicinity, to serve as principal of the new school. On February 28, 1855, the Du Quoin Female Seminary, under supervision of the Presbyterian church, was chartered by the state legislature. On the following April 28, the board bought six acres of land on the low hill southeast of the marker, paying $600 for it. On June 16, the cornerstone of a new building was laid.

Shortly afterwards, Miss Paine, who had been appointed agent of the board, departed for the East to carry "this enterprise directly to the hearts of the Christians there." The results of her trip must have been pleasing since she returned with cash and pledges totaling more than three thousand dollars. Her trip also resulted in the later purchase of an additional six acres of ground and its donation to the school by W. S. Gilman, of New York. Contributions continued to come from the region where Miss Paine had worked until they totaled fourteen thousand dollars.

After Miss Paine's return, the work of building was taken up with vigor. The outlook for the new educational venture appeared rosy. The financial depression of 1857, however, changed the situation. Payment on pledges decreased, creditors began to press for settlement of accounts, and it became necessary to discontinue the work. In 1859, the property of the school was assigned for the benefit of the creditors. Apparently the project was doomed to early failure.

The financial affairs of the school soon took a better turn. Some of the creditors agreed to scale down their claims. Mrs. P. C. Morrison, of Collinsville, completed the rescue. She made a gift of one thousand dollars to the school and loaned it another thousand that later became a gift. She also gave a special gift of five hundred dollars. The board of directors was thereby enabled to satisfy all claims and to make the school debt-free. Other contributions continued to be received until a total of thirty-four thousand dollars had been received before the end of 1866. This enabled the board to complete the central section of their projected building, and again the future of the seminary appeared hopeful.

Some of the early rules and practices of the school are interesting. Pupils might enter at any time if they were capable of taking up the work of established classes. It was desirable, however, that they enter at the beginning of the school year or after the winter vacation. Regular examinations were conducted in each class at the end of the term. At the end of the year a general examination was held, and the public was invited to be present and to question the pupils if they wished.

Each student was required to attend at least one religious service on the Sabbath and all were required to attend the religious services regularly held in the school. No social calls were to be made or received on Sundays, and the usual walks were not to be taken. Pupils were not to arrive at or leave the school on Sundays except for an emergency.

It had "ever been the object of the Institution to place the expenses at the lowest possible point." This is clearly indicated by the following schedule of fees for each ten-week term.

Preparatory Department	$4.00
Higher Department	6.00
Use of Piano	2.00
Incidental expenses	.50
Board per week	3.00
Fuel furnished in room	.50

Special lessons in drawing, painting, and language required extra fees. Rooms were furnished with bedstead, tables, chairs, and stoves. The girls were asked to provide their own bedding. Where this could not be conveniently done, the need would be "supplied at a slight charge." Though it was founded as a Female Seminary, its doors soon were opened to admit men students.

After more than fifty years of service, the school closed about 1910. Six former pupils were in attendance at the dedication of the marker in 1954.

THE COLLEGE AT CREAL SPRINGS

BEFORE THE DAYS of high schools, youngsters who had been fortunate enough to complete the work of the common schools, sometimes went on to attend academies, or they might even go to a "college" with an academic department. One such school that flourished for a time was at Creal Springs, south and east of Marion, in Williamson County.

It was to this town, already widely known as a health resort, that Henry Clay Murrah and his wife, Grace Brown Murrah, moved shortly after their marriage in 1880. Both had received college training and had been teachers. It was natural, therefore, that they should remain interested in education and that they decided to establish a girls' school under Mrs. Murrah's direction.

Grace Brown Murrah was born near the village of Bainbridge, once the county seat of Williamson County, about four miles west of Marion. She attended the Brownsville country school there, and later went to Southern Illinois College at Carbondale, to the State Institute at Flora, and to Ewing College. She also attended the collegiate department of Mount Carrol Seminary at Mt. Carrol, Illinois, from which she was graduated in 1875. After attending these schools, she taught in country schools, in the high school at Frankfort, and in Ewing College before beginning her thirty-two years of service at the school she was also instrumental in establishing at Creal Springs.

The story of this college and of Mrs. Murrah's part in it is well outlined in *Horse and Buggy Days,* a booklet published by her son, Charles M. Murrah, in 1937. From it we learn that in March, 1884, they acquired title to a five-acre tract of land in the village "to be used for school purposes." The construction of the main building—a basement and three stories plus attic structure—was begun immediately. It was completed and ready for use on September 22, 1884, when the first term began.

The school had been planned as one for girls. On the first morning, however, as many boys as girls appeared—three of each. It was therefore decided to make it coeducational. Students continued to arrive throughout the term, and before the end of the first twelve weeks, fifty-nine students had been enrolled. Twelve of these were on the collegiate level, whatever that may have meant. Thirty-one were in the preparatory department, seven in the primary, and nine were special students of music.

The first faculty of the Creal Springs Academy consisted of six members. H. C. Murrah, who also did some teaching, was listed as proprietor, and Grace B. Murrah as principal, the office she continued to occupy until the school closed in 1916. The name of Creal Springs Academy was continued until 1894, when it was changed to Creal Springs College and Conservatory of Music. By this time the number on the faculty had grown to fifteen and the student enrollment to almost one hundred. Baccalaureate degrees were granted in the "Classical," "Latin-Scientific" and "Philosophical" fields. An additional year of study lead to a master's degree.

The curriculum offered was varied. It was boasted that the college offered a strong course in history, including three years of general history preceded by one year of American history. T. O. Hawkins taught "muscular penmanship" that would eliminate the "cramped and tiresome finger movements." In addition to the common branches of learning, the school offered Latin, Greek, German, French, analytical geometry, calculus, typewriting, elocution, shorthand, physical culture, pedagogical studies, music, and art. It had grown into a well recognized school.

The beauty of the region as one in which an artist might work was emphasized, and it was said, "Any girl can, by putting in her spare moments, decorate the walls of her home with paintings made by her own brush." Music courses "followed the methods of the conservatory of Music in Brussels, Belgium."

A department of theology was maintained. In order to be admitted, an applicant was required to furnish a "certificate to his character" from the church where he held membership. He must also have received a "call to gospel ministry" and must demonstrate "intellectual fitness." This course extended over three years during which time the student might pastor churches if it did not interfere with his studies.

There were literary societies, school papers, varied social activities, and above all the annual commencement and reunion. Programs of commencement exercises, at which the Erica Society performed, list a wide range of offerings. Among them are declamations, orations, original poems, vocal solos, duos, trios, and quartettes, piano solos and duets, recitations, and a harp duet. Commencement week was a truly great one.

With passing years, financial problems beset the school; they finally reached such proportions that the institution was forced to close. The last students departed on Christmas Eve, 1916, and the doors of the strange looking three-story frame building were locked, never to open again for school use. Mr. and Mrs. Murrah moved into a near-by cottage. Mrs.

Murrah lived until 1929, never ceasing her efforts to reopen the school to which she had given so many years of unselfish service. The building stood until 1943 when it was dismantled. No memorial remains to mark the site of the Creal Springs College and Conservatory of Music. A few who were students there when the college closed on that Christmas Eve of 1916 remain to talk, almost in reverence, about the school.

🌼 *HAYWARD COLLEGE*

SEVERAL COLLEGES have had their day in southern Illinois and now are only memories. One of these was Hayward Collegiate Institute at Fairfield.

During the period of its existence more than 2,000 individuals were enrolled. In October, 1956, twenty-three of these former students held a reunion in the gymnasium of the Community High School which now stands on the grounds of the old college. It was their first formal meeting since the college building burned on the morning of November 1, 1889.

These former classmates came to renew acquaintances, some of which were made sixty-seven years earlier. They also came to unveil a bronze tablet to indicate the location of the one-time college. Some had traveled considerable distances to be present. One came from as far away as New York State.

A number of these former students went out to attain more than local prominence. One, the captain of the school's long-ago football team, had served twenty-five years as dean of the College of Commerce at the University of Illinois before his retirement several years ago. Some became ministers, attorneys, physicians, and teachers. A number of those returning were housewives, proud of their families.

The marker they unveiled stands near the main entrance to the high school grounds and bears the following legend:

SITE OF HAYWARD COLLEGIATE INSTITUTE CHARTERED 1885.
FINANCED BY SUBSCRIPTION, THE LARGEST BY ROBERT HAYWARD,
1826–1908, FOR WHOM IT WAS NAMED. THE FOUNDERS STATED
IT THE INTENTION TO MAKE IT THE BEST, MOST INEXPENSIVE
AND WIDELY INFLUENTIAL SCHOOL IN THE LAND, ABOUT 2000
STUDENTS ATTENDED BEFORE THE BUILDING BURNED IN 1898

ERECTED BY
WAYNE COUNTY HISTORICAL SOCIETY 1955

The original cornerstone of the college building is set in the lower right side of the memorial as one approaches it. This stone was rescued from the foundation of a barn where it had been for more than fifty years. On the stone's exposed face, it reads: ''HAYWARD COLLEGIATE INSTITUTE,'' and on the exposed end it says "ERECTED A.D. 1886."

Robert Hayward, whose generosity sparked the college's founding, was born in Dorsetshire, England, in 1826, and came with his parents to settle on a farm in Marion County, Ohio, where he grew up. When the Civil War began, he joined the Union Army. After the war, he returned to give undivided attention to farming, at which he was highly successful. In 1880, he moved to a farm near Fairfield.

Hayward, who had been much impressed by the college at Marietta, Ohio, near which he had lived but which he had not been privileged to attend, stated about the end of 1884 that he would give his five-thousand-dollar farm at Fairfield toward the founding of an educational institution. When citizens of the town learned of this, they started a movement to obtain the required additional funds and raised six thousand dollars more. A charter was obtained from the state legislature on May 4, 1885.

With the accumulated $11,000, one building of ten rooms with a chapel, some recitation rooms, and offices was built during the summer of 1886. The first eight-weeks term began September 1 of that year with fifty-one students in attendance. Before the end of the term, the enrollment had reached one hundred, and before the year's end it was 250, representing six states. A student could enter at any time and could begin work on whatever level his attainments would permit—a somewhat strange arrangement, as presently viewed.

The vow of the founders that it should be an inexpensive school was evidently fulfilled. Tuition was set at eight dollars a term. Some courses in music or art required additional fees. Ten lessons in oil painting could be had for ten dollars, and lessons in embroidery were fifty cents each. Those taking lessons on the piano or organ also were called upon to pay added tuition. They could practice one hour each day on their chosen instrument at a cost of two dollars a term.

Prospective students were advised to bring any available textbooks with them because they "might find them helpful." It was not absolutely necessary to bring texts, however, since they could be rented for twenty cents a term. Some of the courses listed in the school's catalogues arouse a bit of curiosity. Just what is meant, for instance, by "Automatic Lettering," "Kensington Painting" or "Decoration of Wares" is not known.

Eighty-five per cent of the boys attending took military training. These boys were asked to wear Middlesex blue uniforms and were advised to delay the purchase of such suits until they came to Fairfield, where the proper blue suit could be bought at a cost of from seven to ten dollars. Though the school was owned and supervised by the local Methodist church, records specifically state that it was not "narrow." Effort and merit, "not wealth nor dress nor high connection," determined the standing of the students.

There were literary societies, debating clubs, a Y.M.C.A., a school paper, and a rousing football team whose exploits still are recounted by very old persons. Dancing was banned, but this loss does not appear to have been so depressing. In its stead they had the "walkaround," where the band played and romantic couples could stroll about, hand in hand, or arm in arm, over a prescribed course. The tendency to play pranks, even then, is revealed by the story related by a former student in which she tells of helping to put an organ in the attic on Hallowe'en.

THE COLLEGE IN THE HILLS

SOME SOUTHERN ILLINOIS schools and colleges had very brief existences. One of these was the College of the Hills which ended in failure twenty years ago—or did it? The venture was highly idealistic, and the success of such an enterprise often is difficult to measure. Anyway, this school was a pioneer one—despite its recency.

It was in 1933, in the depths of the depression years, that a small group of people, most of them graduates of Chicago and Northwestern universities, began plans for the College in the Hills. This college would make available to the youth of the area a liberal education—one that they, poor as they were, could afford.

One may wonder why southern Illinois was chosen as the location. There were several reasons. It was the belief of the founders that conditions in the region afforded excellent opportunities for further study of social problems and for the application of the basic principles of sociology.

Conditions in the Hardin County section of southern Illinois were deplorable. Aside from a somewhat primitive sub-subsistence type of farming, fluorspar mining was the principal industry of the region. Unemployment among the miners was high. Many mines had closed, never to reopen. Others were operating at 25 per cent of capacity or less. The population was, even by standards of that time, desperately poor. More than one-fourth of the people were dependent solely upon emergency relief. Numerous families were living on twenty-five dollars or less per month, which afforded only a starvation existence at best. Malnutrition,

Legends & Lore of Southern Illinois

A *few well-preserved landmarks among
the ruins of what were once thriving
towns and enterprises, the re-enactment
of past events and an occasional map—
these form a part of the pictorial record
of southern Illinois' historical and
legendary past. The scenes depicted in
the pages that follow represent what
the visitor to these places will see today.*

*This lonely spot near Grand
Tower was said to be the
haunt of a forsaken maiden's
ghost.* See pp. 314–15.

William Edgar Borah, native of Wayne County, with his sister, at her home in Fairfield. Borah was then U.S. Senator from Idaho, dean of that body and at the height of his influence. *See pp. 34–36.*

Courtesy of Wayne County Historical Society

William Jennings Bryan, thrice presidential candidate, was a native of Salem, where he was born in 1860.

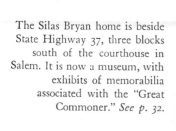

Photographic Service, Southern Illinois University

The Silas Bryan home is beside State Highway 37, three blocks south of the courthouse in Salem. It is now a museum, with exhibits of memorabilia associated with the "Great Commoner." *See p. 32.*

This old courthouse, abandoned as such more than a century ago, is on the bluff overlooking the river at Thebes. For a few years it was the migrating "permanent seat of justice" for Alexander County. It now houses a public library. *See pp. 50–51.*

These Indian carvings beneath a rock shelter near Gorham are typical of many to be found in southern Illinois. *See pp. 101–4.*

The Piasa Bird, one of America's most noted Indian petroglyphs, is mentioned in the accounts of early white explorers who found it on the face of the bluff overlooking the Mississippi at Alton. *See pp. 104–6.*

Several early taverns bore the name "Halfway House." This one
was about midway between Cahokia and Vincennes. A number of
frontier trails, including Clark's, converged in this vicinity. *See
pp. 125–27.*

Photographic Service, Southern Illinois University

Covered bridges were well designed and sturdily built. This well-
preserved one, beside Route 50 near Chester, was built in 1853. It
helps tell the story of early bridges. *See pp. 127–29.*

Illinois Furnace, in Hardin County, was one of the very early ones west of Pennsylvania. From 1838 until 1883 it operated almost continuously. During the Civil War it furnished iron to the Cairo Navy Yard. *See pp. 138–39.*

In the heyday of steamboating, a river could change its channel and doom a town or business. The ruins of a flour mill at Rockwood tell such a story. *See pp. 336–38.*

A good million fence rails, plus years of hard labor, went into the state's 90,000 miles of rail fence. Perhaps less than nine miles of such fences now remain. *See pp. 179–81.*

Courtesy of Leslie R. Cox

A sawmill and its oxen. The motive power most used in earlier Illinois was that of slowly plodding work cattle urged along by highly vocal drivers.

Courtesy of Russell Peithman

The most frequently used "long sweet'nin'" of early settlers was molasses made at the local molasses mill from cane that almost every farmer grew. This mill in Hardin County was one of three reported as operating in southern Illinois in 1962. *See pp. 170–72.*

Soon after 1830 a group of men near Shiloh Hill decided to build a school. The Illinois legislature chartered it as Shiloh College. About 1870 the present building replaced the original one of logs. *See pp. 191–92.*

Schools are often referred to as many-sided institutions. Royal Oak School, with eight sides, is literally so. One of only a few octagonal schools built in America, this was the last to be used. *See pp. 206–8.*

La Guiannée, an ancient European folk observance, was brought to Prairie du Rocher by the French. On each New Year's Eve their descendants re-enact it. *See pp. 216–17.*

Three farmers sat by an earlier building here on the first Sunday in April, 1866, and saw a mother and her children go into the cemetery near by and lay flowers upon a soldier father's grave. From such incidents came Decoration Day. *See p. 223.*

This marker is at the grave of one of the soldier dead in the churchyard of Crab Orchard Christian Church.

The Church of the Holy Family at Cahokia, the oldest church in Illinois, is a continuation of a Catholic mission established in 1699. The present log church, impressive though small, was dedicated in 1799. *See pp. 231–33.*

The church at West Salem is known as the only one of the Moravian faith in Illinois. It was formed by immigrants from Salem, North Carolina, and from Germany. A section of the near-by cemetery is unusual for the manner in which graves are marked. *See pp. 236–37.*

The old brick jail at Elizabethtown had many jail-breakers. Discolored mortar joints show where restless prisoners made their exits. Other walls of the jail bore similar scars. *See pp. 244–46.*

The Old Slave House near Equality was built by John Crenshaw. Here he kept some of the slaves he used at the Nigger Springs salt works. *See pp. 268–69.*

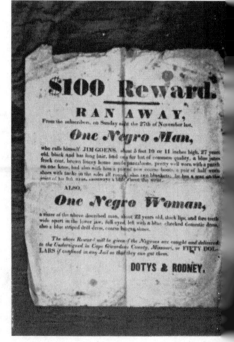

An offer of rewards to those helping capture and return runaway slaves tells its own story. *See pp. 261–63.*

The Burlingame residence at Eden, near Sparta, was a station for slaves attempting to escape by way of the Underground Railroad along which many fled to Canada and freedom. *See p. 262.*

The shipways at Mound City began business in 1856. During the Civil War they were taken over by the Federal government and had an important part in naval operations on the western waters. *See pp. 306–7.*

A formidable earthen fortress at the junction of the Ohio and Mississippi rivers first was called Fort Prentiss for the general in command at Cairo. Later it was renamed Fort Defiance. It controlled traffic on both rivers. *See pp. 287–89.*

The "Majestic" was one of the famous showboats to stop at towns beside the Ohio, the Mississippi, and their tributaries. It is the last still to cruise along the rivers. *See p. 305.*

Brownsville, first county seat of Jackson County, has vanished. The cemetery on a near-by hilltop, overgrown by great forest trees, shows no burial since 1846. *See pp. 344-45.*

Courtesy of Southern Illinois University Museum. Photo by Carl Kiefer

The first bank chartered in Illinois Territory began business in the John Marshall residence at Shawneetown in December, 1816. *See pp. 153–55.*

The Rose Hotel at Elizabethtown began in 1812 as McFarland's Tavern. It now has served continuously for more than 150 years as a stopping place for travelers. *See pp. 330–31.*

The Cahokia courthouse began as the residence of M. Saucier. France, England, and America in turn have used it as a center for local government. *See pp. 333–35.*

KASKASKIA
and the MISSISSIPPI.RIVER

------ IN 1808
——— PRESENT

0   1   2 SCALE OF MILES

NORTH

Old channel of
Kaskaskia River

Old
Kaskaskia

MISSISSIPPI RIVER

KASKASKIA

When the French came to Kaskaskia, the Mississippi flowed against the Missouri bluffs, miles to the west of its present channel. The Kaskaskia River lay against the Illinois bluffs. Then floods came. The Mississippi broke across the narrow strip of land that separated the rivers and took over the Kaskaskia River channel. The old town of Kaskaskia was washed away.

The two maps, one of 1808, taken from the Randolph County records, the other a recent drawing, will give visitors at the Lookout a better understanding of what is meant by "the Island." See pp. 351–53.

After each decennial census the center of population for the United States is relocated. In 1950 it was in a cornfield north of Olney; in 1960 it was in a soybean field near Shattuc, in Clinton County. *See pp. 366–68.*

Flights of passenger pigeons once darkened the American sky for hours. Not one survives today. The last known specimen died more than sixty years ago. *See pp. 384–86.*

Courtesy of Southern Illinois University Museum. Photo by Carl Kiefer

disease, and despair were widespread. Housing was deplorable, with families often living in sheds or abandoned buildings. People were too poor to move. After all, where could they go?

Schools already established offered little in terms of social and recreational life. Most elementary schools were of the one-room type. Southern Illinois University was the only institution offering instruction beyond high school. Though Southern was a comparatively inexpensive school to attend, the costs there were more than many potential and aspiring students could afford. Those were the times and conditions that prompted a dream.

In February, 1934, some interested persons from Chicago made a trip to southern Illinois hoping to make a dream come true. They selected a site on a hilltop south of Herod and on the east side of Route 34. A contract was signed, and a down payment on forty acres of land was made. This group spent some time in securing the interest and approval of educational leaders in the area, in explaining their objectives, and even in the actual labor of building construction. Ground was cleared, underbrush was cut away, a water supply and sanitary facilities were arranged.

School opened on June 25, 1934, with sixteen students and eleven staff members. An eight-weeks session was conducted. Courses were offered in economics, art, speech, psychology, geology, German, political science, and modern civilization. The total cost of this first term was ten dollars per student for room, board, and tuition, but those enrolled also were required to do four hours of manual labor each day. Each student provided his bedding and personal articles, including "high boots, over-alls, and rough warm outdoor clothes."

Staff members received no salary—"only a small allowance for personal expenses." Both faculty and students participated in the actual construction and maintenance of the college. Rock was quarried on the campus, wood was donated by farmers, gravel was secured from the creek bed. Some lumber came from trees on the campus. Much of the food used was raised on the campus farm.

The first building erected served as kitchen, temporary living-dining room, library, and girls' dormitory. Lighting was by kerosene and gasoline lamps. Heating was by the fireplace and by one or two donated stoves that sometimes used coal costing two dollars a ton. The usual fuel, however, was wood obtained from the near-by forest.

Life at this College in the Hills was strenuous. A typical day started at 4:30, when chores, like getting in water and firewood, began. The remainder of the day's schedule continued: 6:00, breakfast; 6:30–10:00, physical work, like building construction, gardening, housekeeping, hauling rock, etc.; 10:00–11:30, study; 11:30–12:00, dinner; 12:00–1:30, recreation or study; 1:30–5:00, classes; 5:15, supper; 5:45–8:00, study and recreation; 8:00, taps and bedtime.

Community nights were arranged twice weekly for children of the community, and a Sunday afternoon forum was held. Children had access to the college library, which contained about 2,500 well-selected books. For recreation in season, the students swam in the swimming holes of near-by creeks, hiked, folk-danced, and engaged in other similar types of entertainment.

When time for the opening of the fall term came on October 15, 1935, the college dormitory had not been completed. The opening of the school accordingly was delayed until January, 1936. The cost of tuition, room, and board for this term of twelve weeks was set at thirty dollars. Despite the utmost frugality of students and faculty, the college was soon in dire financial straits. Indebtedness rose to four hundred dollars and in addition a land payment was due. A concert was arranged in Chicago to raise funds. Personal solicitations were made. In spite of all such efforts, the college was forced to close.

Today, only a small collection of newspaper clippings, a handful of mimeographed literature, a heap of stones and charred timbers, a few letters, and the memories cherished by those who knew the College in the Hills remain to tell its story.

Did the founders regret their venture? Did those who contributed to the meager funds that kept it alive its few years rue their giving? No! A recent letter from one of the instructors who worked in the college is typical. It says: "We do not regret for a minute the years spent on this venture though they left us broke and one of our number is in a TB sanitarium. It was probably as good a way as any to spend the depression, and we weren't the only ones that went hungry. I do remember with horror . . . when our dinner (and only meal) each day consisted of a hamburger and French fries—the price, ten cents per person."

Much credit for the formation of this group and their noble effort toward being helpful to the region belongs to Baker Brownell, who later came to teach at Southern Illinois University and to initiate the program of Community Services that the University offers. Brownell's recent book, *The Other Illinois* grew out of his work in the region.

A MANY-SIDED SCHOOL

It is only natural that schools are many-sided in the purposes they serve. At least two schoolhouses in America are literally and physically

that way, each having eight sides. One of these buildings is a recon-
structed one near Valley Forge, Pennsylvania. The other one is on the
south side of the Sparta-Evansville blacktop road a half-mile west of the
village of Schuline, in Randolph County, Illinois. There is an unverified
report of a third such school in New Hampshire or Vermont. There is
also an octagonal church at Dreghorn, Scotland, and a church of ten
equal sides near Charlottesville, Virginia. However many the total may
be, these many-sided schools and churches are rare.

The Diamond Rock School near Valley Forge, Pennsylvania, was built
in 1818 by donations of materials and labor from the people of that vicinity, and a school was conducted there for more than four decades. Years
after it had been abandoned as a school, it was made into a house museum
by a group of former students and teachers in 1909. An association was
later formed to preserve it.

The Charter Oak brick school house in Randolph County was built
in 1870. The present building was used for eighty-four years, perhaps
longer than any other school building in the county. The name Charter
Oak was selected when the first log school was built more than a hundred
years ago. Someone present when naming time came, saw a large oak
near the building. It reminded him of the historic Charter Oak of New
England and suggested the name that the school has borne for a century.
Abandoned at the close of the school year of 1953–54, when the school
district was combined with others in a program of school consolidation,
it already has begun to show evidence of neglect.

The present brick building, however, is not the first to stand on the site.
The earliest there was one of logs, a typical pioneer school. It was replaced
by a frame building which was destroyed by a tornado in 1870. Tradition
relates that the teacher at that time, an easterner, was acquainted with
the school at Valley Forge, and convinced the local authorities that an
eight-sided building would be the best kind to build. It would be resistant
to wind and would give a more natural lighting—that is, from all sides
instead of from one or two. Anyway, it was decided to build an octagonal
brick school, and this was done.

The new school did not have a cloak room, however, and the present
wooden addition for that purpose was not made until about 1910. Previous
to that, shelves and hooks placed beside the east door served to accommodate lunches and wraps.

It was at first intended that pupils be seated in rows around the walls,
with narrow aisles between the sections, and that they face the teacher's
desk in the center. Despite the old belief that teachers have eyes in the
back of their heads, that plan didn't work. There were always some

pupils who took advantage when the teacher's back was turned, and acted accordingly.

The people living about this school have always maintained an above-average interest in it and in community activities, and the present and previous building were used for numerous purposes. Farmer's organizations met there. Political groups gathered to hear the issues of the day discussed. It has been a meeting place for an afternoon Sunday School and for church services. The local literary society with its varied programs of music, readings, declamations, plays, and debates has come and gone. Likewise, the marble rings, the larger worn circle where the boys played bull pen, the bases about the ball field, the limiting lines for shinny, the mounting block used by those who came on horseback, and other familiar markers of earlier school playgrounds have vanished.

Spelling bees, ciphering matches, and ball games once were common. Many basket dinners have been eaten beneath the shade trees about the school. It has seen many a last-day-of-school observance and leave-taking, when older pupils finished school and when patrons and pupils met to enjoy a festive day and perhaps to speed the teacher on his way— his, because most of the teachers were men.

In earlier years the attendance at Charter Oak School was usually between thirty-five and forty pupils. This number often was increased to fifty or more when the big boys had finished gathering the fall crops. Attendance diminished when time for spring plowing came. In later years, enrollment decreased until the maintenance of a separate school was not considered practical.

When the present building was erected, the school bell was placed in the belfry at the top center. Many very old persons still remark about the pleasing tones of the bell—tones that are perhaps a bit mellowed by memory.

There are some who express hope that this old school can be preserved, partly because it is unique in structure and partly because it represents an educational age that is rapidly passing away. It does not necessarily mean that those persons yearn for a return of the good old days. Nevertheless, the ringing of the old bell brings back a host of pleasant memories to those who once were called to school by it.

Travelers along the roadway still stop to look at one of the strangest schoolhouses in the United States.

THE FIRST TEACHERS' UNION

When Lewis E. York was commissioned as County Superintendent of Schools for Saline County on March 23, 1897, he was the youngest person holding such office in Illinois. Press reports stated that he was the youngest one serving in such capacity in the United States. Perhaps this was true, for York was too young to vote in the election that gave him his office. Despite his youth, he was reasonably daring in his educational policies. This is evidenced best by an innovation which was launched in Saline County during his tenure.

Teachers then were poorly paid—some insist they still are. Low salaries prevailed over all of southern Illinois. Several schools paid as little as $22.50 a month, and then only for a term of six months. Even so, some teachers also were required to serve as janitor without additional pay.

About this time, a new force came to Harrisburg and Saline County—the miners' union. Some teachers of the county observed the workings of the new union and drew ideas from it. Why not form a teachers' union?

A small group eating at Jack's Place during the annual teachers' institute in August, 1904, discussed the proposition of starting a union of the county's teachers. They knew that if the organization was to succeed, they must have the co-operation of Superintendent York. Definite plans for the union were formed and explained to him. York approved and promised "reasonable" co-operation.

The Saline County Teachers' Association accordingly was formed before the close of the county institute. A schedule of salaries that different districts would be required to pay was made, based on the assessed valuation of the district and the legal tax rate. This schedule of salaries was made effective for the next school year. Teachers signed a pledge not to accept a school below the salary established by the "scale committee."

It only remained now to activate the plan, and it was here that the county superintendent became the key figure. The method of certification for teachers in use at that time was suited admirably to the union's purpose if the county superintendent chose to co-operate, and York so chose.

Except for the very rare state certificate, the county superintendent was in full control of teacher certification. It was he who made up the questions to be used, conducted the examination, graded the papers submitted, and passed upon the personal character of the applicant for a certificate. Using some one or a combination of these powers, the county superintendent could give "reasonable" assistance to the union's goal.

Superintendent York proceeded to reduce the surplus of teachers in his county. He also discontinued the general practice of endorsing certificates issued by other county superintendents, requiring that all take examinations given in Saline County, which were noted for their severity. A balance in the number of available teachers and of teaching positions in the county was easily attained in this manner.

As may be imagined, public reaction was heated, but despite all opposition, the plan succeeded. Some districts delayed many weeks in their employment of teachers, but to no avail. They paid the designated salary or they had no teacher.

The Saline County Teachers' Association won the contest, and the first teachers' union in America—one having a definite and controlled plan for fixing teachers' salaries—was in successful operation.

When Superintendent York left office in 1906, he was succeeded by R. E. Rhine, who gave full support to the plan. This union, under the name of Saline County Teachers' Association, continued to influence teachers' salaries even after new state certification laws became effective.

If a member of the association or an outsider purposely or unwittingly accepted a teaching position below the established scale, he was promptly invited to appear before an executive committee. There he was given what could be termed the third degree. Some of these sessions were stormy indeed, but the erring one invariably conformed or resigned.

A NIGHT ON THE OLD SCHOOL GROUND

ABOUT EARLY CANDLELIGHT, this old teacher came with his camp trailer to the abandoned southern Illinois rural school that he attended sixty-five years ago. He decided to spend a night on the grounds where he had spent so many happy days, and accordingly, parked his trailer there.

As darkness came, he went to sit on the well curb and deal in memories. He peopled the scene with long-absent pupils and recalled past incidents. These musings strengthened the realization that the one-room rural school is all but gone to join rail and hedge fences, fence shuttles, gluts, frows, log mauls, ash hoppers, double-shovels, and a host of other objects that have served their purpose and passed.

A generation ago there were hundreds of rural schools beside the muddy roads of southern Illinois. Now, only isolated ones remain. Many of them have disappeared and the few remaining ones little resemble those of earlier years.

At the time when the writer first knew Gholson School, commonly called "Hardscrabble," it had eighty-one pupils enrolled. In age, they ranged from six to twenty-one. School "took up" at eight o'clock. There was an hour of recess at noon, one of fifteen minutes at mid-forenoon and another at mid-afternoon. School was dismissed at four o'clock except, too often, when classes were behind, and the school "kept late."

Among those who came to teach in this school were a few who had no training beyond that afforded by similar country schools, with perhaps two weeks or so in a county normal. One teacher, however, was a college graduate who combined his teaching with the operation of a nursery. Gentle, kindly, scholarly, and inspiring, he left a lasting effect upon the community. It must have been his influence above that of any other that led more than a dozen of Hardscrabble's early pupils to become teachers.

Several pupils from this school, among them the writer, went directly from it into teaching. A few went to college for a term or so. Despite such limited training, about fifteen of those who attended this school or taught there during the writer's time became teachers, principals, or superintendents.

Former pupils from here went to work and lived at various places over the world. They went to China, the Philippines, India, Alaska, France, and far up the Congo in Africa. They entered numerous businesses and professions, including the military, governmental services, the building trades, and the ministry. Hardscrabble was a typical good rural school, fortunate in having an unusual succession of competent and devoted teachers. It did a good work.

Hardscrabble, like many others, had its extra curricular activities. Some of these were the literary societies with their debates, contests, dialogues, declamations, essays, and mock trials, all about forgotten now. It also had its spelling matches, ciphering matches, box suppers, pie suppers, writing schools, singing school, Farmer's Union, and the occasional itinerant showman with his magic, or an early talking-machine.

The playground activities of early years were recalled. Many of the ones popular then are now forgotten. We played hat ball, old sow, shinny, bull-pen, long town, cat, move up, and baseball. We knocked flies, caught, played "andy over," set pegs, played wolf on the ridge, stink base, touch base, rooster, and burn out. Indian wrestling and just plain "rasslin'" were frequently indulged in.

Two pulled at a sack while two "scratched gravel." Sling Dutch, whip cracker, leap frog, one and over, and lap jacket came in for their turns. Marbles were seasonal until thumb nails and trouser knees alike became worn. Those who could afford them brought taws of agate. Many an oldster will recall his favorite taw and center man. The boys, just as they do now, played jail and outlaws.

Girls played the gentler games. They liked "andy over," drop the handkerchief, London Bridge and needle's eye. One teacher, the college graduate, encouraged folk games and dances, leaving some of us with an abiding interest in such. The school ground was never a dull place.

Unless they lived near the school, all pupils brought lunch, generally in a tin pail or small basket. No one then dreamed of a school-lunch program. On a fair day most pupils ate out of doors. Some hardy souls did so throughout the year. The lunches were not well selected; malnourished and anemic children were common. Only one girl in this school wore spectacles, but many doubtless needed them.

The school's first blackboards were the painted planks of the schoolroom wall. Slate blackboards came several years later. Erasers ("Andrews dustless") were shaped wooden blocks with felt glued on. One box of crayon was supposed to last a year. Water was scarce. Some years it was necessary to haul water to fill the wet-weather well. Once this was obtained from a neighbor's pond, but he kept his livestock fenced away. At other times, water was carried by the bucket from a well three-eighths of a mile away and drunk from a common drinking cup or at another time from a gourd, yet somehow, most of us survived.

The rural school definitely is gone. Those who knew it and know present-day schools do not regret its passing. Nevertheless, a glimpse of it across the years arouses a measure of nostalgia. Will another sixty years cause oldsters then to see as much lacking in the schools of today?

Chapter 9

Holidays

❦ *THE NEW YEAR'S ANCIENT CUSTOMS*

OLD AND YOUNG celebrating the New Year in southern Illinois help to perpetuate customs that began thousands of years ago and have been observed by many peoples. Most frequently these observations have been at or near the time of the winter solstice, when the sun ceases to sink lower in the southern sky and begins to move northward, bringing the promises of another growing season.

In the many centuries during which this change has been celebrated, strange practices have come to cluster about the New Year. Some of the customs now followed here have come from very ancient times and from distant countries. Others may have originated here. A great proportion of old beliefs that survive in the lore of the New Year are those that would bring good fortune or would help to foretell and ward off approaching ill fortune. No ceremonial practices were more prevalent than those intended to assure a sufficient food supply in the new year.

More than two thousand years ago the white-robed priests of the Druids in northern France and the British Isles used golden sickles to clip mistletoe from oak trees. This mistletoe, thought to bring good fortune, peace, and bountiful crops, was blessed and widely distributed. Descendants of the French who settled around Prairie du Rocher, St. Genevieve, and Vincennes reflect that belief in the practice of *La Guiannée* on New Year's Eve, and bits of mistletoe may yet be found in cow barns in England and Ireland.

Other practices thought to be helpful toward assuring a bountiful food supply are still observed occasionally. One of these calls for families to eat beans on the first day of the year. These should not be string beans but dried beans of the "navy" or pinto variety. In the event beans are not available, black-eyed peas are considered to be equally effective. In the event there are neither beans nor peas on hand, a herring can be eaten for the same purpose. While beans, peas, or herring indicated good fortunes in food, other items were to be avoided. To have a head of cabbage in the house on New Year's Day was a harbinger of ill fortune and could easily 'offset the combined influences of beans, peas, and herring.

Similar food superstitions much like ours are found among the Chinese. Their people seek the promise of a bountiful food supply by eating soup made from yellow bean sprouts which, when cooked, bear a fancied resemblance to an old Chinese gold coin. American beans were considered by some as more effective if cooked with a bit of "hog jaw." The Chinese served a pig's head, garnished and decorated with colored trappings as a special dish for the day. They even fashioned small cakes to resemble gold coins, and drank tea from cups that resembled other coins. At other times, the Chinese set off firecrackers to frighten away evil spirits. American men and boys also set them off and sometimes fired guns at the same season, perhaps to frighten away evil spirits or just to make a noise. If the gun were fired into or just above the top of a fruit tree, it assured a good fruit crop.

Certain New Year observances could help to foretell the weather. Climatic conditions during each of the first twelve days of the year would indicate conditions of the corresponding months.

Should one wish to know more concerning month-by-month rainfall of the year, it could be learned by a proper use of twelve onions. The top third of each onion was cut away and a cuplike space hollowed out. They then were arranged in a row and an equal measure of salt placed in each depression. The amount of water appearing in the individual onion the next morning would indicate the rainfall for its corresponding month. To provide reliable information, it was necessary that this ritual be enacted on January 1. Personal good fortune came to the man who slept with a horseshoe under his pillow on the first of the year. His dog's general good health and immunity to rabies could be guaranteed by placing some silver filings in the dog's food on New Year's Eve. Some held it was just as effective if the filings were administered on Christmas Eve.

Farm animals were believed to indulge in strange behaviors at the midnight of New Year's Eve. A surprise visit at that hour should find the cows kneeling. Animals could even understand what was said to them on the midnight visit. The proportion of pullets and cockerels in the approaching season's hatch was thought to be greatly influenced by the first visitor entering the henhouse on New Year's morning. If this visitor were a woman, pullets would predominate, but if a man came in first, the larger proportion would be cockerels.

If the wind is from the south at five o'clock in the morning on New Year's Day, the summer will be a dry one. If it is from the north, expect a rainy summer. Wear some new article of clothing on the first day. Listen for a turtledove to coo and foretell good luck, or watch to see if water drips from the eaves.

These are only a few of the almost endless number of beliefs and sayings relating to the New Year.

Shortly after nightfall on the eve of each New Year, a group of people in grotesque masks and beggar-like costumes gather at some appointed place in the village of Prairie du Rocher, in Randolph County. They meet to observe *La Guiannée,* an event which has been celebrated there since 1722. Until recently, the only participants were men, but women are now included. The motley and picturesque group includes some twenty singers and two or three with violins and guitars. Some of the older men in the group have been singing *La Guiannée* for sixty years or more.

When the time comes, generally about seven o'clock in the evening, the celebrants begin their tour. Those at whose homes the singers stop esteem it a mark of courtesy. In earlier years, the celebration was confined to the village, but the singers now go as far as Modoc and to the vicinity of St. Leo's Church, five or six miles away. When the group arrives at a house, always doing so quietly, they gather in front of the doorway. The musicians and song leader immediately begin the song. The leader, tapping out time with his walking cane, sings the first couplet of the song as a solo. The entire group responds, repeating the lines already sung by the leader. This procedure is continued until the first stanza of the song is ended, when the singers pause. The householder, who always shows delight and pretends surprise, opens the door. The group enters and completes the song. All this is done in the French patois, a form of that language in common use during the earlier years of the village.

A visitor hearing it for the first time may not understand the words of the song, but he is impressed by the rapt attention it gets. Though some of the audience may have been listening to *La Guiannée* for a lifetime, they appear to be hearing a new and appealing melody for the first time. When the song, with its strange and plaintive air, has been completed, there is merriment and chatter. The householder serves drinks—never lemonade—and cookies, often made from recipes similar to those used two hundred years ago. After disposing of the refreshments, the singers move on.

Formerly, because of the refreshments consumed, some singers had to be replaced as the evening wore on. In recent years this tendency has been brought under full control. An individual is selected to ration and allocate drinks. The last such master of ceremonies—genial, capable, and answering to the name of "Tiny"—was about six feet two inches tall and weighed a good two hundred pounds. No casualty had occurred at one o'clock when the author left.

Those who observe the re-enactment of *La Guiannée,* depart feeling they have observed a unique event. Once widely observed in the French villages of Canada and the Mississippi Valley, it is now practiced in only a few places. In addition to Prairie du Rocher, it is sung in Sainte Genevieve, Missouri, where there also is a German version. Also, there are a few places in the French provinces of Canada where it still may be heard.

Each New Year's Eve a troupe will go about Prairie du Rocher and once more sing *La Guiannée.* Many of the singers in this group are aging. Charles Clerc, now past eighty, has participated for about his seventieth time. For many years he sang the lead. Now his son, Percy, and Mr. Milliere sing the lead with him. Another son accompanies with a guitar. Few of the singers are any longer youthful. Some are direct descendants of those who sang the old song two hundred years ago. Others answer to German and English names. The number of participants lessens with passing years, but the song lives on with a few other remnants of the happy practices of the early French.

A few years ago it appeared that the tradition might entirely disappear. In recent years, however, there has been a marked revival of interest, and now this quaint old French custom promises to survive. Recordings have been made and the music transcribed. The words in the original French patois and their translation into English also have been recorded. All are preserved in the Congressional Library.

THE EARLY FRENCH WERE A JOLLY LOT

PERFORMANCE OF *La Guiannée* was only the beginning of New Year observances by the early French settlers. Other practices, many of which have disappeared, followed. The careful observer still can see traces of them, and traditions concerning them are easy to find. The early days of each incoming year were filled with festivity and friendship.

Early on the first day of the year, it was the custom to begin a round of visiting. Each person first went to visit the eldest members of the family. After calling on their elders, when kisses and congratulations were bestowed and received, the married sons, daughters, nephews, and nieces returned to their own homes to receive those younger. The day thus became one of almost continuous visiting and being visited. At each place, drinks, cookies, and tidbits were served, but it does not appear that drinking was excessive.

Each visitor kissed not only the master and mistress of the house, but also the old ladies, the young, the boys and girls of all ages as well as the men- and maidservants. All alike received the customary salutation.

If two persons had quarreled during the year, a mutual friend or acquaintance would arrange a time and place for the meeting of the estranged ones. There they would kiss and drink to each other's health and happiness. Old differences were forgotten and they were friends once more—at least until their next quarrel.

It was also on the first day of the year that preparations were begun for holding the series of social affairs known as the King balls. As a first step in this program, some prominent lady of the village attended to the baking of a cake in which four beans were hidden. The eligible young men of the town were then invited to gather. The cake was cut and the pieces were passed among them. The first young man to find a hidden bean was designated as King. Those finding the other three beans became attendants, with seniority established by the order in which they had found the beans. After this, the king selected his queen and the attendants their partners.

It was the privilege of the King to hold the first of the series of balls that were soon to begin. If he did not have a house suitable for the ball, some elder dame of the village considered it an honor to offer her home for the occasion. The men provided and paid the fiddler.

The first ball was held on the night after "old Christmas," January 6. When homes were not large enough to accommodate all who would come, attendance was by invitation. These balls were the social highlights of the year. The elderly, important, and respected came in state, perhaps more to give dignity to the affair than to dance. Today the King balls have disappeared.

🌺 *SAINT VALENTINE'S DAY*

AMONG SPECIAL DAYS that have been observed for centuries is Saint Valentine's Day, February 14. Much of the significance attached to this day is the same as to the Lupercalia, a festival of ancient Rome. Accounts of ancient rites are somewhat sketchy, but about six hundred years ago,

Valentine's Day began to be marked regularly in Scotland, England, and France. From what is known about this special day in Rome and later in the other countries, one concludes that its observance down through the years has had romantic implications.

In Rome, it was the custom of a group of youths to place an equal number of girls' names in a box and to draw them by lot. The youth who drew a girl's name was privileged to court her for the coming year. She was his special friend to whom he gave devoted attention. It was something of a mock betrothal. It appears that the girl had little to say in the matter.

This practice of the Lupercalia offended churchmen and they offered a substitute plan by which a name of a saint would be drawn instead of a girl's name. The one drawing the name of a saint was to exemplify the virtues of that saint for the coming year. Somehow this plan did not meet with the approval of the boys, and the earlier purposes, perhaps slightly modified, returned.

According to the earliest accounts of the day's observance in the British Isles, it was the custom of the lad and of the lass whose name he had drawn to exchange gifts. Later the lad alone provided a present. Gloves appear to have been the favorite one, but others included clothing, trinkets, or jewelry. There is a record of one such gift to the value of eight hundred pounds sterling.

A lad drawing a name also kept the slip of paper on which the name had been written. Sometimes he wore this paper on his cloak, or he might write a bit of sentiment upon it and send it to the lass. It is said that the sending of this missive gave rise to the present custom of sending valentines with their sentimental ditties.

The exchange of comic or mock valentines came into wide practice about sixty years ago. One year, about the turn of the century, the Chicago post office handled more than a million valentines, mostly of the comic variety. Of those reaching the post office, 25,000 were considered to be unfit for transmitting through the mail. It must have been a field day for the postal workers inspecting them. In the same year, the post office at Philadelphia handled about 750,000. Anyone wishing to take a sly dig at another, may still find old-time comic valentines for that purpose.

Although the name of St. Valentine has become associated with the day, there is no apparent reason for such except that he was killed on that day, February 14, A.D. 270. Since Lupercalia was on February 13 and St. Valentine was executed on February 14, the two became associated and Valentine thus innocently became a patron saint of those with love problems.

The date for the Lupercalia was first set on the day when, according to pagan belief, birds selected their mates and flew away to connubial bliss and nesting. This belief is found also in the earliest written mentions of the day in Britain. Chaucer says: "For this is Saint Valentine's Day when every fowl cometh there to choose his mate." Shakespeare alludes to it when he says, "Saint Valentine now is past. Begin these wood birds but to couple now." Another explanation of the name Valentine would have it derived from the old Norman word "galantin," meaning lover of women, the letter *g* taking somewhat the same sound as *v*, but the explanation that the name comes from that of the saint appears to be more valid.

There is evidence that the day was taken quite seriously by some. Dame Elizabeth Drew wrote to John Paston with whom she was trying to arrange a match with her daughter, Margery, in 1477 that he should come to visit them on the eve of St. Valentine's Day and remain for three days. The final results are not known, but two letters written by Margery a few weeks later address John as her "beloved Valentine."

The eve of St. Valentine's day also had its magic. A lass might adorn her pillow with bay leaves, bake a dump cake and place it under her pillow, or burn a piece of paper with her beloved's name and place the ashes on a looking glass under her pillow, or she could boil an egg, remove the yolk and fill the space with salt, then eat the egg, salt and all. In either of the above cases, she should dream of her intended. There were numerous other methods adjudged equally reliable.

It now seems that people have lost faith in the lore surrounding the day, although valentines are still sent. Many a man or lad will casually stop at the corner drug store and buy a heart-shaped box of candy or some trinket that proclaims sentiment and present it to his girl. Parties galore will be held, and some of the age-old practices will be observed.

Best of all, however, will be the joy that the day will bring to kindergarten and primary pupils who will design and make their own valentines to take home to mother, and to give to those whose names they draw. However it started, it is a nice day to observe.

🌺 ALL FOOLS' DAY

Folk sayings have settled several things about the month of April. For instance, the number of frosts for the month will be the same as the number of times it thundered in January. Girls born during this month will grow up to be industrious women particularly devoted to their homes. Also, April boys will become jealous men, but otherwise good husbands.

If hickory timber is cut during the month, it will become badly worm-eaten. This also is held equally true of that cut during the month of May. Bountiful crops of muskmelons may be expected from April plantings if they are made while the sign is in Cancer. To assure the best growth, lettuce should be planted on the fourth day of the month and potatoes on the tenth, which is the hundredth day after the New Year. In leap years this would require that potatoes be planted on the ninth. Oats planted after the tenth will definitely "grow to straw."

With the above items disposed of, there remains the major and strange one of All Fools' Day, April 1. It is puzzling how such a singular observance, now widely accepted, came about in ancient times.

The observance of this day, like others, apparently had no definite beginning. Like Topsy, it just grew up. As early as the year 1200, there was a day of jokes and buffoonery in France, during a part of which the participants overran the churches in a somewhat irreverent way. The feast of Hull in India has been observed for centuries on March 31 of each year. On the day of this feast, tricks are played and gullible persons are sent on foolish errands.

As early as 1700 the custom of observing a fool's day was practiced in Britain. In Scotland, it was called Gowk Day for the gowk or cuckoo that they considered as the silliest of the bird family. Jokesters would send someone to the butcher for such an item as a gill of pigeon milk, or to the shoemaker for some strap oil. In the latter case, the shoemaker administered a few strokes of a strap to the astonished and unsuspecting caller. Always a group would gather to see the "gowk" perform his silly mission.

Perhaps one of the largest mass jokes ever indulged in was on April 1, 1860. A London paper on the previous day had carried an announcement that all who appeared at the White Gate to the Tower next day would receive free passes to the Tower and be privileged to see a special bathing of the white lions of the Tower. At the appointed time, hundreds of London cabs rattled about looking for the nonexistent gate and the equally mythical lions.

Observance of the day began early in America, where it is universally recognized. Within recent years, an advertisement offering to buy black cats appeared in a metropolitan paper. Scores of them were brought to the vacant address given. On April 1, 1946, the Bronx zoo received 2708 telephone calls for Mr. Fish, Mr. Camel and even Mr. L. E. Fant. These were in response to an "if interested call Mr. —— at the number given below" advertisement.

Considering such mass jokes, it is not strange that boys who at other times are determined to become presidents or great ball players, dismiss their abiding ambitions for one day and spend it playing harmless tricks. Purses with concealed strings attached will be drawn away quickly by hidden youths who will guffaw at the unsuspecting finders as they stoop to gather them. Other "lost" objects will be found securely nailed down. And we all have heard, "Goodness! What's that on your cheek? No, the other one." Then, "April fool."

Strange explanations are offered to account for the practice. One tradition connects the bootless mission to the run-around from Annas, to Caiphas, to Pilate, to Herod and back to Pilate when the guilt and punishment of Christ was being considered. Another explanation would connect All Fools' Day with the ancient observance of the New Year which then took place in late March, but neither of these is very satisfactory.

This singular observance of an All Fools' Day or special day for playing jokes is widely known over the world. It is frequently found among primitive peoples. Another common feature of the day is that the resentment felt at being made to appear foolish is less on this special day. It ends at noon. After that, "April Fool done is past—And you're the biggest fool at last."

❧ MEMORIAL DAY

A MONUMENT ON THE Stone River battlefield north of Murfreesboro, Tennessee, erected by the Union troops while they were still encamped there, is said to be the first memorial erected to the soldier dead of the Civil War. This claim has remained unchallenged. There are several places, however, laying claim to the first observance of Decoration Day, now known nationally as Memorial Day.

The practice of beautifying and placing offerings at graves is of ancient origin and has been carried out in a sporadic manner for centuries. Savage and uncivilized peoples mark the graves of their dead and return to them with ornaments. However, the custom of setting aside a special day or days for such purposes is of more recent origin.

Our Decoration Day is relatively new—less than one hundred years old. As a special day, it did not have its beginning until about the end of the War between the States. It was instituted for the placing of floral offerings on the graves of the dead of that war. Soon it was expanded to include the dead of all our wars, and before long, to include all civilian dead as well.

Widely scattered places are contenders for the distinction of having been the first one to set aside a special day. Three such claimants, presented in time sequence, are given here. They are Boalsburg, Pennsylvania, Columbus, Georgia, and Carbondale, Illinois. These are not the only places that would have the distinction. They are the three, however, that contend most sharply.

According to an article written by Herbert C. Moore and appearing in the *National Republic* of May, 1948, the day was first observed at Boalsburg on May 30, 1864. On that day, nineteen-year-old Emma Hunter took flowers to the cemetery to place upon the grave of her colonel father who had been killed leading his regiment at Gettysburg. By coincidence, she met a Mrs. Meyers, who had likewise brought flowers to place on the grave of a son killed at Gettysburg. Miss Hunter and Mrs. Meyers talked together, and, before leaving, each took some of the flowers she had brought and placed them upon the grave the other had come to decorate.

Before parting at the cemetery, these two planned to meet again a year later for the same purpose. At intervals during the year, the idea of decorating the graves in the Boalsburg cemetery was discussed with others. Such a plan appealed to many, and when May 30, 1865, arrived, a community service was held. A local clergyman, Dr. George Hall, preached a sermon, and all graves were decorated with flags and flowers. According to the account cited "not one grave was neglected." When General Logan, then Commander in Chief of the Grand Army of the Republic, issued General Order No. 11 on May 5, 1868, Boalsburg again responded nobly. This is the basis of Boalsburg's claim. Apparently, though, no contemporary accounts have been made public.

Another account of the day's origin appeared in the New Orleans *Times-Picayune* on June 11, 1937. This article was reprinted as a small brochure and distributed by the Alabama State Department of Archives and History. According to this version, the Ladies' Aid Society which had served the cause of the Confederacy became the Ladies' Memorial Association at the end of the war. Even before hostilities ended, the newspaper says, this group of women had decorated the graves of their soldier dead. After the war, the memorial objective became their primary one.

The account cited relates that early in the spring of 1866, Miss Elizabeth Rutherford called a meeting of the members of the group mentioned at the home of Mrs. John Tyler, where plans for the proper observance of a

Memorial Day were made. The date chosen was the anniversary of Johnson's surrender. Thus, according to the *Times-Picayune,* the first observance of Memorial Day was made in Columbus, Georgia, on April 26, 1866, with the Hon. J. M. Ramsey as speaker of the day. A marker at the grave of Mrs. Elizabeth Rutherford Ellis in the local cemetery carries the inscription: "In her patriotic heart sprang the thought of Memorial Day."

Based on the reported dates of their occurrence, Carbondale, Illinois, is the third claiment. The Carbondale claim is supported by records kept by Mr. Green, caretaker of the town's early cemetery, by accounts of those participating in the first observance, and by contemporary church records. This observance was held at Woodlawn Cemetery on April 29, 1866. It was the outgrowth of a similar but somewhat spontaneous observance held at Crab Orchard Christian Church about four miles west and south of Carbondale on a Sunday earlier in the month.

The Carbondale observance apparently was the first in which returned veterans were major participants. Its promotion definitely was in the hands of these men, and the pattern it set was the one afterwards followed. According to Mr. Green's record, there were 219 comrades in the line of march. They were led by Colonel E. J. Ingersoll, "Master of the Day." Rev. J. W. Lane, pastor of the First Methodist Church, offered prayer and Gen. John A. Logan was speaker of the day. Green records one passage, perhaps the highlight of Logan's talk: "Every man's life belongs to his country and no man has a right to refuse it when his country calls for it." After this part of the program had been enacted, graves of the military dead were decorated, including one of an unknown soldier. There was a barbecue for which the Dillinger brothers furnished the hogs and John Borger the bread. There was one fight, Brannon and Russell. It must have been an eventful day. A bronze marker at the cemetery entrance marks the place as the one where Memorial Day observances began.

🌿 *THANKSGIVING*

THANKSGIVING IS THE oldest and most distinctive festival of American origin. Begun at the end of the Pilgrims' first year here, the practice was confined mostly to the New England states for the first two hundred years. After that long period as a somewhat local custom, the practice spread until it became nationwide.

Thanksgiving was first marked by the Puritans in Plymouth Colony, Massachusetts, in 1621. It had been a most difficult year, but their crops had done reasonably well, and the prospects for food during the approaching winter were much better. Health had improved and more comfortable houses had been built. All were grateful for these good fortunes. Governor Bradford accordingly set aside three days in early December for observance of a period of worship and prayer as well as for feasting, games, contests, and the manual of arms. Hunters were sent into the forest and along the seashore for game. They returned with turkey, waterfowl, eels, clams, fish, and mussels. Neighboring Indians were invited, or heard of the feast, and came bringing five "Deere" with them. There was not sufficient space to house the settlers and the eighty or more Indians. Hence, most of the festivities were held about great open fires. All went well, and the first Thanksgiving was successful. From time to time, but not regularly and not always as thanks for a bountiful harvest, other days were picked for Thanksgiving.

These first festivals were naturally All American affairs, except perhaps for the release by the Puritans of small amounts of "comfortably warm water" (Holland Gin). The typical menu of the annual festival is still the same—turkey, waterfowl, cranberry sauce, sweet potatoes, pumpkin pie, nuts, oyster dressing, cornbread, and tobacco to smoke after the meal.

The earlier Thanksgiving observances did not have the great religious significance that later came to be associated with them. They took on much of the family reunion or "to grandfather's house we go" atmosphere. In this way, they carried on much of the "home for Christmas" practices of England. Since Christmas had been legally banned in New England, some of the Christmas customs of England easily became attached to the New England Thanksgiving.

After many years, Thanksgiving became a fixed practice in New England. Some steps also had been taken toward making it a national observance. This is indicated by President Washington's proclamation of 1789, which designated November 26 as a day for national thanksgiving. Perhaps Washington was disappointed in its somewhat boisterous observance. He did not issue a second proclamation until 1795, when he designated a day in March as Thanksgiving Day. John Adams issued two such proclamations during his term of office. Jefferson considered it a religious festival and issued none. Succeeding presidents took little note of it.

These conditions held until 1846, when Sarah Josephs Hale became "the lady editor" of *Godey's Lady's Book*. Mrs. Hale began to advocate a national observance. She wrote many editorials and letters to those of influence, urging the adoption of such a day. After seventeen years, Mrs.

Hale's efforts began to produce obvious results. President Lincoln read the editorial she wrote in 1863 and doubtless received a letter from her. His response was a proclamation—perhaps the best one ever written—on October 3 of that year, asking all people to observe the last Thursday of November as a day for thanks and prayer. Each president since that day has designated a November day as one to be observed.

Illinois settlers from Virginia, the Carolinas, Kentucky, and Tennessee brought Christmas and firecrackers to the state. They considered Thanksgiving as a Yankee innovation, however, and accordingly ignored it. It was left for those of New England origin to initiate the Thanksgiving Day practice in the state. The first recorded observance of the day in Illinois came as a result of a proclamation supposedly issued by Governor Joseph Duncan in October, 1838. This proclamation appears to have been the product of a joke or forgery, but it did result in some observances. The next proclamation by an Illinois governor was issued by Governor Thomas Carlin on November 12, 1842, setting aside the last Thursday in November. Since that time, observance of Thanksgiving Day has been a rather regular practice.

With only the exceptions made by President Franklin D. Roosevelt, the last Thursday in November has been the day set apart. In 1939, he chose a date one week earlier. Many state governors ignored the new date and, following the old practice, set the last Thursday of the month as the proper one. After another unsuccessful effort had been made to move the date forward, national legislation was enacted in 1941 to fix the date permanently as the last Thursday in November. Thus, after 320 years, Thanksgiving was made a legal holiday with a fixed date.

❦ CHRISTMAS ON THE CACHE

THE EARLIEST ACCOUNT found about Christmas and the manner in which it was spent in southern Illinois, outside of the French settlements along the Mississippi, appeared in a paper published in London (England) in 1828. It tells how John James Audubon, the great naturalist, spent Christmas Day of 1810 near the mouth of the Cache River where it joins the Ohio about six miles above Cairo.

Audubon and a Frenchman named Ferdinand Rozier had left Henderson, Kentucky, a few days earlier with a keelboat load of merchandise, consisting of three hundred barrels of whiskey, sundry dry goods, and gunpowder. Audubon was on his way to Sainte Genevieve, Missouri, where he and a man named Herrick planned to establish a business.

When they reached the mouth of the Cache on December 23, Audubon and Rozier came across some other travelers there. They also found about twenty-five families of Shawnee Indians who were camped to gather nuts and to hunt. From the travelers and the Indians, Audubon and Rozier learned that the Mississippi was covered with thick ice and that boats could not use it. They therefore decided to remain at the Shawnee camp.

The second day after his arrival, that is on the morning of December 25, Audubon tells that he was awakened early by the activities of the Shawnee. He arose at once and found that a canoe with a half-dozen squaws and as many warriors was about ready to leave for a large lake on the Kentucky side for the purpose of killing swans.

Audubon was given permission to accompany the Indians in the canoe. He went along, as he states, "well equipped with ammunition and whiskey." He relates that the task of paddling the canoe across the river was performed by the squaws and that "the hunters laid down and positively slept during the whole passage." When they reached the Kentucky side, the squaws made the canoe secure and began to gather nuts. The hunters made their way through the "thick and thin" to the lake, the thick and thin being the thickets of small cottonwood trees and occasional lagoons that bordered the river.

In a short time, they reached the lake where they saw swans "by the hundreds, of a white or rich cream color—either dipping their black bills in the water or . . . floating along and basking in the sunshine." Three of the Indians passed around to the other side of the lake and three remained on the side nearest the river. Audubon joined one of the groups and all hid themselves behind trees. When the hunters on either side of the lake alarmed them, the swans would arise and fly to the other side, where the hunters hidden there would take careful aim and fire. Alternating, the hunters repeated the process until a large number of birds were killed.

In describing the situation, Audubon says: "I saw these beautiful birds floating on the water, their backs downward, their heads under the surface, and their legs in the air, struggling in the last agonies of life, to the number of at least fifty—their beautiful skins all intended for ladies of Europe."

When the sun was nearly even with the tops of the trees, "a conch was sounded and the squaws shortly appeared, dragging the canoe, and went about in quest of the dead game." All was "transported to the River's edge and landed upon the Illinois shore before dark."

"The fires were lighted—each man ate his mess of pecans and bear fat, and stretched himself out, with his feet near the small heap of coals intended for the night. The females began their work; it was their duty to skin the birds. I observed them for sometime and then retired to rest, very well satisfied with the sport of this day—the 25th of December."

❧ *CHRISTMAS LORE*

THE ORIGIN OF numerous customs, practices, and folk beliefs found in southern Illinois today can be traced back through many centuries. The observance of Christmas and the customs connected with it afford some examples that have long survived. More than five hundred years before the advent of Christianity, pagan peoples in widely scattered countries were observing a season that corresponds to our Christmas. Many of their customs were the same as those we now observe. These pre-Christian observances were naturally not to celebrate the birth of Christ. They were held to entreat the gods to turn the sun from its southern course and assure another summer. These ceremonies thus served to express the joy of the people that the winter solstice had passed. Each day thereafter, as the sun rose higher in its course, they were happy to know that another summer with its fruiting season was approaching. The unconquerable sun was returning.

Festivals at the time of the winter solstice were observed in the British Isles, in the Scandinavian countries, in Persia, in Germany, in France, in Italy, and in various other countries before the advent of Christianity. Always they were times of rejoicing. They were marked by feasts, singing of carols, giving of gifts, and general jollity, somewhat paralleling present practices.

The plum pudding, even today a typical Christmas dish, is said to have had its origin in the Court of King Arthur in England. Then, as now, no plum pudding was considered complete until wine or brandy was poured over it and burned. Children long ago must have begun to be good "jes' 'fore Christmas," for it was said even then that "only good little boys and girls" were to receive gifts during the Saturnalia in Rome five hundred years before Christ.

Long ago cakes were prepared at Christmas time with one candle for each member of the family. They survive today as birthday cakes. Then as now, good fortune came to the one who blew out all the candles at one vigorous puff. Festoons on today's Christmas tree are the successors of decorations that represented beneficent dragons more than two thousand years ago. Boughs of evergreens are now woven into festoons at Christmas time; the Romans wove them in like manner.

Slaves were freed and criminals were pardoned at the Saturnalia. Some governors now extend pardons to deserving prisoners at Christmas time. Little girls received dolls at the Saturnalia just as they do at Christmas today. By mutual consent, it appears that many old quarrels were then forgotten. "Peace on earth, Good will toward men" is still echoed. No new wars were then declared during the season of celebration.

In the misty past, groups went from dwelling to dwelling and sang carols. Mummers long ago went about the British Isles and sang. Today, carolers gather and make the rounds on Christmas eve. Then they sang the very best songs they knew. Through the years since then, many wonderful musical compositions have been inspired by the season.

Saint Winfrid vanquished the Druids and cut down their sacred oak with its mistletoe. When he came to inspect the fallen tree, he found a small evergreen undamaged among its limbs, and there declared that evergreens should thereafter be used as an emblem of the season.

In each land the people had a mythical patron who presided over the celebration. It was not until the advent of Christianity and Christmas, however, that a historic individual, Saint Nicholas of Myra, became permanently associated with the annual observance.

Much of the established data as well as the legends associated with Saint Nicholas were gathered by Angelo Fanelli, a retired Wall Street businessman. It is largely through the work of Fanelli, that a connected account of the saint's life was developed. Some of the facts set down by Fanelli, with bits of legend mingled, give us a clear glimpse of the patron saint of Christmas.

Nicholas was born about A.D. 270 in the city of Tacora, province of Lycia in Asia Minor. His parents were members of the Christian group that had existed there since the time when the Apostle Paul had visited the region some two hundred years earlier. The father of Nicholas was a prosperous merchant and left his son a considerable legacy. Nicholas early became a devout churchman. Coupled with the data establishing this fact, there is much of legend. It is said, for instance, that Nicholas rose and stood alone in the bowl of water at his natal bath. Illustrations based on this legend sometimes appear on Christmas cards. Another tradition states that Nicholas, even before he talked, would not take food on Wednesday, then the fast day for Christians.

While still a youth, Nicholas attained a place of respected prominence in the city. Despite his earnest efforts to be anonymous in his charitable acts, his identity as their doer became known to many. When the bishop of the church at Myra died, churchmen met to select his successor. According to legend, a vision directed their attention to Nicholas, and he was immediately chosen. He, pleading youth and inexperience, tried to avoid the responsibility. Not being able to do so, he accepted it and lived an eventful and useful life.

Many and various experiences came to Nicholas. He was cast into prison by the Emperor Diocletian. There he made friends with everyone including thieves and robbers, and became their guide and patron saint as well as that of slaves. On a sea voyage, he stilled great storms and thus became the patron saint of sailors. Legend has it that children gathered and trudged with him along the dusty roads, and so he became the patron saint of children and of schoolboys. Statues still exist commemorating the boy bishops that once were selected in some of the old schools of England. He also was the patron saint of butchers and in some places they paid funds to the church in his name. Perhaps no saint has had more churches named for him.

Nicholas died on December 6, A.D. 34, and was buried at the church in Myra. His tomb was a point of pilgrimage until the Saracens overran it in 1034. People at Bari, Italy, decided to remove the body from the territory controlled by the Saracens, and they set out in several ships to do so in April, 1087. Outwitting the Greek guards at Myra, they secured the body of Saint Nicholas and reached Bari with it in May, 1087, just before an expedition was due to leave Venice with the same objective. His remains now rest in the church at Bari.

Legend has Santa travel in various ways. In Norway and Sweden it is with reindeers, and he drops the presents down the chimney. In Poland and Germany, he places them in stockings hung by the chimney or, perhaps outside the window. In Belgium and Holland, he rides a big white horse and places toys in wooden shoes, around which the youngsters have often placed hay for the horse. Recently, he has been pictured traveling in automobiles and airplanes.

Santa generally travels alone. Sometimes, though, he has a helper, one who finds the disobedient and naughty since Nicholas himself could never punish or deny. In Norway his helper is Kris Kringle. In North Germany it is Knes Rutrecht, who helps deliver gifts to the good, and Pelsnichel, who carries along birch rods for the bad children. In Holland, his helper is Jan Haas, who carries a big black sack of sticks and sand. In Switzerland, his helper is Schmitzle, who goes along to scoop up the bad boys and girls and place them in a big black bag. In parts of Switzerland and Sweden, Santa is accompanied by his wife, Lucy, who helps to distribute presents to the deserving.

Children are now pictured sitting on the knee of Santa Claus. This picture comes from a legend that originated in Poland about the tenth century.

Then a seven-year-old orphan boy named Stasia, hungry, barefooted and in rags, stood watching other children as they made merry. Saint Nicholas saw the lonely child and asked him what he would like most to have for Christmas. Stasia replied, "One thing only I want and that is that once in my life someone will hold me on his knee, pat me, and put his arms around me the way fathers and mothers do." Saint Nicholas took the boy on his knee, patted him, put his arms around him and held him there until he went to sleep. The next morning Stasia awoke a happy boy, with new clothes, new shoes, food, and the great memory of having been loved.

Chapter 10

Churches

🌿 *OUR OLDEST CHURCH*

MISSIONARIES OF THE Catholic faith and French explorers came into the Illinois country together. The missionaries, a most devoted group, came to convert the Indians to Christianity. The explorers came seeking to discover the resources of the new country and the opportunities it offered. The explorers, as explorers must, kept moving onward. The men of the church paused to establish missions or centers that would enable them to go about their work in a more systematic manner.

Tradesmen coming later often would locate about these mission centers. Officials and emissaries of the French government stopped here. Thus it was that the missions established by the church and afforded a measure of protection by the military, became permanent settlements. Few such settlements survive except in name.

One mission, however, has continued its existence through the years since its establishment on May 14, 1699. This one is the Parish of the Holy Family at Cahokia. Though the original log buildings of this mission have been rotted away for a couple of centuries, some of the relics preserved in the present log church have close connection with the mission that Father Cosme established.

Allowing the curiosity aroused by this old building of walnut logs to function, an inquisitive visitor of today will soon begin to glean bits of the long and interesting story centered about the old church. The age of the structure alone makes it of interest to many. The present building erected and dedicated in 1799, an even century after Father Cosme had set up the first mission, is among the very oldest, if not the oldest church building in the Mississippi Valley.

This log structure does not conform to the usual pattern of such buildings. Instead of the logs being laid horizontally—then practically the universal method except among the French—they are arranged vertically. The ends of these vertical logs, hewed both inside and out, are mortised into other shaped logs lying along the bottom and top of the wall. The matching edges of the vertical logs have wide grooves in them about two inches deep in order to retain the mortar and stones used to chink and daub the openings. The corners of the building are sturdily braced. Also, the logs of the wall are leaned inward about eight inches, better to withstand the thrust of the roof trusses. All these combine to give the building a restrained and rugged appearance.

The floor slopes gently, about six inches, from the doorway to the altar. There is no ceiling. The graceful and well-proportioned trusses that support the roof are of hewed timbers and show skilled workmanship. Bronze plaques and printed legends at appropriate places highlight some of the church's history. Emblems used in the worship service of this and of the preceding churches and mission are distributed about the room. The old pews are gone as are the charcoal foot warmers, but candles still are kept burning at the altar.

In the dim light and quietness, it is not difficult to conjure up scenes of the earlier years. These scenes are peopled with a motley group that included stolid, blanketed Indians, French settlers with their kapots and blue handkerchiefs, Indian traders, *coureurs de bois,* explorers, adventurers, hunters, the local French gentry and robed priests that ministered to the local citizens and Indian tribes of the area. In the 264 years since the establishment of the mission that is now the Parish of the Holy Family, this old church and its predecessors at about the same spot have seen a motley crowd pass. The church buildings now serving the parish along with the older ones each have their own interesting stories.

The early burying ground with only a few markers remaining lies behind the old church. An appropriate memorial stands near the center of this spot. A bronze plaque on the memorial says: "Ancient burial grounds of the Holy Family Church of Cahokia. Here were interred from the earliest days of the settlement to about 1840 the departed of this parish and here they lie in peace." This is the oldest marked burial ground for white people in Illinois. In 1839 a new burial ground was selected east of the first one.

At one time about two thousand Indians lived in the vicinity of the mission. Groups often were encamped on the plot of open ground in front of the church. It was on this spot that George Rogers Clark, after his conquest of Illinois in 1778, conferred with various Indian tribes in an effort to have them become friends and allies of the American colonists.

On this same plot in front of the church, services were held on May 14, 1949, to commemorate the founding of the mission just 250 years before. Pontifical high field Mass was celebrated by Cardinal Stritch of Chicago. The whole proceedings were magnificent and impressive.

From the stone steps in front of this log church and its predecessor, proclamations, announcements, edicts, and sales were made, and public discussions were held in accordance with French practices. Now it is only on rare occasions that services are conducted in the log structure.

A few years ago, about 1950, a thorough restoration of the old church was undertaken. The siding that had covered the logs for fifty years or more was removed. Needed repairs and a few replacements were made. The wood was thoroughly treated to ward off decay. In fact, everything known was done to have the building stand for another century and a half or even longer.

This old church may be considered as a kind of national memorial. The roster of devout men who have served it is a long one. Those who should receive the most credit for its restoration are Father Joseph Mueller, parish priest; Joseph Desloge of St. Louis; Guy Stady, St. Louis architect; and the Most Reverend Albert R. Zuroweste, Bishop of Belleville.

Anyone interested in the early history of southern Illinois can well afford to pause as he drives on Route 3, a few miles south from East St. Louis and visit this picturesque church.

❧ PETER CARTWRIGHT

THOUGH PETER CARTWRIGHT was not, by many years, the first Protestant minister or missionary in Illinois, he easily remains one of the most colorful and distinguished of the early group. He was born in Virginia in 1785. When the family moved west, young Cartwright was taken over a trail beset by hostile Indians. The family located on a farm ten miles south of Russellville in Logan County, Kentucky, a mile north of the Tennessee boundary. Here Peter grew up, a somewhat boisterous and venturesome youth. At sixteen he was, by his own accounts, a skilled and somewhat successful gambler, a race-horse owner and rider, and, as he described it, was well launched on a useless life.

In the autumn of 1801, he returned from a night spent at a dance and began to ponder the folly of his way of life. After many days of remorse, meditation, and prayer with his mother, he became a professed Christian.

Almost immediately thereafter the Peter Cartwright of legend emerges. He soon was licensed as an exhorter in the Methodist church. Entering at once upon his chosen work, he showed himself to be fearless, forceful, intelligent, aggressive, industrious, competent, and devoted. Though lacking in formal education, he proved to be a fluent, forceful, and appealing speaker. He soon became a noted preacher.

In 1812, he was made presiding elder of the Wabash district of the Methodist church, including the circuits of Vincennes, Little Wabash, Fort Massac, and some counties across the Ohio River in Kentucky. During his work in this district, he traveled many thousands of miles on foot and on horseback and held an almost unbelievable number of camp meetings.

Cartwright, whose home had remained in Kentucky, became dissatisfied with living there. He did not wish to raise his family in an environment so greatly influenced by slavery. He also thought that the economic advantages offered in Illinois would be better for his children. To these he added the great opportunity that Illinois offered for the advancement of the church.

Having decided to move, Cartwright set out in the spring of 1823 to inspect some regions of Illinois and to seek a desirable location for a new home. He selected a site in the northern part of Sangamon County and bought the improvements that a settler had already made. Arrangements were made to move to the new location in the fall of 1824.

The journey began in October and seems to have gone well until the parents and their children were some distance within the state of Illinois. As they were nearing the northern line of Saline County, one of the wagons was overturned. When it had been righted and reloaded, the sun had set, and they decided to camp where they were until morning. Since the night was pleasant, they did not pitch a sleeping tent. Instead, after the evening meal, all lay about the fire that had been kindled at the base of a tree and slept soundly.

At daybreak the next morning, Cartwright heard the snapping of timber and sprang up. The tree against which the fire had been built had burned almost through and was beginning to fall. The base of the tree which they had thought solid had been hollow and rotten. Despite Cartwright's utmost efforts to divert it, the tree fell upon his nine-year-old daughter and instantly killed her.

The driver of one of his wagons ran to the only two houses in the vicinity to secure help, but the people at neither place would come to the aid of the distressed travelers. Cartwright and the driver then began to cut the log in order to remove it from over the body. Cartwright says:

"We drew her from under it, and carefully laid her in our feed trough, and moved on about twenty miles to an acquaintance's in Hamilton County, Illinois, where we buried her."

The place where this burial was made is near Cartwright Church, five miles west and a mile and a half north of the village of Dale. According to tradition, the child's grave, marked by rough sandstone slabs, is located beneath an oak tree on the west side of the old Goshen Road and about two hundred yards south of the church. A memorial to her is located in the larger cemetery near the spot where the first church stood. The inscription on one face of the memorial states that it was erected by the Mount Carmel district of the Southern Illinois Conference of the Methodist Episcopal Church. The other face carries the following inscription:

CYNTHIA

DAUGHTER OF

PETER AND FRANCES CARTWRIGHT

BORN MARCH 27, 1815

WAS KILLED BY FALLING TREE

OCTOBER 23, 1824.

SHE CLOSED AT NIGHT HER SLEEPY EYES

AND WOKE AT DAWN IN PARADISE

This mention of the burial of Cartwright's daughter could hardly be ended without a condensed quotation from his account of the tragic incident. He says: "There was in the settlement a very wicked family . . . total strangers to me and mine. This old gentleman and two sons heard of our affliction . . . hastened to our relief . . . every act of kindness that they possibly could do was rendered . . . would on no account have any compensation. . . met and conversed with them years afterwards."

In the history of the Protestant church in earlier Illinois, few names are comparable to that of Peter Cartwright.

❧ MORAVIANS

NEARLY EVERY CHURCH has a bell. Some have a series of tuned bells or chimes upon which a melody may be played. It is not common, however, for a church to have two regular bells. In fact, we know of only one Protestant church with two such bells, both in service. This church is in West Salem, Edwards County, Illinois.

It is not the two bells alone that set this church apart. Bells or no bells, it would still be a distinctive church, made so by the fact that it is the only Moravian church in the state. The official name of the denomination with which the West Salem church is affiliated is Jednota Bratraska or Unitas Fratrum, the "Unity of the Brethren." Since this church was first organized on the borders of Moravia in what is now the country of Czechoslovakia, the name Moravian came to be applied and through some centuries has become the popular designation.

The Unitas Fratrum, or, as it will be designated, the Moravian, is an old church group having already celebrated its quincentenary or five hundredth year of existence as a church organization. This observance began in 1952 and ended in 1957, emphasis being placed each year upon some fundamental aspect of the church's program.

The Moravian church, one of the very oldest of the Protestant faiths, traces its establishment to the teachings of John Hus, who died in 1415. Hus was educated at the University of Prague, where he obtained the rank of Magister (M.A.) in 1396. After graduation, he joined the faculty, and became rector of the University in 1402. Because he refused to conform to certain beliefs and practices of the established church of his day, Hus was charged with being a heretic and was burned at the stake on his birthday, July 6, 1415.

The story of the Moravian church is a long one, too long to recount here. Through the early years, it faced a continuous struggle to remain in existence. The story of the Moravian church in West Salem is also a long one. Only enough of its story will be told to account for the presence of the two bells, side by side in the same belfry.

When the region about West Salem was being settled, a few Moravian families from North Carolina located there. They were interested in forming a local church organization. The Reverend Martin Houser, living in Indiana, accordingly came and preached to the group. As a result of his efforts, a church organization was set up in Peter Hinkle's barn on Saturday, May 24, 1844. This group continued to worship in various homes and other places until a building was erected near the present memorial archway at the entrance to the old cemetery. This building was consecrated on May 31, 1846.

On July 20, 1849, a group of forty-six persons, Moravians, from Germany, arrived at West Salem and encamped on the spot where the present church stands. With their coming, a language problem presented itself. This was solved by the two language groups, English and German, alternating in the use of the building. In 1858 these groups separated and the English speaking members erected the building now standing on the south side of the square. The German-speaking group continued to use the old building.

The building on the south side of the square was used by the English-speaking group until 1915, when, the language problem having disappeared with the passing of those who understood only German, the two groups reunited and all went to worship in the building that the German-speaking group had erected and dedicated on April 10, 1902. With the reuniting of the two groups, the bell from the English-speaking church was brought to the present building and placed beside the one already there. These bells may be rung separately. On some occasions, they are rung together. The members of the Moravian church look upon the ringing of the two bells together as a symbol of unity in their church.

Citizens of West Salem, whether members of this church or not, are proud of the 114-year-old Moravian congregation. They point with pride to the present building, with its tall, slender spire and the beautiful new parsonage. One cannot talk with members of the Moravian church there without sensing the existence of a calm and abiding faith.

The first church, long ago removed from its original site to a place about a block west from the south side of the square, is now a storage house. The building used by the English-speaking group still stands on the south side of the square. When one visits West Salem, he thus sees the three churches, each offering its part of an interesting story. These and the older portions of the cemetery, with their distinctive system of burials and grave markings, make a visit to West Salem worth while.

🌿 *MORMONS*

IT SEEMS THAT ABOUT every church of the Christian faith has an organization or adherents in southern Illinois. Something already has been said about the Moravian church at West Salem, the only one of that faith in Illinois. Another faith, until recently little associated with this area, is that of the Church of Jesus Christ of Latter Day Saints, more briefly referred to as the Mormon Church. Perhaps this sect, once influential in Illinois, has always had a scattered membership and had at least one church group in Egypt as much as sixty years ago.

A visit to the Carthage-Nauvoo area, once the center of the Mormon church in America, in the spring of 1957 rekindled our interest and brought back memories of earlier fleeting contacts with members of that sect in southern Illinois. These first recollections of Mormons go back to a time when two young men came into a community north of Raleigh in Saline County about sixty years ago and set up their simple camp.

These two young men were Mormon missionaries. During the day they went about the countryside visiting and talking to people. In the evening, "at early candle light," they held church services near the place where they had made camp. Seats for those attending were arranged by laying planks across sections of logs. A speaker's platform was made in a similar manner, but it is not recalled that either of the men used it. "Early candle light" was provided by kerosene lanterns.

These two young men were missionaries sent out by the Mormons. It is not known whether they were from the Reorganized or from the Utah branch of the church. The interest and discussion they aroused was considerable. They and the church they represented immediately became the principal subject of conversation when people stopped to visit or talk, or when neighbors came to "set 'till bedtime." Much information with perhaps an equal amount of misinformation concerning the beliefs and practices of that church were spread about.

Only confused memories remain of stories told about their travels and migrations, golden plates, and magical stones through which a man had peered to translate engravings on the plates.

There was much talk about their men having more than one wife. So far as is remembered, this talk was made around neighbors' firesides. In fact, it is not definitely remembered what it was that the missionaries said or what it was the neighbors said. However, the various stories aroused an early interest in the Mormons and tended to make them a rather interesting, romantic, and mysterious people.

The two missionaries, referred to by most of those who spoke of them as "two nice young men," have long been gone, but the interest they aroused lingered, at least with one lad. Two or three years after their leaving, it was learned that an old gentleman, a Civil War veteran living beside the roadway toward Eldorado, was a Mormon. Any lingering thought that a Mormon was necessarily evil was quickly dispelled by this smallish, kindly, calm, and utterly inoffensive old gentleman with a family of several children and only one wife.

Some years afterward, it was learned that there was a Mormon church building in Johnson County. In fact, it may even yet be there. From time to time, while rummaging among old books in some attic or smokehouse of southern Illinois, we have found various books concerning the Mormons. One such collection from South Pass contained several volumes, indicating that the one owning them was of that faith. The designation of the owner's address as South Pass would predate 1856, when South

Pass became Cobden. Perhaps southern Illinois has always had some of the Mormon faith.

Today there are two branches of the church: The Church of Jesus Christ of Latter Day Saints and The Reorganized Church of Jesus Christ of Latter Day Saints. There now are eight or more church organizations of the former and at least two of the latter in this section. All members encountered seem pleased to have one know that they are members of that church. From time to time, missionaries still go about in pairs just as they did sixty years ago.

Whatever one's beliefs concerning the church may be, a visit to Nauvoo and to Carthage, where Joseph Smith and his brother Hyrum were slain by a mob while they were being held prisoners in the jail, will be rewarding to anyone interested in the great religious movement referred to as Mormonism. The town of Nauvoo that once had a population of about fifteen thousand now has only one tenth as many. Many of the old houses carry interesting stories of the days when the church was centered there. No matter how well informed the visitor may be, he can glean other additional stories by spending a day in the town. Also, he is likely to come away with an increased respect for the Mormons.

Chapter 11

Law & Order

❧ *PUNISHMENTS*

ON THE FRONTIER, organized law enforcement did not keep up with the advancing fringe of settlement. Until enough settlers came into any region to organize courts and execute their judgments, it might be said that each settler was dependent upon his own strength, perhaps combined with that of his neighbor, if one was near enough to be helpful. When enough settlers arrived, they established some form of government. This government and its laws generally were borrowed from older settled regions. The laws they brought and the punishments prescribed for their violation were severe.

"Thirty lashes on the bare back, well laid on" sounds brutal, and it was. These words appear in many old southern Illinois court records. In addition to lashes, the violator sometimes was placed in the stocks or in the pillory. The whipping post, stocks, pillory, and the lash were regular instruments of punishment. The whipping post was high enough to permit the wrists of the standing victim to be raised high above his head and tied there. Sometimes these posts had a crosspiece to which the extended arms could be bound. Always they were in public view, and the sight of them must have served as a deterrent to would-be law violators. Where there was no whipping post, a tree served the same purpose.

Stocks were made of thick horizontal boards that had notches in their adjoining edges. Into these the extended wrists and ankles of the seated victim were fastened. After he was secured in the stocks, the person being punished was uncomfortable and helpless and often was subjected to indignities by the passers-by. The pillory, fashioned somewhat like the stocks, was made of two boards with three notches in their adjoining sides. The center notch was large enough to fasten around the neck of the victim while the smaller notches, one on either side of the larger one, would close about his wrists. The height of these openings required the victim to stand in a stooped position. Confinement in the pillory was considered very severe, and no sentence could exceed three hours. Only rare mention of another device of punishment, the ducking stool, is found in the laws applicable to southern Illinois, but no record of its use has been found.

Some of the early laws and the punishments visited upon those violating them may be of interest. Murder, defined as killing with malice aforethought, was punishable by death, and the person on trial was either found guilty and hanged or went free. Apparently, there were no degrees of murder. Anyone committing forgery had to repay the damaged person and to stand for a time in the pillory. For larceny or theft of personal property those convicted were required to return the value of the goods stolen and to receive not more than thirty-one stripes on the bared back. Burglary was punishable by thirty-nine lashes. The offender also had to furnish bond guaranteeing good behavior for three years. If he violated this bond, he was obligated to restore three times the value of the goods stolen—one part going to the state and two parts to the person whose goods had been stolen. Rioting, a disturbance in which three or more persons joined to create disorder, was punishable by thirty-nine lashes plus a fine.

A disobedient child or servant could be taken before two justices of the peace. If convicted, the violator was confined in the county jail until he "humbled himself in a manner satisfactory to the parent or master." Should the child or servant assault the master, the two justices could sentence him to receive ten lashes on the bared back. A Negro or mulatto ten miles from home without special consent received ten lashes. A like punishment was due if he entered upon the property of anyone other than his master's without specific permission. A sheriff who willingly allowed a prisoner to escape was required to take the prisoner's place and to receive the punishment the prisoner would have received if convicted of the crime charged. In 1808 the penalty for stealing a horse was death. Anyone convicted of selling liquor to an Indian was fined $5.00 for each quart sold.

Men between sixteen and sixty were required by law to serve in the militia and to meet regularly each week for two hours of drill. Each member had to provide his own rifle, bullet mould, a pound of powder, four pounds of lead, a priming wire, a gun brush, six flints, a powder horn, and a bullet pouch.

The height of fences also was fixed by law. Northwest Territory statutes required fences four feet, six inches in height, but later Illinois Territory laws called for fences five feet, six inches high. The width of cracks between pickets or palings and between the rails in a rail fence likewise were determined by law.

In considering early laws and penalties, one should remember that physical and social conditions were quite different then. For example, jails and space for the confinement of prisoners was limited. Thus, it was more convenient to dispose of the culprit with "thirty lashes on the bare back well laid on" or "three hours in the pillory" and turn him loose. This made space available for the next violator.

❧ SCRAMBLED RECORDS & SPEEDY JUSTICE

THE KEEPING OF county records now is systematized and designated books carry particular types of records. In the earlier days of many counties in southern Illinois, records were not kept in such an orderly manner. It might be said that they were "kept by ear." In some of the older books of county records one finds deeds, contracts, trial records, bills of sale, indenture and apprentice papers, mortgages—in fact, almost anything that was recorded—in the same book. Sometimes the reason for choosing a particular book seems to have been its convenient location at the time; that is, it was the one nearest at hand. This does not mean that records were not accurately and thoroughly set down, only that they were scrambled.

Though this somewhat unmethodical manner of recording may make it more difficult to find and interpret any particular information desired, it certainly furnishes surprises. This is illustrated by a few minutes with Deed Record "A" in the office of the circuit clerk of Crawford County at Robinson. Page one of this book records the fact that on June 7, 1817, a man named William Howard granted freedom to a Negro woman named Fanny. On September 7 of that same year, he granted freedom to a Negro man named David. In neither of these cases is the last name of the freed party given. After these notations on page one, a few deeds and other instruments are recorded. Page nine resembles the first page and records Abraham Hamp's certificate of freedom. It indicates that Hamp's mother was "one of Sir William Johnson's Mohawk Indians." It also says that Hamp had obtained his freedom by court action in Virginia on July 26, 1786.

Hamp appeared in the Crawford County clerk's office on February 27,

1819, and requested that his certificate given by the Virginia court be recopied because "From the long period since it was written . . . the words are somewhat effaced and obliterated." In addition to a copy of the papers granted in Virginia, there is added the information that Hamp had lived on the Wabash near Vincennes for many years and that he was a good citizen. The names of the other members of his family also are listed. At the end of the records concerning Hamp on page nine, an entirely different type of record begins. It relates to a murder trial and indicates the speed with which justice was dispensed. The following is a condensation of several pages.

On June 12 the sheriff was directed to summon twenty-three men to form a grand jury and thirty-six men from whom required petit jurors could be selected. These men were to assemble in the county seat, then at Palestine, on July 7. They evidently were on time; the grand jury returned its first indictment on July 8. This was against John Killduck, Captain Thomas, and Big Panther, three Delaware Indians living in Alliston Township. They were charged with the murder of a man named Thomas McCall a short time previously.

The next day, July 9, the three prisoners were "led to the bar" for trial and pleaded "Not guilty." A jury, composed of the men who had been summoned for jury service, was impaneled and the trial began. It ended on the same day with the verdict, "We the jury find the prisoners guilty in the manner and form as they stand charged in the indictment." A motion for a new trial was immediately made. It was alleged that the verdict was "contrary to law and evidence." It also was alleged that the indictment was defective. At this point, the judge must have decided that a day's work had been done. He adjourned court until seven o'clock on the next morning.

When the court convened on July 10, the judge ruled that the indictment was defective and quashed it. On this same day, however, the grand jury reassembled and returned another indictment against the Indians. The judge then remanded Captain Thomas and Big Panther to jail to await trial at the next session of the court. John Killduck was immediately tried separately. The trial proceeded with all reasonable speed. Before the end of the day, it had ended and the verdict was: "We the jury find the prisoner guilty in manner and form as he stands charged in the indictment." A request for a new trial was made at once. "After argument and due consideration" this motion was denied.

The prisoner was then brought before the court and "was asked if anything he had to say, why sentence should not be pronounced against him, saith that he has nothing to say further than what he has said."

Judge Thomas C. Brown, presiding at this July session of the court, then proceeded to sentence the prisoner.

The balance of John Killduck's story is easily gleaned from the following paragraph taken from the records of the court's proceedings: "It is therefore ordered by the court here understanding all and singularly that the said William Killduck be taken to the gael from which he came and from thence to the place of execution on Wednesday next, the 14th of this inst. between the hours of 1 and 2 o'clock in the afternoon and there hanged by the neck until dead."

After the pronouncement of the sentence, the court adjourned. It was Saturday afternoon. Killduck had been first brought to trial on Friday, July 9. His second trial had been held on the next day, July 10, and sentence had been passed. Four days later the career of John Killduck was ended. The record book contains no further information of the fate of Captain Thomas and Big Panther.

🌿 *OLD JAILS*

When new Illinois counties were formed, it became necessary to have county buildings. Strangely enough, jails held high priority on the new county's building program. In numerous cases, they were built before the courthouses. A room to serve the needs of the county officials and to house their meager records often was found "at the residence of" some citizen. There were no places available, however, to serve as ready-made jails, and it was necessary to erect them.

In almost all cases, these buildings were small, separate structures made of logs. They obviously were intended for security and not for comfort or convenience. No indication has been found of a plan to heat one of them. They were not meant for extended confinement of prisoners—there was no such sentence as "ninety days in jail." Jails were intended only to hold culprits until a speedy trial could be held and those found guilty could receive a prescribed number of lashes or could spend a certain number of hours in the pillory or stocks, or even could be hanged.

A number of specifications for early jails are found among the records of older counties. Those for the jail erected at Brownsville, county seat of Jackson County, in 1825, illustrate very well the manner of their building. Perhaps it was better built than the average. On December 6, 1824, the County Commissioners Court of Jackson County voted to build a new two-story jail at Brownsville to replace the one erected when the county was formed in 1816. They located it in the northeast corner of Lot 75, purchased from Jess Griggs for $4.00.

The Brownsville prison had a "foundation laid of rock 17 feet and two inches square on the outside and three feet and six inches thick . . . said foundation to extend 18 inches into the ground and one foot above." It had a "floor laid thereon of hewn whiteoak timbers one foot square to extend over the whole of said foundation except 13 inches on each side with a floor of white oak planks two inches thick well spiked down to be laid thereon." The first floor thus was fourteen inches thick.

The lower story had a heavy outside wall that really was three walls. The inner layer of this wall was "12 feet square in the clear" and was made of "hewn whiteoak timbers 10 inches thick well dovetailed at the corners." The next or middle layer was of "upright timbers six inches thick . . . well squared . . . with bottoms standing on the rock foundation." The third or outer layer was a wall of "brick and lime 13 inches thick." The total thickness of the walls of the lower story thus was twenty-nine inches. The ceiling of the lower room, which also served as the floor of the second story, was "of hewn whiteoak timbers 12 inches square to extend over the timbers of the lower floor to the brick walls and to be notched down to the timbers of the lower story with a half dovetail and a flooring of inch oak planks well laid thereon." The ceiling height of both the lower and upper rooms was "seven feet in the clear."

There was one doorway located on the south side of the lower room. It was "five feet and a half high and two feet four inches in the clear." The frame of this door, six inches thick, was "well pinned to the timbers and walls with a six quarter (one and one-half inch) auger." Two doors were hung at this doorway, "one door to open inward and one door to open outward." They were made of "two inch oak planks well lined with one inch oak planks and spiked full with iron spikes." Both doors were "well secured with bolts, iron hinges and locks."

The specifications as first written said "there shall be in the lower story a window 12 inches square made by cutting half through two logs and space left in the outer brick wall." This window was to have four one-inch iron bars across it "let into the timbers five inches at each end." A later order added another "window of the same size as the one in the old order."

The second story was much like the first except for the omission of the center layer of the walls. Its ceiling like the floors of the first and second stories was "laid of squared whiteoak timbers 12 inches square . . . well pinned down." The upper room had two windows twelve by twelve inches. Its doorway, "six feet high and two feet two inches in the clear" was "finished in the same manner as the lower door." It was reached by a "flight of stairs from the ground to a platform on a line with the second floor."

The contract for the erection of this building was awarded to David Husband, who agreed to "complete said building in a strong and workmanlike manner and suitable for a jail" for $1,000. The completed jail was accepted by the county on September 29, 1825. Notwithstanding its sturdiness, this jail has long since vanished along with all other buildings of the village. A few stones in the ground outline the old foundation. When last visited, the place was overgrown with tall weeds, and only ground hogs populated the site.

🏵 FLATHEADS & REGULATORS

BEFORE CALIFORNIA HAD its vigilantes to maintain a semblance of law and order in the gold fields, southern Illinois had mobilized similar organizations. The region had had its flatheads, regulators, vigilantes, and perhaps other minor groups at an early date.

Two pairs of early opposing bands in southern Illinois were the Flatheads and Regulators of the Pope-Hardin-Massac area, and the Regulators and Vigilantes of the Gallatin County region. In each pairing the first group named appears to have been formed earlier. In both instances the second group was formed for the announced purpose of controlling and suppressing the activities of the first, and to aid in law enforcement.

The origin of the Flathead-Regulator conflict in the Hardin-Pope-Massac region can be understood better by a brief glimpse of earlier events in the region. A man named Mason came to the cave at Cave-in-Rock before 1800 and established a "Liquor Vault and House of Entertainment." Mason was from a respected Virginia family and had served as a captain in the Continental army. At Cave-in-Rock he became leader of a gang which practiced river piracy, robbery, and murder.

Mason soon transferred his activities to the lower Mississippi, and other men took over at Cave-in-Rock. Mason was followed by a man whom some believed was Mason operating under an assumed name. After Wilson, other men came to reign for varying lengths of time. One of these, named Duff, is said to have been the man who guided George Rogers Clark on his journey from Fort Massac to Kaskaskia in July, 1778. The next man to attract particular attention in the region of the cave was named Sturdevant, who had headquarters in a blockhouse that he built where the water plant of the city of Rosiclare now is located. His specialty was the making and distribution of counterfeit money.

Sturdevant's method of operation was designed to arouse the least amount of local opposition. He wholesaled the spurious money, selling it at the rate of $100.00 of counterfeit for $16.00 of legal money. At all times, the purchaser had to promise to pass the counterfeit money outside the local area. Some of the purchasers, however, failed to abide by this understanding, and the circulation of the worthless money locally, with other crimes committed by Sturdevant's associates aroused unfavorable sentiment. A Regulator group, including many of the most prominent and influential men in the region, was formed to curb their activities. Sturdevant's gang became the Flatheads.

Tension rapidly increased, and the entire area took on the air of an armed camp. While the objectives of the Regulators appeared commendable, their methods of operating soon became extralegal. Men whom they suspected or disliked, and some who hesitated to join them, were threatened, whipped, tarred and feathered, and coerced in various ways. Extralegal or kangaroo courts were set up and enforcement officers appointed. Soon purely personal differences entered into the feuding, and the men who had launched the movement lost control of it.

Within a short time a battle was fought between the two forces at Sturdevant's blockhouse, where the Flatheads were quartered. In this clash, Sturdevant's men used a small cannon and held the Regulators at at bay. A call for reinforcements was sent out. Night came before these reinforcements arrived. The men in the blockhouse escaped in the darkness and fled the area. With the departure of the leaders of the Flatheads, the strife gradually subsided and an uneasy quiet was restored, then settlers began to come to the region in large numbers.

The Regulators and Vigilantes in the Gallatin County area were similar in organization to those of the Pope-Hardin-Massac region. In this case, though, the name of Regulators was applied to the group outside the law. The Regulators first were formed to "regulate" the Negroes and those who appeared friendly to them. They were charged with threatening and whipping Negroes, with kidnaping free ones, and with stealing slaves being moved across the state. They also appear to have engaged in other law violations.

Practices of these Regulators led to the formation of the Vigilantes to oppose them. The new group was led for a time by Michael K. Lawler, who later became a captain in the Mexican War and a brigadier general in the Civil War. Lawler, a capable and energetic leader, ably controlled the Vigilantes. They were not accused of engaging in the excesses charged against the Regulators in adjoining counties. Both the Regulators and the Vigilantes in the Gallatin area faded away before the Civil War. The Regulators were led by a man called "Leather" Moore, a name assigned because he was charged with stealing leather.

Perhaps the activities mentioned here are indicative of the growing pains of a new country, one where the settlers arrived in numbers before the processes of local government had been established, or where local authorities were grossly indifferent or negligent. Several parallel groups operated at other places in southern Illinois.

❧ PEOPLE DISLIKED HORSE THIEVES

PERHAPS THERE IS not an active anti–horse-thief association in America today, but such associations once were common over the country, and southern Illinois had its quota of them.

People evidently considered horse thieves very, very bad and showed them little mercy. In fact, the earliest laws effective in the Illinois country prescribed severe penalties for those convicted of stealing horses. As punishment for the thief's first offense, the law prescribed "40 lashes on the bare back, well laid on." For a second conviction, the penalty was the same as that for murder: death by hanging. These drastic punishments were later lessened in severity, but men still gave more than passing attention to those who would steal horses and grouped themselves together to discourage such activities.

Some of these anti–horse-thief associations sought to protect their members against losses of other livestock by theft. There were even anti-chicken-thief associations, and at Murphysboro there was the "Jackson County Anti–Horse- and Mule-Thief Association." The territory covered by this organization lay within five or six miles of the town.

The "Constitution and Bi-Laws" of the Murphysboro group, printed by the "Era Print" in 1884, may be considered typical of those governing such organizations. According to the by-laws, "any male person above the age of 18 years and possessing a good moral character and living with the bounds of the association" was eligible for membership.

The organization required that anyone desiring to become a member "shall have his name presented by a member in good standing at a regular meeting." If the one proposed for membership received the unanimous vote by ballot of all present and "paid to the secretary the regular initiation fee of $1," he became "entitled to all the benefits of the Society so long as he conforms to its rules and regulations."

Numerous such associations appear to have held monthly meetings. The one at Murphysboro, however, held regular meetings only quarterly, the scheduled dates being the first Saturday in March, June, September, and December of each year, "at one o'clock P.M." Any member missing a regular meeting without a justifiable excuse was to be fined twenty-five cents, and if he missed three regular meetings in succession without proper excuse, he "shall lose his standing and be refused the benefits of the Society until he pays all fines and assessments." If a member wished to withdraw, he could do so by paying all dues and assessments and filing his resignation with the secretary at a regular meeting.

The duties of membership in an anti–horse-thief association were naturally those required to apprehend thieves or to recover stolen horses. A standing committee of three members appointed and working with the president was to notify members of the respective routes assigned to them in case a search for stolen property was made. In event of a theft and a call for search by members, the standing committee was "to remain in consultation with each other and with members as nearly as possible through mail, telegraph and otherwise." They also had the "power to change the route of any member should evidence warrant them in doing so."

It was "the duty of each member immediately upon receiving notice of a theft from a member in good standing to take the route which had been assigned to him by the standing committee." The pursuit was to be continued two days or even longer if there was reasonable hope of arresting the thief or recovering the stolen property.

If evidence from reliable sources warranted, the searchers might continue the search more than two days. In that event, they were to receive "expenses for the first two days and $2 in expenses per day thereafter." Those not assigned to search in particular areas or along designated roads were to "search in the surrounding woods and places where thieves would probably find a hiding place." Any member failing to perform the duties assigned to him and not having a valid excuse was to be expelled from the organization.

A little association booklet with blue paper covers shown to the writer by Clyde Smith of Carbondale affords an interesting glimpse of a practice common in southern Illinois seventy years and more ago. The crime of stealing horses now seems to have gone out of fashion. In fact, horses themselves have practically passed from the picture along with the anti–horse-thief associations.

✿ SELF-DEFENSE

AN ABANDONED SOUTHERN Illinois cemetery near the center of the present city of Benton, in Franklin County, occupies about two acres of ground and contains several hundred burial plots. Only five markers are left standing, however, to name those buried there. One of these stones is a tall, tapering shaft surmounted by the conventional carving of a draped urn. It marks the burial place of Judge William K. Parrish, who died in 1861. The name of Judge Parrish suggests an interesting story relating to the legal definition of self-defense.

Parrish attained an early prominence. When less than thirty years old, he was elected to the office of circuit judge and was the presiding judge at the June term of the Circuit Court of Metropolis, in Massac County, in 1854. Among the cases docketed was one charging a man named Campbell with the murder of another named Parker. It was this case, where Judge Parrish was overruled and the final decision made by the Illinois Supreme Court, that furnished the most cited decision of its kind in Illinois. It also has been cited in many other states and only recently before the United States Supreme Court. After more than a century, the clarity with which the Illinois Supreme Court sets forth the rights of an individual to employ self-defense to preserve his life, makes it a much used precedent.

The case against Campbell was prosecuted by John A. Logan, later to attain national prominence as a politician and Civil War general. Logan was then serving as district attorney before the establishment of the office of state's attorney. Campbell was defended by another competent attorney, J. Jack, who often appeared as defense attorney when Logan was serving as prosecutor. Both Logan and Jack were capable and aggressive, and they were widely known as spirited contenders.

Court records show that Parker and Campbell had developed strong feelings against each other. These appear to have been greater on the part of Parker, who, one day, publicly made threats against the life of Campbell and vowed to settle the score that night. Apparently intent upon carrying out his threat, Parker took three companions with him and went to the home of Campbell's father looking for his victim. Leaving his companions thirty or forty yards behind, Parker went to the door of the Campbell home to see if the man he sought was there. Learning that Campbell was at home, Parker called the ones accompanying him to come forward.

A scuffle between Parker and Campbell began immediately in the darkness near the front door. The mother and sister of Campbell apparently tried to help him, and perhaps the companions of Parker came to his assistance. Whatever may have occurred, Parker was stabbed and died immediately. Campbell emerged from the affray with his head "gashed to the skull," evidently by a hatchet that Parker had brought with him. No pretense was made that there was any justification for the assault upon Campbell.

To this point, the case had not assumed any more than usual significance—the freedom, or perhaps the life, of the accused. Campbell's attorney entered a plea of self-defense. He offered proof that the slain man had threatened the life of the accused on the day of the killing. Judge Parrish held that the evidence was not admissible and ruled that any threat was not of significance. The defense took exception to this ruling.

As the trial progressed, exceptions were made to other rulings of the judge and to parts of the instructions he gave the jury or refused to give them. The trial went on to its end, and Campbell was adjudged guilty. An appeal was taken to the Illinois Supreme Court. It was the opinion of the higher court that the decision of Judge Parrish should be reversed and Campbell freed.

Before that time, it generally was held that one pleading self-defense had to establish the fact that the danger of losing his life or suffering great bodily harm was real. Therefore, being threatened by an unloaded pistol or a wooden sword or a rubber dagger—no matter how realistic the danger might appear—would not justify killing in self-defense. The pistol must be loaded, the sword or dagger real.

The Supreme Court ruled in this case that actual and positive danger is not indispensable to justify self-defense. It rules that "if one is pursued or assaulted in a way to indicate reasonable, well-grounded belief that he is in actual danger, actual and personal danger is not indispensable to self-defense." The court held that if the appearance and actual state of things were such as would convince reasonable and judicious men that there was danger that the assailed would lose his life or suffer great bodily harm, then necessary self-defense was justifiable.

There were other court cases in southern Illinois that are judicial firsts. The first plea of temporary insanity as defense against a charge of homicide is found in a case at Shawneetown, and the first admission by a court that the identity of one accused could be established solely by the witness recognizing his voice is reported from McLeansboro. In this case, the witness was a blind man.

❦ *A DUEL*

SOME SOUTHERN Illinoisans once believed that a proper way to uphold one's personal honor was to fight a duel. A tragic result of this belief is seen in the following story.

Alfonso C. Stuart and Timothy Bennett were living near each other in Belleville in 1819. Bennett had a breachy horse that often got into Stuart's cornfield. After several protests, Stuart warned Bennett that his horse would be shot if it kept breaking into the field, but the break-ins continued. Stuart did not personally carry out the threat he had made, but his hired hand did it for him, using a gun loaded with salt instead of shot. The wound inflicted was painful but not fatal. Bennett became highly incensed and did little to conceal the fact. He went about the community making threats against Stuart.

Two other men, Nathan Fikes and Jacob Short, according to the account they later related, decided to turn the whole affair into a great joke. They would have the principals fight a duel, but the firearms used would contain only powder charges and no bullets. Short began to play upon the feelings of Bennett and suggested that he challenge Stuart to fight a duel. Fikes strove to arouse the anger of Stuart. Both Short and Fikes were successful in their endeavors. Bennett issued the challenge, Stuart accepted it, and plans were laid for the affray. Arrangements of the usual details were completed, weapons were selected, and the date set.

The duel was fought on a vacant town lot. Short served as second for Bennett and Fikes in like capacity for Stuart. The weapons were rifles. The distance was twenty-five paces. After the participants had taken their proper positions, each would be privileged to fire at a given signal. All this was in conformity with the code duello as then observed.

When time for the duel arrived, the contestants, their seconds, and apparently some onlookers went to the chosen spot. The principals and seconds took proper positions. When all was in readiness, the signal to fire was given. Bennett fired first and Stuart fell forward across his weapon, mortally wounded. Bennett's rifle had been loaded with live ammunition. Fikes ran to the prostrate Stuart, rolled him off his rifle, seized it and discharged it into the air. Bennett, Short, and Fikes were promptly arrested, lodged in jail and charged with murder.

An event so sensational attracted much attention and drew varied comments. Men hearing the report made by Stuart's rifle when Fikes discharged it, insisted that it also contained a bullet; because, they contended, the sound made by a loaded gun and another containing only a powder charge were definitely distinguishable to the practiced listener. One witness, a ten-year-old girl named Rachel Tannehill, stated that she had seen Bennett place something in his rifle, presumably a bullet, as he passed near the end of the courthouse on his way to the dueling ground. Whatever had happened, the surviving duelist and both seconds were held to trial, but the seconds soon were released.

The Illinois legislature passed an act that called a special session of the circuit court to try the case. John Reynolds, the "Old Ranger," then Chief Justice of the Illinois Supreme Court, served as circuit judge in the case. When court convened on March 8, 1819, the sheriff was forced to report that the prisoner had escaped from the log jail on the previous night.

Nothing more was heard of Bennett until July, 1821. Then it was learned that he had been living in Arkansas Territory and that he was coming to meet his wife, who was preparing to leave with her household goods in a wagon. Citizens of Belleville trailed Mrs. Bennett's wagon to St. Genevieve, Missouri, where they met Bennett and arrested him. He was returned to Belleville, lodged in jail once more, and the murder charge was reinstated. He was brought to trial in July, 1821, and found guilty of murder under a law that had been passed by Illinois Territory on April 7, 1810. He was sentenced to be hanged on September 3, 1821. The hanging was a public affair, and hundreds came to witness it.

This duel between Stuart and Bennett was neither the first nor the only duel fought on present Illinois soil. A low sandy island near the Illinois shore at East St. Louis was known before Bennett's trial as "Bloody Island." It was perhaps the most noted dueling ground of the Midwest. Some insisted that it belonged to Missouri and others that it was a part of Illinois. Apparently, neither wanted to own this no man's land.

Chapter 12

Slavery & Servitude

🏵 *EARLY SLAVERY*

No ONE KNOWS WHEN the practice of slavery began in Illinois. It is known that when the French explorers, Louis Jolliet and Fr. Jacques Marquette, came in 1673, they found slavery in existence among the Indians. When the explorers gave gifts to the Illinois Indians as evidences of friendship, the Indians responded by presenting gifts to the Frenchmen—a calumet or decorated ceremonial pipe and a "little Indian slave." Incidentally, their records indicate that the Indians considered the calumet as the more valuable of the gifts. The holding of slaves by the Illinois Indians was not unusual. They generally were women and children that had been captured or stolen from other tribes. Many of the slaves held by the Illinois Indians were from the Pawnee, a tribe living west of the Mississippi. In fact, so many of the slaves came from the Pawnee that the French spelling, "panis," came to mean slave. These and other occasional references in existing French records give a glimpse of slavery here when white men arrived.

The first Negro slaves of record in Illinois were five hundred brought from the West Indies by the French promoter, Philippe François Renault in 1719. Many of these were settled at a place known as Saint Philippe, in present Monroe County. They were to be used in the growing of food for other slaves and for laborers at mines that Renault planned to develop in Missouri and Illinois. Mining did not prove as profitable as expected, and some of the Negroes were sold to farmers in the region about Kaskaskia and Cahokia. Thirty years later, when the French population in Illinois was 1,100, most of them in the Kaskaskia-Cahokia region, there were also three hundred Negro and sixty Indian slaves.

The King of France issued edicts legalizing slavery in the territory. Regulations, known as *code noir* or Black Laws, also were established for the control of slaves and slave trade. Punishments prescribed for lazy, disobedient, or insolent slaves were severe and brutal. For misbehaviors that would now be considered as somewhat trivial, slaves could be put to death.

Some records of the trials of slaves remain. One case concerns a Negro named Jean Baxe at Fort de Chartres, in Randolph County. Owned by the orphaned children of a man named Texin, he was charged with resisting an overseer named Bastien. Since the court regularly prescribed by the *code noir* was nonexistent in Illinois, Baxe was tried before a group of officers of the French garrison at the fort. It is recorded that Baxe, "a baptised Christian," was made to "raise his hand to tell the truth." Evidence in the trial indicates that the overseer, Bastien, struck Baxe to punish him. To shield himself from the blows, many of which he had already received upon his left arm that he had raised in protection, Baxe seized Bastien with the evident intention of holding him until help could come. They, Baxe and Bastien, were shortly found by M. La Lande. No evidence was offered that Baxe struck back at Bastien.

The court decided that Baxe should "make public reparations to the above mentioned Bastien on his knees and be whipped three different days short of death." It also decreed that "having determined to mitigate and soften the punishment of the above Negro by reason the prayer of Mant [. . . . . . (illegible)] in the name of his village we commute the punishment of death, even if merited, to that of whipping." Quoting further, the judgment says: "We forbid all persons of whatever quality or condition they may be, to augment or diminish the above mentioned punishment in any manner whatsoever."

This trial was held on December 22, 1730. Perhaps it is the oldest record of the trial of a Negro slave in Illinois. There are numerous later records of similar trials.

🍃 SLAVE LAWS & PRACTICES

PRACTICES DO NOT always conform to existing laws. This was especially true about slavery and Negro servitude in Illinois during its territorial and early statehood days, as is shown by a study of records in some of the earlier counties. Those of Pope County offer interesting illustrations of what actually happened. A few selected items from the Golconda records are given here.

The first entry found there was an indenture dated June 22, 1815, between Silvey, a Negro woman twenty-five years old, and John Morris, of Gallatin County, which then included a portion of Pope County. This indenture was filed for record June 25, 1816, a few months after the county of Pope had been formed. Silvey bound herself to serve Morris "for a term of forty years next ensuing." The records state that Silvey received "$400 in hand paid, receipt of which is hereby acknowledged." In addition to the $400, which it is doubtful that Silvey ever received, she was to be given "good and sufficient meat, drink, lodging and apparel, together with all other needful conveniences fit for such a servant." Silvey pledged herself "faithfully to serve, obey, not to absent herself from her work and not to embezzle or waste or lend her master's property."

The second entry is a "Bill of Bargain and Sale," showing that Thomas Ferguson, living at Golconda, bought a Negro man named Jeffery, about thirty years old, from Jessie Jones, Caldwell County, Kentucky, for $525. This bill of sale was filed in the office of Joshua Scott, recorder of Pope County, on November 26, 1816, and thus shows ownership of Jeffery in the county.

Numerous other transactions of similar nature are recorded. Louis La Chapelle, of Randolph County, sold Isaac, a servant about twenty-three years old, bound to La Chapelle for forty years, to Thomas Ferguson on April 2, 1811. Then Wiley Davis of Eddyville, Kentucky, assigns his interest in "Letty, a slave," and her one-year-old son to Ferguson. On December 18, 1816, John Ditterline transfers his rights to Mary, "a slave for life" to Ferguson for a consideration of $500. This transaction, ackowledged before Joshua Scott, county clerk for Pope County, shows that the transaction took place in that county. Numerous other sales were legalized in this manner.

In addition to the records of sales, many of indentures are found. A Negro man named Anthony was bound to Thomas Ferguson for a period of thirty years for "a certain lot numbered 163 in Sarahville," now Golconda. Anthony was to have immediate possession and "enjoy the rents and profits" of said lot during his term of servitude. The value of Anthony's lot must have been negligible, since near-by lots numbered 161 and 168 sold within the year for three dollars each. On February 13, 1818, Linda, about nineteen years old and "last out of Missouri Territory," bound herself to William Wilson for a period of ninety-nine years for a consideration of $400 "in hand paid, receipt of which is hereby acknowledged." This indenture would have ended in 1917. On December 14, 1820, John Henry, of Pope County, sold Anthony, about eighteen years old, to Elizabeth Henry, of Logan County, Kentucky, for $612. This bill of sale was certified by Craven P. Hester, a justice of the peace in Pope County. Another record concerning Fannie Mac, "a woman of color" and her son, Caesar, "a man of color" is somewhat singular. It shows that Fannie Mac, on September 16, 1835, purchases her son, a slave, from Stephen Smelser of Calway County, Kentucky, for the sum of $550. About four months later, Fannie, "for love and affection," emancipates Caesar. During the intervening period, Fannie Mac obviously held her own son as a slave.

These are only random samplings of the legal records concerning slavery and Negro servitude in one southern Illinois county. They show that laws to regulate slavery were openly flouted.

🌿 *BINDING OUT*

"READING AND WRITING and the ground rules of arithmetic . . . a new Bible . . . two new suits of clothes (dresses) suitable to his (her) position in life . . ."—such phrases are found in many old southern Illinois records. They came from indentures, the legal forms used to "bind out" white children as clerks, apprentices, or servants and to indicate the rewards that the master agreed to give to the one bound if he or she satisfactorily completed the term of service.

The rewards listed above were those generally mentioned, but others were sometimes added. A girl might receive additional awards such as a feather bed, two blankets, pots and cooking utensils, or perchance a dress "suitable for the Sabbath" or for "going out." A boy might receive a horse, saddle, and bridle, $50 in cash, a set of tools used in the trade he was apprenticed to learn, or one of his two suits might be "proper for the Sabbath." In all cases, the rewards were to be given to an apprenticed boy when he was twenty-one years old and to a girl when she became eighteen.

It was required that a copy of indenture papers be filed with the proper county official, and it is from the copies of these old papers that a glimpse is afforded of the treatment accorded orphans and other unfortunate children.

Binding out was a general practice, and hundreds of records relating to it are in existence in county archives. More than one hundred records of indentures were found in Edwards County, one of the smaller ones in this section of the state. It would be easy to find a thousand or more in the southern Illinois area.

Orphaned children without means of support, those who sought alms or whose parents had become public charges, those whose fathers had deserted them, or had been committed to prison or had become habitual drunkards, and children termed illegitimate were subject to being bound out. In fact, any child could be apprenticed with the consent and approval of the father. This provision of the law later was revised to include the consent of the mother. If the father were dead or had deserted the family for six months or more, the mother was allowed to bind the children out.

The laws governing the practice of apprenticing did not originate in Illinois. They came from old laws that operated in England at the time when the colonies were founded. These English laws were adopted by the colonies with little change and later applied in turn to the Northwest Territory, Indiana Territory, and Illinois Territory; they finally were adopted by the State of Illinois. Laws relating to apprenticeship, basically unchanged from the ones first in force in Illinois Territory, remained on the statute books of the state until their repeal in 1931.

The apprenticed child was entitled to the rewards set by law when he had satisfactorily completed the term of service. He also was entitled to "meat, drink, lodging, washing, apparel suitable for working and for holy days and to all other things necessary in sickness and health and neat and convenient for such a servant." In return for the considerations given him, the apprentice was to "well and faithfully serve the said master, during said term, keep his secrets and obey his lawful commands, shall do no harm to said master, he shall not waste the goods of his master nor lend them without his consent, he shall not play at unlawful games, contract matrimony during his term of service, frequent lewd or gaming houses, absent himself from services without his master's consent, and shall in all things demean himself as a good and faithful servant unto said master."

The bound child was subject to discipline and "suitable punishment" by the master or mistress. In cases of extremely cruel or inhuman treatment, the apprentices could have recourse to law, but this privilege was so hedged about by various requirements that the apprentice was practically helpless unless some man served as "next of friend." The penalties for aiding, advising, or sheltering a runaway apprentice were severe.

The same form of indenture used to bind white children could be used to bind Negro children, but such was not the usual practice. Other procedures that allowed longer terms of service were naturally more attractive to masters and generally were used. If a Negro child was apprenticed by the same provisions used for white children, it was permissible to omit the "reading, writing and ground rules of arithmetic" provision legally required for whites.

The lot of the unfortunate pioneer child must have been a rugged one. Perhaps circumstances of the times afforded little opportunity for better treatment.

🏵 *PRISCILLA*

STORIES OF A FEW individual slaves are preserved. Among these is the story of Priscilla, a young quadroon girl who came to live at the home of Brazilla (Basil) Silkwood near Mulkeytown, in Franklin County. Silkwood, emigrated from Pennsylvania in the 1820's and settled beside the Shawneetown-Kaskaskia Trail about a half-mile north of Mulkeytown. He built a large log house that still stands beside the sunken roadway.

In the mid–1830's, Silkwood went to visit a friend in Georgia. While there, he became acquainted with many of the plantation slaves, among whom was Priscilla. A short time after Silkwood's visit, the master of the plantation died, and his property was sold. Priscilla was bought by an Indian chief living on the near-by Cherokee reservation.

In 1838, many of the Cherokee were moved from their reservation in the Great Smokies to the Indian Territory. On their way, they passed through southern Illinois and stopped to camp near Jonesboro, in Union County.

At that same time, Silkwood went on a business trip to Jonesboro. While standing in front of the Willard Hotel on a winter day, Silkwood noticed a Negro girl who seemed strangely familiar pass by with a group of Indians and look intently at him. Upon her return, she paused and timidly asked, "Are you Marse Silkwood?" He then recognized her as one of the slaves he had known on the Georgia plantation.

Silkwood learned that Priscilla was the property of an Indian chief camped on Dutchman Creek. Her plight appealed to his sympathy. He accordingly obtained a conveyance and proceeded to the Indian camp, where he bought the girl from the chief, paying a reported one thousand dollars for her.

Taking the girl with him, Silkwood returned to his home near Mulkeytown. There she became as one of the family and lived at the Silkwood home until her death in 1892. A reminder of her stay at the Silkwood home returns each year. When Priscilla prepared to leave the Georgia plantation for the Indian reservation, she gathered seeds from the hollyhocks that grew about the plantation home to carry with her and plant about the Cherokee chief's cabin. When the Indians were forced to leave the reservation, she again took hollyhock seeds with her. She had these when Silkwood bought her and planted them at the Silkwood home where they have grown for 120 years and are now known as the Priscilla hollyhocks.

In 1950, seeds were gathered at the Silkwood place and sent to the daughter of the last chief of the Cherokee. The Indians completed their journey in 1838. One hundred twelve years after the Indians reached Oklahoma along the Trail of Tears the Priscilla hollyhocks were growing about Indian homes in Oklahoma.

Priscilla lived to be a very old woman and still is remembered by a few elderly people. She is buried in the family plot beside Basil Silkwood and his wife in the Reed Cemetery near the old roadway north of the old home. An unlettered sandstone marks her grave. The freedom papers given her by Silkwood are recorded in the county clerk's office at Benton.

🌸 BLACK JOHN

AMONG THE SLAVES ONCE held in present-day Hardin County was one named John, better known as Black John. The farm where Black John lived is located on the east side of Illinois Highway 1, then noted as Ford's Ferry Road, where a roadway led eastward from a point near Potts' Tavern toward Saline Tip Ferry.

At the death of Black John's owner, whom tradition names as Lambert, his Negroes were given their freedom, whereupon they took the name of Files. Tradition tells us that after being freed, they were well treated by the children of their former owner. This must have been true since Black John, his brother, and two sisters continued to live on the farm where they had been held as slaves. Black John's brother was called Bill, and one of the sisters was Haly, but the name of the other one is not known.

Black John and his brother worked as farm hands, and the sisters did housework in the homes of the vicinity. Haly, even then an old woman, was helping in the home of a Mr. Oxford when Lou Oxford, now popularly referred to as "Aunt" Lou Pinnell, was born some ninety years ago. Haly returned at times to help with the housework or visit in the Oxford home, and Black John worked on the farm. In this way the girl, Lou Oxford, came to know them both.

The Files family evidently was a kindly and thoughtful one. Stories of their helpfulness, especially of Black John, are still related. When misfortune came to a home in the vicinity, Black John, strong, genial, kindly, competent, and thoughtful would be among the first to arrive and to quietly and efficiently go about doing the things that obviously needed to be done.

John also was a mischievous person and enjoyed practical jokes. He could imitate the sounds of wild animals as well as mimic many persons. On one occasion, he chose to frighten a herd of cattle by imitating the cry of the panther, then frequently heard in the hills of the area. His imitation had the desired effect. The herd stampeded but becoming confused among the rocks, charged directly for the bushes where Black John was hidden. He escaped with only minor injuries. At another time when a few Indians had been seen, alarm spread through the settlement. Some feared an attack. Knowing that a Mr. Abner Dutton was much concerned, Black John decided to give him a real fright. After nightfall, John accordingly began to go from hillside to hillside near the Dutton cabin, stopping periodically to emit a series of Indian war whoops. Dutton became frantic, barred his house, and spent a night of fearful suspense.

Black John and his sister Haly lived to be very old. John farmed, hunted, and trapped. He located many bee trees and sold the honey. When not hired out, John and Haly lived on the south side of the Saline Tip Ferry road. Their old cabin, still well preserved, is about one-fourth mile east of the pavement on a farm now owned by James Porter.

The original cabin, sixteen feet square, is of logs and has a stone chimney at the north end. A boxed side room was later added on the east. About fifty years ago, other additions were made on the west side of the original cabin. The entire house is now covered by weatherboarding. Before the building of a schoolhouse for Lambert School District, this cabin was used as their school. Mrs. Mollie Dutton Grace, of Golconda, who lived in the vicinity when a girl, attended school there. Joe Hindall, once owner of old Potts' Tavern, was another pupil.

Though Black John and Haly have been gone for a long lifetime, the stories older persons tell about them make them very real. The small field that John cultivated between his cabin and the Saline River is still referred to as Black John's field.

A QUIET RAILROAD

A LAW VIOLATOR WHO could be subjected to a fine of $550 for each offense committed would naturally not announce his legal misdeeds. If he knew that he also could be held for personal damages, he would be inclined even more to silence. While a few might applaud and strive to defend his action, others would bitterly condemn. Along with these risks of punishment and censure was also to be added the realization that knowledge of the lawbreaker's deed would be injurious to those he strove to help. Persons indulging in legal violations that might bring such penalties had to be particularly careful not to leave any evidence that might "tend to incriminate." These hazards and threats of stiff punishment were apparently ineffective against the operation of the Underground Railroad in pre–Civil-War days. Those helping to maintain the mythical railroad by which many runaway slaves were helped in their flight to freedom were prudently silent. They did little talking and left few written records. Yet enough fragments of information remain to piece together some of the methods and tactics employed.

The Underground Railroad was not a single line along which runaway slaves were advanced. There were many routes that ran northward at irregular intervals from a line separating free from slave states and extended westward from the Atlantic seaboard to Kansas. One Illinois route began at Rockwood, then called Liberty, in Randolph County, and extended northward through Carlyle. Runaway slaves, coming across the Mississippi from Missouri first were hidden at the farm of a Mr. Clendenning, north and east of Rockwood. From this point, they were taken, generally at night, to Eden, a village adjoining Sparta. At Eden they were hidden in a house, still standing, then occupied by a Mr. Burlingame.

Burlingame operated a shop that manufactured, among other things, farm pumps. The pipes and other parts of these pumps were made of sassafras logs or poles, often twelve to fourteen feet long. When a number of such pumps and sections of pipe were completed, they were loaded on a wagon and taken to market. The region about Carlyle apparently was an excellent sales field, and loads of pumps accordingly were sent in that direction. The round trip to Carlyle could not be made in one day. It was therefore necessary to take along feed for the horses or oxen used to pull the wagons. Since a wagon box was about three feet wide, nine or ten feet long and perhaps two feet deep, the space it afforded was more than was needed to carry feed. It was in this surplus space beneath a covering of hay or fodder that passengers over the Underground Railroad were carried.

Any runaway slaves that had been assembled at Eden were hidden beneath the hay in the wagon box, and the pumps were carefully laid lengthwise on top of the wagon. With his cargo thus arranged, the driver would set out for Carlyle. There he would deliver his runaways to the local "station agent," dispose of his pumps, and return to Eden. All the while, the making of pumps had been going on apace. When more pumps were ready for sale and more runaways were available, the process would be repeated.

The number escaping along this particular route was not large. However, when the relatively small trickles along the various routes were combined, the number became significant. It is estimated that a total of about 75,000 slaves thus escaped to Canada and freedom.

There are yet vicinities in Canada with large Negro populations, descendants of the slaves who reached freedom by way of the Underground Railroad. The community of Dresden, about forty miles north and east of Detroit is an example. The grave of the Rev. Josiah Henson, designated as the individual used by Harriet Beecher Stowe for her character of Uncle Tom, is in the cemetery there. The house where the Reverend Henson lived is pointed out as the real Uncle Tom's Cabin.

Stories concerning incidents on the Underground, passed down in local lore, may still be heard from very old Negroes living about Dresden.

MONUMENT TO A SLAVE'S MASTER

IT IS SELDOM THAT a former slave erects a monument to the man who once held him in bondage. Likewise, it is not often that slave and master are, by previous mutual agreement, buried side by side. Both of these unusual occurrences did happen, however, in the village of Otterville, in Jersey County, Illinois.

The slave in this case was George Washington, or Black George. The master was Dr. Silas Hamilton, a native of Tinmouth, Vermont.

Dr. Hamilton was vigorously opposed to slavery, but he felt that its abolishment would be a long and difficult process. He, therefore, decided that in the meantime he could best promote the welfare of slaves by operating a model plantation in the Black Belt—a plantation where slaves would be treated with the utmost kindness and consideration. Hamilton accordingly bought a plantation in Adams County, Mississippi, stocked it with slaves, and began his experiment. His adventure, apparently successful within itself, did not induce the practices he had hoped for on other plantations in the area. He therefore sold his plantation, freed his slaves, and emigrated to Illinois. Three of his former slaves accompanied the doctor. These were a Negro man and his wife, house servants, and a boy named George. It was the boy who is the other principal in this story.

George had first come to Dr. Hamilton's attention when the latter, on the way to Mississippi, was traveling through Virginia in a wagon. Stopping at a plantation that belonged to a family named Washington, the doctor heard the continuous crying of a child, apparently in great distress. Thinking that the child was physically ill and in need of a physician's services, Dr. Hamilton made inquiry. He learned that George's mother had recently been sold to a slave-buyer and had been taken south.

The evident distress of the child aroused the sympathies of the doctor. He accordingly approached the owner of the plantation and offered to buy the boy. The owner, convinced that this bit of property would certainly grieve itself to death, sold George to Dr. Hamilton for one hundred dollars. The boy, when he learned that he was to be taken south and that he might find his mother, became somewhat reconciled. George was carried to the Hamilton plantation in Mississippi, where he proved to be an exceptionally intelligent, trustworthy, and capable boy.

When Dr. Hamilton and his three former slaves came to Illinois, they first stopped in the New Design settlement in Monroe County. After thoroughly exploring several other sections of the state, a site on Otter Creek Prairie, in Jersey County, was selected. Here Dr. Hamilton and the three Negroes lived until the death of the doctor in 1834.

Dr. Hamilton bequeathed four thousand dollars for the establishment and support of a school in Otterville to serve a territory four miles square. This school, built in 1835, became widely known as the Stone School House. It is said to be the first "free" public school in Illinois. Since there was no color barrier at this school, George attended it and obtained a good common school education.

Upon attaining manhood, George, "Black George," or George Washington became a successful farmer. He became a member of the Baptist Church, and served many years as its caretaker, as Sunday school teacher, and as song leader. He also served as grave digger for the community, refusing pay for such services. Traditions still relate incidents concerning his many acts of kindness.

People over a wide area came to know and respect George. He was once arrested in Calhoun County where there was strong anti-Negro feeling, was lodged in jail, and held as a runaway slave. A businessman who knew George secured his release. At another time, some boys set about stoning him when he came to their county, but the county judge came to his rescue.

At his death in 1864, George left one thousand five hundred dollars for the erection of a monument to honor his former master, Dr. Hamilton. This monument on the grounds of the Old Stone School was dedicated on May 22, 1876, the birthdate of Jason Humiston, now the oldest native

resident of the village. The scroll on the shaft above the base block records
the fact that the memorial was

ERECTED BY GEORGE WASHINGTON

BORN IN VIRGINIA A SLAVE

DIED AT OTTERVILLE, ILL., APRIL 15, 1864

A CHRISTIAN FREEMAN

The base block of the memorial continues the inscription:

TO THE MEMORY OF DR. SILAS HAMILTON

HIS FORMER MASTER

BORN IN TINMOUTH, VT., MAY 19, 1775

DIED AT OTTERVILLE, ILL., NOV. 19, 1834

HAVING IN HIS LIFETIME GIVEN FREEDOM TO

TWENTY-EIGHT SLAVES

AT HIS DEATH BEQUESTED FOUR THOUSAND DOLLARS FOR THE

ERECTION AND ENDOWMENT THE HAMILTON PRIMARY SCHOOL

George also left seven thousand dollars as a fund to be used for the
education of "colored persons, or Americans of African descent." This
fund still functions for its original purpose. Each Memorial Day a group
of Negroes comes to Otterville to pay tribute to the memory of George.
Now, almost one hundred years later, local lore yields stories of Dr. Silas
Hamilton and George.

❦ *ABOLITIONIST LOVEJOY*

AN IMPOSING MONUMENT erected to the memory of a tragic figure in the
history of Illinois, stands in the cemetery at Alton. It honors the memory
of Elijah P. Lovejoy, noted in the history of American journalism.

Elijah Parish Lovejoy, eldest son of a Presbyterian minister, was born
in Albion, Maine, on November 8, 1802. Elijah was a precocious youngster, being able to read the Bible fluently when four years old. He received a liberal education and was graduated from Waterville College,
now Colby College, in Maine. Afterwards, he taught in Vermont until
May, 1827, when he emigrated to Missouri, where he taught and wrote
for a St. Louis newspaper.

Lovejoy was typical of numerous young men who came west from
New England during that period, sent by churches or educational societies

to teach or preach. They did much to shape opinion and to influence thought in the new state.

Though he was the son of a minister and had been reared in a distinctly religious atmosphere, young Lovejoy was known as a skeptic. In 1832, casting doubt aside, Lovejoy fully embraced the teachings of the church and began preparation for the ministry. After a year of study at Princeton Theological Seminary, he was licensed to preach by the Second Presbyterian Church in Philadelphia.

Lovejoy returned to St. Louis in 1833 to serve as editor of the *St. Louis Observer,* the far western organ of the Presbyterians. In his work as a minister, he was an ardent crusader against dancing, drunkenness, and intemperance of all kinds. He considered slavery as an evil and was opposed to it. He was not, however, an abolitionist. His expressed opinion apparently was the same as that of numerous prominent citizens of Illinois. He thought slavery a blight but thought abolition inexpedient.

As time passed, Lovejoy became more outspoken in his opposition to slavery and in his criticisms of court actions that he considered as unduly favoring it. This practice aroused opposition toward him and his paper. This opposition, accompanied by threats of violence, caused him to discontinue publication of a paper in St. Louis and to move his press to Alton.

The press arrived in Alton on Sunday, July 24, 1836, and was allowed to lie on the wharf. During that night, it was broken to pieces and thrown into the Mississippi. A second press was obtained only to be destroyed in the paper's office on August 27, 1837. At the same time, threats were made against the life of Lovejoy.

Even though the first two presses had been wrecked, a third was ordered. It arrived on September 21, 1837, and was stored in a warehouse on Second Street between State and Piasa. It was almost immediately taken from the warehouse, smashed, and tossed into the river.

When it became known that a fourth press had been ordered, a meeting of those opposed to the publication of the paper was called for the evening of November 2. Lovejoy appeared before the group and vigorously defended his previous actions and the right of freedom of the press.

Five days later, that is, on November 7, 1837, the new press arrived at three o'clock in the morning and was put in the riverside warehouse of Godfrey, Gilman and Company. News of its arrival spread, and threats of mob violence grew. That evening the militia met for drill at the warehouse. It was apparently the regular place and time for such drill.

After they were dismissed, most of the men went home. Several, perhaps twenty, remained as guards, including Lovejoy and Winthrop S.

Gilman, a part-owner of the warehouse. An armed and threatening group soon gathered outside. Gilman addressed them from an upper-story window and asked that they disperse. They refused, and tension rapidly mounted. Shooting soon began, and one of the outside group was killed. The mob then grew in numbers and made an effort to burn the building, but the defenders succeeded in preventing the fire.

A second attempt was made to burn the building. Lovejoy and others came out to extinguish the fire and drive away those kindling it. They were fired upon by men behind a pile of lumber. Lovejoy received four or five bullets and died immediately. Two of the men with him were severely wounded. The warehouse defenders asked for a truce and free departure. Both were promised and all departed except the two severely wounded men, and one or two others who remained to attend them and watch over Lovejoy's body. A passer-by extinguished the fire. The press was thrown out of the warehouse and followed its predecessors into the river.

No inquest was held. Lovejoy was buried the next day, November 8, 1837, the thirty-fifth anniversary of his birth, on the bluff where the city cemetery was later located. Few attended the funeral. His grave was marked by two boards. A few years later, a roadway was laid out across Lovejoy's grave and stones were lowered in the roadway where the oaken boards had been. Some time later Major Charles W. Hunter had the Negro who dug Lovejoy's first grave, dig a second one and move the body to it. The new grave has been kept marked.

Indictments were returned against members of the mob and against the warehouse guards. Speedy trials were held, but no one was found guilty. People apparently wanted to square accounts and forget it all.

The abolitionist movement continued to grow. Lovejoy's death, perhaps more than any other single event, gave it impetus. It also furnished America with its first martyr to the cause of a free press. Some questioned the wisdom of Lovejoy's persistent efforts. All, however, recognized his heroism and high purpose.

A portion of the broken frame of one of Lovejoy's presses stands against the wall in the office of the present *Alton Telegraph*.

❧ OLD SLAVE HOUSE

JOHN HART CRENSHAW, WHO came to this region in the 1830's, built a fine three-story residence on Hickory Hill about a mile south and west from the crossing of Illinois highways 1 and 13, east of Equality, in Gallatin County. From the time of its building, this residence has been a landmark. For almost a century, it has been called "The Old Slave House."

Those wishing to visit it may do so by turning west down a lane beside the railroad less than a mile south from the highway crossing. When the visitor reaches the end of this lane, he notices that the deeply gullied hillside between there and the home is littered with refuse and bits of discarded equipment from abandoned coal mines and is pitted with abandoned shafts and entries. Snags and broken limbs show that time and storms have dealt severely with the large trees that once were numerous about the house. The three-story frame house itself looks its age. Though it shows much evidence of neglect, the house that John Hart Crenshaw built in the 1830's still carries a look of distinction. Numerous stories and legends coming out of the most vicious chapter concerning Negro slavery in Illinois touch this old house and the salt works that once were operated south of it on Saline River.

As the visitor turns up the hill toward the house, he is impressed by its large wooden columns, each turned from an entire tree trunk that support the second-floor porch and roof. They give to the front of the building an appearance somewhat like that of a Greek temple. The wide doorways with transoms above them and glass panels at their sides are suggestive of a southern mansion.

Though the general appearance of the house attracts the visitor's attention, it is the third floor, reached by a steep narrow stairway, that is most interesting. It is here, where great patches of plaster have fallen or been torn away, that the methods employed in building the house are most easily observed. Hand-shaped timbers, hand-riven plaster lath, wrought iron nails with square heads, and plaster made of sand, lime, and hair are evident.

The manner of dividing the third floor into several small rooms indicates the use once made of it. There are numbers of doors on either side of the long, central hallway that reaches north and south across the building. Some lead into small rooms that are said to have been used for entire families of slaves. Other doorways open into narrow cells fitted with shelves, one above another, that are thought to have served as bunks for single slaves. These shelves, about six feet long and two feet wide, must have been cramped sleeping quarters. Neither the family rooms nor the cells mentioned have windows opening to the outside. There once were some iron rings attached to the floor, supposedly to fasten slaves that might escape at night. The last of these rings disappeared several years ago, presumably with souvenir hunters. There also are two queerly constructed racks of frames that are said to have been used as devices for punishing slaves, but it is not easy to see the manner of their use.

Naturally, there is a considerable amount of conjecture concerning incidents connected with the use of the third floor, but there can be no reasonable doubt concerning the use to which it was put. It is a matter of record that John Crenshaw used much Negro labor at his salt works. Some of this came from slaves leased from their owners in Missouri and Kentucky. Other labor came from Negroes indentured to Crenshaw, to whom he evidently neglected to give certificates of freedom when they had served out their terms.

There are some indications that Crenshaw kidnaped free Negroes and held them to labor or sold them into slavery. Court records at Shawneetown show that he was indicted for such kidnaping. Since a Negro could not appear as a witness against a white person and most white men hesitated to appear as "next of friend," Crenshaw escaped conviction.

A visit to the old house on the hilltop and to the near-by cemetery where Crenshaw and General Michael K. Lawler, his son-in-law, are buried, suggests an interesting chapter in local history.

🏵 EMANCIPATION DAY

No one seems to know definitely why Emancipation Day first came to be observed on August 8. Likewise, no one tells just when, where, and how it began. Nothing has been found concerning its observance on the August date outside of the southern Illinois–Paducah, Kentucky, region. Nevertheless, it once was a great day in this area, the greatest gathering day of the Negroes. One explanation of the August date, given by two elderly Negroes, states that it was because the time was one of slack labor, and weather was suitable for picnicking. The small grain crops would have been harvested, corn laid by, and turnips sowed.

Farmers—and nearly all Negroes then were farmers—thus would have a few weeks of rest before time to strip cane, cut shock fodder, sow wheat, gather in the fall crops, and arrange a wood supply for the winter. It was a good time to hold picnics, reunions, revival meetings, and other celebrations.

One newspaper states that the date in August was selected because it was the one on which the slaves of Santo Domingo, now the Dominican Republic, were freed. We have not been able to establish either of these explanations as the more valid one, but we are inclined to believe the first. Likewise, we have been unable to learn definitely when the celebration began. Though the day may have been celebrated earlier, the first observance at Elizabethtown, Hardin County, came in 1882. Moses

Barker, a former slave and one of the many Negroes owning farms in the county at that time, met with some of his friends and talked of observing an Emancipation Day. They discussed it with leading white citizens, who readily approved and offered their help. Businessmen and farmers agreed to furnish cattle, sheep, and hogs for the occasion.

Long pits were dug, and when the eighth of August came, barbecuing began before daybreak. At noon an ample supply of meat was ready. Whites were invited, and many of them came to visit together, to look on, and to eat barbecue. They continued to attend these yearly meetings and provide the food.

The first Elizabethtown celebrations were held at the site of the old brickyard in the northwestern part of the village. The dancing floor was a smooth plot of hard ground covered with sawdust. Music was furnished by an old-time fiddler, sometimes supplemented with a banjo-picker. Square dances were then, as now, a main feature of the celebration, which is still observed in a grove beside the Ohio.

As the Negro population of the region decreased, so did the number of Negroes attending. The proportion of whites who came to look on, to visit, and to share in the delightful barbecue increased. In 1940, when the writer first attended Emancipation Day at Elizabethtown, there were about twenty Negroes present.

At this meeting, a Negro man past eighty years of age was seen sitting against a tree and looking on somewhat wistfully. He told of attending the first celebration held almost sixty years before. He told of the wagons that stood about and of the horses and oxen tied to them. He told of the long barbecue pits, of the men working at them, and of the Negro women who danced barefoot in the sawdust. The observance must have meant much to this old man.

Other places in the area, including Metropolis, Brookport, and Carbondale, in Illinois, and Paducah, in Kentucky, also observed the day in a somewhat similar manner. The observances at Metropolis and Brookport drew most of their attendance locally.

The one at Carbondale was begun by the late Frank B. Jackson in 1911. It never reached the scope of the Paducah observance it was patterned after, but it drew many hundreds of people and became quite an occasion. Various contests and games were held, and it was a gala occasion. Noted bands came to play for dances. After the passing of Mr. Jackson, the Carbondale observance was discontinued in 1954.

The celebration at Paducah, still held regularly, once reached great proportions. At its height, thousands came by excursion trains and by river steamers. Special trains filled the sidings near Eleventh and Broadway, and steamers were tied to the wharf. These excursions brought people from places as far away as St. Louis, Chicago, Louisville, Cairo, and Memphis. In 1905, special trains from Memphis alone brought two thousand persons to a meeting attended by more than ten thousand. It remains even yet a day looked forward to in Paducah.

Chapter 13

The Military

🏵 *FORT DE CHARTRES*

SOUTHERN ILLINOIS NEVER has been a major battleground. Aside from a few clashes with the Indians, the military accomplishments of George Rogers Clark, and such minor affairs as mine wars, organized gang warfare, and a few Regulator-Vigilante skirmishes, it has gone quietly along its somewhat turbulent way. It has, however, as one may see, contributed to other military activities.

George Washington never visited Illinois, but he did have unpleasant visitors from here. These were "a hundred select men" who went from Fort de Chartres, in Randolph County, to help capture the father of his country at Great Meadow, Pennsylvania, in 1754. But this was only one of the numerous significant events that occurred at or were closely associated with the old fort.

One of these events took place in 1720, the year that Pierre Duc de Boisbriant completed the building of the first fort. In that year, Philippe François Renault brought engineers, skilled workmen, and five hundred Negro slaves to the vicinity, intending to develop a great mining industry. When mining did not prove very profitable, many of the slaves were sold to the settlers, thereby establishing Negro slavery in Illinois.

Another event, and a tragic one at that, came in 1736. In that year Pierre d'Artaguette, commander at the fort, received orders to lead an expedition against the Chickasaw Indians. He accordingly took thirty regulars, one hundred volunteers, and several hundred Indian allies from Fort de Chartres and started down the Mississippi in February, 1736. Chevalier Vincennes from the French post on the Wabash, with twenty additional soldiers and one hundred Indians joined d'Artaguette at the mouth of the Ohio. These combined forces continued toward the Chicka-saw country. The expedition ended in disaster. d'Artaguette, Vincennes, and Father Senat were captured by the Indians and held for ransom. When no ransom was forthcoming, the captives were slowly roasted at the stake, the process taking almost all of a day.

In 1751, Richard MaCarty, an Irishman, became commander. The old fort had fallen into decay and it was decided to replace it. Work on the new fort began in 1753 and was finished in 1756. Built of stone, it cost five million livre, about one million dollars, a great sum of money for that time. The outer walls, fifteen feet high and more than three feet thick, enclosed an area of four acres. A powder magazine, storerooms, barracks, quarters for officers, and other essential buildings were sufficient for four hundred soldiers. It was well built and impregnable to any but artillery attacks.

In 1754, while the fort was being rebuilt, a group of French explorers operating in Pennsylvania were attacked by Virginia militia under the command of George Washington. The French commander, Coulon de Jumonville, was slain. Some historians believe that this act should be considered as the opening one of the French and Indian Wars. Neyon de Villiers, senior captain under MaCarty at Fort de Chartres, asked for and received permission to lead a party to avenge the killing. It was as a part of this plan that "a hundred picked men" and Indian allies started on the long journey to Pennsylvania. They were joined by other French forces at Fort Duquesne. Washington and his men took refuge in a makeshift fortification at Great Meadow, Pennsylvania. There they surrendered on July 4, a date later to become a marked one in American history. France, defeated in war, ceded the Illinois country to the British in 1763. The hostile attitude of the Indians, encouraged by Chief Pontiac, prevented the British from taking possession until October 10, 1765.

Dark days came under the British. Many of the more prosperous and influential of the French moved across the Mississippi from the Illinois country into Missouri. In 1772 the river flooded and water stood seven feet deep within the fort. The river channel also shifted, and the west wall of the fort was carried away. The military garrison was transferred to Kaskaskia, and Fort de Chartres was never officially occupied again. It ceased to be of military significance.

Occasional glimpses indicate the gradual decay of the fort. In 1804 one writer states that the walls were practically intact. In 1805 another observes that the natives had begun to haul the stones away for buildings. A visitor to the ruins in 1817 tells of flushing a flock of wild turkeys within the walls of the fort. In 1829 James Hall visited the site and wrote: "It was curious to see, in the gloom of the forest, these remnants of the architecture of a past age."

On October 10, 1854, exactly eighty-nine years after the day when Captain Stirling and his Highlander troops took charge of "the great fort that had never fired a shot in anger," John Reynolds was there and described the scene as "a pile of moldering ruins." Fifty years after Reynolds' visit another writer says: "At one time all roads led to Fort de Chartres. Now, not even a cowpath guides one to the old fort."

Today, the original foundations have been exposed by the removal of flood deposits, and some of the buildings have been restored, including the original powder magazine which appears much as it did two hundred years ago. With the flags of the three nations that ruled there fluttering in an afternoon breeze, it is easy to sense some of the romance that clusters about the ruins of old Fort de Chartres.

❦ FORT MASSAC

PERHAPS NO STATE PARK in Illinois has a more varied assortment of stories, legends, lore, and accounts of historical events associated with it than Fort Massac State Park. Some of the names connected with it mean much in American history, and they range from the great to the infamous and depraved. However, the man whose name did much to turn attention toward the historic spot said or did nothing about the place he helped to make prominent. He spent only one day in the vicinity and perhaps never actually was on the site of the fort. Despite all this, George Rogers Clark's name is one that adds great luster to Fort Massac.

The ruins of the old post, located in Fort Massac State Park at the up-river side of Metropolis, make it an appealing historical site. Stories and legends concerning it go back many years. The earliest one would have the Spanish explorer, De Soto, stop there in 1542. No documentary evidence has been found to support this legend, and it is highly doubtful if he even was near the place.

According to later legend Father Mermet, a Jesuit priest, preached a sermon there on August 15, 1701 or 1702. He was in the region with M. Juchereau de St. Denis. Since that was Assumption Day in the Catholic church, the place first was designated as Fort Assumption. There is no record of further occupation of the spot until 1757. It is possible, however, that it was used at intervals as a trading post.

Massac's authenticated story begins in 1757, when Charles Philippe Aubrey led a French force to intercept an English force which was said to be coming down the Tennessee River from the southern English colonies. Though Aubrey went many miles up the river, he heard nothing of an English expedition and returned to the north bank of the Ohio, where he built a temporary fort near the mouth of the Tennessee. Since the first stone of this fort was laid on Ascension Day, the fort he built was called Fort Ascension. This post was in a strategic location—one that could oversee the coming and going of Indian tribes and traders who followed the river.

The site selected by Aubrey for a temporary fort met the approval of MaCarty, Commander at Fort Chartres. It also met the approval of the French Ministry of Marines in Paris. Aubrey accordingly rebuilt the fort in 1758 and called it Fort Massac in honor of M. Massiac, the Minister of Marines. This is the valid explanation for the naming of the fort.

There also is an interesting legend that offers another explanation. According to this story, the Indians, wishing to attack the fort, employed a ruse. A group of them wrapped in bear skins, crawled about on a sandbar across the Ohio. Members of the garrison saw these "bears" and set out to kill them. The soldiers remaining at the fort left their posts and gathered along the river to see the sport. This allowed other Indians hidden near by to surprise and massacre the garrison. The legend would then name it Fort Massacre. There is no apparent basis in fact for this story.

The French continued to occupy the fort until they surrendered the region to the British in 1763. The territory, however, was not occupied by the English until Captain Stirling stopped there on his way to Fort Chartres. The English shortly abandoned the fort and it remained so until 1794, when Washington ordered it rebuilt. The name was changed from Massiac to Massac. It again served as an important military post until its armament and stores were removed in 1814.

During the years that the fort was maintained, a number of names prominent in American history became associated with it. Among those were Commander MaCarty, St. Ange de Bell Rive, Father Mermet, Juchereau, Zebulon M. Pike, Captain Bissell, General Wilkinson of ill fame, George Rogers Clark, Blennerhassett, Tecumseh, Pontiac, John Duff, Big and Little Harpe, and that brilliant conspirator, Aaron Burr.

When time came to locate a United States arsenal in the Midwest, the Fort Massac site was seriously considered. It was rejected, however, in favor of the location at Rock Island.

❦ *AN INCREDIBLE MARCH*

THROUGH THE EFFORTS OF the Daughters of the American Revolution, the grounds about Fort Massac at Metropolis were made into the first Illinois state park in 1903. The recent addition of several hundred acres to this park rekindles interest in the old fort and also in Colonel George Rogers Clark, whose name is inseparably connected with it. This close association continues and is justified despite the very strong likelihood that Clark was never on the actual site of the fort.

Clark, born in Virginia on November 19, 1752, remains one of the great figures in early Illinois history, and the dominant one here during the period of the American Revolution. It was through his efforts more than those of any others that Illinois, along with the remainder of the Old Northwest, became a part of the United States. Most of the military activities that Clark conducted to accomplish that objective were enacted in southern Illinois.

Before coming to the Illinois country, Clark had already attained a measure of distinction as a frontier leader. Since he was twenty, he had been a land surveyor, Indian fighter, and explorer. At twenty-four he wielded much influence in having the Kentucky country set aside as a county of Virginia instead of an independent state· of Transylvania, as some planned. Clark was made a major of militia in the new county and given the task of defending the settlements against Indian attacks.

In appearance Clark was an imposing figure. He was six feet tall, of strong and symmetrical build, red-haired and dark-eyed. He had that personal magnetism and dignified appearance evident in great leaders. His portraits show much of the same self-confidence and calmness evident in those of Washington. Many remarked upon this, and Clark took pride in the resemblance he bore to his great contemporary.

When given the task of defending the frontier, Clark made bold plans. He would drive the British from their posts at Detroit and Vincennes and from the Illinois country. To accomplish this, he would have preferred to move directly against Detroit. The distance, difficulties of transportation, and shortage of men and supplies prevented such a bold approach. He therefore decided first to attack the British posts in the Illinois country.

When his plans were submitted to Governor Patrick Henry and other Virginia leaders, they approved. Clark was commissioned as a lieutenant colonel, given orders for some essential military supplies, and authorized to enlist 350 men. He gathered men and supplies on Corn Island in the Ohio just above the falls where Louisville now stands. When all was in readiness, the soldiers were told that the expedition was to proceed against Kaskaskia. That night a number of them deserted. Others were eliminated because they were not considered physically equal to the arduous campaign that lay ahead. These desertions and eliminations reduced his forces to a scant but highly competent 175 men. Clark promptly set out on the mission that was to win a great territory for the nation being created and eventually to bring undying fame to its leader.

The falls of the Ohio were shot by Clark's men during a total eclipse of the sun, and all due haste was made downstream. They soon arrived at the mouth of the creek about a mile above Fort Massac. Here they hid their boats and spare equipment and spent the night. On the next morning, they met John Duff and two other hunters who had recently been in Kaskaskia. Taking these men as guides, the little army set out in single file through the forest toward their objective. In three days they reached the open prairies west of Marion, in Williamson County, where the trail was lost. Clark suspected treachery, and told Duff that he would be shot if he did not promptly discover the way. The trail was quickly found and the march resumed. On the evening of July 4, 1778, his forces reached the Kaskaskia river about three miles above the town, where they found boats and crossed to the western side of the stream.

Clark divided his forces into two groups. One of these surrounded the town to cut off all avenues of escape. The others went directly to the fort, found the gate unlocked, surprised the commander, de Rocheblave, and captured him. Before morning the town had been disarmed—all without the firing of a shot or the injury of a man. Cahokia, Prairie du Rocher, and St. Philippe likewise fell without a struggle. Emissaries to Vincennes accomplished equally easy conquests without incident. All pledged allegiance to the American cause, and Clark was in full possession of the Illinois country.

Indians, hearing of the manner in which Clark had supplanted the British in the region, came to smoke the pipe of peace. Fortune had smiled upon the venture. The first part of Clark's campaign in the Illinois country had been successful. The second part of his campaign, one of the most incredible in American history, followed in a few months.

The ease with which the twenty-five-year-old Clark had wrested control of the Illinois country and Post Vincennes from the British in the summer of 1778 was amazing. Perhaps it even amazed Clark himself.

Five months later, Governor Hamilton, in the British post at Detroit, struck back. He led a force of British soldiers and Indian allies, totaling about eight hundred, against the American garrison that had dwindled to only two men at Vincennes and retook that post. This was on December 17, 1778, and winter had begun. Flood waters covered much of the bottom lands and flat prairies between Vincennes and Kaskaskia, where Clark's forces were stationed. Hamilton decided that an expedition against the American forces would not be advisable before spring. Indian allies, therefore, were dismissed, and many of the soldiers were returned to Detroit.

With Hamilton in possession of Vincennes, the plight of the Americans could easily become hopeless. After conferences with his officers, Clark decided that he must attack and retake Vincennes immediately or lose control of the country. This decision launched one of history's most storied military adventures. Though thoroughly documented and proved, the account of that 180-mile march from Kaskaskia to Vincennes across the flooded prairies and woodlands of southern Illinois remains hardly credible.

On February 1, 1799, preparations for the expedition against Vincennes were begun. A "galley or batteau" which they called the "Willing" was built and placed under the command of a Lieutenant Rogers. It was, until then, the most heavily armed boat that had appeared on the western rivers. With a crew of forty-six men, the "Willing" left Kaskaskia at two o'clock on the afternoon of February 4, laden with ammunition and supplies that Clark would need when he reached Vincennes.

The next afternoon, Clark crossed the Kaskaskia River with a force of 170 artillerymen, pack-horsemen, longknives from Kentucky, and French militia recruited locally. On the first night they encamped about three miles east of the town. The night was "rainy and drisly" and there were no tents. March was resumed on the morning of the seventh when they traveled "9 leagues" over roads "very bad with Mud and Water." Next day they marched "thro' the water . . . in those large and level plains." On the ninth "it rained most of the day." A day later they "crossed the river of Petel [Petit] Ford upon trees we felled for that purpose." It was "still raining and no tents." On the twelfth they marched across flooded prairies, where they saw and killed numbers of "buffaloes . . . the Men much fatigued."

On February 13 they arrived at the two Wabashes that "altho a league . . . A sunder now make but one." They finished a canoe and on the fifteenth, "ferryed . . . across five miles of water to opposite hills." It was "still raining." On the sixteenth they "marched all day thro' Rain and Water . . . our provisions began to grow short." On the seventeenth they "traveled till 3th o'clock in mud and water but could find no place to encamp on." They finally found the "Water fallen from a small point of ground" and "staid there the remainder of the Night . . . Drisly and dark weather." On the eighteenth "at Break of day heard Hamilton's morning gun." The water became deeper, the weather colder. Men were "starving . . . cast down . . . no provisions of any sort . . . two days of hard fortune." The next day "the camp was very quiet, but hungry." The men were openly murmuring and there was talk of turning back. On the twenty-first they "plunged into the water, sometimes to the neck, for more than one league . . . rain all this day no provisions." On the twenty-second "Col. Clark encourages his men which gave them great Spirits." They heard the evening and morning guns from the fort, but there were "no provisions yet, lord help us." The next day February 23, they crossed a plain "about four miles long covered with water brest high." It was now bitter cold, sheets of ice "having froze in the night." About "One O'Clock we came in Sight of the Town and halted on a small Nole of dry land." From a captured duck-hunter Clark learned that his approach was unsuspected. He sent a letter into the town warning the citizens of danger should they resist and sternly advised them to stay in their homes. At sundown Clark's men marched into the town. At 8 o'clock they began to fire on the fort. "Not one of our men wounded. Seven Men of the Fort badly wounded."

On the next day, February 24, "About 9 o Clock the Col. sent a flag to Govr. Hamilton. The firing then ceased during which time our Men was provided with a Breakfast it being the only meal of Victuals since the 18 Inst." While deliberation was going on between Clark and Hamilton, a raiding party returned from an assault on the Kentucky settlement, bringing scalps and two prisoners with them. Clark's men heard of this returning party and met them outside the town. Several were killed and others were taken prisoners. Four of those captured were taken to a spot in full view of the fort, where they were tomahawked and their bodies thrown into the river. This act surely had its effects, for the next day Hamilton accepted Clark's terms and surrendered Fort Sackville. Two days later the "Willing" arrived.

Vincennes and the Illinois country remained in the possession of the Colonies. The Old Northwest became a part of America. The story of the midwinter's march of the 170 men across Illinois remains an American legend. But long years of misfortune, ingratitude, neglect, dire penury, and shattered health lay ahead for George Rogers Clark.

We wish it could be said that Clark, the man who gave Illinois and the Northwest Territory to the nation, lived his remaining forty years enjoying the rewards he had so richly earned. Such was far from true.

It was almost the opposite. Unrewarded, harried by debts, beset by creditors, broken in health, and even having his character repeatedly attacked by self-seeking men, Clark's life after 1783 was one of increasing misfortunes. Perhaps a few glimpses will indicate the tragedies that followed.

In 1779, after his midwinter march across the flooded lands of Illinois from Kaskaskia to Vincennes, Clark sent a special messenger to Virginia with his reports and accounts. These arrived safely, but they shortly disappeared. It was assumed that they had been burned by Benedict Arnold on his raid through Virginia.

The end of the Revolutionary War came, and Benjamin Harrison, Governor of Virginia, dismissed Clark from the military services on July 2, 1783. Left practically penniless, Clark set out in borrowed clothing, on a lonely trip to Virginia to press his claim for repayment of personal funds he had expended. His mission and plea ended in complete failure.

During the next twenty years, Clark engaged in varied activities, at one time holding a commission as a general in the French army. In 1803, his claims still unpaid, Clark returned to the falls of the Ohio where he had gathered his little army just twenty-five years before. Here, on an Indiana hilltop that overlooked Corn Island and the rapids, he built a two-room log cabin, the first house he had owned since the half-faced camp at the mouth of Fish Creek when a youth. Two faithful slaves, Venus and her husband Kitt, came from his father's estate to keep house and do the chores for the already broken Clark.

At this cabin, on a small porch toward the river, Clark often sat, rocked in a creaky chair, and gazed across the falls of the Ohio and Corn Island, doubtless musing on earlier and better years.

Many visitors came to sit and talk with him. Some were those who had served with him in one of the many military expeditions he had conducted. Others came to talk of the incidents of earlier years. Some came for help in locating lands awarded them for military services. John Audubon came to discuss the bird life of the Ohio-Mississippi region. Indian chiefs, both former friends and former foes, came to smoke with him and to converse in scant words and meaningful gestures, or perhaps to sit in eloquent silence. Meriwether Lewis and William Clark, his brother, stopped on their way to begin their memorable trip to the Pacific. About three years later, returning from their long journey, they again visited the intrepid warrior.

Years of hardship and exposure had made Clark old. His abundant red hair was thinned and gray, his calm dark eyes registered sadness and disappointment. His face was deeply seamed and he was stooped. Crippled by rheumatism, it was difficult for him to hobble down hill to the small water mill that he operated to help eke out a living. Venus kept the house while Kitt tended the garden and did the chores.

Life for Clark moved along in about this same plane for some years. Greater misfortunes, however, were in store. In 1809 he suffered a paralytic stroke that left him hardly able to move about. Independent in spirit, he refused to go and live with his brothers or sisters though they were able to care for him and a welcome awaited him there. A few months after his stroke, he fell into the fireplace. When Venus and Kitt found him, his right leg had been burned badly. Infection set in and it became necessary to amputate the limb. The operation, two hours long, was performed without an anaesthetic. By Clark's request, a fife and drum were played during the ordeal. That night at ten o'clock four violinists, two drummers, and two playing fifes came to march about the house for two hours and to play the tunes Clark loved best.

After the operation, Clark went to live with his sister, Lucy Croghan. In February, 1812, the Virginia legislature voted him a pension of $400 a year. In February, 1813, he suffered another stroke that left him speechless and all but helpless. His remaining days were spent in a wheel chair. His dark eyes grew dim, his mind wandered, his once powerful physique collapsed. Tenderly cared for by loving relatives, Clark died on February 13, 1818, shortly before Illinois became a state, and was buried two days later amid a heavy but gentle snowfall.

In 1838, twenty years after his death, the national government voted to pay to his estate the sum of thirty thousand dollars. In 1913, a sack of old papers was found in a storeroom in Richmond, Virginia. They were the papers that Clark had sent by messenger 135 years before. On regular forms and on assorted scraps of paper the memoranda of his Kaskaskia-Vincennes days were recorded. Clark was fully vindicated, but 135 years too late.

Today, a memorial that cost a million and a half dollars stands on the site of the old Fort Sackville at Vincennes. A statue of Clark is in the center of the rotunda. Seven murals, high on the walls, tell the story of the conquest of the Northwest. Clark's niche in history is secure.

🌿 LEWIS & CLARK AT WOOD RIVER

MANY PLACES ALONGSIDE Illinois highways tell interesting stories to those who pause to question, but most are unmarked. One marked historical site passed by thousands each day is located on the west side of Highway

67A toward the south edge of Wood River, in Madison County. This marker was placed there by the Illinois State Historical Society to indicate the locality where Captain Meriwether Lewis, private secretary to President Jefferson, and William Clark, younger brother of George Rogers Clark, gathered, organized, trained, and equipped a very select company of forty-three unmarried men for a long journey to the Pacific and return. Known as the Lewis and Clark expedition, it still remains the most significant exploring mission ever sent out by the United States.

Even before the Louisiana Purchase had been completed, Jefferson had formed plans, and funds had been allocated for sending a select group of twelve men west and north along the Missouri Valley to explore possibilities for trade in that region. When the purchase of the territory had been completed, the President's earlier plans were extended to the Pacific. Louisiana Territory had been purchased, practically sight unseen. Now it was time to know more about the new lands that had doubled the nation's area.

The expedition recruited at the mouth of Wood River was to become a memorable and significant one. It was to pass through extensive territories about which there were very meager or no written records and little of oral accounts. It was to reveal much concerning an area that was later to make up fifteen states of the union.

The expedition was to gather information concerning unknown rivers, mountains, and mountain passes, of wide expanses of prairie and forest, and of strange plant and animal life. Hitherto unknown Indian tribes were to be encountered. It was to mark the beginning of one of the more romantic chapters of American history, one to which additions are yet being made as more records left by those making the trip are discovered.

Also, this expedition was to bring to attention one of the most noted women in American legend, the little Shoshone squaw Sacagawea (also spelled Sacajawea), or "Bird Woman." She was the wife of Toussaint Charbonneau, a French Canadian, who joined the expedition as interpreter while it was encamped at Fort Mandan during the winter of 1804–1805.

Sacagawea soon became one of the expedition's most important members. Without the help that this wise and diplomatic Indian woman gave and the aid that she was able to secure from other Indians, the mission could not have succeeded. It was she, then eighteen years of age and with her first papoose strapped on her back, who guided the party through the unexplored mountain passes toward the lands on the western slopes where she had spent her childhood and where her relatives lived. The recognition of her services is partially indicated by the fact that more memorials have been erected to her memory than to any other woman in American history.

The first winter after leaving the Wood River camp was spent at a Mandan Indian village just west of Bismarck, North Dakota. The second winter was at Fort Clatsap, near Astoria and within sound of the Pacific. No ship came to the mouth of the Columbia as had been promised, and it was necessary to make the return trip overland. This the expedition did, reaching St. Louis on September 23, 1806, almost two and a half years after setting out from the Wood River camp. It must have been with mingled feelings that they passed the site of their starting point on that September day.

Only two of the men starting on the long journey to the Pacific failed to return with the group. One was Sergeant Floyd, who died and was buried on a hilltop near Sioux City, Iowa, where a shaft marks his grave. The other man was John Coulter who, on the return trip, asked for and received a discharge near the headwaters of the Missouri, in order to trap, hunt, and explore. It was he who first reported the geysers of the Yellowstone.

Today the forest that stood at the Lewis and Clark Illinois camp is gone. Another forest made of spreading oil tanks, chimneys, and weird structures of cracking plants has replaced the original one. The land lying along the Mississippi and about the mouth of Wood River on the west of the highway is used by an oil company as an area for the storage and loading of oil products on river barges. All the early buildings in the area have long since vanished, and apparently no object standing on the site in 1804 remains. A tornado destroyed most of the old trees in 1948. Men have completed the job and left a wasteland.

Much of a significant legend still clusters about the site. Those with reasonable imagination like to pause at the sign while they recall the story of the mission that departed from there on May 14, 1804. One such visitor said: "This place reeks with history."

Courteous guards for an oil company now keep a round-the-clock watch over the area. But a few days ago, one was heard to say: "We sometimes wish that Lewis and Clark had selected some other site for their training camp."

🎖 A MEXICAN WAR DIARY

ON JULY 7, 1847, THE First Regiment of Illinois Foot Volunteers, commanded by Col. E. W. B. Newby, drew out of Fort Leavenworth for the

Spanish town of Sante Fe, more than eight hundred miles distant. The Mexican War was on, and they were on their way to the conflict.

With a heavy and slow moving train of eighty-five ox-drawn wagons to carry military supplies, equipment, and food, and with the prairies, deserts, mountains, rivers, the intense heat of summer, and with hostile Indians to encounter along the way, the men knew that it would be a difficult march.

Ben L. Wiley, a young man from the vicinity of present-day Makanda, in Jackson County, an enlisted man of Company B, kept a diary through the days consumed in the westward march. Too long to publish in full, parts of it have been selected to afford glimpses of the experiences and feelings of a southern Illinois boy, one of those who blithely marched away to war.

The first entry in his diary is for July 6, 1847, and records the fact that "This day was given to preparation for our march on the morrow." Clothes were washed and "a wagon and two yokes of steers to haul our knapsacks" were bought "for $2.50." This undoubtedly was meant to be $250, since Wiley often used decimal points where not required.

On Friday, July 8, they were "up early—got our breakfast over—and started in regular column of Marches . . . over a beautiful rolling prairie enlivened occasionally by its stands of timber." He "saw the small huts and patches of the Delaware Indians." Along the way they camped "at a place called Gum Springs," with "heavy clouds and much thunder."

Some broken wagons forced the company to remain in camp the next day. Starting early on Saturday, however, they continued their march and "about 10 o'clock A.M. reached the Kansas River and were ferried over by the Delaware Indians." Continuing "four miles through a finely improved country we camped at a delightful place where there was one of the finest springs I ever saw." Throughout his diary Wiley continues to pay glowing tribute to springs and "good cold water."

On the next day, Sunday, "with several of our officers and volunteers I went to church in as fine and comfortable a meeting house as I have seen anywhere in the country. . . . The congregation was composed of the Wyandot Indians who live here. . . ."

In the next two days, they met some returning soldiers, had their work cattle stampede at night and "break out of the corral—with a noise like thunder" causing "some of the men to spring out of bed in their shirts and shout Indians! Indians!"

Wiley's entry for the next day, July 14, records a tragedy, one of several such that occurred on the march. Perhaps it can best be told by quoting from the diary.

"This morning we buried John W. Collins, from Marion, a private in Captain Van Trump Turner's company. His grave is located on the east side about 150 yards east of the 'Lone Elm'—the only tree to be seen on the prairie for many miles around. . . ."

Wiley's diary continues through ensuing days, telling of difficult marches, lack of water and wood for cooking, of a violent and unexpected rainstorm at night, a stop at the spot where the Indians had recently attacked a caravan of travelers, of wide expanses of plains "without a stick of timber," of one day's march of twenty-five miles "without wood or water"—indicated as the hardest day's marching thus far encountered—of the use of "buffalo chips" for fuel, of herds containing many thousands of buffalo and extending for miles across the plains, of buffalo hunts, and of eating juicy buffalo steaks.

He tells of false alarms "when the rattling of drums and the call To Arms, to arms sounded through the camp." Old landmarks, inseparably connected with the legend of the Santa Fe Trail are mentioned. Some of these are Gum Springs, Lone Elm, 110-Mile Creek, Council Grove, Diamond Spring, Big Bend of the Arkansas, Pawnee Rock, Cimarron, Rabbit Ear Creek, and Wagon Mound.

Wiley's company was at Diamond Spring, a noted stopping place on the old trail, on July 25. He was on guard duty with a group of men on that evening when a sentry stopped an express guard, a group so designated because they were supposed to move with all possible speed. This group proved to be under the command of the celebrated plainsman, Kit Carson, and was on its way to California. Wiley indicates his admiration for Carson, and when the war was over, he returned with a herding contract signed by Carson as a witness. This remained one of the highly valued of Wiley's souvenirs.

Ten days after parting with Kit Carson at Diamond Spring, Company B was at Pawnee Rock, where some travelers had recently been attacked by the Indians. The litter was still lying about. All was not bad, however, for they "had a fine mess of Buffalo steak fried for supper, which with good coffee and biscuit 'Wasn't bad to take.'"

The manner in which the group of soldiers on duty spent the evening at Pawnee Rock may be of interest. Wiley writes: "I will give you a description of the occupations of our party. Four of them are at a game of 'Old Sledge,' one is looking on, one is reading his Bible, two have just finished singing 'Am I a Soldier of the Cross?' and are now at 'On Jordan's Stormy Banks I Stand,' one is standing sentinel and your humble servant is engaged in making up this journal."

For August 11, he sets down: "This morning all was ready and our long train commenced crossing the river. By ten o'clock all were over and we had performed the far-famed exploit of 'Wading the Arkansas.' "

The first fifty miles beyond the river was one of the most difficult and dangerous stretches of the old trail. When they reached it, however, instead of a desert with drifting sand and no water, they found numerous ponds left by a recent freakish downpour. Traveling mostly at night to avoid the great heat, they traversed this portion of the trail with relative ease.

Wiley's comments concerning the country through which they were passing indicate that the experience was not altogether unpleasant. He tells of finding groves of "plumb" trees along Rabbit Ear Creek, and says that "the boys gathered a fine mess" and that "this morning we had a fine 'plumb' pie which was most delicious." Again, "I this evening made a fine large 'Plumb Cobbler,' Oh! delicious."

On September 7, they were in sight of Las Vegas, New Mexico, and were meeting long trains of wagons returning to Fort Leavenworth. He comments upon the fine appearance of the fruitful valley and upon the large fields of corn, wheat, and onions. He judged the people to be about two-thirds Indians and one-third Spanish and thought, "A little more cleanliness would not be detrimental to either their health or morals."

On Sunday, September 12, Company B was ready to enter Sante Fe. "All were rigged up in their best bib and tuckers this morning and started at a lively pace for the goal of all our toils during the long and wearisome tramp across the plains. . . . We pitched our tents about a half mile from the town on a fine hill to wait for the rest of the regiment." In fifty-three marching days the expedition and its heavy train of eighty-five wagons had covered the 803 miles from Leavenworth to Santa Fe—a remarkable feat.

On October 27, when the First Regiment resumed the march southward, Wiley had become acting quartermaster sergeant for the regiment. On a trip to procure grain for the mules and oxen, he fell ill and was cared for by a Mexican and his wife. Perhaps this incident is best told by extracts from his diary.

It says: "During the night I felt strong symptoms of a fever . . . and arose in the morning with my fears fully realized. I repaired to the house of a Mexican where I had bought 'Mais' for the mules and cattle. . . . I was kindly received and made comfortable. . . . Dr. Tunny visited me. . . . I was visited by Major Donaldson and other officers . . . and kindly waited upon by Pvt. T. J. McKinney of Company B."

Concerning the Mexican and his wife in whose *casa* he stopped, Wiley says: "A brother or sister could not have showed more solicitude or tenderness than was exhibited by this kindhearted couple. In taking leave of them it was with difficulty that I could prevail upon them to receive a trifle in return for their kindness to me. I never shall cease to think of these kind Mexicans who acted the true Christian to a sick stranger."

The trip toward Mexico continued. On November 15, Wiley records that the rabbits were numerous and large and that the boys had killed many of them as well as many geese and ducks that were abundant along the river.

On November 17, they "did not move on this day because of holding a 'Court Martial' to try some Regular and Volunteer teamsters [who] had misbehaved at the town through which we had passed. Charges were stealing chickens and abusing the owners. One of the Regulars was fined $25 and the volunteer teamsters about $6. I hope that this lesson will learn them to demean themselves as Gentlemen and Soldiers."

On November 19, the army lay in camp and "of course had the camp full of Mexicans all day. At night we had a 'fandango' where the fair 'Senoritas' were seen in all their glory."

On Christmas Day they had "as fine a plumb pudding as ever graced any table, also grape pies, and plenty of chickens. In fact we lived as well as any of our fellow citizens in the state of Illinois."

The march continued until December 27, when "an express arrived from Sante Fe with orders for us to return as quick as possible." The war was over and Wiley's diary ends here, without an account of the homeward march.

Military records show that Wiley was discharged at Alton, Ill., on October 11, 1848. During the next forty years, he remained a prominent and influential citizen of southern Illinois. He helped to found the Republican party in Illinois and became a lieutenant colonel of cavalry in the Civil War.

The home in which he lived is standing yet, where the road to Makanda leaves Highway 51, about eight miles south of Carbondale.

❧ FORT DEFIANCE

THE EDGE OF THE Civil War came to southern Illinois. Some who visit or pass through Cairo, at the junction of the Ohio and Mississippi rivers, often do not realize that it was a most useful and used military post during the war. It was a springboard from which significant military expeditions were launched.

At the beginning of the conflict, each side realized the advantages that the control of this point would give. The Confederacy assembled forces farther down the Mississippi in the spring of 1861, and began an unopposed advance northward toward the coveted point. The local company of militia met to decide its course of action. It was decided to maintain an attitude of "armed neutrality." Cairo thus would be an easy prize for the first armed forces to reach it.

This was the situation on April 19, 1861, when Governor Yates, of Illinois, with the approval and urging of authorities in Washington, asked that the Chicago militia garrison Cairo. The troops requested were assembled, placed on Illinois Central trains and started southward. The Cairo Expedition was on its way.

One company was left to guard the Illinois Central railway bridge four miles north of Carbondale. The others continued south and were in possession of Cairo on April 22, three days after Governor Yates had issued the call for troops. This was none too soon, for the Confederate forces were only a dozen miles away. Had roads not been so bad, they might easily have been there first.

Those first Union troops to reach Cairo were a motley group. Their uniforms were not uniform. They were armed with assorted weapons ranging from squirrel rifles to shotguns. Other equipment was nondescript. Their training was very meager. Only a few of the officers among them had knowledge of the military. Despite these obvious deficiencies, they secured a point vital to the Union cause. With this small garrison of men awaiting them and with the difficulties of approach, the Confederate forces did not continue their advance. They remained in the vicinity for some time, however, as a constant threat.

Other Federal forces were dispatched to Cairo. By May 10, 1861, troops had been assembled, and Camp Defiance was definitely in existence. Outposts were established and patrols were set up along the levees on the Illinois side of both the Ohio and Mississippi. Fortifications were built at the junction of the rivers, and on the Missouri side of the Mississippi, artillery was placed at these posts to control the passage of steamboats on either river.

The principal and strongest of the forts was the one located on the point of land where the rivers then joined. This point is less than a hundred yards from the place where the New York Central roundhouse now is located, at the corner of Washington Avenue and First Street. It first was called Fort Prentiss for the general then commanding the camp, but the name was changed later to Fort Defiance. It was a rather massive earthen fortification and was well supplied with the heaviest artillery that could be had. The Union forces thus were in full control of the rivers at their junction.

It is interesting to note that for years before the Union forces built the fort, the site was guarded by one lone cannon used on special occasions to salute approaching steamers. One sizable building, Arlen's distillery, stood on the point, but the troops wrecked it to clear space for the fort.

General Prentiss was in command of the camp until September 4, 1861, when General U. S. Grant was placed in charge. Grant lived at the St. Charles Hotel, later to be known and to attain note as the Halliday House. A portion of the old hotel still stands a hundred yards or so north of the site the fort occupied. The military offices of Grant were located on the second floor of a stone front building which is still standing, but has been condemned, on Ohio Street, about midway between Seventh and Eighth. It was at Cairo that Grant first attracted attention and indicated the aggressive qualities that carried him into military eminence.

Cairo's Ohio Street alongside the river was once one of the busiest streets in America. It is now in ruins and practically deserted. Only at rare intervals may a large boat be seen moored at this river port that was at one time among the more important ones in the world. There is no evidence of the gunboat flotilla that lay in the river. An occasional bronze plaque remains with the written records to indicate the town's importance as a military post during the Civil War.

Some of the romance of river days may yet be felt by the imaginative.

🌿 *A LEGEND OF THE CIVIL WAR*

Two men were taking turns at carrying a strange object up and down last year's corn rows in a field near Mill Creek, in Union County. Their somewhat unusual actions naturally aroused the curiosity of observers. The device they were carrying was the same as that used by engineers to locate buried water and oil lines, or by soldiers to locate land mines. These men were not looking for a pipeline or land mines, but for buried treasure —that is, if an old cannon could be considered such.

They were trying to verify or disprove a local legend concerning some buried artillery. According to a persistent story, three field pieces had been buried near the junction of two streams in that vicinity in the early years of the Civil War. Tradition would have them hidden by a group of men being recruited for service in the Confederate Army who did not want them to fall into the hands of the Federal forces.

Of course, it is possible that these cannons never were buried, or they may have been buried and later removed. The general belief in the story, even by those not prone to listen to such tales, makes one think that there is a basis in fact for it. Whether true or untrue, it vividly illustrates the condition of divided loyalties that then existed in southern Illinois—a condition that is not difficult to understand.

A large proportion of the settlers in the southern section of Illinois, in fact a majority of them, had come from the South and thus looked favorably upon slavery. In fact, many slaves were held, bought, and sold in the state until about 1840, regardless of laws to the contrary.

When the crisis came in 1861, it was only natural that these people should express their beliefs. Some openly and forcefully became advocates of the cause of the South. Mass meetings of these Southern sympathizers were held at various places, one of the largest of such gatherings being in Carbondale early in 1861. A number of men from the southern counties left to serve in the Confederate forces. Not less than thirty went in one group from Marion to join Company G of the One Hundred and Fifteenth Tennessee Volunteers. Smaller groups and several individuals are known to have gone from other places.

Within a short time, Federal forces came into full control of the southern counties of the state, and persons favorable to the South were forced to go underground. By their own naming, these friends of the South were as has been stated previously, Knights of the Golden Circle. By others they were termed "Copperheads," so called for the deadly snake that strikes without warning.

Getting back to the story about the cannon, it was a group of these Southern sympathizers who had obtained the three pieces, formed a company, and prepared to go south to join the Confederate army. Their plans became known to the Federal forces, who set about to disperse or capture the men. Fearing apprehension and loss of their equipment, the recruits decided it was best to disperse, at least temporarily, and to hide their cannon. They accordingly took them into the deep woods and buried them. No tradition concerning removal of the cannon has been found, and therefore, they may yet be buried.

This is only one of the many stories of Civil War days that were current some sixty years ago. For a generation or more after the end of the war, it was not unusual to hear someone in bated breath say when some older man was mentioned, "He was a Copperhead." Though a number of organized groups of the Knights of the Golden Circle are known to have existed, written records made at that time are practically nonexistent.

Divided loyalties did not entirely disappear with the end of the conflict. Citizens were somewhat sensitive on the subject for many years. Throughout the war a company of Federal troops was kept to guard the railway bridge across Big Muddy River north of Carbondale. Vigilant watch was kept for "subversives." A number of prominent men, including judges, physicians, and politicians, were arrested by the military and taken to Washington, D.C., often by way of the military posts at Big Muddy and at Cairo. After a few weeks in prison, those arrested appear to have been released, generally without trial or punishment, upon taking an oath of allegiance. The publication of one newspaper was suspended for a time. Night riders visited places where slaves fleeing northward had stopped and warned those with whom they were staying to send them on.

This large number of Southern sympathizers in the area did not keep the southern counties from contributing their full quota of men to the Union forces. In 1862 all men in Illinois between the ages of eighteen and forty-five years were registered. On the basis of this enrollment, Hamilton County, a reputed center of disaffection, led the state in the percentage of registered men enlisted. Franklin and Williamson counties, likewise known as Copperhead centers, ranked high in percentage of eligible men enlisting; Franklin had the fourth highest ratio in Illinois. Other southern counties far exceeded the average for the state. Most men apparently were "for" or "against" and acted accordingly.

Two books relating the Civil War period in southern Illinois provide interesting glimpses. One is *The American Bastile,* written by John A. Marshall and published in 1880. It tells of many of the men arrested and imprisoned for alleged opposition to the program of the Federal government. Though obviously biased and written in a dramatic style, it still is interesting. The other book, *The Flag on the Hilltop,* by Mary Tracy Earle, is connected with local happenings about the village of Makanda, in Union County.

MOUND CITY NATIONAL CEMETERY

THE MOST WIDELY KNOWN burying ground in southern Illinois is the Mound City National Cemetery. This cemetery, at the junction of Highways 51 and 37, about six miles north of Cairo, was authorized by an act of Congress on July 18, 1862. Ten acres of land were purchased, and the task was begun of removing the soldier dead from several smaller cemeteries—scattered from the site of the old village of America several miles to the east and from Cairo at the junction of the Ohio and Mississippi rivers, and even from other burial places in Kentucky. By 1864 the removals were practically completed.

Grave markers are simply and rather uniform in appearance, with only slight differences to indicate the branch of the military and the time of service. The graves of Confederate soldiers, forty-seven of them, are indicated by pointed stones. These include one "Confederate spy" who remains nameless. This is not strange since many identities were never established, and 2,759 markers at the graves of Union soldiers carry only the one word, "Unknown."

Those who stop and walk through the grounds see a series of bronze markers that carry stanzas of the well-known poem, "The Bivouac of the Dead," written by Major Theodore O'Hara to honor the Kentucky soldiers killed in the Mexican War when their bodies were brought back to the cemetery at Frankfort. O'Hara's poem is the most widely known and quoted dirge written in tribute to the soldier dead of America.

The bronze markers, each carrying a stanza of the poem, are distributed in sequence along the walkways. The first one, found near the caretaker's residence, has the opening lines of the poem that begins with, "The muffled drum has beat the soldier's last tattoo. . . ." Other markers carry additional stanzas until a final one declares:

> Nor wreck, nor chains, nor winter's blight, nor times
>   remorseless doom
> Can dim one ray of light that gilds your glorious tomb.

Some insist that the entire poem is overly charged with sentiment. This may well be true, but it could hardly be otherwise and be appropriate.

Near the center of the cemetery, there is a large granite memorial, seventy-two feet high and with a base twenty-four feet square. This central marker carries assorted legends and the names of many dead. A short way south of this prominent marker is a section of the cemetery where burials are less ordered and uniform. One stone in this section marks the grave of Brigadier General John B. Turchin, "the Mad Cossack," once a trusted officer in the Russian Tsar's army. His checkered career in the Union forces indicates that he was an efficient but sometimes obstreperous officer. After the end of the conflict, Turchin went to live in somewhat straitened circumstances near the small village of Radom, in Washington County. His wife, who accompanied him throughout the war, against rather strict military regulations, is buried beside him.

In addition to the men buried in the cemetery there are about fifty women, many of whom nursed at the military hospital that stood in Mound City, about a mile to the east. Fifty-eight additional civilian employees who worked at the hospital and ship yards are among those

buried in the same plot. One grave having no military significance whatever is that of a local citizen's child.

Mound City National Cemetery is the largest of its kind in Illinois; it
is about twice as large as all the others in the state combined. Since its
beginning, burials have been made regularly, and many serving in later
wars rest here. The only restriction to burial now is that one has been
honorably discharged from the military service. Plans to secure more land
and enlarge the cemetery are being discussed.

Old accounts tell of the Memorial Day services that once were held
here when hundreds of Civil War veterans were present. Observance of
the day still is made, and thoughts turn to the War between the States,
but no Civil War veterans are left to attend.

❧ THERE WERE NO NEUTRALS

DIVIDED LOYALTIES AMONG Southern Illinoisans at the outbreak of the
Civil War caused great bitterness. This bitterness did not end with the
military victory of the North. Some men living near Walpole, in Hamilton County, decided to celebrate the news of President Lincoln's assassination by firing anvils, an accepted method of noise-making. To increase
the volume of sound, they placed a larger charge than was usual. When
the explosion occurred, the anvil split. These broken pieces were still lying
behind Henson's blacksmith shop in 1903, when Mr. O. A. Kane, the
writer's teacher, pointed them out to us.

A somewhat different reaction to the news of Lincoln's assassination is
shown by the records of the circuit court of Pulaski County. Court was
in session at Caledonia on Monday, April 17, 1865, with Judge Wesley
Sloan presiding. The first case called was a request for change of venue
in an insurance case to Sangamon County. This request was granted by
Judge Sloan. At this point, John Dougherty, prominent attorney in the
region, requested the court's attention and the privilege of presenting a
petition signed by sixteen "members of the Caledonia bar."

Among other statements the petition said: "The condition of the public's mind occasioned by the assassination of the President . . . is such
. . . as to suggest . . . an adjournment of . . . court." Judge Sloan considered the petition and appointed a committee to draft appropriate
resolutions. The resulting resolutions stated:

> We have heard with profoundest emotion . . . of the assassination of
> President Lincoln . . . and it is therefore resolved that we mourn
> deeply and beyond expression the death of the President . . . and we
> utterly detest such acts as . . . subversive of all that is good and dan-

gerous to the security of the Government. . . . The assassination of President Lincoln stands . . . as a bloody, damning crime . . . against the American people and . . . calls that measures be taken to detect and punish the person and all connected with him. That we declare . . . our utter detestation of the crime and humbly turn to God and mercy to deliver our people from . . . the dangers shown . . . and resolve that this court and members of this bar will wear the usual burden of mourning.

Upon reading of the foregoing resolution it was ordered by the court that the same be spread on its records and that the court do now adjourn until the next regular session of the court.

Wesley Sloan, Judge

The two incidents cited represent the wide divergence of feelings that still lingered at the end of fighting.

❧ GRAND ARMY OF THE REPUBLIC

At the close of the Civil War, there were more than a million men living who had served in the military forces of the nation. It was the thought of some of these that there should be an organization to preserve the memory of departed comrades, to promote their own mutual interests, and to aid the deserving widows and orphans of the soldier dead. Among the leaders of this movement was Dr. Benjamin F. Stephenson, of Springfield, who had served as a surgeon in the Fourteenth Illinois Infantry.

Dr. Stephenson began his efforts to form such an organization in Springfield early in 1866, but he met no ready response. He accordingly transferred his attention to Decatur, where the first post of the projected organization, made up of twelve veterans, was established on April 6, 1866. This post was named for Amos Duncan, the first Macon County soldier killed in the war, and was designated as Post Number One.

Those who travel that way may still pause in Decatur to read the inscription on the tablet at 253 Park Street. It says:

BIRTHPLACE OF THE GRAND ARMY OF THE REPUBLIC

IN A SECOND FLOOR ROOM ON THIS SPOT THE GRAND ARMY OF THE REPUBLIC WAS ORGANIZED ON APRIL 6, 1866, BY DR. BENJAMIN F. STEPHENSON. THIS TABLET IS PLACED BY THE DEPARTMENT OF ILLINOIS WOMAN'S RELIEF CORPS, AUXILIARY TO THE GRAND ARMY OF THE REPUBLIC, APRIL 6, 1915.

When it was first formed, someone asked why the name "Grand Army of the Republic" was chosen. The ready response was, "Because it was a grand army."

After the establishment of this first post, the movement spread rapidly. Other units were formed in Illinois and adjoining states. Before the end of the year, it had become nationwide. The first national meeting was held at Indianapolis, Indiana, where representatives from ten states and the District of Columbia met on November 20, 1866. They elected General Stephen A. Hurlbut as the first national commander. The second commander was General John A. Logan, of Illinois, who served two years. Perhaps it was he more than any other one who cemented the organization together and gave it definite purposes. His General Order No. 11, proclaimed in the early spring of 1868, established a Decoration Day or Memorial Day, already being observed in a few places.

A few years later—1877—the G.A.R. had its first newspaper established by George E. Lemon, a pension attorney in Washington. Through this and other papers established by state and local units, the G.A.R. wielded great influence. Hundreds of towns and villages had their posts where, on special days, members paraded in their blue uniforms with polished brass buttons while fifes and drums played and flags waved.

Practically all men who had served in the military forces of the national government between April 12, 1861, and April 9, 1865, and who had been honorably discharged, came to join the organization. The peak of its membership was reached about 1890, when the number belonging reached a total of 408,487. It was said to be a nonpolitical group, but it was actually a great power in politics from about 1872 to 1904. Much of the national legislation benefiting Union veterans and their survivors came through efforts of the G.A.R.

After 1890, death began to rapidly thin its ranks. In 1930, forty years after its largest enrollment, the membership had decreased to 21,000. On August 28–31, 1949, its last national encampment was held in Indianapolis, the place where it had been organized eighty-three years earlier. Only six of the sixteen surviving Union veterans attended this last meeting. No member now survives.

A similar organization of Southern states veterans was formed in 1889 and named the United Confederate Veterans. This group never had a membership greater than fifty thousand. Their stated objectives were about the same as those of the Union veterans organization. The United Confederate Veterans, now disbanded, likewise held annual meetings until recent years.

❧ *SOLDIERS' REUNIONS*

MEMORIES OF THE Grand Army of the Republic held by a few oldsters cannot be separated from those of the Soldiers' and Sailors' Reunions that were held regularly until the early years of the present century. At these reunions, the men who had served in the armed forces during our Civil War met to visit and to recount the episodes of their service. They also nibbled once more at hardtack and drank steaming coffee from the large kettles arranged above fires similar to those about which they had gathered in the war years.

At first these reunions were principally for the purposes named. Many persons, however, came to see them as occasions that afforded commercial opportunities. This was the stage of their development when the author first came to know them. With the passage of time and the thinning ranks of the veterans, the commercial aspects became greater and the re-unions less frequent. Their rate of disappearance after 1900 was rapid, but in their heyday, they were the most significant gatherings held during the year in many communities.

Some time time before the dates chosen for the reunion, posters would appear on roadside trees or upon walls, and handbills or even booklets would be circulated. The local papers would carry notices, and news of the coming event would be passed along by word of mouth. Even yet some of this literature is found among old papers in trunks and attics to tell the reunion's story.

The site chosen was invariably a woodland or grove, generally near some town. Much emphasis was given to the importance of speakers who were to appear. A "brass band" could be expected. The author has vivid memories of the Roland Cornet Band that regularly played at the Broughton reunion in southern Hamilton County, and also of the large band wagon with its upsweeping ends and tiers of seats. It was about the only time when a band concert could be heard in the region, and these concerts were impressive—at least they were to country boys, many of whom had never before heard a band.

As the commercial aspects of these reunions came to take on greater significance, they began to resemble present-day carnivals. Actually, they were a blend of carnival, reunion, and political rally.

Those at Broughton were held in the grove just east of the state high-way. The general layout was about a hollow square having perhaps a few stands within it. Various liniments and lotions were offered. Jaynes electric belts, "guaranteed to cure rheumatism or money back," were sold, and the seller signed a warranty with a flourish as "Jaynes, B.D." He said B.D. was for Boy Doctor.

These stands, in and around the square, offered assorted refreshments and some novelties. For five cents one might get all the pink lemonade he could drink from a dipper or tin cup hanging on a string from the side of the tub or barrel. At another stand one could get "Hokey Pokey Jersey Ice Cream" in slabs, or a "Delicious Milk Shake," flavored with vanilla, and even ice cream cones. Sandwiches could be had, or a full meal could be bought at "Young's Dining Room," which was really one continuous table arranged about a hollow square and covered by an awning.

After a call at the food stands, the ambitious ones could try their strength at maul racks or their marksmanship at a shooting gallery. One could throw balls at forward-leaning hinged dolls arranged along a board—"one down – one cigar, two down – two cigars, three down – a quarter of a dollar." At another place, a thrower could fling eggs at a cleverly dodging victim whose head was thrust through a slot in the canvas which protected his body. The most fun here came when an occasional thrower gripped the egg so tightly that it burst in his hand.

For several years at the Broughton reunion, the highlight of the day came with the balloon ascension about two o'clock in the afternoon. This was particularly exciting when the balloonist made a parachute leap. The parachute never failed to open, though here and there was a small boy who wished it wouldn't—"just to see what would happen."

For other amusement, the visitor could see the "two-headed calf," or watch "Bosco the Snake Eater—Half Boy, Half Ape—eat them alive." Those with some spare cash could buy "Magic Spot Remover" that a boy in the know said was really Lennox soap wrapped in tin foil that he had gathered at the places in town where plug tobacco was sold. One could visit "The Wonder Working World—Never Out, Never Over, Going on all the Time. Stay as long as you like." The gasoline engine that operated this "Wonder Working World" was outside the enclosure and always had its full quota of youngsters listening to its put-put and trying to understand what made it tick.

Every large reunion had its steam swing, carrousel or merry-go-round. The earliest one remembered had for its "steam" a pony running around in the circle enclosed by the swing. A tingle could be felt as one watched the knife-thrower pin the trusting lady to a heavy board with a number of long criss-crossed knives hurled with force and amazing precision.

One unforgettable thing seen at the Broughton reunion was the very latest motion picture, at that time the only full length film, "The Great

Train Robbery." When this picture was presented in observance of the motion picture industry's golden anniversary, it aroused many memories in a "boy" who saw it when it was new.

The layout of a reunion ground might vary somewhat, but one feature could always be expected. This was the speaker's stand, gay in bunting and flags, and with seats made of rough sawed boards laid across logs in front of it. The speakers followed the patriotic theme, even to "waving the bloody shirt" and never failing to lambaste political rivals.

The author well remembers peering through an opening at the rear of the stand and watching the trembling knees of an eighteen-year-old boy he knew making his first speech. This nervous youth evidently grew out of his nervousness in later years, since he was elected and served with distinction as president of the American Society of Newspaper Editors.

The animosities of the Boys in Blue lessened with the passing years. The bitterness of the struggle in which they had engaged disappeared and wounds had healed fully. There were even a few "rebels" at later reunions, mingling with their one-time enemies, any hatreds forgotten.

Reunions of Civil War veterans have ceased to be, and most personal memories of them have likewise passed.

Chapter 14

Along the Rivers

❦ BOATS THAT SELDOM RETURNED

THE AGE OF FLATBOATS began on the western waters at about the close of
the Revolutionary War. Yards for their construction became common on
the upper Ohio. The industry spread, and boats were built alongside many
streams, at almost any place on the bank near where they were to be
loaded. Flatboats varied in size, some being only ten feet wide and perhaps twenty feet long. Larger ones were more than twenty feet wide and
eighty feet or more in length. They were designed to draw three feet or
more of water; both large and small were called "broadhorns." Many of
the better-built boats had full decks with cabins. Some cabin sides were
pierced with loopholes so that the crew could better defend themselves
against river pirates or Indians. Oars mounted on long sweeps were used
to steer them.

Downstream trips did not require great physical effort, but they were
beset with dangers that included storms, sandbars, rapids, waterfalls, snags,
pirates, robbers, mosquitos, and an occasional band of unfriendly Indians.
Altogether, the river boatman's was a hazardous occupation. The current
that made the trip down river easier also made the return more difficult.
On upstream trips, sails were sometimes used. Otherwise the boat was
rowed, poled, warped, or cordelled upstream, and it was slow going—only
five or six miles a day at best.

Most flatboats carried produce to lower river markets. Others transported the families, goods, and chattels of settlers. All boats upon reaching
their destination were generally broken up and the lumber used for
buildings. These were the boats that never returned.

There are many accounts of flatboats on the streams of southern

Illinois. An early and tragic one concerns a band of immigrants on their way to settle near Kaskaskia in 1786. After floating down the Ohio from Pittsburgh, they had gone up the Mississippi to the rapids at Grand Tower, where the passengers went ashore while the crew prepared to cordell past the rapids. Indians hidden among the near-by rocks attacked and killed all passengers and the crew excepting one boy. This is the largest massacre of whites recorded in the southern end of the state.

Most boats were commercial ventures. A loading list among his papers shows that Pierre Menard shipped more than $30,000 worth of furs on one boat from Kaskaskia in 1800. William Boon took a flatboat load of produce from the point where Big Kinkaid Creek joins Big Muddy River west of Murphysboro in late December, 1811.

Daniel H. Brush, prominent citizen of early Jackson County, made two trips from Jenkins' Landing, at Grand Tower, in the spring of 1834. Several of his later trips began at Brownsville, Jenkins' Landing, or Murphysboro. Interesting accounts of these appear in his autobiographical journal.

A Doctor Mitchell loaded flatboats on the Saline River at Mitchellsville, in Saline County, about 1840 and sent them to New Orleans. Boats also were taken from the old watermill on the North Fork of the Saline River, two miles southeast of Broughton, in Hamilton County. Countless other boats left from various places along the Wabash, the Little Wabash, the Skillet Fork, the Saline, the Kaskaskia, the Big Muddy, the Ohio, and the Mississippi rivers.

A nice brick home, the Hosick House, on the south side of Illinois Highway 146 east of Elizabethtown was built with the proceeds from a flatboat load of produce. The bill of lading and cargo insurance for this boat are treasured by Mr. Hosick's descendants. Joseph Shetler, "Potato Joe," shipped many boatloads of potatoes from the landing at Shetlerville, a few miles above Golconda.

James McMurry, known as "Hopping John," taught school at Brownsville, Jackson County, and accepted pay in produce which he took down river to market each spring until he disappeared on such a trip about 1830. Abraham Lincoln was a flatboatman on both the Ohio and Mississippi rivers.

When steamboats came, the use of flatboats decreased, but some were used until after 1870. Today both the flatboats and the steamboats that supplanted them are gone. Mike Fink and other hardy and picturesque boatmen also are gone—leaving many a legend to enrich river lore.

✿ THE KING OF THE KEELBOATMEN

"I'm a Salt River Roarer; I'm chuck full of fight and I love the wimen. I can out-run, out-jump, out-shoot, out-brag, out-drink, out-fight, rough-an'-tumble, no holts barred, ary man on both sides of the river from Pittsburgh to New Orleans and back ag'in to St. Louiee." With this broad statement, Mike Fink took in a lot of territory. It is not known that any man definitely disproved his claims, though many tried.

Born in Pennsylvania in 1770, Fink became an Indian scout on the Pennsylvania frontier at the age of seventeen, and he soon was widely known for his boldness, cunning, and skill with the rifle. At about the end of the Revolutionary War, Fink was a pole-pusher on an Ohio river keelboat. Strong, active, and daring, he soon became known as "king of the keelboatmen," a designation he held for more than thirty years. He remains one of America's noted folk figures, the greatest in the lore of the rivers.

Many stories indicate Mike's great skill with a rifle. One tells of his shooting the scalp lock from the head of Proud Joe, an Indian who stood at a river landing across the Ohio from Louisville. Proud Joe's scalp lock was thin and tightly tied, so much so that the bullet completely severed the lock and it fell to the ground. So did the Indian who was stunned by the grazing bullet but was otherwise unharmed. At another time Fink saw a barefooted Negro sitting astride a barrel on the wharf at St. Louis. Remarking that the owner of such a "jaybird" heel could not wear a genteel shoe, Fink picked up his rifle, took careful aim and shot away a portion of the offending heel. When arrested and brought into court, Fink pleaded that he only meant to perform an act of kindness and thereby enable the victim to wear proper shoes.

Stories about the "wimen" whom Mike loved have been preserved. One was winsome Mary Benson, living on the Ohio near Louisville. Between Mike's passings, Mary's father succeeded in marrying her to a man named Taggart, only hours before Mike's arrival. Learning of the boatman's approach, Mary's new husband and her father abruptly fled taking Mary with them. Mike and Mary were to meet again many years later as she lay dying. At this meeting, being deserted by her husband, she gave her son, Carpenter Taggart, to Mike. Fink later affectionately calls him "my boy."

Mike paid court to another girl named Mira Hodgkiss, daughter of a tavern keeper. The father, so far as he dared, opposed the match. Openly and dramatically rejecting Mike in the presence of a crowd one night—probably a pre-arranged plan—Mira left the apparently crestfallen suitor and went to bed. Early the next morning Mike departed without seeing Mira. A mile or so down the river, someone on the shore called out, "Mike, I want to go with you." The keelboat drew to shore and Mira Hodgkiss went aboard.

The number of steamboats increased rapidly, and Mike's beloved keelboats became obsolete. This left him bitter and determined to wreak vengeance. Legend has him deliberately ramming one of the last keelboats he captained into an approaching steamboat rather than yield the channel to it.

On September 20, 1822, the *St. Louis Missouri Republican* carried an advertisement asking for one hundred men to go up the Missouri on a trapping and trading expedition. Fink and Carpenter, and also Taggart, as we later see, went along, Fink serving as captain or patroon on the largest of the three boats—the only one that reached the mouth of the Yellowstone.

At the new location, Mike was restless and disgruntled, so much so that he and Carpenter shortly withdrew and went to live in a cave they hollowed out in a near-by hillside. Relations became strained when Carpenter paid court to the daughter of Mike and Mira Hodgkiss, and the two men quarreled. Effecting a reconciliation, they arranged to demonstrate that fact to the world. They would re-enact a feat that they had performed many times before and shoot filled cups of whiskey from each others heads. It was Mike's turn to shoot first. When Fink fired, Carpenter fell dead. He had been shot in the middle of the forehead. For the first time, Mike had missed, whether purposely or by accident, no one knows.

Mike heard that a man named Talbott, really Mike's old enemy Taggart, whose face had been so badly scarred in a shooting affray that Fink did not recognize him, was spreading reports that Carpenter had been shot on purpose and not by accident. Fink went to call upon Talbott, whether to make inquiry or to settle a score is not known. Advancing in a threatening manner, Fink was warned to stop. When he failed to heed the warning, Talbott shot him. As he lay dying, Mike learned that Talbott was really his old enemy, Taggart, Mary Benson's husband. Thus passed the King of the Keelboatmen.

Taggart was drowned in the Yellowstone a short time later.

❦ FERRIES

IN THE SUMMER OF 1956, a bridge over the Ohio at Shawneetown was opened and another ferry 150 years old ceased to operate. This ferry, an historic one, was among those having the longest records of continuous operation in the Midwest.

There were other Illinois ferries across the Ohio, some of which, likewise, became widely known. Apparently few of them really were planned. They simply began where groups of emigrants from the earlier settled areas, principally the Carolinas, Tennessee, and Kentucky, reached the river on their way to settle in Illinois. Among these earlier and more important ferries were the one at Shawneetown, which began operations about the mid 1790's, and those started at Cave-in-Rock, Elizabethtown, Golconda, and Metropolis, slightly later. They were the principal gateways for settlers entering the Illinois country, as well as for those going across Illinois to points farther west.

Legends gathered about these crossings. No one of them bears more stories than the one operated by James Ford a short way upstream from Cave-in-Rock. In addition to operating the ferry, Ford, who also had a tavern in Kentucky a few miles south of his ferry, improved a roadway long known as Ford's Ferry Road from this establishment to another tavern kept by William Potts ten miles north of the river. Along this roadway many travelers were robbed, some disappeared, and others definitely were murdered. The mention of Ford's Ferry Road suggests many a weird story.

The ferry at Elizabethtown began when a band of settlers from the Carolinas came to the Ohio at that point and found no means of crossing the stream. Led by a man named Barker, this group built a boat and crossed into Illinois. Barker continued to operate the ferry until 1812, when it passed into the possession of James McFarland.

The ferry at Golconda, established in 1797, was first licensed by Kentucky. After more than a century and a half of service, it ceased to operate, then was briefly revived a few years go and closed again in 1957. The Golconda ferry was established by Major James Lusk, who had settled on the Kentucky side of the river. In 1798, despite lack of approval from "William Henry Harrison, Esqr., Governor and Commander in Chief of the Indiana Territory," Lusk moved across the Ohio and built a house, mostly of discarded flatboat timbers, on the crumbling Illinois bank of the river. After removal to Illinois, he obtained a license from the authorities at Kaskaskia. This ferry became widely known, and Lusk, like Ford at Cave-in-Rock, laid out and improved roadways approaching his landing. While opening one to Greene's Ferry on the Mississippi, in 1803, Lusk contracted the illness that killed him. His widow, Sarah, continued to operate the ferry and was granted a license by Governor Harrison on May 7, 1804, becoming the first woman so licensed in Illinois. After her marriage to Thomas Ferguson on April 2, 1805, the license was transferred to him.

In 1816 Ferguson laid out a town and called it Sarahville for his wife, and a post office was established. According to postal records, neither Sarah Lusk nor Ferguson was ever postmaster. This office retained the name of Lusk's Ferry until 1825, when it was changed to Golconda. In the meantime, the town had several names. First locally called Fiddler's Green, it became Lusk's Ferry, Sarahville, and for at least one day, it was Corinth before the present name of Golconda was chosen.

During the century and a half it operated, many settlers entered Illinois by way of Lusk's Ferry. Many thousands of Cherokee Indians, forced along the trail of tears from the Great Smokies to the land assigned them in Indian Territory, crossed the Ohio here.

❧ SHOWBOATS

SHOWBOATS HAVE DISAPPEARED from our rivers, leaving a great stock of legends and lore. Their passing also marks that of another distinctly American institution.

The first showboat of record appeared on the upper Ohio in 1817. It was a large keelboat owned by an actor named M. M. Ludlow. Other boats had carried lone performers and even groups of entertainers from town to town along the rivers, but Ludlow's was the first one where the audience came aboard. Shortly after the appearance of Ludlow's boat, Sol Smith built a complete theater aboard a river barge, and the typical showboat was born.

Showboats were new, but strolling entertainers were not. In medieval times, it was the practice of minstrels to go about singing their songs and telling their stories. No description of life in an olden castle is complete without such a character, generally pictured as owning nothing but his rudely contrived harp of strings and the clothes he wore, who always had a great stock of stories and ballads. Modes of life changed through the centuries, but the counterpart of the roving medieval minstrel continued.

In our earlier days, he was represented by the fiddlers, ballad singers, and story tellers who followed the frontier. The pioneer welcomed them just as the lord of the castle had welcomed the strolling minstrel.

With the river at hand and people wanting to be entertained, Ludlow and Smith were reasonably successful. Numerous other boats followed these first ones. There were floating menageries and museums, assortments of freaks and trained animals, acrobats, jugglers, magicians, minstrels, and musicians. P. T. Barnum, the great showman, took his circus down river from St. Louis to New Orleans in 1836. Many stage plays were presented on boats, melodramas being the most common. Actors and entertainers of note often were in the showboat troupes. Red Skelton is said to have learned the buck and wing dance on the "Golden-rod," and Ted Mack is reported to have played the part of an off-stage bloodhound aboard another of these boats.

An early boat that gave pattern to the many that followed was Captain French's "New Sensation," followed shortly by Captain Price's "Wonderland." In a few years, others that have become part of the showboat legend appeared. They include the "Princess," the "Cotton Blossom," the "Water Queen," the "Sunny South," and the "Majestic." Another great craft was the "Floating Palace," a circus boat. The names of these boats, when mentioned to those oldsters who lived along the river fifty or more years ago, revive many memories.

In the heyday of showboating, there were many such crafts on our western waters. As late as 1931, eighteen of them were regularly stopping at river towns. There was intense rivalry to see which could be the largest and most luxurious. Today only two of the famous craft around which legends of the showboat cluster survive. One is the "Goldenrod," minus its calliope and somewhat the worse for wear, that has been anchored at the foot of Locust Street in St. Louis since 1937, where it gives nightly performances. Here one may again see such plays as *East Lynn, Ten Nights in a Barroom, The Drunkard, Hamlet, Uncle Tom's Cabin, The Trail of the Lonesome Pine, The Hatfields and the McCoys,* and *The Stuttering Cowboy*—the melodramas familiar to showboat audiences seventy years ago.

The wooden hull of the "Goldenrod," decaying and ready to sink, was replaced by a steel one in 1947. Those managing it say that some day they may give the "Goldenrod" a new coat of paint, loose its moorings, restore the calliope, and again follow the river. This vague promise has been repeated for about twenty years. The "Majestic" is the last of the many showboats to tour the rivers. It was on regular schedule about 1950 with a troupe of players from Hiram College, in Ohio.

An American institution in the entertainment world has all but disappeared.

🌺 *SHIPWAYS*

THERE WAS A TIME when Cairo, in southern Illinois, could have claimed distinction as a great "seaport." Then the Ohio and the Mississippi swarmed with steamboats. It was not unusual for a hundred boats to dock at Cairo in one day. The wharves at St. Louis were sometimes lined five deep with boats loading and unloading. Steamboat landings were found at frequent intervals along the banks of the principal rivers. It was definitely the heyday of river traffic.

This great traffic required that hundreds of river craft be built and kept in repair. An important place for this work was the Marine Ways at Mound City, ten miles above Cairo. This shipyard, completed in 1859, was built by the Emporium Real Estate and Manufacturing Company of Cincinnati as part of their plan to establish a great city at the site where they had sold over $400,000 worth of city lots. The confidence of those buying lots in Emporium City must have been sublime, since they paid as much as $113 a front foot for some of them.

Records of the old shipyards were destroyed by fire many years ago. Only one small book, the docking register, appears to have escaped that that fate. This record book gives interesting data concerning the craft that came to the ways. The names of many boats noted in river lore appear upon its pages. According to this register, the first boat serviced there was the barge "Memphis," which was hauled upon the ways on May 26, 1859, and returned to the water on the following June 9.

When the Civil War began, the ways were taken over by the national government and used as a part of the naval station at Cairo. During the time that the yards were in the possession of the nation, the names of many noted gunboats appear. Three, the "Carondelet," the "Mound City" and the "Cincinnati," were built there and several steamers were converted into armored boats.

It often was necessary to repair and outfit naval vessels. Some that came to the yards were the rams "General Price," "Monarch," and "Switzerland." The last served as flagship for the fleet. Maj. James S. Robarts, of Carbondale, was Chief Surgeon on this boat.

Among the gunboats repaired at Mound City were the "Tyler," "New

Era," "Pittsburgh," "Carondelet," "St. Louis," "Mound City," "Cincinnati," "Eastport," "Alfred Robb," "Chillicothe," "Queen City," "Signal," and the "Pawpaw." The last name on the register is the "Romeo."

This brief mention of the Marine Ways could hardly end without mentioning one entry for 1863. On July 15 of that year "Submarine No. 12" was docked. It was returned to the water on August 3. Little appears to be known about this strange boat. Something of the romantic, the heroic, and the puzzling comes to any person who scans the old docking register.

⚜ THE SHIPYARD BELL

ADMIRAL DAVID DIXON PORTER, commanding Union naval forces on the western rivers during the Civil War, brought ten bells upstream from the State of Mississippi to Mound City in 1864. One of these bells was a bronze one cast by the Buckeye Bell Foundry at Cincinnati in 1853. It came from a plantation in Mississippi where it had been used to arouse the slaves in early morning, send them to the field for work, and later call them back to their rude cabins and homely fare. It also rang the curfew to end any gatherings the slaves had been allowed to hold.

Because its tones were loud and pleasing, this bell was placed in use at the Marine Ways. It served as a ship's bell, being struck at half-hour intervals to indicate the time of day or night. It also served as the master bell for the naval station, its signals being picked up and repeated on all others ships' bells within hearing. With the departure of the naval forces from the Marine Ways after the close of the war, the prescribed strokings of the bell and John Schuler's measured and powerful call of "—— bells and all is well" ceased. The bell and other items that the naval forces did not choose to remove were left at the five large buildings donated to the city.

During the next sixty years, it served many uses. It remained on its wooden platform near the group of buildings until they were destroyed by fire in 1879. The timbers that supported it were burned, and it fell to the ground. Undamaged, it was removed to the schoolhouse–city hall building on Main Street. In this location, it called youngsters to school and rang curfew to hasten them home at night. It also summoned volunteers to fight fires.

In 1889, after serving ten years at the schoolhouse–city hall location, it was removed to a wooden tower made of four posts about forty feet high in front of Fireman Hall on the plot where the Pulaski County Memorial Park now is located. In 1910 it was again moved and placed on a tower in front of the firehouse. When the city installed a fire siren in 1924, the bell was no longer required. The local Woman's Club, remembering that the bell had served the city for sixty years and knowing the lore gathered about it, caused a stone platform to be erected beside the Illinois Central Railroad just north of the station. The bell was placed on this platform where it remained for thirty years.

When Mound City observed the centennial of its establishment in 1954, interest in the old bell was revived. A new stone platform was arranged at the Memorial Park, and the bell was removed to that location and placed above a time capsule to be opened in the year 2054. The clapper of the bell was restored, and the present generation has opportunity to hear a bell that has summoned many forgotten slaves to their labor, sailors and workmen to their duties, signaled the change of guards, indicated the arrival and departure of gunboats during the Civil War, called pupils to their studies at school, and sent them scurrying home with its curfew. It signaled many fires and called the volunteer fire fighters. Perhaps it also has served other purposes.

THE SIX SULTANAS

THE GREATEST MARINE disaster in American history is brought to mind by the name "Sultana." There actually were six Sultanas that operated along the Ohio and Mississippi borders of southern Illinois before tragedy came to rest upon the final one. The first bearing the name was built in Cincinnati in 1836 and operated from that port until it was abandoned in 1844. A second and somewhat larger one was built at Jeffersonville, Indiana, and registered at New Orleans. The latest record of this second boat indicates that it left St. Louis for New Orleans with a part of the Fourth Illinois Infantry bound for the Mexican War.

The third and smallest "Sultana," also known as "Sultana No. 2," was built at New Albany, Indiana, in 1848 and operated out of St. Louis until abandoned in 1852. The fourth and largest "Sultana," known for its splendor and luxury, was built at Cincinnati in 1848. It burned at St. Louis on June 12, 1851, with the loss of one life. A fifth "Sultana" was built at Paducah in 1852, operated from its home port of Evansville until destroyed by fire at Hickman, Kentucky, on March 25, 1857.

The sixth and last of the Sultanas was built at Cincinnati and commissioned there on February 7, 1863. On March 11 of that year, its registry was transferred to St. Louis, and John C. Mason became its master. This steamer was 210 feet long, 41 feet wide and 6 feet 6 inches deep. It had one deck, a plane head cabin, four boilers and two engines with 25-inch cylinders and strokes of 8 feet. Its tonnage was 660.38. There were accommodations for seventy-six cabin and three hundred deck passengers.

In April, 1865, the "Sultana" left New Orleans carrying a total of 250 passengers and crew, and a cargo of 250 hogsheads of sugar. It stopped at Vicksburg to take on two thousand Union prisoners recently released by the defeated Confederacy and assembled there. This made a total of more than 2,200 passengers on a steamer licensed to carry only 376. It also took about sixty horses and mules aboard, despite the fact that the "Pauline Carroll," an unloaded steamer as large as the "Sultana," was lying at the Vicksburg wharf and sought vainly for one thousand of the troops at the government rate.

While stopped at Vicksburg, it had boiler repairs made. A section 26 inches by 11 inches was cut from the worst part of its bulged plates. A makeshift patch was placed over the hole by boilermaker R. G. Taylor. Taylor later testified that he was not allowed to press the bulged section back into place because that would have delayed the boat. The plate used for patching was only ¼ inch thick while the regular plate was $^{11}\!/_{48}$ inch. The boat's officers insisted that the work be done in this manner and promised to cut out the bulged section and install thicker plate at St. Louis.

Overloaded beyond reason, the steamer left Vicksburg for St. Louis. Having already flouted many safety regulations, the "Sultana" proceeded to ignore still others. The engineers did not lower steam pressure to compensate for the thinner section of plate. Regular operations and accustomed speed were maintained until the boat reached a point about seven miles above Memphis, when the patched boiler suddenly exploded, killing many outright and hurling others into the river. The boat immediately burst into flame, trapping hundreds of passengers. Perhaps no large steamer was destroyed in so short a time; few survived. Passenger lists and rosters of released prisoners vanished in the explosion and fire.

According to the most reliable estimates made at the official investigation, at least 1,900 persons perished. This tragic marine disaster of April 27, 1865, still is unparalleled in American records.

Very old persons in southern Illinois may recall an elder's occasional remark concerning some local Civil War soldier: "He was on the 'Sultana.'" No other boat has been named "Sultana," it being an established tradition of the river that the name of a boat meeting a disastrous end be discontinued.

❦ THE "LEE" & THE "NATCHEZ"

IF THE "law ag'in it" had been rigidly enforced, history's classic steamboat race never would have been run. The handicap of illegality was evaded, however, and two steamboats along with their captains made their niches in river history.

Captain John Cannon of the Steamer "Robert E. Lee" was a man of medium height and build. He dressed well and tastefully, but never gaudily. He was calm, courteous, gentle, and courtly in behavior. Some even termed him retiring in disposition. When the chips were down, however, Cannon was a decisive, forceful, energetic, ingenious, and daring man. He was a Southerner reconciled to Reconstruction.

On the other hand, Captain Thomas Leathers of the steamer "Natchez" was a large man, well over six feet tall, of powerful build, and had a booming voice. His striking dress included ruffled shirts and diamond stick pins. He moved with force and with a certain degree of majesty. No one accused him of being a retiring person. Until the end of his days, he was an "unreconstructed rebel."

The event that was the beginning of the later rivalry between the two men came in the summer of 1866, when Captain Cannon had a large and luxurious steamer, one of the finest ever to grace the rivers, built at a New Albany, Indiana, shipyard and named it the "Rob't E. Lee."

The "Lee" had a hull 285 feet 6 inches long, 46 feet wide, and a draft of 9 feet. It carried eight boilers and, being a sidewheeler, it had two engines, the cylinders of which were 42 inches in diameter, with a stroke of 10 feet. Its paddlewheels were 39 feet in diameter and had buckets 17 feet wide to give an over-all width of 95 feet.

This steamer began to attract attention and to arouse controversy even before its completion. When Captain Cannon selected the name, "Rob't E. Lee," and had it painted on the wheelbox of the new craft, feelings mounted and threats of sabotage were made. As a safeguard, the unfinished vessel was taken to the Kentucky side for completion and fitting.

On October 7, 1866, the "Lee," with a large list of passengers anxious to travel on the new and luxurious craft, began its first downstream trip to New Orleans, there to begin its regular run between that city and Memphis. Afterwards, Captain Leathers arrived, leased a rival steamer, and entered into competition with Cannon. They quickly became bitter rivals, and their rivalry increased when Leathers went to Cincinnati and had the steamer "Natchez" built in 1869.

The "Natchez" was a magnificent craft. It was 303 feet long, with a hull 46 feet wide and a draft of 9½ feet. It also carried eight boilers and two engines. The bore of these engines was 34 inches and their stroke 10 feet. The paddle wheels of the Natchez were 43 feet in diameter with buckets 11 feet wide. Its over-all width was 83 feet.

Established records on the Mississippi were challenged. Among them was that of three days, twenty-three hours, and nineteen minutes set between New Orleans and St. Louis by the steamer "J. M. White" in 1844. Urged by personal pride and perhaps nettled by the taunts and dares of others, the captains arranged a race between the two steamers. It began shortly after five o'clock in the afternoon of June 30, 1870, when the "Rob't E. Lee" left the wharf at New Orleans followed a few minutes later by the "Natchez," thus avoiding the appearance of the race that it really was.

They did not at any time race side by side, despite the beautiful Currier and Ives prints that show them in such a position. The fact is that the "Natchez" was never near enough to catch a glimpse of the "Lee" after the beginning. They were not, however, very widely separated until after they passed the mouth of the Ohio, where the "Natchez" trailed by only an hour and ten minutes. It still could have been anyone's race.

Beyond this point, misfortunes came to the "Natchez." A heavy fog forced Captain Leathers to lay by for several hours. Engine troubles caused additional delay. In the meantime, the "Lee," ahead of the fog, raced on and reached the St. Louis wharf at 11:25 o'clock in the forenoon of July 4, having completed the run in three days, eighteen hours, and fourteen minutes, the all-time steamboat record between New Orleans and St. Louis. Seven hours later the "Natchez" docked.

The race was over, but the poems, stories, songs, legends, and controversies it aroused go merrily on. After the race, the two craft returned to their regular runs and continued their rivalry, even striving to see how many bales of cotton each could haul ("Rob't E. Lee," 5,741; "Natchez," 5,511).

At intervals each of these boats came to the shipyards at Mound City for service and repairs. The last visit of the "Lee" was in the summer of 1876, when an entry in the little ledger kept at the yard records the fact that the "Steamer Robert E. Lee" was docked. Another entry, about three weeks later indicates that the "Wharfboat Robert E. Lee" was launched. It was thus that the hull of the grand old steamer ended its days at Memphis. The chandeliers from its cabin hang in the Presbyterian church at Port Gibson, Mississippi. The fine pair of deer antlers, the only prize of the race, are in the Kentucky State Museum at Frankfort. Other articles that graced the "Rob't E. Lee" are at Cannon Acres not far from Frankfort.

The "Natchez" continued in service until 1879, when it also was dismantled. On the afternoon of July 3, 1879, the "Natchez" tied up at the foot of Ludlow street in Cincinnati. The next day, exactly nine years after the day when the great race had ended, workmen began to remove its machinery, superstructure, and fittings. The hull, like that of the "Lee," became another wharfboat for an oil company below Vicksburg.

Legends continue to grow about two famous steamers. Perhaps this should be so, for they undoubtedly represent the high point of steamboating on the western waters.

Chapter 15

Landmarks

🌸 *THE DEVIL'S BAKE OVEN*

Two TALL IRON TOWERS, one on either side of the Mississippi, stand a short way north of Grand Tower in Jackson County. These towers carry a strange bridge high above the river. Instead of being a bridge to accommodate rail or vehicular traffic or even foot travelers, it carries only large pipes. These pipes, in turn, bring natural gas from the Texas and Oklahoma fields to cities north and east of the bridge. The tower on the Illinois shore is near the south side of a small rocky hill known as the Devil's Bake Oven. This separate prominence is north of a longer rocky hill known as the Devil's Backbone. The Devil evidently came in for his due when local names were being passed out.

Construction of the Illinois tower for the bridge changed the appearance of the local scene. The building of the tower also served to bring the Devil's Bake Oven and one of its stories to attention once more.

The rocky point has been a noted landmark since the coming of white men more than 285 years ago. It marks the eastern end of a submerged rocky ledge that extends diagonally across the river toward Tower Rock, sometimes referred to in early records as the Rock of the Cross. At lower river stages, the rapids caused by this ledge made the upstream passage of keelboats and flatboats difficult. Crews often had to disembark, walk along the shore and, using long ropes, pull their boats through the rapids. When going downstream, it was often necessary to reverse the process and employ ropes to ease boats through the rapids.

During steamboat days, this rocky point served as a landmark for pilots. It also afforded an excellent lookout point from which approaching boats, miles away, could be seen. Both the Devil's Bake Oven and the Devil's Backbone afforded ideal places where Indians or river pirates could hide and wait for victims.

River piracy once was common along this portion of the Mississippi. In 1803 a detachment of United States Cavalry sent to drive the pirates from the Grand Tower section of the river was stationed here. It camped near the Devil's Bake Oven from May until September of that year. Tradition recounts that when the soldiers came, the pirates simply moved a few miles to the east and hid beneath an overhanging ledge of rock beside the Big Muddy River and there awaited the departure of the military. The place where they are supposed to have hidden is still known by the somewhat appropriate name of Sinner's Harbor. With increased settlement in the region, piracy disappeared.

The Devil's Bake Oven, aside from serving as a landmark for steamboat pilots or others taking crafts along the river, apparently waited idly by until the establishment of an iron industry at Grand Tower. With the coming of the new industry, several attractive residences were built in its vicinity for officials of the company. The house for the superintendent of the furnaces was built on the oven.

Foundation walls of the old house still may be seen near the top on the eastern side of the hill. In addition to definitely marking the site of the residence, they also provide the setting for a widely known ghost story. This ghost lurks, or at least was reported to have lurked, about the ruins. It may have departed ere now since no reliable observer has encountered it for some years.

According to an old, old lady, the story gained substance in the following manner. The superintendent of the iron works had a beautiful and winsome daughter upon whom many a swain cast longing glances. The young lady, however, returned the admiring glances of only one of her numerous suitors. As so often is the case in stories, the one she smiled upon was a handsome, roguish and irresponsible chap—not bad perhaps, but one for whom most people predicted no particular good. The father of the young lady, as fathers so often do, strongly disapproved of the young man she liked.

The daughter, kept much at home and not allowed to see her lover, died as storied maidens do. She began to pine away, and shortly she fell seriously ill and died, all for the love of the roguish youth.

The spirit of the maid, however, lingered about the scene of her unhappy days. For many years after her death, on those nights when the hill was flooded with gentle moonlight, visitors would report that they had seen a weird and mistlike creature much resembling the departed girl, float silently across their pathway to disappear among the rocks or in the dense bushes on the hillside. This disappearance was often followed by moans, wails, and shrieks such as only a ghost can make. In swirling storms, particularly at night, her cries were reported to be blood-curdling. Some claim that the spirit of the young lady could be heard long after her house was removed and the timbers had been carried away to build a railway station.

A visit to the Devil's Bake Oven is interesting enough even if the visitor fails to hear or see the ghost. As a matter of fact, some people may even find the unusual ferns on the face of the bluff along the river more interesting than the elusive ghost.

✿ BIG HILL

BIG HILL, ABOUT TWO miles wide and seven miles long, lying just north of Grand Tower, is a prominent Jackson County landmark. Precipitous sides where it borders the Mississippi and at its north end often are two hundred feet high. Heavy woodland on top of the bluff makes them appear even higher. The wide river on one side and level farmland on the other add to its prominence.

Early settlers came to this hill to build their cabins against its base, and thus many names prominent in the early history of the region are associated with it. In addition to its historical appeal, it has various other features that interest visitors.

Those interested in geology are intrigued by it. By what strange workings of time and nature did this lonely hill come to stand where it is? Did the Mississippi River once flow on its eastern side? If so, what caused its change to the western side? Other puzzling questions are posed. Even though the visitor may know little about geology, this rocky hill offers many other attractions.

Those interested in plant life find Big Hill to be a rich hunting ground. Specimens native to regions much farther north and south can be found on the hill and in the sheltered coves along its borders. The botanist discovers upland and lowland plants as well as those common to regions lying at a considerable distance to the east and west. A count of the annular rings in an increment boring taken from one gnarled old oak growing on a rocky ledge near the river indicates that it was probably standing when Columbus came to America. There are many other trees that saw the first French explorers pass this way as well as all the river pageant since that time. Thin soil and a scanty water supply have kept these trees relatively small, but many of them are truly venerable.

Big Hill is also a haven for birds. It is a stopping place for migrants on their seasonal trips. A diverse plant and insect life attracts many of them as regular residents. Nature lovers, amateur or trained, watching here find birds that they otherwise would seldom see.

This higher land, with fine springs and lush grazing grounds about it, was a favorite living place of the Indian. Many of their burial grounds are located at various points on the top of the hill. Their rock carvings along the bluff are among the most noteworthy found in southern Illinois. One particularly interesting group is beneath an overhanging rock ledge about midway on the river side. Here, overlooking the river below, one finds carved symbols that give him pause. Preliminary inspection indicates that this shelter was used for many centuries, perhaps for thousands of years, by primitive man.

Carved arms and hands point to mystery, and footprints suggest vanished trails. Numerous eyelike symbols, whose meaning no one seems to understand, peer at visitors. There are swastika-like signs with arms reversed and circles about them.

Some suggest that one group of markings may be a crude map representing the Mississippi flowing on the east side of the hill. A row of arched carvings suggests the huts of an Indian camp. Other scars show where the long gone artisans sharpened their tools. A chairlike depression with queer marking upon it may symbolize the throne of a forgotten deity.

It is a beautiful, lonely, and quiet spot where these carvings are found. Except for an infrequent train passing on the railway at the foot of the bluff, little is heard except those sounds peculiar to the forest.

At one point against the rocky wall of the bluff near the Indian carvings, sounds of the waters rippling about the jetties on the Missouri side of the river—and even the conversation there, three-fourths of a mile away—are easily heard. Could it be that the Indians hearing sounds at this spot, thought their Great Spirit was speaking and made the place into a shrine?

❦ AN ABANDONED MAUSOLEUM

THE RUINS OF A fifty-six-vault mausoleum that stands at a lonely and seldom-visited spot on the brink of Eagle Cliff—near the place where Dug Hollow leads downward from the hill to the fertile flood plain of the Mississippi in Monroe County—illustrate the truth of the poet Burns's assertion that the best laid plans of mice and men gang aft agley. This mausoleum is about eight miles north of Valmeyer, at the place where

Stephen W. Miles opened a farm and established an estate of feudal proportions.

Miles was no ordinary individual. Born in 1795 in Cazenovia, New York, he had received a liberal education. He also was a student of music and an accomplished performer on the violin. Though not of great wealth when he came to Illinois, his resources were far beyond those of most persons here at the time. Legend began to gather about the man almost from the time of his arrival.

The large group he led came down the Ohio on flatboats and landed near Cave-in-Rock. They brought along much livestock, many teams, and wagons carrying farm equipment and household goods. Trails leading from their landing place on the Ohio to Eagle Cliff were vague, indirect, and difficult to follow. Miles carefully selected the better portions of the old trail, linked them with new sections of road, and clearly marked the route that is often referred to in old records as Miles's Trace. It is among the traditional roadways of the region and once was designated as the boundary line between counties.

Miles prospered and soon came to own several thousand acres of fertile farmland in the region where he had settled. It is reported that he would stand at the high point where the mausoleum is now located and, extending his arm toward the valley, say, "For miles and miles it is all Miles'."

It apparently was Miles's hope to establish an extensive landed estate, a kind of feudal empire. He bought much land at the government land office in Kaskaskia. Other land came from his purchase of the claims of those who had entered land and made improvement. Tradition has it that strangers, apparently co-operating with him, would come into the region and file on land they claimed for military service. These men would disappear, sometimes mysteriously, shortly after transferring their claims to Miles.

Only the mausoleum now remains to remind us of Miles. An inscription on the large marble panel at the right of the walled-up doorway states that it was built by Stephen W. Miles, Esquire, son of the elder Miles, in 1858 as a memorial to the S. W. Miles family and descendants. It also says that the eldest son of each generation was to care for it and to hold it "through this succession in trust for the above family." The bankruptcy of Miles's son, the builder of the mausoleum, disrupted the plan.

A similar panel on the left of the doorway is entitled "To the Visitor." Much of the inscription here is weathered away and illegible. The legible portions are mostly scriptural citations. The name of Stephen W. Miles appears in large letters above the door.

The front of shaped stone, the high arched doorway, the column and the frieze lend a certain architectural distinction. Earth over the top, however, makes the mausoleum practically unnoticeable except from the small level spot between it and the brow of the bluff. Remnants of a somewhat massive iron fence lie all about among sections of fallen wall and misplaced headstones.

If the visitor clambers to the arched opening at the top of the doorway and peers within, a strange sight greets him. There are fifty-six vaults, twenty-four on each side and eight at the farther end. All are open except one in the top tier at the left. This one evidently contains no burial since the marble slab in its opening shows no signs that it has ever been sealed.

The floor is littered with pieces of broken marble slabs, rotting bits of wood from walnut coffins, and some of the decorations from them. There are numerous bones with shreds of dried flesh still clinging to them, cloths that may be the remains of shrouds, bits of glass that once sealed the coffins, and other assorted debris. A musty smell pervades all. Ghouls and vandals certainly have done a thorough job.

Enough pieces of the marble slabs remain to enable one to piece together some of the records once engraved on them. The slabs that sealed the wall of Miles and of his two wives, Lucretia and Sahra, are in pieces large enough to rearrange and read. Another slab of interest carries the following legend:

ANNY,

A PIOUS, HONEST AND UPRIGHT COLORED SERVANT OF

S. W. MILES, SENIOR

DIED OCTOBER 18, 1847

AGED ABOUT SEVENTY-FIVE YEARS.

Dates on the broken slabs indicate that some of the bodies had been buried elsewhere and later moved to the mausoleum. As the visitor peers about the dismal ruins and listens to the stories that tradition relates, he catches glimpses of an interesting character and wishes to know more about the one who said, "For miles and miles it is all Miles'."

A DESERTED CEMETERY

OLD CEMETERIES FREQUENTLY suggest interesting stories. This is particularly true of the one located a block west and a block south of the

Christian church in Benton. Only a few of its grave markers are left standing. Some have fallen and lie in disorder among the weeds and tall grass. The broken parts of others are piled beneath a large oak. It is said that some have been hauled away. Despite its appearance of neglect and isolation, this small cemetery is rich in legend.

The first impressive thing one sees in the burying ground is a large oak tree that must be older than any of the graves. Beneath this tree, a number of broken grave markers are piled in confusion. It is in the plot of ground around this tree that some of the most interesting stories that the cemetery suggests are clustered. A few of them are told here.

Very old persons recall two plain, unlettered wooden crosses that once stood near the tree. These crosses marked the graves of two boys, Weldon Dillon and Emory Bennett. The boys had grown up together, had always been steadfast friends, and had enlisted together in the Union army. Before leaving, they had vowed to each other and to their parents that neither would ever forsake the other.

From Benton they were sent to Camp Butler, near Springfield. One night the building in which they were quartered burned. Most of the soldiers reached safety. Dillon, who had escaped, found that his friend Bennett was still in the burning building and dashed back in an unsuccessful effort to rescue him. Both perished. They were brought back to Benton and buried in a common grave that was marked by two wooden crosses that rotted away many years ago.

Beneath a large oak at the cemetery's entrance is the prominent marker to honor Judge William A. Parish, mentioned elsewhere. Beside the grave of the Judge, but unmarked, is that of his father, the Reverend Braxton Parish. The father, an Easterner, came to Franklin County early in its history from Kentucky, where he had stopped for a year or so. His first trip to the county where he knew some settlers was to view it and to decide if it would be a desirable place to settle. While here, he borrowed a horse on which to fetch his Kentucky bride and their worldly possessions to a new home that he was yet to build.

On the return from Kentucky, Parish—who was a devout Christian—decided that no home should be without a copy of the Bible. His bride heartily approved and prompted him to procure one. Parish accordingly bought one with the last of their money. His action caused a man who witnessed the transaction to remark, "You'd a d—— sight better buy a grubbing hoe."

Parish entered the ministry of the Methodist church. Having very little formal education, but possessing a good mind, he read and studied diligently until he became a well-informed man and one of the outstanding pioneer ministers of southern Illinois. He lived to be a very old man, widely known and highly respected.

A small but staunchly built log cabin with a clapboard roof sheltering two other graves once stood near the oak tree in this Benton cemetery. It was built over the grave of two small boys who contracted diphtheria, died on the same day, and were buried side by side. The heartbroken parents wished to go back to their former home in Tennessee, but the mother was reluctant to leave the graves of her only children unprotected. The father accordingly erected a small cabin over the common graves. This partially assuaged the mother's grief, and the couple returned to Tennessee.

Sixty or seventy years ago, while the cabin was still standing, many a boy demonstrated his courage by going into the cemetery at night—while all other boys remained at a respectful distance—and staying alone inside the cabin long enough to convince the others that he was not a "fraidy."

A visit to Benton's deserted cemetery, especially if the visitor has Judge Thomas A. Layman along to recount stories of the incidents it suggests, is like a trip into a storied past.

❧ THE HENSON HOUSE

Visitors to old homes are sometimes heard to say, "If this house could only talk!" To those equipped with proper hearing aids, old houses do talk. The things they say for themselves, plus supporting records and traditions, often add up to interesting stories. One such old southern Illinois home, a double log building that has been deserted for many years, stands in majestic loneliness on the west side of Illinois Route 3, about four miles north of Grand Tower in Jackson County. It has been standing there for about 150 years. Since pre-Civil War days, it has been called "the old Henson house."

Allen Henson and his son, George Washington Green Henson, came from North Carolina to settle in the vicinity of Tower Rock, or Rock of the Cross, in 1808. The son settled near the mouth of Big Muddy River south of Grand Tower. The father came a few miles farther north and located his home beside the trail that led along the foot of Big Hill on its eastern side.

More than usual interest attaches to both the builder and his house. While living in North Carolina, the elder Henson had fought Indians. In one conflict, he was tomahawked and scalped, but he strangely survived both misfortunes. When the scalping wound healed, it left a portion of his bare skull exposed, arousing curiosity and wonder among those who saw the scar. In his later years, this injury was thought to have caused some mental derangement since "he often went about and sang funny songs." He remained, however, a gentle and kindly old man and lived to an advanced age. These are parts of the story furnished by records.

For those equipped with proper hearing aids, the house provides further information. The first part to be built, sixteen by sixteen feet and a story and a half high, faced the trail on the east. It was constructed on a stone foundation made from rocks found on the hillside. Some of these, evidently, were used as they were found, while others bear chisel marks where they were roughed to shape and size.

Logs for the house, excepting one persimmon, are of oaks from the hillside. They are carefully and accurately shaped, being hewn on two sides to about six inches in thickness. The bark remains on the unworked edges to tell us that it was not a springtime or early summer job, for the bark would have peeled. The floor joists, likewise, were of oak logs that had been sloped to a narrow ridge on the top side, thus making it easier to level them with an adz for the random width, hand-matched flooring of oak.

Many details about the building show that Henson was a competent and careful craftsman. The corners were saddle-notched and so accurately fitted that the walls are still plumb. The sills that carry the floor joists are twelve inches thick and fourteen inches wide to furnish sturdy support for the floor. The top logs that carry the roof rafters are the same size as the sills. They are carried on end logs one foot longer than the others, thus allowing the plates to overhang the wall line six inches on each side. There plates are pegged down to the top pair of end logs to prevent the thrust of the rafters from displacing them. Altogether, it was a sound job of construction.

Space between the wall logs was chinked with wooden batts often arranged in a herringbone design. All was then carefully daubed with a clay-lime mixture that still remains hard. Both the inside and the outside of the wall evidently were left exposed for many years. Later, however, some portions of the interior were whitewashed and others ceiled. The finish lumber is of poplar and there are indications that it was whipsawed. A corner stairway of poplar timbers led from beside the back door to the attic. Knots are conspicuous by their absence.

Poplar joists about three inches thick and eight inches wide, hand chamfered on their lower edges, support the matched-edge beaded flooring of the upstairs. Mortises were "axed out" through the side logs to receive the ends of the floor joists, and the wedges driven to fix them rigidly in position are still there. The clapboard roof that once was carried on the four-by-four rafters has long since been replaced by sheet iron, much of which has been blown away.

The original ground level beneath the building indicates that wind and water have carried away three feet or more of the soil about the house. The front porch has disappeared, but its protecting roof still droops. The well-worn front door sills lead out into space about six feet above the eroded ground.

Square nails in the sides of the first-floor joists and the roof rafters suggest images of the clothing, strings of pepper pods, and pokes of seeds that once were hung there for protection from rodents. A sawed-out space marks the location of the fireplace that heated the room and was used for cooking. Scorched timbers around the spot where the chimney stood hint at narrowly averted fires.

With reasonable imagination, the viewer can reconstruct one of the better pioneer homes. The old house will talk if the visitor will only listen.

The pioneer era of southern Illinois passed many years ago, and few of the physical evidences of that period remain. The old Henson house is one of these. The typical log house of the pioneer will soon have disappeared with the ash hoppers, smoke houses, rail fences, well sweeps, and other objects typical of the period they served.

🏵 *AN OVERSIZED WASHSTAND*

In the days when most wash basins were movable equipment, perhaps there were advantages in having one that weighed about a thousand pounds. In addition to being a substantial fixture, such a basin would not tempt the user to carry it away nor to casually misplace it. Southern Illinois University has just such a basin and, to the writer's personal knowledge, no one has misplaced it for more than fifty years.

Southern's basin is a block of sandstone, roughly diamond shaped, about thirty inches on the edge and sixteen inches thick. It lies against the hedge a short distance south of the central entrance on the east side of Old Main. Except for two rounded depressions in its top, there is nothing about this block of reddish-brown stone to mark it as unusual. Many people pass by it each day, but few see it among the shrubbery.

Having observed the depressions in the top of the stone, the casual observer might conclude that they were shaped by Indians for grinding corn. Closer inspection, however, reveals sharp markings evidently made by a metal chisel, which identify the depressions as the work of a modern man.

The facts are that these two depressions—the larger about ten inches in diameter and perhaps half as deep, and the smaller one being some four inches in diameter and two inches deep—are respectively the basin and soap dish of this early-day washstand.

More than a hundred years ago this block of sandstone stood at Benningsen Boone's home beside the large spring on the east side of Big Hill between Gorham and Grand Tower, in Jackson County. It was his washstand.

Water for washing was placed in the larger of the depressions. The problem of filling and emptying the bowl was solved by dipping a bucket of water from the spring and dashing it vigorously into the depression. Fresh water was poured in to refill it. The water supply was plentiful, and the brook that leads from the spring carried the waste water away. Soft soap made with lye leached from wood ashes was kept in the smaller depression. Though somewhat crude, it was not an altogether bad wash bowl—at least it was substantial.

According to an account given by Mrs. Maude Wilson of Ava, Benningsen Boone's great-granddaughter, who personally knew the stone's history, it first was used at the White House, home of Joseph Duncan beside the Mississippi at the north end of Big Hill. After Duncan moved away and the house was dismantled, the stone was taken to the spring at Benningsen Boone's home, from whence it was brought to the University on a wagon.

The story of the stone's use by Duncan is strengthened by a reference made to it in a report by George Hazen French to the president of the University in May, 1908, when he refers to it as the "Governor Duncan's wash basin."

Its transfer could be explained by the fact that when Duncan moved away from his home, the White House, on the Mississippi at the north end of Big Hill, William Boon, father of Benningsen, moved there and established a woodyard for steamboats, operating it for many years. Benningsen removed the stone from the home of his father after the death of the elder Boon.

The old washstand, now more than sixty-five years on the campus, bespeaks the ingenuity and the ruggedness of the pioneer.

❧ *A BOY CARVES HIS NAME*

ALMOST ANY TIME IN the year, there are people looking for a place to picnic for a day or to camp for a longer time. Southern Illinois abounds in such places, places that also have a scenic appeal. One such place, easily accessible, is Bell Smith Spring on Hunting Branch, in Pope County.

This spring is reached over an excellent gravel road leading west from Highway 145, about twelve miles south of Harrisburg. It also may be reached over another gravel road through the village of Eddyville farther along the state highway toward Golconda. Either route affords an interesting drive.

The motorist passes through stretches of natural forests and considerable areas of pine plantings made about twenty-five years ago. He looks across rolling hills and glimpses abandoned homesites and overgrown trails that beckon the curious and venturesome to get out and follow them. About a mile before he reaches the turn-around at the picnic area, where steps lead down to the valley floor, a marker indicates a side road on the right that leads to Hunting Branch.

The streams that converge near the Hunting Branch approach have nice, rock-bottomed wading pools—some even deep enough for swimming. Between the pools are rocky shoals over which the waters ripple and chatter. Tulip, beech, oak, cedar, hickory, and other trees are all about. High rock walls are on either hand. Mosses, ferns, lichens, and wildflowers are plentiful in season. The fresh green of some mosses and the ruddy blossoms of other plants are attractive as early as mid-March.

Animal life is plentiful, including deer, which often may be seen in droves. Fortunate visitors may spot wild turkeys. Along the branch, the careful and quiet watcher may see a raccoon feeding at dusk. Strange birds are seen and heard, including the pileated woodpecker, which is about the size of a crow.

The Bell Smith picnic area is practically unspoiled. While it has not been given entirely back to the Indians, the valley remains much in its native state, without hot-dog or concession stands. Yet there are picnic tables, benches, piped water, inconspicuous garbage pits, and comfort stations for the visitor's convenience. Pathways and steppingstones to cross the streams from side to side allow easy travel along the valley.

There are some places in the valley that all visitors should see. One of these is the Bell Smith spring beneath the rock wall a short way below the overhanging lodge at the Hunting Branch approach.

The Smith family was among the early settlers there. Their son, Bell—the mother's family name—decided to carve his name on the rocky wall above the spring. Evidence indicates that he began with determination by carving a large "B." The task must have been more than he had expected, for as the carving proceeded, the size of the letters diminished and the name tapered off. The lettering, deeply carved and still showing little evidence of weathering, gave the area its name.

Another object of interest that should not be omitted is the natural bridge farther downstream. It spans about 125 feet, is 25 feet wide, more than 30 feet high and 8 or 10 feet thick at the key of its arch. When viewed from the valley, the bridge is impressive. Those who wish to reach the top of the bridge and walk over the arch may do so by climbing a flight of stone steps and an iron ladder. It is well worth the effort. The top of the bridge is flat, and the entire structure curves away from the face of the bluff. One sunken spot in the top has collected some soil and leaf mold that supports a scrubby bush or two and some moss. During rainy spells, a small rivulet falls over the bluff and flows under the arch of the bridge. A quantity of rubble has fallen and lies beneath the arch.

In addition to the bridge, there are other interesting rock formations. At many places, large blocks of stones have fallen from the bluffs and lie in grotesque patterns. At numerous sites along the valley, one finds overhanging ledges of rock where shelter may be had.

At one time the region of the spring had many settlers. Now the nearest house is a mile or more away, and the forest is coming back.

More than forty years ago, when the writer was a scoutmaster, he camped here with a troop of Boy Scouts from Harrisburg, walking out from the railway station at Stonefort. It began to rain about the time the spring was reached and the downpour continued during almost all the two days spent there with the boys. Camp was made under the sheltering ledge beside Hunting Branch, and a roaring fire was kept going. The group remained cheerful but thoroughly sodden. Recently, just forty years after that visit, the old scoutmaster revisited the scene and spent a night there. Once again it rained in torrents, but taking refuge in his trailer, he kept dry. This time the experience was slightly depressing and the rain seemed wetter. Perhaps it was because the boys were not there.

🌿 MILLSTONE KNOB

NUMEROUS POINTS OF interest lie hidden away in southern Illinois, sometimes with stories only half-known to the region. One such seldom visited place is Millstone Knob, lying on the left of the highway between Robbs and Glendale, in Pope County, where a convenient gravel road leads from the highway to an unworked quarry at the foot of the hill. The hill itself is in the wild.

The name of Millstone Knob was derived from activities at the site a century or so ago. An unfinished and broken millstone lies on a level rock outcrop just below the brow of the hill on the northern side, where tradition says it was left about a hundred years ago. Bits chiseled from the stone as it was being shaped lie about. Near by one sees the place from which the sandstone block to form the stone was quarried.

This millstone, the upper or running buhrstone, was never finished. It was smoothed on its top and bottom sides and formed into a disk about a foot thick and more than three feet in diameter. A smooth round hole about five inches across was made through the center of the circular slab. The top side was sloped upward and outward from the center hole to form an inverted cone-shaped depression that would cause the corn to pass readily from the hopper of the mill to the grinding surfaces of the stones.

Work was stopped short of completion, however, and one must guess at the remainder of the story. The stone may have been allowed to fall and break as it was being turned face upward to make the cuttings for the saddle irons to carry it. There are no markings to show that carvings of serrations on the grinding surfaces were begun. Perhaps one of the very first strokes for this purpose was misplaced or too vigorous, for it split the almost completed stone. Anyway, the broken pieces still lie there, much as if the breaking had occurred only a few months ago.

Two other stones, likewise unfinished, have been found some distance away at the foot of the bluff. There is about them a kind of ageless look. Those who have visited the place would hardly be startled to return and find that Mr. Benar, who was shaping the stone a hundred years or more ago, had returned with heavy iron bands to bind the broken parts together.

It is not the millstone alone that makes the Knob interesting. There are many other appeals. If the visitor is botanically inclined, he will find a profusion of plants, shrubs, and trees. Mosses, lichens, ferns, and strange flowering plants—strange at least to the unbotanical—lie all about. Dense forest growth now covers the hilltop.

There is little evidence to show that white men have ever made much use of the crest of the hill. Indians of the later Mississippi culture left evidence that they had a large village on the hilltop. Numerous excavations show their house sites. A larger pit, perhaps forty feet in diameter, must have been used as the council house. The careful observer will see the symmetrical arrangement of the pits. Competent persons estimate that this village disappeared from 350 to 400 years ago.

Stone-lined Indian graves, perhaps numbering into the hundreds, are on the brow of the hill near the village site. Smooth limestone slabs, evidently brought from a distance—for there is no similar limestone near by—cover some of these graves. Many of them have been opened and pilfered by the curious; more careful work by competent persons might have added to our knowledge of the manner in which a primitive people lived here before the coming of white men.

A number of curious carvings on a rock ledge toward the north brow of the hill causes the visitor to pause and wonder. There are connected lines that may be maps and others that are symbols. There are carvings of wild animals and men. There is a large outline of an eagle, or it may be that of a buzzard—anyway, one of their very few rookeries remaining in southern Illinois was found in a small cave almost beneath the carvings in which there was one very plump, young buzzard still wearing its white plumage.

A few gravestones standing in the woodland not far from the carvings indicate that some families named Benar and Hazel were living in this vicinity as early as 1810.

If the visitor does not feel equal to clambering about over the hill, he may amuse himself by collecting interesting fossils, plant and animal, from the exposed overlay near the quarry where he parks his car. The variety seems endless. If the tourist will take along some drinking water, properly saturate himself with chigger repellant during the months when these bugs hold open season on man, and perhaps entice a Boy Scout to go along and serve as guide, he can spend an interesting afternoon on Millstone Knob.

❧ BRICKEY HOUSE

NEARLY EVERY TOWN HAS an old house with an interesting story. Prairie du Rocher has several, one of which is the Brickey house. Unoccupied for many years, this large three-story, square-frame house with its wide porches, stained glass, shuttered windows, and mansard roof attracts the attention of the most casual visitor to the village. Standing among large trees on a generous plot of ground below the bluff, it silently proclaims the hospitality that once was known there. The fine iron fence that encloses the grounds emphasizes its air of detachment.

To know the story of this old home one must go to the Chicago of the late 1860's and learn something of another building that Uranus H. Crosby built there in 1865. Crosby, a wealthy distiller, decided to contribute to the culture of Chicago by erecting a magnificent opera house. W. W. Boyington, a noted architect, designed a splendid structure that Crosby had constructed on the corner of Dearborn and Washington at a cost of more than $600,000—a great sum for that day. It quickly became a showplace of the pre-fire city.

Chicago was proud of the new building. Crosby quickly learned, however, that owning an opera house was expensive. In 1867, less than two years after its completion, he announced that he was broke and also expressed an intention of disposing of the opera house and 305 works of art through a nationwide lottery.

Elaborate preparations for the event were made. Some 210,000 tickets—each of them numbered and bearing a nice engraving of the opera house—were printed and offered for sale at $5.00 each. These were sold within a few weeks, and on January 21, 1867, drawings were made in the opera house before a large and interested audience. The number drawn for the grand prize was 58600, and the owner of the winning ticket was Abraham Hagerman Lee of Prairie du Rocher.

There being no telegraph in Prairie du Rocher, a notice that Lee was the winner was sent to a law firm in St. Louis and relayed from there to Belleville. From Belleville a messenger was dispatched on horseback to notify Mr. Lee. Before this messenger reached him, however, two men who had seen a news report of his good fortune in a St. Louis paper hastened to Prairie du Rocher to relate the good news or perhaps with hopes of doing some fast trading.

The two men found Lee reading to his sick wife. Neighbors soon heard the news and hastened to offer their congratulations. The messenger from Belleville arrived later in the evening. It is said that Mr. Lee answered the door in a long nightgown, and the messenger bowed low before him as he delivered the official notice. None of the messages, official or otherwise, seemed to disturb or excite Mr. Lee unduly. He even indicated a slight vexation and remarked, "I wish they had to swallow the opera house." But he carefully guarded his ticket while he continued to care for his ailing wife.

A few days later, when his wife's health had improved somewhat, Lee went to Chicago to meet Crosby, requesting at the outset that publicity be avoided. Lee indicated a willingness to sell his claim for $200,000. Crosby accepted the offer and paid that amount to Lee, who quietly went back to Prairie du Rocher. Crosby once more was in full possession of the opera house, and he had profited to the extent of about $600,000 from the sale of lottery tickets.

Shortly after his return from Chicago, Lee built the residence standing today. Two years later he died in Cincinnati, Ohio, and the house was bought by F. W. Brickey, Lee's partner in the operation of the Prairie du Rocher grist and flour mill. Since that time it has been known as the Brickey House, noted for its hospitality and sociability and as a local center of culture.

Before his death, Brickey expressed a wish that if none of his children chose to make it their home, the house should be given to some charitable organization. In the event no such use was made of it, Brickey asked that the home remain unoccupied or be dismantled. Today it stands empty and neglected.

✿ WILEY-ROSSON HOME

Edgar Guest said "It takes a heap of living to make a house a home." Six generations of the same family living in an unbroken sequence in the same home should amply supply that heap of living requirement for the Rosson home, long known as the Ben L. Wiley house, which stands just south of the roadway that leads from Illinois Route 51 to Giant City State Park.

This home originally was a single room of logs, which later became the central or living room at the front. The log house was being lived in as early as 1830 by a man named Brandon, who sold the farm to Winstead Davie in 1851. John Wiley was living in the home at that time.

In 1856 Davie gave the farm to his daughter Emily and her husband, Ben L. Wiley, the son of John Wiley. They came to live there in 1859. Before moving into the house, however, the new owners built an additional room for his parents on the east side of the original one. The south wing, now used as a kitchen and dining room, was added at about the same time. The present enclosed hallway between this addition and the original building was first a breezeway or "dog trot." Except for brief absences, Ben L. Wiley lived here until his death in 1888.

When children were born and additional living space became necessary, another room with an upstairs was added on the west of the first log house and the breezeway was enclosed.

Throughout the years, the house has been carefully kept. Today with its shaded lawn and that calm, ageless look which nicely arranged old houses seem to acquire, it draws more than a casual glance from passers-by.

There is nothing of the gaudy appearance sometimes seen, where misguided efforts have been made for effect. The inside of the house is as natural and tasteful as is the outside. Most of the furnishings in the home have been there for a long lifetime. Old bedsteads, lamps, chinaware, tables, desks, a baby's cradle, and almost priceless hand-made afghans are so harmoniously arranged that the visitor who is appreciative of home furnishings of earlier days finds the home delightful. The baby grand piano in the living room also appears to "belong." When the visitor comes to know Mr. and Mrs. Frank Rosson, they, too, belong in the Wiley house.

The chronology of occupancy of the home is as follows: First there was John Wiley, then his son Col. Ben. L. Wiley, followed by the Colonel's son, Ben Wiley, whose daughter and her husband, Frank Rosson, still live there. The daughter of the Rossons grew up in the home, and she often returns, bringing her son for extended visits in the home where his great-great-great-grandfather lived. One wonders if there is another southern Illinois home with such a long and unbroken occupancy by one family.

ROSE HOTEL

IN ADDITION TO sheltering travelers, early-day taverns served as community centers. The guest coming from a distance brought news, and the local gentry gathered to hear it. Men met to discuss questions of interest. Some came for a few social drinks, to visit, and to swap stories. The tavern-keeper often was the postmaster, and people visited the tavern to receive and send their infrequent mail. Those licensed to keep taverns furnished bond to warrant the proper and legal operation of their places.

As far as can be learned, only one of the many early-day taverns in southern Illinois still operates. This one opened in 1812 at Elizabethtown, in Hardin County, and survives as the Rose Hotel. Its first owner was James McFarland, who had settled there about 1808.

McFarland's Tavern is the oldest continuously operated hotel in Illinois and one of the very old ones of the Midwest. Despite its many years, the building is well preserved, is clean, and is a pleasant place to stop. The family burying plot behind the hotel and a slight acquaintance with local lore, enable the visitor to almost literally sit in the past.

In 1812 McFarland built the first part of the present brick building and began to care for travelers. In the spring of 1813, he secured a license and filed bond to assure legal and proper operation of his establishment. This license also set the charges that McFarland might make, as follow:

Breakfast, dinner, or supper . . . . *25¢*

Lodgings . . . . *12½¢*

Oats or corn, per gallon . . . . *12½¢*

A half pint of whiskey . . . . *12½¢*

Small Beer, one quart . . . . *12½¢*

The tavern's practice of dispensing drinks was discontinued a lifetime ago. The thirsty soul now must go downtown. The prominence given the prices of drinks in the license indicates that they were considered an important part of the tavern business even at this early date. The names of some drinks listed, like taffia, cherry bounce, and cider royal leave this unschooled writer wondering about their contents.

After the death of McFarland in the 1830's, the tavern was operated by others. In 1884 a widowed woman named Sarah Rose bought the tavern and gave it the present name of Rose Hotel. Mrs. Rose operated it until her death in 1939, a period of fifty-five years. Since then, her daughter, Mrs. Gullet, has been its manager. Currently, the hotel is being offered for lease, and it is hoped that someone will take over the delightful old place.

The cook and general helper about the place is a Negro woman, Frankie Wood. Frankie's mother began to cook at the Rose Hotel when Mrs. Rose bought it. Upon her mother's death, Frankie became the cook. Mother and daughter thus served as cooks since 1884—seventy-four years.

Because of the scarcity of help, meals are no longer served. When food was served at the old hotel, a meal there was a delightful experience. Good meat was offered with a bewildering array of side dishes, and the atmosphere of the better early taverns was well preserved.

Anyone who stops at the Rose Hotel, who sits in the evening on the wide veranda, strolls over the shady lawn, or loiters in the summer house that also serves as a lighthouse to guide river traffic, naturally feels something of the glamor of the past. There are few more delightful river views in America. After all, a traveler in the Midwest has few opportunities to stay at such an old and storied place, so clean and well kept and in such a beautiful setting.

The Rose Hotel, *née* McFarland's Tavern is probably the last of a once noted line of river hostelries.

✤ *THE JARROT MANSION*

IN ADDITION TO THE old St. Clair County courthouse, the village of Cahokia has two other interesting, well-preserved buildings. They are the log church and the former residence of Nicholas Jarrot, often called the Jarrot mansion. Each of these buildings appeals to a different interest. The courthouse is associated with the history of local government in the region. The church reminds the visitor of the mission established by the Catholic church there in 1699. The mansion is associated with the social and commercial activities of an interesting family.

Nicholas Jarrot, sometimes spelled Nicolas Jarreau, was born in France in 1764. Member of a prominent family, he received a fitting education. Jarrot came to America about 1790, stopping briefly in Baltimore and in New Orleans before appearing in this region, where he acquired a stock of goods and became highly successful.

Jarrot first married Mademoiselle Marie Barbeau, daughter of a prosperous French family at Prairie du Rocher. The first Mrs. Jarrot lived only a short time. The widower next married the wealthy, cultured, and gracious seventeen-year-old Mademoiselle Julia Beauvais, of Sainte Genevieve, Missouri, and brought her to Cahokia, where they began housekeeping in a frame building across the roadway from the log church.

Jarrot, then carrying on a thriving Indian trade, began the construction of a new dwelling east of the church. The building, some materials for which were imported from France, was not completed for a number of years. It is a large Colonial-type dwelling, 38 by 50 feet, two stories high, with a basement and attic. It is massively built, the walls being 16 inches to 2 feet thick. The framing timbers are fastened together with wooden pegs. According to some accounts, bricks for the building were burned near the site. Other accounts state that they were brought from Pittsburgh. The sixteen-foot-wide hallway through the building, which includes a large fireplace against the west wall, was the center of the Jarrot's social life. Guests were received here, and it was used as a dining room for frequent banquets. In season slaves stood at each end of the hallway and wielded huge fans to keep flies from annoying the guests.

The Jarrots entertained lavishly. The Bonds, John Reynolds, Ninian Edwards, and doubtless Pierre Menard were regular guests. Tradition would have Lafayette visit the mansion, but no record supports the claim. The mansion seems to have been the scene of a continual round of receptions, parties, and formal balls. It was an exceptionally gay place at all times, and especially about the time of the New Year.

Jarrot was a devout churchman. In addition to his regular attendance at mass—and it is recorded that he never failed to attend—he gave liberal support to the local church and also gave the large Indian mound, now known as Monk's Mound, to the Trappist order, which occupied it from 1809 until 1813.

Jarrot served as a militia officer, a court judge in several capacities, as member of the Orphan's Court, and as a justice of the peace.

Despite his penchant for lavish entertainment and his attention to social affairs, Jarrot remained an astute businessman. In 1815 the government confirmed to him titles to more than 25,000 acres of land in Illinois. Only one person, John Edgar, held more. During the War of 1812, Jarrot operated a horsemill in Cahokia, from which he supplied flour to the army. He established the first school at Cahokia in one of the rooms of his house, with Samuel Davidson as teacher. Jarrot owned numerous slaves and other personal property and was among the wealthier men of Illinois.

The mansion stands on land that is flooded at high stages of the river. It is said that a canoe was kept in the wide hallway of the building during the great flood of 1844 and that the Jarrot children, with ropes tied to them and to the bannisters, learned to swim in the hallway of the house. Cracks in the back wall of the house and in those of the stone powder magazine in the back yard are said to have been caused by the earthquake that centered at New Madrid, Missouri, in the last days of 1811 and the first of 1812.

The mansion is now used as a home for the Catholic sisters teaching in the parochial school.

❦ OUR OLDEST COURTHOUSE

WHEN ARTHUR ST. CLAIR CAME to Illinois in 1790, he issued a proclamation establishing a new county named for himself. Its northeastern boundary was a direct line from the site of present-day Pekin, on the Illinois River, to the mouth of the creek that empties into the Ohio at Fort Massac. The Illinois, Mississippi, and Ohio rivers completed the borders of the newly formed county. This proclamation also designated three places where courts would be held. They were Kaskaskia, Prairie du Rocher, and Cahokia.

In a short time, a portion of St. Clair County was detached to form a county named Randolph, with its seat at Kaskaskia. Cahokia then became the county seat of St. Clair County. The courthouse and jail were located in the same building. Near the courthouse were grim devices of punishment including stocks, a pillory, and a whipping post. The courthouse is still standing, looking much as it did more than 150 years ago. In addition to being the oldest courthouse in the state, it also is typical of the houses that the early French built in Illinois.

This house of vertically arranged logs is one of only three or four known buildings of this type left in the state. Two others are the Church of the Holy Family in the village of Cahokia, and a residence in Prairie du Rocher, which, now covered with weatherboarding, is generally unnoted.

A unique feature of the Cahokia courthouse is its extended eaves entirely around the building, a feature common to French colonial dwellings in Illinois. Many of the French settling here came to Illinois from the West Indies, where it was customary to extend the eaves for protection against the hot sun and rains. They seemed to like the idea and brought it to Illinois with them.

Two methods were used in the construction of the vertical log buildings. By one method, trenches conforming to the desired wall outlines were dug about two feet deep. Logs, sometimes hewed, were placed on end in these trenches to form the house walls. The tops of the vertical logs then were sawed to an even height. By the second method of construction, a stone foundation was laid, and hewed sills were placed upon it. The logs to form the walls stood upon these sills. The spaces between the logs were regularly filled with straw and clay or perhaps with small stones and lime mortar. Logs with their ends imbedded in the earth naturally rotted away sooner than those placed upon sills. This should explain the fact that each of the surviving buildings is of the post-on-sill type.

The Cahokia courthouse is the oldest of the three buildings mentioned. Its age is not known with certainty; one writer, however, says it was built as early as 1716, but this is doubtful. It is definitely known that it was erected by Jean Roy Lapance for a residence at least several years previous to 1790. It later passed into the possession of François Saucier, who had married into the Lapance family. Saucier sold it to St. Clair County on October 8, 1793, for a consideration of $1,000. This or another Saucier house had been used for court purposes at an earlier date. A jury held its deliberations in a room of his residence on June 9, 1785.

From the time when the county bought the Saucier property until the removal of the county seat from Cahokia, the building served as a courthouse and as a military center. When the county seat was moved to Clinton Hill, sometimes called Comton Hill but now the city of Belleville, in 1814, the county advertised the old courthouse for sale, and it was bought by François Vaudry on October 16, 1814, for $225. The ownership of the building from 1814 is not difficult to trace. In addition to being used as a residence, it also has served other purposes; in the earlier 1870's it was used as a warehouse. In 1881 a writer said: "For several past years it has been utilized as a saloon."

When the World's Fair came to St. Louis, John Palmenier, the owner at that time, sold the building to Alex Zella for exhibition there. After the closing of the fair, the building was removed to Jackson Park in Chicago. It stood there until 1939, when the State of Illinois acquired it for reconstruction on its original site in Cahokia. Careful study of some early photographs, excavations made at the site, and a few bits of documentary materials enabled those charged with the responsibility to make accurate restoration of the building.

The stocks, pillory, and whipping posts are long gone, as well as the palisade of mulberry posts that enclosed the grounds. The orchard on grounds back of the courthouse also is gone. No one knows the location of the open well into which a colt fell, for which the county paid damages to the owner.

The old courthouse stands as a highly faithful restoration. A visit to it helps to make more vivid an interesting period in the history of Illinois.

Chapter 16

Towns–Old
&
Older

❧ *A SHIFTING RIVER DOOMS A TOWN*

AN ODD ASSORTMENT OF papers given to the writer by Clyde Smith, of Carbondale, contained several lists of produce shipped by steamer from the river port of Rockwood, in Randolph County, in 1857, when that village was on the Mississippi River bank, instead of a mile or more away as it now is. The village is still in its original location; it is the river that has moved.

Rockwood has always aroused interest, and a look at the old papers revived that interest. First, the village has had three names. Its earliest name was Jones Creek, for a man named Emsley Jones, an early settler in the area. Next, it was Liberty, for the river island which had in turn received its name from Negroes fleeing from slavery in the state of Missouri. Later, it became Rockwood—the first syllable referring to the rocky bluff alongside the river, and the second to the woodyard which supplied fuel to steamboats.

In 1857 three men were listed as wood dealers. Rockwood was one of the larger woodyards on the river, selling as much as $100,000 worth of fuel to passing boats each year. At the price then current, this would represent one hundred or more cords each day, enough to make an ordered rick 4 feet wide, 4 feet high and 800 feet long, which is a goodly amount of firewood for one day. A year's supply would have built a rick about fifty miles long.

In 1855 a group of local men began construction of a flour mill, which was completed and began operation in 1856. Partially destroyed by fire in 1863, it was rebuilt at a cost of $20,000. It was a three-story building of cut stone with a brick smokestack sixty feet or more tall. This mill had a daily capacity of 250 barrels.

The opening of the Rockwood mill brought several business and professional men to the town. Among these were three millers, a number of laborers, and coopers and helpers to make the loose barrels for the flour. The demand for wheat in the surrounding countryside increased the importance of farming. Even so, additional needed grain was brought to the mill from other regions by boat. The Rockwood mill was conveniently located. The barrels of flour could be rolled from the mill to the waiting boats. Wheat, too could be unloaded easily.

After 1880, the river began to shift its channel; it is now more than a mile away. The inconvenience and added labor resulting from this shift increased labor costs and made milling less profitable, so much so that after several years operations ceased. Only the tall square brick smokestack and bits of the stone walls, both vine-covered, remain to mark the site of the once flourishing industry.

At the time when the village was most prosperous, its population was about 300. It was then the largest corn market in Randolph County. Some thought that it would become a business rival of Chester. Old bills of lading and shipping records indicate that Rockwood made large shipments of fruit and other farm products in season, much of which went to river towns between St. Louis and New Orleans. One may wonder concerning the condition of "barrels" of eggs shipped to New Orleans in June, 1857, before the coming of refrigeration.

A list of the business and professional men in Rockwood in 1857 indicates that there were five dry goods stores, two grocery stores, four blacksmiths, one boot- and shoemaker, one dressmaker, one tailor, one plasterer, two school teachers, and three physicians.

There was one chairmaker, Tuthill, whose product is even yet sought by collectors. There was a "large" hotel, a wagon shop, a schoolhouse, and one or more churches. There was considerable river traffic. Many merchants having stores away from Rockwood came here to receive shipments of goods, including one who came regularly from as far away as Red Bud.

As indicated, Rockwood was a crossing place for runaway slaves from Missouri in pre-Civil War days. One of the stations of that mysterious and muted Underground Railroad was at a farmhouse which stood until recently a short distance along the roadway toward Sparta.

Several substantial old buildings remain. Others are far along toward decay. Parts of stone foundations, chimney bases, rock-walled wells, fragments of stone walkways and retaining walls indicate the sites of vanished homes.

❧ BOWLESVILLE

PEOPLE WHO WANT TO visit Bowlesville should cross the railway track at the north side of the high school grounds in "new" Shawneetown, go one mile south around the east end of Gold Hill, and turn west along the south side of the hill. Two and a half miles beyond this point and just before reaching a school and church on the right hand side of the east-west road, another gravel road leads one-fourth mile south to Bowlesville. One also may leave "old" Shawneetown by the down-river road and travel along the same roadway on the south side of Gold Hill as directed above. The visitor will not find Bowlesville along either of the routes, but he will see old houses, with some railway dumps, foundations, and shade trees.

The records of the village are meager. It was an early "company town" which came into existence with the establishment of coal mines in the vicinity. With the decline of the industry, the village deteriorated. It was never incorporated, and there is no plat of it in the county recorder's offices.

At one time, however, Bowlesville was an important town credited with a population of 350. It got its start in 1854, when Joseph Bowles purchased land about Coal Hill and with a Dr. Talbot and Thomas Logsdon formed the Western Mining Company. Talbot and Logsdon soon sold their interests to Louisville, Kentucky, parties. Little coal was mined and the property was allowed to be sold for taxes. Bowles bought it and began operations alone.

The Civil War came and cut off much of the coal supply from Kentucky. The mines near Bowlesville thus became an important source of coal for the Federal gunboats on the lower Ohio and Mississippi and for the naval yards at Cairo and Mound City. During the period of greatest demand, coal brought high prices. Slack sold for ten cents a bushel and lump coal for twenty-five cents. As many as nine steamboats are recorded as waiting at one time in Saline River to load coal at these high prices.

At the end of the Civil War, the Kentucky mines reopened and others were developed. Those at Bowlesville no longer yielded a satisfactory profit, and before 1885 they ceased operations. After the closing of the shaft mines, Mike Carney and Bonena Hansha opened a slope mine at an outcropping on a hillside and continued mining on a small scale for a few years. A post office was established on September 12, 1871, and Ezra T. Elliott was appointed as postmaster. He was succeeded by Frederick H. Sellers on October 8, 1872. Thomas B. Logsdon succeeded Sellers and served until the office was discontinued on November 5, 1889.

Little of the early village remains. The building that served as a hotel is still standing. Though the guests have been departed for more than a half-century, the numbers above the doorways of the eight upper rooms are still distinct. The treads of the stairs leading up to these rooms are deeply worn, and its handrail shows a peculiar pattern of wear where guests grasped it as they climbed the steps. The old hotel lobby at the foot of the stairs is now the dining room of a farmhouse. A large front room on the first floor, once the hotel parlor, is now the living room. A portion of the building that was used as the kitchen and dining room of the hotel has been torn away.

Despite decay, removals, and neglect, the old building with its strange roof lines, general unconventional design, its long front porch with clapboard roof, and walls of oversize handmade bricks, is still impressive, standing on a rise of ground as it is approached from the north. Knowing nothing of its story nor that of the vanished village of which it was a part, most observers still pause for a careful look. Once there were nine of these large brick houses, arranged along what was often referred to as "brick row," that ran north and south. They were the homes of the operators, officials, and foremen of the mines.

South and west of these brick houses were about twenty nice log houses arranged along a street—now only a dimly marked lane—that led toward the west. Only two of these, bearing that ageless look that comes to good hewed log houses, are standing. This street was then generally known, and is even yet termed "log row" by older persons. A score or more boxed houses, none of which remains, made up another group known as "box row."

A few stones that were once part of the tipple foundation and a small pit where the shaft has fallen in mark the spot where there was a coal mine. The powder house on posts four or five feet high has disappeared. Some scattered stones and an occasional scrap of rusty iron indicate the location of the machine shop. Depressions where clay was removed, and some rubble from the kilns show where bricks for the buildings were made.

The narrow gauge railway from the Bowlesville mine to the loading tipple on the Ohio became useless with the closing of the mines and was abandoned. Cuts through rises in the ground and fills across the valleys point the route it followed. At one place where the coal was mined at an outcropping on a hillside, the crossties and wooden rails of the old railways have been preserved by the mineral waters flowing over them.

Cisterns and wells, shade trees in patterns, with here and there a clump of hardy shrubs or flowers, or perhaps a chimney base indicate vanished homes. A large cemetery on the west side of the road a short distance south of the village site is the final resting place of several hundred of the one-time citizens of Bowlesville and vicinity.

As the demands for labor decreased, people continued to leave the village and so did the grist mill, blacksmith shops, company store, shoe shop and other businesses. However, the log school where Robert Ingersoll made his first political speech is still there. But the salt works about one and a half miles east of the town finally closed and Bowlesville disappeared, gone to join a host of other deserted villages.

✺ *VANISHED EWINGTON*

EWINGTON, COUNTY SEAT of Effingham County for the first twenty-five years of its existence, is listed as a vanished town. It lay alongside the historic National Highway that ended at Vandalia, Illinois. The overpass that carries U.S. Highway 40 across the railway about three miles west of the city of Effingham now occupies part of the site of the one-time village. A small marker calling attention to the county's first seat of justice was placed beside the paved highway some years ago.

A well in the cornfield south of the overpass was sunk in what once was the courthouse square. A farm home an eighth of a mile south of the well is built with bricks from the last courthouse that stood in Ewington. The burying ground of the local pioneers is near the farmhouse. No building of the vanished town remains, however.

The first houses of the early village were the rude huts of those who came to build the National Road and to bridge the Little Wabash. This workmen's village continued to be only a cluster of huts until September, 1835, when a town was platted by Thomas C. Kirk on land given to the county by Joseph and James M. Duncan. This newly platted town was named for Wm. L. D. Ewing, one of the first attorneys practicing in the county.

Effingham County offered lots in the new town for sale, and orders were given for building a new courthouse and jail. County offices were set up and the projected village became a reality. Even before the establishment of the village, several had come to live in the vicinity. Among these were the McWhorter, Moore, Trapp, and Rentfro families, who lived a somewhat rugged life. Their cabins were of logs and puncheons. Much of their meat came from the plentiful game found in the surrounding forests and on near-by prairies. The nearest horsemill was on the Okaw River, about thirty-five miles away. Stump mills and wooden mortars were used to pound corn for meal and hominy. Their principal source of sweets was the maple trees, many of which were near at hand.

Eli Cook apparently was the first man to open a tavern. He was followed shortly by a man named Kinzey, whom tradition accounts as one of the unique characters of the early town. He was city bred and exhibited city airs. It is recorded that he wore fine clothes, a "plug" hat and patent leather boots, and that he drove "fine rigs." In fact, "he looked like he had just stepped out of a bandbox."

Any account concerning Kinzey would be incomplete without mention of his wife, an Englishwoman, who was somewhat stern and decisive. Stories of the manner in which she controlled her husband are part of the traditions of the village. Kinzey was inclined to tipple. His wife often would march into the tavern and lead him away, sometimes by an ear or by the hair. On more than one occasion accounts have her bringing along a carriage whip from his "fine rig," and she applied it with telling effect.

Ewington's first schoolmaster was Dr. John Gillenwater, who opened a school in his home until enough settlers arrived to support him in his medical practice. Samuel White then became the village schoolmaster, and the school was moved to a two-story log house, the upper floor of which was the Masonic hall.

The following school notice, dated 1838, may be of interest:

The residents of this township shall each pay the sum of two dollars per quarter for each scholar they send to school, and non-residents shall pay the sum of two dollars and fifty cents for each scholar they may send.

Costs of education have certainly increased.

The first courthouse in the new county was built in 1835. It was a log structure and cost the county $580.37½ The county commissioners were slow in building a jail, in fact so slow that they were brought into court and charged with contempt after the county had paid far more than the jail would have cost to have their prisoners kept in the Fayette County jail or under constant guard in Ewington. The cost of guards for prisoners was more than the combined salaries of all other county officials.

Ewington fared as well as other early county seats. It once had a tannery, a cooper shop, two blacksmith shops, a sawmill or two, and a gristmill. It was incorporated on April 10, 1855, and the village officials assumed their offices after solemnly swearing that they had not fought a duel nor sent a challenge to fight one nor had been a bearer of such a challenge since the constitution debarring the practice had been adopted.

Despite the town's earlier prosperity, some became dissatisfied with Ewington as the county seat and sought to move it. An election was accordingly held, and Effingham won the prize by a margin of seventy-four votes—though the usual complaint of "fraud" was raised. With the removal of the county offices, the old village soon vanished. Today few persons know that such a town existed.

❦ BAINBRIDGE

The last of the buildings that once were a part of the village of Bainbridge are gone. The old town has joined the list of southern Illinois' vanished towns.

Bainbridge was located about three miles west of the present city of Marion. It was near the edge of Phelps' Prairie, where one of the trails from Fort Massac to Kaskaskia—the one along which George Rogers Clark passed on his way to capture the British post at Kaskaskia in July, 1778—crossed a later trail from Frank Jordan's Fort to Jonesboro. Other trails from Shawneetown and from Lusk's Ferry at Golconda joined the Fort Massac–Kaskaskia trail a short distance south of the village site.

It was only natural that a trading post should spring up at a place where these important trails converged. The first merchant of record was a man named Kipps, who operated a small store there in 1818. The next one mentioned was named Thompson, who left the place about 1821. Records show that he sold coffee for seventy-five cents a pound and calico at fifty cents a yard. Other merchants and traders followed.

When Franklin County was divided in August, 1837, and Williamson County was established, Bainbridge was chosen as the temporary county seat of the new county. It served as such until October, 1839, when the county court held its first meeting in the newly created village of Marion.

Bainbridge Post Office was established on February 18, 1837, and Allen Bainbridge was appointed postmaster. Doubtless it was for him or his brother John that the town was named. The second postmaster was Doctor George L. Owen, who served until the office was discontinued. The post office and a grocery store were kept in the east wing of the old residence before the west or main portion was built.

Various craftsmen came to ply their trades. Among these was a youngster named Samuel Dunaway. Dunaway had been apprenticed to a man in North Carolina to learn the hatter's trade. He ran away from his master there and came with a group of immigrants to southern Illinois. Stopping at Bainbridge, he began to make hats, and was probably the village's first manufacturer. Dunaway later became a highly successful man and was president of the company that built the railway which passes near the site of the old village. It was he who gave the name "Bainbridge" to the now vanished railway station.

Bainbridge had its quota of taverns. One was kept by John Bainbridge, a brother of the postmaster, another by F. F. Duncan and William T. Turner. Others were owned by D. Dempsey, John Davis, and James T. Goddard. Taverns and houses of entertainment always seemed to have been plentiful there.

The militia of the region held muster at Bainbridge. At such a meeting in 1845, liquor flowed freely and the assembled troopers seemed on the verge of a war among themselves. Just when they appeared ready to begin the conflict, lightning struck a large cottonwood tree near which the belligerent groups were gathered. In the face of this common threat, the impending war was forgotten and all fled for shelter.

The people in the vicinity were interested in education, and Bainbridge Academy was chartered by the state legislature in 1839. A school of higher grade was accordingly opened by a Professor Buff in 1840. It appears to have operated on a limited scale until the mid-1840's.

A noted citizen in the village of Bainbridge was Dr. George L. Owen, who started practicing medicine there as early as 1840. He also conducted a store and served as postmaster for thirty-nine years. In addition to these activities, Dr. Owen was internal revenue collector for a time, land agent for the sale of lands given to the Illinois Central Railroad by the state of Illinois, and was a member of the commission that located and built the state hospital at Anna.

He was intensely loyal to the Union cause during the Civil War. Learning in April, 1861, that plans were afoot to burn the railway bridge north of Carbondale, Dr. Owen rode on horseback to the telegraph office at Carbondale and notified Gov. Richard Yates of the plans. The governor ordered a company of soldiers with some artillery, part of a force en route to Cairo, to stop at the Big Muddy River and guard the bridge. This is mentioned as the first place west of the Alleghenies and outside of a regular military reservation to be fortified during the Civil War. Big Muddy bridge was closely guarded during the remainder of the war.

No houses of old Bainbridge remain. The last to disappear were a combination cook house and carriage house, the first hut occupied by the doctor and long known as the ice house, the old post office and grocery, the well house and the later residence of Dr. Owen. These buildings presented interesting structural features. The large hand-hewn framing timbers were fastened together with wooden pegs. The plaster laths were split from oak. Clapboards were used for siding on the doctor's first residence, which later became the ice house. Plaster was made of lime, sand, and hair. The fine old stair rail was of walnut.

Most picturesque of the old buildings was the one long referred to as the ice house, since it was used in later years to store a summer's supply of that commodity. Its outside walls were covered with clapboards, apparently the original ones. The spaces between the outside and inside walls and that beneath the floor were packed with ground tanbark that came from the early tannery located near by.

The village plat was abandoned in 1847. Now, the last of the buildings that were a part of the old town have been removed. Bainbridge has completely and finally disappeared, gone to join a host of southern Illinois' vanished villages.

❧ *BROWNSVILLE*

TRAGEDY SELDOM COMES on an anniversary. Such happened, however, when fire destroyed the courthouse at Brownsville, first county seat of Jackson County, January 10, 1843, exactly twenty-seven years from the day when the county had been created and Brownsville designated as its seat of government.

Perhaps no one watching the dying fire on that January morning realized that the hopes of a prominent southern Illinois town were likewise fading.

Rumors intimating that the courthouse had been purposely burned soon began to circulate. The County Commissioners Court accordingly named a committee to determine the cause of the fire and report. No evidence of arson was found, however. It was decided that the fire came from hot coals and ashes that had been stored in a wooden box in a room used for a school.

Even before the fire, there had been some talk of moving the county seat to a new location. Afterwards, action to do so was initiated, along with efforts to divide Jackson into two counties. Petitions for both were circulated. The petition to relocate the county seat was recognized and an election was scheduled. The proposition carried by a narrow margin, accompanied by the usual cry of "fraud."

Today about all one can see of the departed village is a couple of stone-walled wells, a few low mounds of brick-filled rubble from old chimneys, a trace of the foundation of the county jail, some stretches of sunken roadway, scattered bits of blue-flowered china, a few slight depressions that once were cellars or cisterns, and an old cemetery on a near-by hill where the latest recorded burial was in 1844.

One of the earlier free public schools in Illinois, possibly the first one, was established at Brownsville on June 25, 1825. This was under the first free public school law, introduced by Joseph Duncan, who was then state senator from Jackson County and was later to become governor of the state. One of this school's teachers, a legendary figure named James D. McMurry and commonly called "Hopping John," long ago loaded his flat boat with produce taken in payment for his teaching and passed to his death down the river.

Widely known attorneys came to practice in the court at Brownsville. Sidney Breese, later a noted jurist and prominent citizen of Illinois, tried his first case in the court here. The dark-eyed Logan boy mentioned and described by Daniel H. Brush, often came to the village with his father, grew up to ride the family race horses, engaged in numerous youthful escapades, and finally became a famous Civil War general and national figure.

William Boon's company of Rangers for the War of 1812 was recruited in the vicinity, and the soldiers that Alexander M. Jenkins assembled there for service in the Black Hawk War have long since answered the last roll call. Numerous Jackson County veterans of the Revolutionary War, who doubtless gathered at the local tavern to recount their experiences in the conflict that gave the nation its freedom, are forgotten.

The town with its estray pen, county jail, ferry boat, tanyard, gristmill, shoe shop, wagon shop, doctor's office, hatter's shop, and numerous other establishments that were part and parcel of the typical pioneer village now may be seen only in the visitor's imagination. The distinctive sounds of the heavily-laden ox wagons that lumbered up from the ferry and crept slowly along the roadway that led to the north are no longer heard.

The silent, beaten, blanket-wrapped Indians, who came from the Kaskaskia Reservation at Sand Ridge to wander about the town, likewise have vanished. The militia no longer meets at the old drill grounds and politicians no longer assemble to plan campaigns. Today, no stagecoaches stop at Meehas' tavern, for there is no Brownsville.

🌸 *ELVIRA*

THE NAMES OF ELVIRA AND Palmyra sound much alike. From the similarity of the names, it might be suspected that they were sisters. Figuratively speaking, they were. In many ways they were so much alike that they almost could be thought of as twin villages. Both were county seats, Elvira for Johnson County and Palmyra for Edwards. The name of Elvira appears to be the older; it became a matter of record when a region lying about the future village was designated as "Elvira Township" and was described as having "the bounds of Captain William Thornton's Company," that is the militia company. The township was thus about seven or eight miles square.

A brief account of Palmyra has been given elsewhere. Something of the story of Elvira, located one mile north and two west of Buncombe, is told here. However, before going ahead with the story of Elvira, it might be of interest to note some of the parallels in their brief reign as county seats. Each was the seat of county government for a territory much larger than any present-day county in the state. They were in existence at the same time. Each lost the county seat to a younger town. Both have vanished as villages and at each site only stone markers remain.

The first settlers are said to have come to the Elvira region in 1806, and to have located in the vicinity of an excellent spring. This spring, one-fourth mile north of the marker mentioned, is walled with rock and still flows freely. Some of the first white inhabitants in this region were the Bradshaw, Thornton, Wiggs, and Worley families. There must have been a number of other families in the vicinity before long, since John Bradshaw was appointed a justice of the peace there in 1809.

The manner in which Elvira received its name is not known. It evidently comes from a feminine Christian name, but no knowledge has come to light of any local lady named Elvira. The first post office was established in 1817 and was named Johnson Courthouse. It, too, later took the name of Elvira. After moving its location from one country store to another over a considerable range, it was discontinued on June 24, 1904, and mail was sent to Buncombe.

The second courthouse called Elvira, was built in 1814. The contract for this building was awarded to William Simpson for a contract price of $260 to be paid in three annual installments. Simpson must not have finished the job, however, since he was paid only $175.75 for his work. The jail, constructed in the same year, was evidently deemed more important, for it cost the county $500. When the boundaries of the county were changed in 1818, the seat of government was moved to Vienna. County offices were removed to the new town, and county officers went to live there. The old village steadily declined.

Little evidence remains to show the location of the first county seat of a county that once included all of the present counties of Alexander, Pulaski, Massac, and Johnson, and portions of Hardin, Pope, Saline, Williamson, and Jackson. A person who walks across the field from the stone marker beside the roadway to the spring will see a few scattered and broken building stones and assorted bits of debris that indicate former building sites.

Some of the stones on a little knoll near the spring are from the foundation of the log courthouse that the county disposed of in 1823. One of the chimneys that stood at opposite ends of the courthouse was removed and used on a log house about a quarter of a mile west of the spring. Logs from the old courthouse were put into a barn constructed beside the present gravel road south of the spring. Some stone doorsteps at farmhouses over the countryside came from the foundations of other Elvira buildings.

The marker indicating the site of old Elvira is on the north side of the road one mile north and two west from Buncombe. It was placed there by the Daughters of the American Revolution in 1924. When one stands at the marker and looks north toward the line of bluffs that extend from east to west beyond the site of the village, it is easily seen that the founders of Elvira selected a beautiful spot.

❦ *PALMYRA*

In 1815, ANYONE LIVING at the places where Chicago or Milwaukee later were to appear and needing to transact business at the county seat would have journeyed to the now vanished village of Palmyra that then stood about two miles north of present Mt. Carmel, in Wabash County. Palmyra was the county seat of Edwards County, Illinois Territory. This county extended along its present southern boundary to about midstate and northward to an indefinite place in mid–Lake Superior, that is, to "upper Canada." In this vast territory of about 80,000 square miles, only a few hundred white people lived. The county was created by an act of Illinois Territory legislature on November 28, 1814, and a nonexisting town, Palmyra, was named as its seat. But the village was soon platted; in fact, there were two plats made, both of which were recorded on April 22, 1815.

Promoters of the newly established village, in order to encourage the settlement of skilled tradesmen there, agreed to give to each such person one of the uneven-numbered lots. The only stipulation was that each newcomer would erect a hewed log house, sixteen by twenty feet, one and a half stories high, with stone or brick chimneys, before July 4, 1816. Those who had already bought lots were to have two years in which to comply with the requirements for building.

With no courthouse, the first session of the County Commissioners Court was at the home of Gervase Hazleton on January 23, 1815. Their first action authorized the establishment of a ferry across the Wabash at Palmyra and fixed its rates as follows: "vehicles, 18¾¢ per wheel; each horse drawing same, 12½¢ man and horse in winter, 25¢ in summer, 12½¢; footman or cow, 6½¢, hogs or sheep, 3¢ the year around." The court's second action established a road from Palmyra "by the nearest and best route to the Gallatin County Line." Other roads were approved and more ferry licenses were granted.

Provision was made at their meeting of February 25, 1815, for the building of a jail, which is always high on a new county's priority list. Permits were granted for damming some streams at mill sites. More taverns were licensed and the rates they might charge were fixed, but they never got around to erecting a courthouse. Necessary space for the county offices was rented from Gervase Hazleton for 6½ cents a year. Why build? For this sum the court's clerk and sheriff were to have the use of one room in Hazleton's home.

Palmyra was off to a fair but not sensational start. The most optimistic accounts credit it with a peak population of five or six hundred, though it is to be doubted if the village was ever so large as that. It soon became apparent that it had been established in a most unhealthful spot. Malaria was rife, and an epidemic which the doctors called yellow fever killed many. Tradition states that at times there were not enough well persons to dig graves, and that the dead were thrown into the Wabash River with little ceremony.

However, the English settlement which had recently sprung up in the vicinity where Albion is now located was growing. In a short time, the greater part of the population of the county was centered there so a movement to relocate the county seat was initiated. On February 1, 1821, the Illinois legislature appointed a committee of three to select a new site. On April 10, 1821, an order was issued that the county seat be removed to Albion and the last recorded meeting of the County Commissioners Court was held at Palmyra a week later.

Palmyra naturally was not happy to lose the county seat. Tradition reports that three or four companies of militia—perhaps it may have been only a mob—met in the vicinity of Palmyra with the avowed purpose of marching to Albion, repossessing the county records, and returning them to the old town. The people around Albion heard about the armed group and dispatched a committee to find and placate it. This committee is said to have found the Palmyra partisans encamped about a bonfire on Bald Hill. A compromise was arranged. Edwards County would be divided and the eastern part would become a new Wabash County with Mt. Carmel as its county seat.

Palmyra continued to exist for a few more years; at any rate as late as March, 1824, the county court granted Gervase Hazleton a license to keep a tavern there. Hazleton must have been the last resident of the village, for an account written in March, 1825, states that there was but one occupied house in the town. All others had been abandoned.

An article in a century-old copy of the *Vincennes Gazette* described the village in 1828, at which time it was entirely deserted. Whole streets of "large frame buildings" and numerous others of hewn logs stood empty. Much of the weatherboarding had been torn from the frame dwellings. The weatherworn straw-clay mixture that had been used to fill the walls added to the desolate appearance.

Today no buildings are left and only faint traces of any home sites are to be found. No markers remain at the village burying ground. A large irregularly shaped granite boulder about six feet long and three feet high stands beside the roadway two miles north of Mt. Carmel and carries a bronze plaque about sixteen inches by eleven inches. On this plaque is the following inscription:

THIS TABLET MARKS THE SITE OF PALMYRA

THE FIRST COUNTY SEAT OF EDWARDS COUNTY.

SETTLED APRIL 22, 1815.

EDWARDS COUNTY AT THAT TIME EMBRACED

ONE-THIRD OF THE STATE OF ILLINOIS

AND A PART OF MICHIGAN AND WISCONSIN,

EXTENDING TO UPPER CANADA.

TWENTY INDIAN MOUNDS WERE

ALSO LOCATED ON THIS SITE.

PLAQUE BY THE MT. CARMEL CHAPTER

DAUGHTERS OF THE AMERICAN REVOLUTION

Except for this marker, the site of vanished Palmyra would be passed unnoticed.

❦ *AMERICA*

IN 1818 THE VILLAGE OF America was platted on the north bank of the Ohio River about six miles above the mouth of the Cache and twelve miles above the place where Cairo later was to appear. When the new county of Alexander was established on March 4, 1819, America became the county seat. The new village was located on ground high enough to escape frequent river overflows. The founders as well as many others thought it would grow into an important city.

Indeed, America's beginning was auspicious. Lots were sold to settlers, and those promoting the villages built "many frame dwellings and twenty-four double log cabins to accommodate settlers." Streets carried all the names of the states of Union at that time as well as the names of some noted people. Blocks were set aside for churches, a school, a jail, and a courthouse. The latter two were built of brick—the jail first. Roadways were laid out leading north and west toward other settlements.

The main street of the town, leading down to the steamboat landing at the lower end of Hodge's Bayou, was Maryland Street. Wagons from the countryside passed down this street carrying produce to be shipped on the river boats. Arriving merchandise was hauled up from the boat landing on creaking and slow-moving ox wagons. Numerous travelers as well as the idle and the curious passed this way. By standards of that time, Maryland Street was a busy one, and America's future looked promising.

Despite its early progress, America lived but a few years. A fickle river built a sand bar and soon only boats of very shallow draft could reach the landing. A few business failures, not uncommon to any new village, occurred. Fire set by an arsonist destroyed some warehouses and stores. Men influential in promoting the progress of the village died, moved away, or transferred their interests to other projects. Malaria attacked practically all the people living there. These misfortunes made the lot of America a difficult one, but the worst was yet to come.

In the autumn of 1820, a steamboat from New Orleans tied up at a point about three miles below the village. Its engineer, a man named Lough, was very sick and was brought to the town for better care. He was found to be suffering with a malady that the doctors diagnosed as yellow fever. Whatever it was, the disease spread rapidly through the village and many people died. Records state that two others died on the same day as Lough and that eventually only four men were then well enough to dig graves and make burials.

People began to desert the town and seek more healthful localities. The county seat was moved to Unity. The courthouse and jail were abandoned. The movement away from America continued, and in 1843, the place where the village had stood was returned to farmland. Many years later the cemetery, containing several hundred graves, was abandoned and plowed. Now, more than a hundred years after it was deserted, hardly a sign remains to indicate the location of the one-time promising village. Maryland Street is a deeply sunken, impassable roadway overarched by the trees growing beside it. Bits of chinaware and broken brick from fallen chimneys indicate home sites. Small parts of grave markers and ornaments are found at the village burial ground; elsewhere in the vicinity grave markers serve as stepping stones at doorways.

When the railroad came in the 1870's, thirty years after the old village had completely vanished, a station was established and the name America was revived and a few houses were built. Now these are gone, the station has disappeared, and the village has vanished a second time.

The site of the old village may be reached by crossing the railway at the abandoned station site, then turning east and following the road to the north about a quarter of a mile. A sunken roadway on the right is Maryland Street.

❦ *A VANISHED CITY*

THE VANISHED TOWN of Kaskaskia was founded by the French and named for an Indian tribe that lived in the region. It once was the metropolis of the Mississippi Valley and a merchandising center for an area large enough to be an empire. It also served as a springboard from which numerous adventures toward the west were launched. It became, in time, the territorial and the state capital for Illinois. Many activities and incidents of national significance centered in the old town. Today it has vanished. Only by careful and guided observation can traces of it be found.

On top of a bluff, the visitor will find low, grass-covered mounds that once were parts of the palisades fort erected to guard the city that lay below and to the west beyond the Kaskaskia River. A bronze marker at the point where visitors enter the ruins of the fort briefly tells its story, which has been recounted (see pp. 6–7).

Some years ago the State of Illinois erected a shelter and lookout on top of the bluff north of Garrison Hill Cemetery. It is from this point that one has the best view of the site of old Kaskaskia. Three sonnets written by the blind poet, Louis William Rodenberg, appear on bronze tablets that are mounted on the low stone walls of the lookout. Perhaps they voice, as well as anything that has been written, a lament for the city that now lies in the river below. It follows:

TRIPTYCH TO A SUNKEN CITY KASKASKIA
by L. W. Rodenberg

[LEFT PANEL]

O Mississippi, monarch of the plain,
Despoiler old! we mourn your victim low
Now stay the mighty minions of your train
That this poor vale may no more havoc know:
Bid not far mountains burst torrential spleen
Nor tempests wreak their lightning souls in woe.
For here, beneath your flood's dissembling sheen
A city lies, her walls and spires down-hurled;
No stone is left whereon some chisel keen
May tell her ravished fame unto the world.
And though your ruthless fury her defiled,
Now o'er her miry tomb your waves are pearled
With sunbeams, all too fair to be reviled
In dance ironic o'er her ruins piled.

[CENTER PANEL]

Father of Waters, native god, forget
The yesterday of ages you were free,
Nor count tomorrow's aeons you will yet
Remain untrammeled in your majesty.
When bold invaders came, with boast profane
To make you slave, you bore them languidly:
Till, with unwonted fear for your domain,
A city here you grappled to your breast,

Plunging her towers in your torrent's lane
Where still they lie, man's weakness to attest.
Nor spared their graves, whose ghosts now stalk the tide,
Bewildered who their sleep should thus molest;
In vain they seek the city where they died,
Her glories vanished and their rest denied.

[RIGHT PANEL]

God's temple floor these level waters pave,
And by these hills His altars are defined;
The azure-ceiling'd heaven domes the nave,
While, far below, to wat'ry crypt assigned
The mother of a thousand cities lies,
In Nature's vast cathedral deep enshrined.
But never on that barren floor our eyes
May find inscription o'er her sodden cell:
How she arose a star in western skies;
How on her hope there broke a dreadful knell;
Aghast with fear from doom she could not stir;
She paled, her glory clutching as she fell,
Despoiled forever! Yet the soul of her
Went not into the sunken sepulchre.

❦ ELIZABETHTOWN

THE ONLY COUNTY SEAT in southern Illinois that never has had a railroad is Elizabethtown, in Hardin County. This village is located on the river ten miles west from the south end of Illinois Highway No. 1. Before the paved highway was built, the river was its principal contact with the outside world.

The name of Elizabethtown was given to the village by James McFarland for his wife Elizabeth. He came to the site in 1806, and in 1812 he built a comfortable brick house on the rocky point beside the Ohio. This house became a popular stopping place for travelers and now, 147 years later, it is still used as a hotel.

The town was a favorite stopping place for showboats. Old newspapers
carry accounts that such famous boats as French's "New Sensation," the
"Cottonblossom," the "Golden Rod" and other boats which contributed
to the legend of the showboat on the Ohio, regularly tied up there. When
one of these boats came to town, the steam calliope would be played at the
landing and the band paraded through the streets. These were gala occasions. In addition to the showboats, which were equipped with stages and
gave plays, there were menagerie boats that much resembled the wild
animal displays of the present-day circus. Old advertisements tell us that
one could see lions, tigers, bears, and even elephants on these boats. There
were trapeze artists, tumblers, jugglers, and sleight-of-hand performers.

The first post office, known as McFarland's Ferry, was established on
November 15, 1830, with James McFarland as the postmaster. This office
was discontinued on August 23, 1834. The next office, known as Elizabethtown, was established there on May 8, 1840. Mail came to this office twice
a week by carrier.

Several houses in Elizabethtown have interesting stories. One of these
is a building once owned by a Mrs. Litzenberger and now known as the
Litzenberger Building. According to the current story, Mrs. Litzenberger
had been reduced to dire financial straits and had only enough money
left to buy one keg of whiskey, which she did, and she began to sell it
by the drink. With the proceeds from this keg, she bought two more,
which she sold, using the proceeds for additional stock. In a short time,
the profits she made enabled her to erect the building now bearing her
name.

An annual event at Elizabethtown is the celebration of Emancipation
Day on August 8 of each year. This practice was begun in 1882 by some
Negroes under the leadership of Moses Barker. Barker and his friends suggested the idea to some men about the town, and it met with popular approval. Farmers over the county donated animals to be barbecued. The pit
was dug, the animals were killed, and the barbecue prepared. All white
people were invited to attend, and many came. From 1882 until the present, this celebration has been a well-attended annual affair. Because the
Negro population of the county has decreased greatly since 1882 and only
a few are now present, the name of the annual observance has been
changed to the Hardin County Homecoming.

Elizabethtown once was noted for its annual old soldiers' reunion. An
account in the local paper tells of such a gathering in 1904, when there
were thirty-eight Civil War veterans present. The newspaper account also
states that there were eighty-three others, five of whom were Negroes,
living in the county at that time. Among the total of 121 Civil War

Veterans then living in the county, one had served in the Confederate Army.

The last veteran of the Civil War in Hardin County, William Winters, died May 14, 1942. Winters was a native of Germany, where he was born October 29, 1845. It is claimed that Anne Walters, who died in Hardin County on June 2, 1948, was the last surviving widow of a Mexican War veteran.

Among the postmasters for Elizabethtown is one of the storied characters of southern Illinois. This man was William Potts, noted as the owner and operator of Potts' Tavern, which stood north of Elizabethtown on the widely known Ford's Ferry Road. Potts was appointed postmaster on May 9, 1849, and served until December 8, 1853.

Much of the calm and unhurried air of the typical river town of an earlier day continues in Elizabethtown.

🌼 COBDEN

PRESENT-DAY COBDEN WAS laid out by Ben. L. Wiley in 1857 and given its first name of South Pass. The name was appropriate since the town is located at a gap in the hill range through which the new Illinois Central Railroad passed. Another town, North Pass, became Makanda.

In 1859 Sir Richard Cobden, who had led the movement to repeal Britain's Corn Laws and who had helped supply English capital for the building of the new railroad, came to America to inspect the properties in which capitalists there had invested heavily. It was on this, his second visit to the United States, that he stopped in South Pass. Cobden and the group traveling with him came by special train. The countryside about the young village, even then attracting attention as a fruit- and vegetable-growing center, impressed the distinguished visitor. The wide view afforded from the high point east of the town, now referred to as Bell's Hill, was particularly appealing to Cobden and his companions, so they spent some time there hunting and picnicking. The people of the vicinity evidently liked Sir Richard, too, for they soon changed the name of their town from that of South Pass to Cobden.

In addition to its association with the name of Cobden, numerous other persons and incidents added interest to the town. One of these was William Henry Harrison Brown, operator of the town's first store. Brown inadvisedly sold a deck of playing cards, which was a law violation. For this he was indicted by the grand jury and thereby so disgraced that he felt forced to sell his business and leave town.

As early as 1866, the fruit-growing industry had been developed to an extent that warranted the running of special trains from this point to Chicago. It was from Cobden that Parker Earle, a large grower of strawberries, sent out the first refrigerated car shipment of that fruit in 1858. Earle's car was a large box with space around it for ice. This shipping box is on display in the Museum of Science and Industry at Chicago.

The growing of tomatoes, begun by David Gow in 1858, became a major industry. Twenty-two carloads of them were shipped on one day in the fall of 1882. At different times, Cobden has been designated as the largest tomato-shipping center in the nation.

Older persons still tell of the time when long lines of farm wagons extending up the hillsides awaited turns to unload fruit and vegetables at the railway shipping platforms. Early fruit and vegetable growers about the town formed the Cobden Fruit Growers Association, said to be among the very first in America. This market still operates.

While Cobden was developing its fruit- and vegetable-growing industries, it was not neglecting other things. In 1867, at a cost of $10,000, it built a brick schoolhouse, the best and perhaps the first in the county. In 1882, the town had a library of more than 1,400 volumes. It also had a temperance club and a large Sunday School.

Since the handling and shipping of fruit required many containers of different kinds, the making of boxes, baskets, and crates soon became important. Machines, devices, and methods developed here marked a great advance in the industry.

The parents of Harold Bell Wright, prominent author of fifty years ago, moved to South Pass shortly after their marriage. Here they became good neighbors with the Bells, who lived on the hill east of town. After a few years, the Wrights moved back to New York state, where their author son was born and given the middle name of Bell for his parents' former neighbors.

Today, Cobden is a quiet, but prosperous little town. In season, the market is a busy place. Millions of assorted containers come from the box factories. Traditions concerning Sir Richard Cobden still linger. One recorded remark of his, however, remains somewhat puzzling. Was he referring to their physical appearance when he said that American women were "deficient in preface and postscript"?

🌱 *ELSAH*

ELSAH IS DIFFERENT. You go to Elsah because you want to go there. No billboards or neon signs lure you, nor is the village cluttered with either when you arrive. It is not difficult to reach. A well kept loop of blacktop leads south from Illinois Highway 100 about five miles east of Grafton. At the state highway end of the loop, an inconspicuous sign with an arrow and modest lettering shows the way to one of the most distinctive communities in the state.

For more than one hundred years this quaint town has nestled in the narrow, mile-long ravine that cuts into the Piasah bluff facing the Mississippi. Before it became Elsah, it was Jersey Landing, a busy river port where steamboats stopped for fuel. In fact, the first men settling there were woodcutters. It remained Jersey Landing until the early 1850's when a Scotsman—born in Kentucky—named James Semple, bought land in the vicinity and platted a town in just about the only ravine in the area large enough to shelter one. Its founder would have named the village Ailsah for the Scotch town of his ancestors, but somehow Ailsah became Elsah when a post office was established.

Semple was a strange man. By turns he was U.S. chargé d'affaires at Bogotá in Colombia, and author of unpublished histories of South America and Mexico. He was U.S. senator from Illinois, appointed by Governor Ford. He also was the maker of the first automobile in Illinois, a steam-powered vehicle. In addition, he left a creditable military record, attaining the rank of brigadier-general.

Semple offered lots in his new village for reasonable prices. Better than that, he gave some away. To get a free lot, the recipient was only required to build a house of native stone on it. This explains the presence of several quaint old stone buildings there today.

Whether of wood, brick, or stone, the style of buildings remained plain and functional. One sees little of "gewgaws or gingerbread" on Elsah's buildings. Whatever the material employed, those who came to make homes in the new village built well, and houses put up a hundred years ago are still standing and in use. Time naturally has taken its toll, particularly of the wooden structures. Alongside the fifteen-foot–wide streets that meander with the ravine, the houses, perforce, snuggle closely against its rocky walls.

Beside the main street a short way up from the stone schoolhouse is a small memorial park with a shapeless granite marker. On the smooth side of the marker are the names of the twenty-two men who went from Elsah Township to serve in World War I. A spring of good water pours into the brook from beneath the bluff back of this park. It is good water, but a visitor must be careful, for those who drink from it, it is said, will always return to the quaint village.

There are two well kept active churches, one Methodist and the other Church of Christ, Scientist. Their friendly relationship and mutual help-

fulness are cheering. No antagonism is sensed, and if there is an element
of rivalry, it comes solely from an effort to best serve. By a strange coincidence, the very attractive Church of Christ, Scientist and its reading
room occupy the site where a distillery once was located. There is not
even a tavern there now, and no one expresses regret for the omission.

Many of Elsah's houses have interesting stories. One of them is known
as River View House. The older portion of this building, erected in
1848, is of logs. It still is heated by the original stone fireplace. Its small,
paned front windows look out across the river. Mrs. E. L. Rhoads, who
lives here, began to make record of the passing river craft sixteen years
ago. Night or day, each commercial craft passing along the river sounds
its greeting and plays its spotlight on the doorway, and its passing is
noted in the log she keeps.

Many of the interesting structures of earlier times are gone. No longer
are there the large flour mills which stood beside the Mississippi and
rolled their barrels of flour directly to the decks of the steamers. Likewise
the large riverside distillery is gone. There are no longer any cattle pens
and no livestock is held for river shipment. The one-hundred-room hotel,
with its fine dancing pavilion that once stood atop the bluff and commanded a wonderful river view is also gone. Likewise, the tramway leading up the steep hillside to the pavilion where passengers went to dance
while their boats were loading or unloading has disappeared.

One often sees an artist or a group of them gathering in some pleasant
nook to sketch the scenery.

A visit to Elsah will turn the wheels of time backward and make one
want to return even though he may not have drunk from the magic
spring.

❧ NEW HARMONY

NEW HARMONY, INDIANA, first called Harmonie, is just across the Wabash
River from Illinois. Its close relationship with the English settlement in
Edwards County warrants its inclusion in this series of southern Illinois
articles.

The first settlers coming to New Harmony were led by George Rapp,
usually referred to as Father Rapp, originally from Württemberg, Germany. He was an active dissenter from the established Lutheran church,
opposing many of its doctrines and practices. Convinced that the privilege of unfettered worship would not come in Germany, Father Rapp

came to America, selected a site about twenty-five miles north of Pittsburgh, Pennsylvania, where in 1805 he founded a successful and prosperous settlement called Harmonie.

After nine years, Father Rapp decided to establish a new settlement farther west. He and two companions accordingly set out on horseback. They reached Vincennes, Indiana, in May, 1814, where they began to explore the surrounding region. The site of New Harmony was selected as the one best adapted to their purpose. Father Rapp bought 7,000 acres of land and wrote back to his followers in Pennsylvania: "You will not believe what a rich and beautiful land is found here."

In less than a month, more than one hundred workmen from the Pennsylvania settlement were on their way to the new Indiana site. Father Rapp disposed of all the community holdings in Pennsylvania and gave his full attention to the development of the new community on the Wabash.

Land was cleared and a complete town was built. It included a fort, a church, dwellings, shops, mills, and other buildings appropriate for a village of that time. All property at the new settlement was held in common, with Father Rapp in unquestioned control. Everyone worked. Each was assigned to tasks at which it was thought he could render the best service.

Industries at New Harmony were many and varied. There were hatmakers, shoemakers, saddlers, tinsmiths, farmers, coopers, brewers, blacksmiths, boatmen, butchers, shepherds, candlemakers, weavers, and millers. Others engaged with some success in the raising of silkworms and the manufacture of silk. The community was a self-supporting and prosperous one. Even though local citizens did not use its produce, they had a distillery which they turned to profit.

In 1824 Father Rapp decided that the group should once more move to a new location. On April 11 of that year, they engaged Richard Flower, a member of the English settlement in Edwards County, to find a buyer for their property at New Harmony.

Flower soon aroused the interest of Robert Owen, a wealthy and philanthropic weaver of Lanark, Scotland. He came to America in January, 1825, to view the property. After several conferences with Father Rapp, and for a total consideration of $190,000 Owen bought the "Town of Harmonie with 20,000 acres of first rate land . . . one large three-story merchant mill, extensive factory for cotton and woolen goods, two sawmills, one large brick and stone warehouse . . . two large granaries, one store, a large tavern, six frame buildings used as mechanics shops, one tan yard of 50 vats, three frame barns 50 x 100 with one threshing machine, three large sheep stables, six two-story brick dwellings 60 x 60, 40 two-story brick dwellings, eighty-six log dwellings, all houses having stables and gardens, two large distilleries and one brewery."

The Rappites departed a few days later, and the entire holdings came into the possession of Robert Owen and his sons. No one would have dreamed that the fortune Robert Owen was to expend here would be listed as one of the seven fortunes in all history which exerted the greatest influence for the betterment of human relationships.

Under the direction of Owen and his sons, New Harmony gave numerous firsts to America. Among those claimed for it are the first kindergarten in America, the first infant school in America, the first trade school in America, the first free public school system in America, the first woman's club in America, the first free public library in America, the first civic-dramatic club in America, and the seat of the first geological survey in America. The first printing taught in a school in America also was said to be here.

Perhaps Owen was too lenient with those who came to join the colony. It was not self-supporting as Rapp's colony had been. After some years, but not until it had made great contributions to social and educational causes, the colony lost some of the characteristics that had made it a distinctive community.

Today the walled burying ground with its unmarked graves, the old fort, a few of the early buildings, some memorials and markers, bits of scattered ruins, an excellent museum, many a golden raintree, and countless bits of lore serve to remind the visitors of the significance of the quiet old town.

🌿 NEW HAVEN

AN EARLY ILLINOIS TRAIL led from Shawneetown on the Ohio toward Vincennes, Indiana. It crossed the Little Wabash at the rocky rapids near its mouth. Shortly after 1800, settlers began to locate near this river crossing. Among early arrivals were John Pond, Joseph Boone, Samuel Dagley, Robert Grant, "Paddy" Robinson, the Pearces and Trousdales.

John Pond is said to have been the first to open a farm in the community which later became known as the Pond Creek settlement—a name heard occasionally even yet. Joseph Boone, a brother of Daniel, chose a site on the south side of the Little Wabash at the rapids, where he built a palisaded fort, a grist mill powered by a water wheel, and was licensed to operate a ferry. Samuel Dagley, whose sister Boone had married, brought his wife and fifteen children to live near the Boones.

Robert Grant laid out the first town of 161 lots, setting aside one lot for a church, another for a school, a third for a mill and a fourth one for a burying ground. He called his town New Haven. Grant also opened a general store which prospered. "Paddy" Robinson became a flatboatman and noted trader, buying and shipping almost anything salable from the boatyard at the foot of the rapids. Paddy also built an eight-room log building as an inn. This building was staunchly constructed and was intended to double as a fort if such became necessary. It was heated with five large fireplaces.

Another man settling near New Haven was the Rev. R. M. Davis, a Presbyterian minister, who located about three miles northwest from the village and founded Union Ridge Church where he served fifty-two years as pastor. It is in the burying ground of this church that the man who served as General Washington's baggagemaster during the Revolution is buried.

The town of New Haven has passed through several periods of prosperity and adversity. At one time, it had two widely known hotels to accommodate travelers, a large sawmill, four saloons, six general stores, a tanyard, a distillery, along with blacksmiths, coopers, gunsmiths, and other pioneer craftsmen. At the height of its prosperity it had five banks, and it is said to have had more cash available than any other place in the state. At that time, it also was a river port of importance.

When railroads were built, they by-passed New Haven by some miles, river traffic diminished, improved highways did not reach the town soon enough, and gradually it began to decline. A new section of the state highway now passes at the edge of the town and crosses the river near the place where Boone had his ferry. The large three-story mill and its water wheel are gone. Some bolt holes in the ledge of rock across the stream show where the timbers of the dam were anchored.

The Graddy House and Paddy's large eight-room log inn with its five great fireplaces passed long ago. Until it was blown down by the wind a few years ago, however, there was one reminder of the days of the fort. That was a large catalpa tree known as the Elizabeth Boone Tree. It had grown from a riding switch that Boone's daughter stuck into the ground near the palisade wall upon her return from a horseback ride. Other large catalpas now there are seedlings of the tree that Elizabeth unwittingly planted.

A few stories of New Haven and earlier days are still related. One of these concerning the Pond family and some Indians is briefly told here.

In the fall of 1812, Pond went early one morning to help raise a house for a new neighbor, leaving his wife and two small sons at home. When he returned at dusk, he found his wife murdered and scalped in the house. His two sons had been tomahawked and scalped and were lying against the house by the stick and clay chimney. One was still alive. The attack evidently had occurred in the forenoon.

Neighbors were notified of the crime. It was learned that three Piankashaw Indians had been seen lurking in the vicinity. The next day, about twenty hours after the crime, Pond and two men named Pearce and Trousdale set out to find the Indians. By observing broken wild pea vines, they were able to pick up their trail. When the prairie was reached, the trail was easily followed through the tall grass. Pond and his companions were mounted so they gained on the Indians fleeing on foot. On the third day, signs became fresher, and it was evident that they were about to overtake the Indians. When they did, they found three Indians making a meal from a wild turkey. Pond and his companions crept forward, each selecting an Indian as his target and fired. One gun misfired, but two of the Indians were killed. The third escaped and was not apprehended though his pursuers hunted all day. Seaching the dead Indians, Pond recovered the scalps of his wife and sons.

The Pond story does not end here, however. A short time after the tragedy, Pond moved from New Haven to western Missouri, where the surviving son grew to manhood. Pearce remained at New Haven until he was an old man, when he too decided to move farther west. Passing through Missouri on his journey, Pearce stopped to spend the night at a farmer's home. Learning that his visitor earlier had lived at New Haven, the younger Pond, now middle aged, asked if Pearce had once known a family there named Pond. Pearce assured him that he had, and told the story of the killing and scalping. At the end of the story, Pond calmly walked to the mantel, opened the clock and took from it a carefully wrapped package. From it he removed a scalp about the size of a dollar with blond hair. He pointed to the scar on his head where the scalp had been removed.

Incredible as the coincidence may seem, the story is documented.

❦ *SAINTE GENEVIEVE*

THOUGH WE CANNOT say of Sainte Genevieve "It Happened in Southern Illinois," there is, nevertheless, a connection. Those who gave the town its beginning went there from the older Kaskaskia settlement to mine lead in the hills near by and to make salt at the salt springs a short distance beyond. Soon tiring of crossing and recrossing the Mississippi, they built a row of cabins along its western side as early as 1735 and thus began the town.

From the time of its founding until now, Sainte Genevieve has had its marks of distinction, evident even today. No other place in the Mississippi Valley, after New Orleans, displays more specimens of French Creole architecture. Also, few other towns so obviously and, at the same time, so placidly and surely, go about their own ways, and few communities have so varied a cultural background. All this did not just happen.

The lead deposits west of the town were known and apparently worked as early as 1715. In 1720 Philippe François Renault, a French promoter, came by way of New Orleans with the intention of developing mines in upper Louisiana. He brought the necessary machinery and equipment as well as miners and other artisans. On his way from France, Renault stopped at Santo Domingo in the West Indies and bought 500 Negro slaves. Some of these were to work in the mines, but most of them were to be used in the vicinity of the village of Renault in Monroe County, Illinois, to grow the food for the miners and other workmen.

Sainte Genevieve was located in a strategic position. In addition to its lead and iron deposits and the saline springs, it was rich in game and fur-bearing animals, and had fertile farm lands. The town had a prosperous beginning. In 1772 there were 264 free males, 140 females, and 287 slaves, making a total population of 691. At the same time, the total population of St. Louis was 597.

The first houses standing beside the Mississippi were menaced by floods and a crumbling river bank. Even before the great flood of 1785 had covered the village site to a depth of fifteen feet or more, some had removed their houses to higher ground about four miles to the northwest. Along with these old buildings, they took their customs, social attitudes, practices, beliefs, traditions, and folklore. These remain and combine to give the community a calm and poise that one person describes as "a serene tempo."

A brief mention of one old house will indicate the enjoyment in store for the one who leisurely walks through the older section of Ste. Genevieve. The Bolduc House, named for the French merchant who built it, has been faithfully restored to its original condition. A high palisade fence of cedar posts encloses the house and grounds, just as such fences did many other houses 170 or more years ago. It is fitted with furniture and household equipment that belong to the period of its earlier existence. Once inside the enclosure, it is not difficult to feel that you are in one of the nicest of the old French homes still standing. The way of gracious living that these people enjoyed is evident.

The restoration of the Bolduc House resulted from the efforts of the National Society of Colonial Dames of America with the co-operation of the Missouri Historical Society and other interested groups and individuals. Other of the city's historic landmarks are zealously and carefully preserved.

A visit to Sainte Genevieve, starting with a visit to its museum to get a map of the town and a leaflet that briefly tells of its significant landmarks, can provide a delightful day to those who are interested in the local past.

❦ CAHOKIA

CAHOKIA, SLUMBERING peacefully beside Illinois Route 3 a few miles south of East St. Louis, is the remnant of a storied village. It was established in 1699, the same year that saw the naming of Williamsburg, Virginia; it is the oldest town in the Mississippi Valley. For several years before it became a white settlement, the Tamaroa Indians had their village there. It was a regular meeting place for Indian traders, merchants, *voyageurs, coureurs de bois,* explorers, and assorted adventurers.

During the first two centuries of its existence, Cahokia varied little in size. In 1767 Captain Pittman, serving with the British forces in Illinois, wrote: "The village is long and straggling, about a half mile from north to south, with 45 dwellings." In 1914, some 147 years later, there were forty-two dwellings in the village. Only within recent years, as industries have located in the area, has the population varied from its long-time average of about 250 to its present 16,000.

In addition to being a very old village, Cahokia has other claims to distinction. The log church on the east side of the highway, built in 1799, is the oldest church building in the Mississippi Valley. Another house built of vertical logs in the same manner as the church stands a block or so west of the paved highway and almost opposite the church. It was the residence of François Saucier about 1785; its story is told more fully elsewhere. A third landmark is the brick residence that was built by Nicholas Jarrot about 1800. Its story, likewise, appears in another place.

Names of many persons prominent in the early history of the region are associated with that of Cahokia. Henry Tonti, faithful lieutenant of La Salle, guided the group that set out from Quebec to establish the Catholic mission around which the village grew. Bois Briant, St. Ange,

Father Marquette, Father St. Cosme, Chief Pontiac, John Todd, General St. Clair, John Reynolds, Dubuque, d'Artaguette, MaCarty, Gratiot, Jarrot, and a host of others came and went.

When France was defeated in the French and Indian War, the Illinois country was ceded to the British, whereupon many of the French living in the Kaskaskia–Prairie du Rocher–Cahokia region moved across the Mississippi River into Missouri, which was then under Spanish rule. After thirteen years of British occupation, Virginia troops under the command of Colonel George Rogers Clark gained possession of Illinois in 1778. During these troublous times, the French settlements in Illinois declined greatly, but Cahokia and the region about it appear to have suffered the least of any.

When St. Clair County was created in 1790 and a local government was set up, Cahokia came upon better days. It continued, however, to be a distinctive French village, clinging to the customs of its earlier years. A visitor to the town in 1848 says that the village, even at that date was but little changed from the time when it was under French rule.

Now most evidences of its French origin have disappeared. In a few more years, the old village will doubtless lose its physical identity and become merged in an expanding industrial area. Even though this may come, Cahokia's story will remain an interesting part of the historical lore of southern Illinois. With Prairie du Rocher and the now vanished Kaskaskia, it was an important part of the French colonial veture in the Mississippi Valley.

Chapter 17

Random Stories

🏵 *CENTER OF POPULATION*

ON MANY DIAGRAMS and pictures an "X" is placed to mark the spot where something happened. Anyone naturally assumes that such a spot once definitely located would not immediately go wandering. However, there comes to mind one migratory spot that doesn't stay put. It was first used in southern Illinois in 1950 to mark the center of population of the United States.

If an east-west line extending from coast to coast were drawn through this spot, there would be as many people living north as south of it. Likewise, if a north-south line through it were extended to the nation's borders, it would make an equal division of the eastern-western population. A glance at a map shows that this would allow more persons to become Southerners or Westerners—that is colonels or cowboys.

The center is calculated after each decennial census. After the census of 1790, it was located at a point twenty-three miles east of Baltimore. From this first location, it began an erratic course westward, following closely along the thirty-ninth parallel. It was farthest north when first established and farthest south in 1940. The extent of its north-south wandering has been small, slightly more than twenty-two miles.

In 1950, after 160 years of westward progress, it appeared in a cornfield beside Illinois Highway 130, about eight miles north of Olney, in Richland County. An appropriate and substantial marker that attracts the attention of passers-by was erected and parking space was arranged. Many travelers seeing the marker stop to read the inscribed legend, also to feel that they are really at the heart of the nation.

This westward progress of the center has been at an irregular pace. Its ten-year distance record came in the period between 1870 and 1880 when it spread a distance of 57.4 miles. The least movement was made in the decade from 1910 to 1920 when it moved only 9.8 miles, or an average progress of less than a mile a year. In the 160 years since it began its westward meander, its average annual advance has been slightly more than 4.5 miles.

In 1800, ten years after it had first appeared east of Baltimore, it turned up eighteen miles west of that town. Another decade, and it was forty miles west of Washington D.C. By 1840 it had reached a location sixteen miles south of Clarksburg, then in Virginia and now in West Virginia. In 1870 it was forty-eight miles east by north from Cincinnati, and evidently spent a part of the next decade wandering unnoticed through that city to appear eight miles west by south from there in 1880. In 1890 it made its first appearance in Indiana, choosing a point twenty miles east of Columbus. Evidently liking that state, it loitered across it for sixty years before appearing in the Richland County, Illinois, cornfield.

With only one recorded exception, this center has chosen rural and often isolated spots for its appearance. This one exception occurred in 1910 when it settled down in the city of Bloomington, Indiana, choosing a coal yard in which to locate.

The present, that is today's actual center of population, is not known. Those who have studied its movement over the years appear to agree that it is now wandering somewhere west from the latest marker, but none hazard to guess how far it has moved. Many are reluctant to predict its north-south progress.

As people are born, die, or change their places of residence, the center moves accordingly. When the decennial census of 1960 was completed and necessary calculations made, the wandering center had moved to a farm about seven miles northwest of Centralia. Then, even before the engineers, mathematicians, and others had calculated the spot and men had opportunity to place a marker, the center doubtless had moved away. It truly may be said to be like the Irishman's flea: When you put your finger on it, it is not there.

Students of population trends predict that the center will continue a slow progress westward in Illinois. Many think that it will be many decades before it leaves the state, if it ever does. If it should decide to locate permanently in Illinois, why not move the national capital here where it would be equally accessible to all citizens? We'll vote for the move.

There are many other centers in the United States most of which are like that of the center of population in that they are always moving about.

There is one center, the geographical one, which has stayed in the same place for a long time, but it is subject to change now that Alaska and Hawaii have come into the Union. Before 1958, the geographical center was located about three miles northwest of the small town of Lebanon, in Smith County, near the midway point on the northern border of Kansas, and about fifty miles north of an east-west line through the center of population. If the productive farmland and other natural resources of the nation were evenly distributed perhaps the population and geographical centers eventually would come to settle in the same vicinity.

With the center of population now located within it, southern Illinois can partially justify the claim, "Here is the heart of America."

❧ CHOLERA

Even a casual visitor to some of the older cemeteries in the lower counties of southern Illinois can hardly fail to observe the frequency with which "died—1847" occurs on grave markers. One of these is to be found a short way west of Pomona, and another is on Walker Hill near Grand Tower. The 1847 dates are out of proportion to those of other years, for that was the year when the area had a severe epidemic of cholera.

The very name, "Asiatic cholera," sounds remote; nevertheless, it was for several years a scourge in Illinois. Epidemics of it occurred over the state at irregular but rather frequent intervals from 1832—when it came to Chicago among the troops that General Scott brought there to aid in the Black Hawk War—until 1873, when the last recorded case occurred at Sandoval, in Marion County.

The disease had long been known in India. About 1800 it began to move westward along the routes of trade and travel and was raging in Europe about 1830. Before long, it had taken a million lives there.

The outbreak among General Scott's troops at Chicago, where there were some two hundred cases, soon spread to the civilian population. In a short time, it appeared at several points along the line of travel to New Orleans. It seemed to prefer younger victims. Since doctors did not know the method by which the disease was spread nor effective remedies to employ against it, little could be done. The most widely accepted explanation for its spread was that its cause was a "miasma" or vapor that arose from decaying vegetation.

Once contracted, the course of the disease was rapid. Death often occurred in four or five hours. One instructor addressing a group of medical students said: "Gentlemen, cholera is a disease the first symptom of which is death."

Records to indicate the cause of death were not regularly kept at that time. Also, there was an obvious tendency to suppress the news that a region was infected, for such news would keep travelers and settlers away. Information in local newspapers often told about an epidemic in some other town and glossed over the fact that it was prevalent in the town where the paper was published. These items in the newspapers, plus a few physicians' day books—like the one still in existence at Jonesboro—old family letters, oral tradition, and grave markers indicate the heavy toll the disease took.

The epidemic of 1833 was particularly severe. It began in towns along the Mississippi and shortly moved to inland places. Quincy, not even incorporated at that time, had thirty-three deaths in five days. Carrollton, Springfield, Belleville, Bloomington—in fact, almost all the towns of any size in the downstate Illinois—suffered greatly. St. Louis had 3,262 deaths from the disease between January 2 and July 9 of 1833. Each summer it recurred with varying degrees of intensity.

The *Cairo Delta* of May 16, 1849, states that there were deaths on practically every steamboat passing along the river. The same paper in its issue of May 29, 1851, again makes a similar statement and says that there were many cases on the steamer "Iowa" and that several persons afflicted were put ashore at the quarantine station a short way south of St. Louis. Tradition relates that a group of rough stone markers on the river bank south of Chester show the place where steamers stopped to bury the cholera dead.

The *Cairo Democrat* of September 9, 1866, reports a number of cases in Marion and says that there had been eight deaths there in the previous week. Among the victims in Marion was Mrs. Elizabeth A. Cunningham, mother-in-law of General John A. Logan. The same paper in its issue of September 19 states that cholera had entirely disappeared in Marion and that there had not been a death reported there in the past week. It also says that there had to date been twenty-three deaths and that it had "threatened" to become an epidemic.

Many remedies were offered for treatment of the disease. Among these were calomel, opium, castor oil, powdered mustard seed, spirits of camphor, red pepper, hot rocks, brandy, and tea made of snake root. A number of patent medicines were advertised and wonderful claims were made for them. Dr. Jaymes' Carminative Balsam, Wells' Cholera Specific, Gould's Cholera Specific, and Percy Davis and Son's Pain Killer were offered. Perhaps the most sensational of all remedies advertised was

Egyptian Anodyne. This latter remedy was compounded, according to
the advertisement, from a formula recorded in Egyptian hieroglyphics on
a papyrus scroll found beneath the head of an Egyptian king buried five
thousand years before. This reputed remedy was sold by a druggist in
Jonesboro.

As late as 1900 many older persons still were living who remembered
the later epidemics in the state and related stories concerning the time
when the disease was abroad. Now, with a thorough knowledge of the
method by which it may be spread and with more effective methods of
control and treatment, the word no longer arouses as great a feeling of
fear as it once did. The record of its prevalence in the state, however,
is not pleasant to recall.

❦ *EPITAPHS*

STYLES CHANGE, EVEN in southern Illinois cemeteries. Epitaphs, very much
in vogue on grave markers or tombstones erected a century ago, have
all but disappeared from markers erected in recent years. Newer stones
still carry bits of biographical data, but even this is not so complete as
it was when the years, months, and days of the deceased were carefully
recorded. The words of tribute to the departed with his gentle admonitions or solemn warnings seldom appear now.

The present tendency in carving indicates greater restraint and recordings are more matter of fact; but enough of the old markers with their
inscriptions remain to provide much interest to those prone to prowl in
cemeteries—once called "graveyards." As these earlier markers fall and
are broken or removed, the one-time plentiful stock of epitaphs dwindles.
Since about the time of the Civil War, their number has declined greatly.

At an earlier time it was not unusual for one to direct what he would
have recorded on his gravestone. Two of our presidents, Jefferson and
Jackson, left such instructions. Strangely enough, neither asked that his
marker record the fact that he had been President of the United States.
Each evidently thought his election to the high office was less important
than his other accomplishments or, perhaps, each knew that history
would record the fact.

Epitaphs may be placed in a few general classifications. Many evidently
intend to tell bits of a story, while others sound a warning, often a somewhat grim one. An occasional one voices a plea, and some are expressions
of faith. Their wording ranges from the most stately prose and genuine

poetry to the simple rhyming of the unlearned. Occasionally there may even be a bit of humor.

Some markers plainly tell a story. A marker at a grave of a three-year-old boy in Union County Cemetery says that he "Was killed October 16, 1857 by a wagon running over him while playing with six other playmates." Another Union County marker tells that the man buried there was scalded to death when the steam drum of the Union gunboat "Mound City" exploded on January 17, 1862 during the attack upon the "rebel batteries" near St. Charles, Arkansas.

In other cases, the story may be inferred. Two stories are suggested by six markers in another southern Illinois cemetery. Three of these markers, side by side, record the fact that three sisters, Louisa, Nancy, Maria, differing some years in age, each died on the same day, January 21, 1860. In the same cemetery, three other stones again side by side record the fact that Augusta, Edward, and Alida, brother and sisters of different ages, died on October 23, 1867. A visitor is left to guess at the stories.

One of the more common themes is that of the admonition. Such an epitaph, occasionally varied somewhat in its wording, says:

> Take warning friend as you pass by
> As you are now, so once was I
> As I am now, so shall ye be
> Prepare for death, and follow me.

To this particular epitaph there occasionally is added a postscript that says "To a better world." This warning epitaph, so one story goes, prompted a waggish rhymster with a somewhat morbid sense of humor to add: "To follow you I am not bent until I know which way you went." Another common warning says "In the midst of life we are in death."

Many epitaphs appeared to have migrated westward with the settlers. One of these carved on a stone in a cemetery near Cooperstown, New York, voices a plea and says "You must talk to the children as I should have done had I lived." A marker near Dongola, in Union County, erected a century after the Cooperstown one, records the fact that the mother left young children and repeats the exact words of the earlier marker. It is interesting to observe the solemn pause that comes when visitors read this epitaph. In the words of the poet Gray, it evidently "Implores the passing tribute of a sigh."

Tributes to the departed are many and varied. Recurring specimens record the virtues of men. "He was an affectionate and loving father, a loyal friend, a staunch lover of his country, a loyal member of the church." One even says, "He was a lifelong Democrat."

Tributes to women are even more varied: "She was a tender mother"; "She hath done the best she could"; "A prudent wife." One inscription occasionally found in southern Illinois says, "Lord, she is thine." This one, evidently, was brought west by earlier settlers too, for its counterpart is found in a mid–New York cemetery. There, however, time and erosion have erased the final letter *e* and the inscription now reads "Lord, she is thin–."

That thoughts of peace have always interested people is evident from the many times one finds such phrases as "May his soul rest in peace," "He giveth his beloved peace," "At peace." A visit to an old cemetery and a study of the epitaphs one finds is always interesting, often in a somewhat sad way.

THE NIGHT THE STARS FELL

IN ADDITION TO recording information concerning the individuals they are designed to honor, gravestones often suggest other stories to those acquainted with local incidents. Such stories are seldom recorded, but nearly every cemetery can supply a few of them.

An interesting story is brought to mind by a broken marker in an unprotected cemetery located on a farm between the site of Jordan Brothers' Fort or blockhouse, about three miles south and one east of Thompsonville, and historic Bethel Church. This burying ground, perhaps the oldest one in Franklin County, has long been deserted, and there is no indication that a burial has been made there within a lifetime.

Only one marker that memorializes a soldier who served in one of our earlier wars is left standing. Many are broken, and hogs have rooted the pieces about; some have gone into the branch that flows beside the plot.

One of the fallen and broken stones carries the inscription: "Z. Mitchell Died November 13, 1833." Zadoc, for that was his first name, was an early settler in the vicinity. So far as records and traditions indicate, he was a substantial and exemplary citizen leading a rather quiet and uneventful life. He would doubtless be entirely forgotten had not the time of his death coincided with a most spectacular shower of meteorites that came on "the night he lay a corpse."

No one knew that literally hundreds of "falling stars" would appear. They understood little of the principles involved, but it was an awe-inspiring sight. The loneliness of the thinly settled Illinois country, the natural grief felt at the loss of an esteemed neighbor, and the general air of solemnity coupled with the dead helped to make the meteoric shower even more impressive in Franklin County.

Neighbors, going to pay their respects to the deceased man or to "set up with the corpse" on that November night in 1833, were greatly impressed with the fiery flashes and traces left by the speeding meteorites. "The night that Zadoc Mitchell lay a corpse" and "the night the stars fell" thus became inseparably connected.

For many years after his death, one had only to mention the name of Zadoc Mitchell and the response would be, "He lay a corpse the night the stars fell." If allusion was made to the meteoric shower, the response would be, "That was the night that Zadoc Mitchell lay a corpse." They were much like the method used to designate time in the South in relation to the Civil War, when the expressions "befo' de wah" and "afta' de wah" were commonly used to date events.

❦ A HORSE RACE

The sports of pioneers were based on individual performances. Horse-racing fitted well into this pattern. Tracts constructed in many localities were "straight-aways," often no more than a quarter-mile long—hence the expression "a quarter horse." A noted one of these tracks was located a short distance south of Benton.

This Franklin County track was among the more popular ones, and many of the region's best horses raced there. Among them was one named Fremont, owned by Truman Thing.

Fremont, a frequent winner, also was difficult to handle. In fact, his owner had found only one rider who was able to control the spirited steed. This jockey had one grave defect—that of going on periodic "toots." This was not so bad unless the toot and the race occurred at the same time, as happened on at least one occasion.

Time for the race came and it was obvious that the jockey was unable to ride, whereupon Uncle Truman sent for a Negro boy living in Du Quoin. This boy was considered an able rider, but Fremont evidently had not heard of his ability and didn't co-operate; in fact, he became practically unmanageable and spilled the new jockey.

With no one else to ride and with race time approaching, Uncle Truman decided upon a bold course. He would ride Fremont. Truman disappeared for a brief time, returning to the track without shoes, coat or hat and with a heavy whip in his hand. While helpers held Fremont, he climbed astride the racer, settled himself in the saddle, ordered the helpers to release the horse, and calmly awaited the starting signal.

With heavy beard, longish hair turning gray, shoeless and hatless, the rider and his mount presented a unique picture. Fremont sensed evidently that he had met his master, and from that time was well behaved. The horses came to the starting line, the signal was given, and the race was on.

Uncle Truman applied the lash vigorously and Fremont was away to a fine start. It was a great race. People who saw it continued to recount the story. They could not forget the barefoot rider with long beard and gray hair stringing in the wind. Fremont, it is said, ran the best race in his career and finished some lengths in the lead.

❦ BIG STAKES AT THE RACE TRACK

ANOTHER LEGENDARY RACE concerns a horse owned by Dr. John Logan. Dr. Logan, living on a farm where the city of Murphysboro now stands, owned many horses and raced a number of them. These horses were ridden by his son, John Alexander, later General John A. Logan, one of the region's most competent and daring jockeys.

Among Dr. Logan's horses was a black stallion named Walnut Cracker. He was such a consistent winner that his owner thought him unbeatable, but there were others who held a different opinion. One who did not agree with the doctor's thinking was a Mr. Dillard who lived near Benton, in Franklin County. Dillard was the owner of another consistent winner called Bald Dillard that had not been raced against Walnut Cracker.

Banters, challenges, and dares began to pass between the prideful owners of the two horses, and soon plans were being laid for a matched race between the highly touted steers at a well-known straight-away near Benton. Interest in the race steadily mounted and heavy bets were made. Dr. Logan wagered practically everything he had on the outcome. The race was held as scheduled, and the doctor's Walnut Cracker lost.

Ordinarily the bets would have been paid off and the episode forgotten, but the prominence of the men, the reputation of the horses, the magnitude of the bets, and the dramatic nature of the race combined to keep the story alive. This was particularly true with a man named Thomas Biddle, who as a youth had witnessed the event and loved, throughout the remainder of life, to relate the story. One of his most colorful renditions was made in the home of Thomas J. Layman, Sr., the father of the present Judge Thomas J. Layman, of Benton.

On the day when Biddle did such a good job, the elder Layman had as his guest an aged and highly regarded minister, the Reverend Jacob Cole. Biddle, noted for his florid and unrestrained language, had come to pay a neighborly call on the Laymans. In the combined presence of Mrs. Layman and the minister, the caller kept his usual manner of speaking under control even if it did somewhat cramp his style.

The name of General Logan soon came into the conversation, and Mrs. Layman, unthinkingly, asked Biddle to tell the Reverend Cole of the famous race that he had seen. Always ready to retell the story, Biddle immediately launched into his account. As the narrator developed momentum, he also began to lapse into his familiar speech patterns. The minister seemed to be thoroughly enjoying the tale, but the listening Laymans grew apprenhensive. As Biddle continued, he increased his volume and animation. The horses were brought to the starting line, maneuvered into position, and the race was under way.

At about this point, Biddle became so enthused that he began to act out the story. Soon all restraint was cast aside and in gestures and pantomine, the race was re-enacted. The story-teller figuratively rose in his stirrups, grasped an imaginary whip in one hand, the reins in the other, and loudly shouted Logan's starting cry of "Go, damn you, go." Then swearing, lashing, shouting, and careening along the track of his imaginary steed, Biddle completed his account of the race with the words, "He rid that thar black stallion like a demon out of hell."

With the ending of the story, Biddle suddenly realized that perhaps he had caused the minister and his hosts some embarrassment. Looking somewhat startled and confused, the story-teller grabbed his hat and hastily left without another word. But, the minister seemed to have enjoyed the story all the more for the way it was told.

🕸 BEFORE ALCOHOLICS ANONYMOUS

ALCOHOLICALLY SPEAKING, Carbondale began as a very dry town. A condition inserted in each of the first deeds to town lots given by those who promoted the village was a provision that it was not to be used as a place for the sale of alcoholic beverages. Should such use be made on the land, it was to revert to the city, then be sold, and the proceeds given to the schools. A few years later, a court invalidated this provision, but court action did not open the town to purveyors of drink. Early records indicate that those attempting to operate saloons or to sell liquor received prompt and decisive treatment.

Perhaps it was Carbondale's record as a temperance town that influenced Dr. Keeley, who already had established the Keeley Institute at Dwight, Illinois, in the early 1880's, to select this town as a place to start a branch, which began operating in 1892. The Carbondale branch with its business office in St. Louis, occupied the large building, then known as the Allen homestead, that stood on a plot of about six acres where the Holden Hospital now is located. It housed about fifteen patients, the supervising physician and his family, while others here for treatment boarded in the town. Treatments at Carbondale were identically the same as those given under the supervision of Dr. Keeley at Dwight.

After a few years, Dr. Keeley's Carbondale branch ceased operations. The initial impetus given the temperance movement by the town's founders apparently has never waned. At intervals through the more than a century since Carbondale came to be, the "saloons or no saloons" issue has been bitterly contested. Even yet, the city has its hard core of militant drys.

❦ RIFLES & SHOOTING MATCHES

A SOUTHERN ILLINOIS "shooting tree" is in a wooded hollow on the south side of the highway at Waltersburg, in Pope County. It suggests the story of a vanished sporting event—the cap and ball rifle shooting match. Most pioneer sports were those that measured personal skills and strength, and a favorite one of these was the shooting match. These contests offered the opportunity not only to display shooting skill but also to demonstrate the particular excellence of each marksman's long rifle.

The old-time shooting match now has disappeared, and few of the cap and ball squirrel rifles remain, except in museums or in the hands of collectors. Only on rare intervals does one find someone with one of these rifles with its scraped, translucent powder horn, charger, bullet mold, and a leather pouch, all of which were standard equipment.

The pioneer's small bore rifle with its thin short stock and very long barrel—sometimes as long as five feet—was an unbalanced and awkward appearing weapon. It was heavy, at times weighing as much as fifteen pounds. A handmade product, it represented the most thorough workmanship.

For many years the production of these rifles centered in the region of Lancaster, Pennsylvania. Later there were gunsmiths in almost every locality to make, repair, and recondition rifles. Rifles were essential and gun-making was a major industry.

Shooting matches were held in many places. Often they became localized about some favorite shooting tree against which the target was rested. Since the bullets fired into the tree were cut out after each match and remelted, the shooting tree came to have a pit or depression over the area where the bullets had been imbedded. The tree visited in Pope County several years ago had such a depression about a foot across and perhaps half as deep. Some short sections of logs, a few rocks, and a smaller tree about sixty yards from the target tree indicate the place from which the shooting was done. When the shooting was "freehand" men stood at this same place to shoot.

The man holding a shooting match provided assorted prizes for the winners. There might be a beef that came to the match on foot, a half-barrel of whiskey, turkeys, geese, or even lowly hens. Shots were sold at unit prices and generally in groups of three or five. The target used had a mark or bull's-eye, generally a blackened circle about an inch in diameter with concentric circles about it. At other times, the target was made by crossed lines on a sheet of paper or a clean, light-colored board. The point where these lines crossed was the bull's-eye. Other bull's-eyes could be made by drawing additional short lines across the main horizontal and vertical ones.

The shooter was allowed to load and shoot in a deliberate manner. He might even take time to carefully swab his rifle between shots. The accepted code of ethics frowned upon any attempt to annoy or distract the shooter when he came to fire, and an air of suspense generally prevailed.

Great care was taken in loading the rifle. The bullets were scrutinized, and any irregularities or ridges left by molding were trimmed away. Powder was measured delicately in the charger made from a hollowed bear's tooth or the tip of a deer's antler. The charge was poured into the muzzle of the rifle. A few taps of the hand near the breach of the rifle made doubly sure that the powder filled the nipple and tube.

The next step in loading was to place a light patch greased with tallow across the muzzle. The bullet was then forced to the level of the muzzle with the finger or with a hollow-ended hickory stick which many carried for that special purpose. It was next rammed to the breech with a hickory ramrod, because a metal rod might injure the delicate rifling of the soft iron barrel. The contestant worked cautiously to prevent the bullet becoming battered or flattened, for that could make it sail. Some riflemen were known to slightly hollow the ends of their ramrods to conform to the curvature of their bullet.

With loading properly made, the shooter next gave attention to his flint and firepan. After the coming of percussion caps, it was the cap that was attended to next. When these preparations had been made, the shooter took his position, cocked his rifle, pulled his release trigger, and thus brought the hair trigger into play. He now was ready to sight and fire. For each of his shots, this deliberate procedure was repeated.

When a beef was the prize, the best shot got his choice of hind quarters. The second best shot, the other hind quarter. The third and fourth place winners got the two fore quarters and the fifth took the hide and tallow. An occasional expert shot would win all places and cart the entire beast away. A consolation prize, the lead in the tree, went to the one placing sixth, if he chose to chop it out.

When turkeys were offered as prizes, they provided their own target by unwittingly thrusting their heads through a hole in the top of a box in which they were placed. The marksman fired at this. Blood drawn from the neck or head was considered a hit, but "bill shots" did not count. Geese were disposed of in the same manner. Instead of being placed in a box, turkeys and geese were sometimes tied behind a log. At a call, they would thrust their heads up to give the marksman something to aim at. Men came to look upon this shooting at live targets as unsportsmanlike, and the practice was discontinued.

The last old-time beef shooting match coming to our attention was held on August 23, 1954, near Waynesville, North Carolina, the locality that knew the youthful Daniel Boone, David Crockett, and Tom Collins, whose name was given to a drink he mixed. The best score there was made by a bright-eyed man of sixty-eight, whose three shots were placed within the one and one-half inch bull's-eye at sixty yards. The best shots were still driving one out of three nails at forty yards.

❦ *RAG-WHEEL BOY*

MANY OLD TERMS ARISE to puzzle us. One that persisted in our curiosity group, "rag-wheel boy," found an explanation in a book, *The Life and Works of F. F. Johnson, M.D.*, given us in Harrisburg. In this book, the doctor describes the work of a "ragwheel boy," a job he held as a ten-year-old. The book also affords interesting sidelights into life in this region at the time when he lived.

Before the Johnson family moved to Illinois, the father bought and operated a water mill near Lebanon, Tennessee. It was necessary to have someone care for the bolting or "sifting" device, otherwise the rag wheel.

This became the son's task and allowed him ever afterwards to refer to himself, evidently with pride, as a rag-wheel boy.

The rag wheel was a cylinder covered with closely woven bolting cloth; it was operated with a hand crank. Almost every old-time grist mill had one. The cylinder operated on a horizontal axle with one end very slightly elevated. Into the higher end the operator placed the freshly ground grist with one hand, meanwhile turning the crank with the other. The flour or meal would fall through the bolting cloth into a trough or bin, and the larger bits of bran would pass to the lower end of the cylinder and fall into another container. Thus the flour and meal were "sifted."

The doctor tells us that the first school he attended was a "blab" school—one where the pupils conned over their lessons aloud—held in the sideroom of a dwelling in Lebanon, Tennessee. He also tells that he sometimes used the blab method in schools he taught at Raleigh after coming to Illinois. From Lebanon, Johnson "went away" to school, first to an academy six miles from his home and next to a school thirty miles away. In each case, he would "commute" by foot on weekends.

When twenty-one years old, Johnson and a brother came to a farm near Raleigh. The brother farmed while F. F. taught a subscription school in one room of their double log house. The next year he was teacher in the "free school" at Raleigh at a salary of $24.00 a month. The low log schoolhouse was about 16 by 16 feet with a puncheon floor, slab benches, a stick and clay chimney, one door, and it had no ceiling. Its one window was made of 8 by 10 inch glass set in a space where a section of log above the writing desk had been removed. The roof was of clapboards three feet long, evidently laid in the light of the moon, since they had curled up.

While teaching, Johnson also studied medicine under the direction of Dr. V. Rathbone and clerked in a drug store the doctor had. Two years later, F. F. attended the winter term of a medical school in Louisville, Kentucky. In the spring, he returned to Raleigh and began to practice medicine with one young man "reading medicine" under him. A year later Johnson decided to complete his medical training and spent one term at Philadelphia, the medical hub of the country.

After returning from his sojourn in Philadelphia, he combined teaching, farming, and the practice of medicine until the outbreak of the Civil War. When a local company was recruited, Johnson enlisted and left Raleigh on August 15, 1861. After being examined by a medical board, he was appointed Assistant Army Surgeon and was stationed at Cairo.

Some of his comments concerning the camp in Cairo are vivid. He tells of the filthy conditions there, occasioned by such deficiences as the lack of spittoons for the three hundred men from the regiment, sick with measles and resulting complications. He tells that the chaplain, ignoring usual procedures, stormed headquarters and secured enough tin pans to meet the spittoon needs.

He also tells of the bitter cold night of January 30, 1862, when the regiment on a march into Kentucky was forced to camp with eight inches of snow on the ground and with no tents. One fortunate group found a spade and dug a "grave" (now termed a fox hole) in which to sleep. The next day was warmer and sloshy. That night they slept on brush piles. He tells how men attached long ropes to cannons and dragged them from bogs when the horses mired, and how he often refilled his canteen with whiskey and doled it out to those on the verge of collapse, despite the fact that he was a consistent temperance advocate.

His description of mass burials after the battles of Fort Henry and Fort Donelson lend reality to war's carnage.

Upon his release from military service, he returned to Raleigh and was elected county superintendent of schools, serving eight years. His comments concerning schools and his reports to the state superintendent's office are interesting. Then, as now, it was difficult to find qualified teachers. His efforts to hold a county institute elicited little response until he threatened to revoke the certificates of those failing to co-operate. Under this duress, a one-week institute was held at Harrisburg.

Johnson's life was anything but dull. When very young, he survived an attack of Asiatic cholera. He narrowly escaped numerous accidents, and his varied career included serving as a rag-wheel boy, farmhand, teacher, country doctor, army surgeon, county superintendent of schools, druggist, ordained minister, and a militant apostle of the Seven Day Baptists. He lived to be a very old man, spending his latter years in Stonefort.

Johnson's book is one of a long list of those about earlier southern Illinois by southern Illinoisans. A few others are *The Flag on the Hilltop, From Timber to Town, Deluvium, The Boy of Battle Ford, Fifty Years in the Schoolroom,* and *Logan Belt.* These books generally are not profoundly written, but many times they afford revealing glimpses of a somewhat rugged way of life. Even though they are of small value, measured financially, they still are a rich reward to those who like to delve into the past.

❦ *THE MUSICAL FORTY*

IN EARLIER DAYS IT was not unusual for a tract of land to take a particular name. Thus, in any community you might hear of the Jones eighty or the lost forty, and of course, there always was the lower forty. In this case, the land carrying a peculiar name is located in Franklin County not far from Benton. It was long known as the "musical forty." It all came about because of a Saturday afternoon incident on a street corner in Benton.

On this particular afternoon, an Italian with a hand organ and a monkey named Jocko appeared on the corner of the public square. The Italian with a stolid and unchanging face turned the crank of the organ and Jocko with a cup begged for coins from the listeners. Among those who stopped to observe the monkey and listened to the music was a man named William Johnson. The more he looked and listened, the more charmed he became. When the Italian and his monkey moved to another street corner, Johnson followed along. Whether it was the unusual music, the sad face of the monkey, or some other appeal, we do not know, but Johnson decided that he must have the monkey and organ.

Beyond a few small coins in his pocket, Johnson had no money, but he did have a forty-acre tract of land a few miles from town. Since land was plentiful and he felt no particular need for this forty, would it not be possible to exchange it for the monkey and hand organ? When the Italian started to the next corner, Johnson accosted him and began to talk trade. It was difficult for the Italian to understand that anyone would want to trade good land for a hand organ and a monkey. The thought of owning a farm appealed to the Italian, however, so he and Johnson began to discuss terms. After some haggling, it was decided to swap evenly. The Italian received the deed to the forty acres of land. The new owner took the organ, strapped it on his neck in the approved manner, took the chain attached to the monkey's collar, and moved away.

We do not know the later history of Jocko and the hand organ. Neither do we know of the Italian. But the tract of land that had figured in this queer deal is even yet referred to by very old persons as the "musical forty."

❧ *BUFFALO*

To MOST PERSONS MENTION of the buffalo brings memories of pictures of vast herds of these animals that roamed our western plains, pictures that were literally landscapes of buffalo. Their number was almost beyond reckoning. Competent observers estimate that at one time there were more than five million of them between the Mississippi River and the Rocky Mountains.

All buffalo, however, were not west of the Mississippi. They once were common in the eastern United States and very plentiful in Illinois. In fact, the earliest account found concerning the buffalo in America is in a report of explorations that Cabeza de Vaca made in the Florida country in 1530. It may strike some as a strange coincidence that this particular Spaniard should make that first report concerning the cowlike animals, since Cabeza de Vaca means "cow's head" in Spanish.

He tells of the excellent flavor of the meat and says that Indians slaughtered the buffalo for food, using the hides of younger ones for robes and dress. They made moccasins and other leather products from the hides of the older animals. Accounts of the later explorers and travelers repeat this. Records of De Soto's explorations contain references to the buffalo in regions east of the Mississippi. Herds then were common in the southeastern states, ranging south to the Gulf of Mexico and east to the Atlantic.

The first mention found concerning buffalo in Illinois is in the writings left by Father Marquette, early missionary-explorer who came to the region in 1673. On his voyage down the Mississippi in that year, he recorded the fact that buffalo were plentiful on the prairies along the river about where Nauvoo now is. In his writings, Marquette calls them "pisikous or buffaloes," saying they somewhat resembled the buffalo of Europe. He often saw herds of four hundred or more coming down to the river to drink. He wrote, "I never saw a more beautiful country than we saw on this river. The prairies are covered with buffalo, stags and goats." The buffalo and stag are not hard to identify, but the reference to "goats" is somewhat puzzling.

La Salle came through the Illinois country about 1680. On this journey, his party portaged from the St. Joseph River to the Kankakee, then floated down the latter and the Illinois. La Salle, much impressed with the Illinois country, wrote: "Far and near the prairie was alive with buffalo." He tells of their snorting, wading, wallowing, and wending their way in long files across the land. Other French explorers and missionaries tell of seeing herds of many hundreds in Illinois, and all mention the great use made of them by the Indians.

That buffalo were plentiful in southern Illinois also is indicated by the fact that an early French trader named Juchereau established a trading post and tannery on the north bank of the Ohio near present-day Grand Chain about 1700 and collected thirteen-thousand hides there in one year.

Audubon and Bachman, early naturalists, state that in their childhood and youth, about 1790, numerous buffalo ranged the open woodlands of Kentucky and Tennessee, and there are records of buffalo being killed a few years earlier near Columbia, South Carolina. Other travelers and explorers tell of them in the states east of the river. In fact, buffalo once ranged over most of the United States where there were suitable feeding grounds.

The heaviest buffalo population in Illinois was naturally in the prairie regions where ideal grazing was available, but southern Illinois offered several features attractive to them. Its plentiful vegetation, open woodland with grassy glades, canebrakes, and salt licks were among the attractions. Until the woodland was cleared and the fields cultivated, distinct trails, sometimes deeply worn, led to numerous licks where buffalo and other animals came to lap the salty earth.

With the advance of white settlers and hunters, the buffalo withdrew from the eastern regions. By 1790 they had become very scarce in Illinois but had not entirely disappeared. André Michoux, traveling between Fort Massac and Kaskaskia, records: "The 7th of October, 1795, my guide killed a buffalo which he considered to be about four years old. . . . Thursday, the 8th [of October] saw another buffalo about 30 toises [approximately 60 yards], from our road." A buffalo cow and calf were killed south of Vincennes in 1800. The last recorded killing in Indiana was in 1810. There is a traditional report, unverified, that the last Illinois one was killed in 1808. The last recorded killing in Wisconsin was in 1833.

A few place names remain to remind us that the great beast once was here. A town named Buffalo, earlier known as St. Marian, was prominent in the Black Hawk War. Buffalo Rock is near Starved Rock on the Illinois River. A carved and colored outline of a buffalo is on the face of a rock ledge north of Simpson, in Johnson County. Older persons sometimes refer to a Buffalo Wallow in Hardin County. There is also the refrain of a very old song used in a play game that says, "Then we'll rally round the canebrake and chase the buffalo."

Barely saved from going the way of the passenger pigeons, a few small herds now are kept on protected reserves and in zoological gardens. Of the millions that once roamed America, only a few hundred remain. With the protection now afforded them, however, there is little likelihood that they will become extinct.

✿ *PASSENGER PIGEONS*

IN 1941 A VERY OLD man living near Olive Branch in Alexander County was directing us toward a local landmark, one he had known seventy years before. Perhaps thinking as in the times of his boyhood, he said, "It is just north of the old pigeon roost," and then he paused. The pigeon roost immediately became more interesting than the landmark sought. His reminiscences concerning it were detailed and vivid.

The old gentleman's mention of the roost suggested other localities like Bear Track Hollow, Rattlesnake Ferry, Goose Creek, Beaver Dam, Eagle Cliff, Otter Slides, Deer Lick, Buffalo Wallow, Possum Flat, Coon Creek, and Panther Hollow. It also brought to mind two more pigeon roosts known to have existed in southern Illinois—one in Hardin and another in Hamilton County. There were surely several others, now forgotten. His mention of the Alexander County roost also revived interest in the greatest bird tragedy in all history.

The passenger pigeon, resembling the common mourning or turtle dove though much larger, was once the commonest bird in America. Competent ornithologists estimate that their number was at one time as great as five billion, which would be more than thirty birds for each person now living in the region they ranged. They made up about one-third of the bird population of North America. Their regular range was over the forested regions of the continent east of the Rockies and north from the Gulf of Mexico to the Hudson Bay country. The beech and oak trees that furnished the bulk of their foods were common in southern Illinois, and millions of these pigeons came here to feed. They were voracious birds, and in addition to the beech nuts and acorns they ate almost all kinds of seeds, fruits, and insects.

They were also very gregarious—migrating, nesting, roosting, and feeding in flocks of many millions. The first report found regarding these pigeons in Illinois tells of a massed flight observed at the mouth of the Ohio on October 16, 1700. After that, missionaries, explorers, travelers, and settlers mention them and tell of their almost inconceivable numbers. These reports, with the flights gradually growing smaller, continued until about 1890. No records of massed flights have been found since then.

In early September, 1914, a St. Louis newspaper carried a short paragraph or "filler" between larger articles. This terse announcement of about twenty words said that the last surviving specimen of the passenger pigeon had died on the first of that month in the Zoological Garden at Cincinnati, Ohio. So far as is known, the death of this bird, called "Martha" for Mrs. Washington, marked the end of the species. This was 380 years after their first mention by Cartier, the French navigator, who had observed them at Prince Edward Island in the Gulf of St. Lawrence on July 1, 1534, and said that he saw "myriads" of them.

Three great flights observed and recorded by competent men help to a realization of the once great passenger pigeon population. The first of these was made by an ornithologist, Alexander Wilson, at Benson Creek as he journeyed from Shelbyville to Frankfort, Kentucky, in 1811. The column he stopped to observe was over a mile wide and was more than four hours in passing before Wilson resumed his journey. In the time he observed the flight—and he left before the entire flight was passed— Wilson estimated he had seen 2,230,000 pigeons.

John James Audubon observed another flight in Kentucky in 1831 and estimated that it contained more than a billion birds. Major King, commander of a fort in the province of Toronto, Canada, observed and made record of another flight that was more than ten hours passing over his post and contained an estimated 3,717,000,000 birds. Writers commented upon the smooth gyrations and graceful maneuvers of the pigeons in flight. Careful observers credited them with a speed of a mile a minute. They were sometimes referred to as "blue meteors."

By the mid-1850's, a decrease in the number of passenger pigeons was becoming apparent to careful observers, and efforts to afford them some protection were begun. Not much favorable sentiment was aroused, however. The report of a committee appointed by the Ohio State Legislature is typical of the general reaction—or rather, inaction. This committee said in 1857, "The passenger pigeon needs no protection. Wonderfully prolific, having the vast forests of the north as its breeding grounds, traveling hundreds of miles in search of food, it is here today and far away tomorrow. No ordinary destruction can lessen the myriads that are yearly produced."

Other states assumed about the same attitude. Massachusetts, one of the first states to legislate concerning the passenger pigeon, enacted a law that was somewhat ironic. This law forbade anyone to use firearms within a half mile of the baited grounds where nets were set to entrap the pigeons. It was not to protect the birds, but to benefit the trapper. No legislation to protect the pigeon has been found for Illinois.

Men continued to destroy pigeons at their roosting and nesting places—particularly at the nesting places, where they were shot, netted, clubbed or trapped by the use of stool pigeons whose eyes were sewed shut. The squabs were punched from the nests by long poles or jarred from them by battering rams, applied against the trees. In some cases the trees in the roosting or nesting areas were chopped down at night while loaded with pigeons and nests containing squabs. Sulphur was burned beneath the roosts to smother the birds. Adult birds roosting on shrubs and the lower limbs of trees were clubbed to death. Millions of live birds were used by "sportsmen" at trap shoots. These live birds often had their tail feathers cut or toes clipped. This was said to have made them livelier.

Millions of birds were shipped to city markets where a plucked bird would sometimes sell for as little as one cent, seldom for more than a nickel. Live birds, netted and stall-fed, brought more. Some of the birds killed were salted or smoked to preserve them. Squabs were cooked, packed in jars or barrels, and covered with hot grease.

A marker dedicated on May 11, 1947, is found in Wyalusing State Park at the junction of the Wisconsin and Mississippi Rivers. It reads:

DEDICATED TO THE LAST WISCONSIN PASSENGER PIGEON SHOT
AT BABCOCK, SEPTEMBER 1899.

So far as records have been found, this was the last passenger pigeon killed in America.

❦ BELLS

SOMEONE ASKED, "Why are church bells no longer tolled at funerals?" The answer was a return question, "Why were bells ever tolled at funerals?" Talk then turned naturally to the history of bells and to the legends that the centuries have given to them. In doing this, it was found that interesting stories are attached to some southern Illinois bells.

One local bell that suggests much that is interesting in the early history of Illinois is in a bellhouse near the Church of the Immaculate Conception on Kaskaskia Island, a few miles north and west from Chester.

This bell, a gift from King Louis XV of France, came to the Catholic mission at Kaskaskia more than two hundred years ago when the region was one vast wilderness peopled with a few French settlers and many Indians. This alone should give it distinction. It has another claim, that of being the first church bell in the United States brought west of the Appalachian Mountains.

There may have been small hand bells for use within the church during the services, but this was the first campana or principal bell intended to be heard throughout the countryside.

It served the church and community for more than two centuries, calling the faithful to worship and proclaiming events. Since clocks were practically unknown, its ringing told the hour of the day. Its early Angelus awakened people to a day of activity. Its ringing at midday called the laborer from his task to his midday meal. In the evening it signaled the close of the day's work. At all these ringings, the hearers paused for a moment of prayer. It signified observance of the Church's holy days. It heralded the opening of court, the issuance of new proclamations and ushered in the new year. Its ringing announced births and weddings. It tolled the passing of many a citizen. In these and other ways, it long served the church and community.

When the shifting channel of the Mississippi began to carry away the old French town and it was necessary to relocate the church building, the bell went to serve in the new location. It continued in use until a larger one came to replace it. Then those mindful of the many associations clustering about this first bell, attended to its preservation.

The Kaskaskia bell was in use many years before the one in Philadelphia, later to become known as the Liberty Bell, was cast and brought to America. Like the Liberty Bell, and in fact many other bells, it has lettered legends upon it. This lettering, briefly recording a few facts about it, is in French, the language then in use in Illinois. Strangely, the inscription on the Kaskaskia bell contains the word "Liberty."

Another first in church bells is the one in the Presbyterian church at Vandalia. It was brought to Illinois in 1830—almost one hundred years after the first one came to Kaskaskia. It is proclaimed as the first bell used in an Illinois Protestant church.

The Vandalia bell was a gift from Romulus Riggs, a Philadelphia merchant, and his wife, Mercy Ann Riggs. It was given in the name of their daughter, Illinois Riggs. The story of its giving is well told in the excellent "Documentary History of Vandalia, Illinois," compiled by Joseph C. Burtschi.

On August 27, 1830, according to Mr. Burtschi's account, Riggs and his wife wrote, "To the minister and sessions of the Presbyterian Church in Vandalia, Illinois." They mentioned that the congregation has found "their means not sufficient . . . to procure a bell." In the daughter's name, they offered to supply that need.

A copy of the *Illinois Monthly Magazine* published by James Hall at Vandalia in December, 1830, tells of the arrival of this bell and of its installation in the frame church. After justly lauding the donors and expressing the community's gratitude for the gift, Mr. Hall says, "This bell, which was hung on the fifth day of November and announced its own arrival in joyous tones, bears the following inscription:

ILLINOIS RIGGS TO THE PRESBYTERIAN
CONGREGATION OF VANDALIA, 1830.

There are numerous other bells in southern Illinois with interesting stories. The two bells in the slender and graceful spire of the Moravian church at West Salem are of considerable interest. The bell on the courthouse at Shawneetown has rung to announce the opening of court through many decades. The church bell at Cave-in-Rock first was a steamboat's bell. The shipyard bell at Mound City likewise has an eventful record.

Man has used bells for many centuries. They have ranged in size from those almost too small even for toys to ones large enough to crush freight cars. They have been made of wood, bamboo, shells, bones, stone, pottery, and metal. They have ranged in size from the smallest jingles to the Great Bell of Moscow that weighs 180 tons. They have appeared in almost every conceivable form from hollowed logs to the conventional bell shape.

For centuries their pealings have announced joys and sorrows, victories and defeats. Their ringings have inspired poets and have given musicians themes for melodies. Their tones have aroused men to great actions and are said on various occasions to have moved both William the Conqueror and Napoleon to tears.

The Chinese record the use of bells more than 4,600 years ago. Bells have been found in the ruins of many ancient civilizations. They are found in the ruins of Egypt, likewise in excavations at ancient Inca and Aztec sites in America, and on isolated islands of the seas.

The bells of St. Bartholomew's Church in Paris rang on August 24, 1572, to mark the beginning of a massacre of many thousands. The sounding of the vespers in Sicily once signaled another such orgy that cost many thousands of lives. Bells have called people to wars and have proclaimed peace. They have announced the hours of day and night. They have called men forth to labor in the early hours of the morning, have sounded the time to pause for prayer, and to close labor at the end of the long day. In our own towns sixty years ago the curfew bell sent youngsters scurrying home at night. Some towns are again employing bells for the same purpose.

Bells were used to call the Romans to their baths and watchmen to their posts. They have announced the openings of courts, and for centuries have assembled people of many faiths to worship. The town criers of Europe as well as those of New England called attention to their messages by clanging hand bells. This practice still is observed in a few places.

In early England the curfew (cover fire) bell signaled the covering of fires for the night. Later the curfew bell marked the time for execution of criminals, who, passing to the place of execution, were forced to wear bells about their necks, thus warning others to avoid them.

War horses of ancient Assyria were festooned with small bells. The Greeks made similar use of them by decorating the funeral car of Alexander the Great. Roman guards rang bells instead of punching time clocks. Mohammedans do not use bells in their religious services fearing they will disturb departed souls, but they must like them, since they say that bells will hang from the limbs of trees in Paradise.

Perhaps another historic southern Illinois bell should be mentioned. This one is in the chapel of McKendree College at Lebanon. According to available information, this bell was cast in Spain in the eighth century, recast in the sixteenth century and later was taken to serve as a mission bell near Santa Fe, New Mexico. From the old mission, it was brought to St. Louis about 1850, again recast there in 1858 by David Caughlan and taken to the Illinois State Fair. President Cobleigh and Professor Moore of McKendree liked the bell, bought it, and took it to the college where for more than a hundred years, its ringing has announced many activities about the campus.

This is only a smattering of the lore concerning bells. Bells definitely have a place in history. Through many centuries a great body of interesting lore has grown up about them. The odd beliefs, superstitions, and strange practices in their use lend appeal to the study of bells.

Epilogue

❦ *I RETIRE*

THE WRITER BELIEVES that anyone who has spent a lifetime at a particular task should be allowed to halt and cast a backward glance when the time comes for parting. That time is here for the writer, and he wants to claim the privilege. After all, his experience is typical of the many, many thousands of youngsters who attended country schools, and the countless ones who taught them.

A lifetime ago, a barefoot lad trudged along a dusty southern Illinois road to his first day in a country school and into a new world. That youngster had no thought whatever that the "book larnin" to which he was introduced that day would remain a first interest through life, and that before he left it, time would sprinkle his head with chalk dust until his hair was white—but such proved true.

It was these recollections that caused him, during the afternoon of his "last day of school," August 31, 1956, to travel back in memory over the years during which he had been associated with school work in various ways.

The memories of those years are pleasant ones. Admittedly, there were unpleasant things occasionally, but time somehow has dulled their sharp edges. In retrospect, the good far outweighs the bad.

Thoughts of retirement and of the many years spent in schoolrooms bring few regrets. Such regrets as there are arise chiefly from things not done, sins of omission rather than those of commission. Altogether, retirement is welcomed. This is particularly true since it comes while reasonable health and vigor remain.

The financial rewards of teaching have been very modest, but on the other hand, the pleasant memories, the friendships, and the associations formed during the years have reached astronomical proportions and somewhat compensate for the money shortage. Anyway, by strict observance of the latter half of Benjamin Franklin's admonition, "Earn more or want less," a reasonably comfortable life has been lived.

Many of the features of the schools I first knew have disappeared, and their passings have aroused momentary regrets, now only dimly remembered. It has been pleasant, however, to see the improvements that have come.

The entire school pattern of that day was different from the present one. Then, with muddy and sometimes almost impassable roads, school districts were small. One-room schools dotted the countryside. Now, those one-room schools have almost disappeared. Despite their handicaps and deficiencies, they did a good work.

These earlier schools with their strange bits of equipment and fittings appear odd today. Gone are the long, home-made recitation benches, the double desks, the blackboards painted on the walls, the wood-burning box stove that was red-hot one instant and almost cold the next.

Gone also are the clusters of wraps and lunch pails that were found beside the front door. Sometimes these were stored in an anteroom where food would freeze before the noonday intermission. Gone also are the pointer and the switches that once rested upon nails or pegs above the teacher's desk as silent admonitions to better behavior. Likewise, the wooden water bucket with its common drinking cup, dipper, or even a gourd is no longer seen. Neither are the wooden-backed erasers and the soft crumbly chalk that preceded the "dustless" brand.

With these have gone the shattered and patched window panes, the rough untreated floors, often littered with gobs of mud carried in on boots and shoes. Along with all these have passed the old-time legendary teachers, men who farmed in summer and taught in winter. They often had little training beyond that provided in a country school similar to the ones in which they were teaching.

The dress of the youngsters then would appear odd now. Some came barefooted until frosty weather. Straw hats for boys and poke bonnets or hoods for girls were common wearing apparel. Much of the clothing was homemade; often it was made over from the outgrown clothes of older brothers and sisters. High top leather boots and button shoes were the style.

The well-nourished look of pupils now was absent then, when "peaked" children were common. Eyes were "weak," but spectacles were very uncommon. Personal cleanliness was at low ebb. Scabies and head lice were occasionally found. The contrast in the looks of both pupils and school-houses then and now is striking.

The games played were different from the ones of today. Their sports were mostly those that emphasized individual strengths and skills. There were not many team games. Among the almost forgotten games were hat ball, bull pen, old sow, shinny, rooster fighting, Indian wrestling (rasslin'), burn out, mumble peg, whip cracker, sling dutch, Spanish leap frog, setting pegs, wolf on the ridge, stink base, and one and over. Perhaps boys still play jail, war, policemen, or outlaws.

Pupils of those one-room country schools varied greatly in age. There were those barely old enough to go and others "of age." There was no organized course of study, and pupils accordingly went at their own pace. There sometimes were "B" and "A" classes. One who could "solve every problem in Ray's Third" was considered a mathematician. When a pupil had finished the work the school offered, having no other place to go, he often "took it over again." Older boys began attendance after the fall work was done and quit when spring plowing began. The very young often dropped out during the severe parts of the winter.

Qualifications of the average teacher, aside from a certain earnestness, often were very limited. A few grown-up boys and girls left the equivalent of today's eighth grade, took the county superintendent's examination, and obtained a teacher's certificate. With this, they began to teach. The writer entered the profession in that way.

This could go on indefinitely. During the years since he went wonderingly down the dusty road to his first day of school, that one-time barefoot boy has seen schools transformed. He wonders what another lifetime will bring. We cannot end, however, without answering a question oft repeated. "If the opportunity could be had to live life over, would you be a teacher?" The answer is "YES, but a better one."

After sixty-six years of direct connection with schools, as pupil and teacher, the impulse to close on this note could not be resisted.

Index

Index

Index

White, Samuel, 341
White, William Allen, 35
White County: origin of name, 49
Whooping cough: cures for, 83–84
Wiley, Ben L.: diary of, 284–87; home of, 329–30; mentioned, 287, 355
Will, Conrad: migration to Illinois, 8, 9; business ventures, 9, 10; political career, 9–10; first stock drive in southern Illinois, 158; mentioned, 147
Williamson County: witchcraft in, 57–58
Wilson, Alexander, 385
Winters, William, 355
Witches: defined, 56; differed from ghosts, 56; powers of, 56; to break spell of, 56; to destroy, 56; stories about, 56–58
Wright, Harold Bell, 356
Writing schools, 187

Yellow fever: at America, 350–51
Yellow jaundice: cure for, 86
York, Lewis E.: in Saline County Teachers Association, 209–10
Young Ladies' Friend, The, 195

Zodiac, signs of, 92–93
Zuroweste, Albert R., 233

SHAWNEE CLASSICS

A Series of Classic Regional Reprints for the Midwest

*A History of the Ninth Regiment
Illinois Volunteer Infantry,
with the Regimental Roster*
Marion Morrison
New Foreword by John Y. Simon

Tales and Songs of Southern Illinois
Collected by Charles Neely
*Edited with a Foreword by
John Webster Spargo*

*Eight Months in Illinois: With
Information to Immigrants*
William Oliver
New Foreword by James E. Davis

The Outlaws of Cave-in-Rock
Otto A. Rothert
New Foreword by Robert A. Clark

When Lincoln Came to Egypt
George W. Smith
New Foreword by Daniel W. Stowell

*Afloat on the Ohio: An Historical
Pilgrimage of a Thousand Miles in
a Skiff, from Redstone to Cairo*
Reuben Gold Thwaites

A Woman's Story of Pioneer Illinois
Christiana Holmes Tillson
*Edited by Milo Milton Quaife
New Introduction by Kay J. Carr*

*Autobiography of Silas
Thompson Trowbridge, M.D.*
*New Introduction by John S. Haller Jr.
and Barbara Mason*

*Life and Letters of General
W. H. L. Wallace*
Isabel Wallace
New Foreword by John Y. Simon

*Army Life of an Illinois Soldier:
Including a Day-by-Day Record
of Sherman's March to the Sea*
Charles W. Wills
*Compiled by Mary E. Kellogg
New Foreword by John Y. Simon*